PRAISE FOR *TRUMP AND POLITICAL PHILOSOPHY*

"Bringing the wisdom contained within the history of political philosophy to bear on the shocking events of the past few years, these essays give us what we need most of all: illumination in place of obfuscation."
—Damon Linker, Senior Correspondent, *The Week*

"Anyone who believes that philosophy has the ability and responsibility to reflect upon the concerns of the present will find these volumes utterly compelling."
—Jeffrey Bernstein, Professor, *Philosophy, College of the Holy Cross, USA*

"Certainly we have had a plethora of books speaking about the rise of Trump… but there is nothing from this timeless perspective."
—Bryan Paul-Frost, Associate Professor, *Political Science, The University of Louisiana at Lafayette, USA*

D1601082

Angel Jaramillo Torres
Marc Benjamin Sable
Editors

Trump and Political Philosophy

Leadership, Statesmanship, and Tyranny

Editors
Angel Jaramillo Torres
National Autonomous University
of Mexico
Mexico City, Mexico

Marc Benjamin Sable
Universidad Iberoamericana
Mexico City, Mexico

ISBN 978-3-030-08993-1   ISBN 978-3-319-74445-2   (eBook)
https://doi.org/10.1007/978-3-319-74445-2

Cover design by Fatima Jamadar

This Palgrave Macmillan imprint is published by the registered company Springer International Publishing AG part of Springer Nature.
The registered company address is: Gewerbestrasse 11, 6330 Cham, Switzerland

To Leslie Rubin, a fine scholar and a good friend

PREFACE

To edit a volume that is a compilation of essays on the hypothetical opinions of classical and modern philosophers on the 45th Presidency of the United States is undoubtedly a challenge.

The predicament is compounded by the inescapable fact that Donald Trump is unlikely to be interested in philosophy. According to his own public testimonies, Trump's favorite books are the Bible and *The Art of the Deal*—not necessarily in that order. Perhaps this book will find a place on the bookshelves of citizens interested in the fate of American democracy, and more generally the world they are living in as the twentieth-first century approaches its third decade.

This volume is divided into three parts: Ancient and Medieval Political Thought, Modern and Liberal Thought, and Continental Perspectives.[1] The quarrel between ancient and moderns can help us to better understand statesmanship, tyranny, and leadership—themes critical for the America which has witnessed the rise of Trump. Political philosophy is, among other things, a meditation about real and desired regimes.

It should be noted that this book has a companion volume, *Trump and Political Philosophy: Patriotism, Cosmopolitanism and Civic Virtue*, and the project was originally intended as a single volume. If the reader finds some great thinker or political stance lacking here, we hope that they will look in there for insights.

This collection is undoubtedly diverse, not only in terms of the thinkers with whom our contributors engage, but also in their politics. We have included authors who believe, explicitly or implicitly, that Donald Trump lacks the moral, political, and technical capacities to govern the United

States. We have decided to give voice as well to those who are optimistic about Trump and believe that he deserves a chance to demonstrate that he can deliver the goods.

Our decision is likely not to garner much assent from either side of the political spectrum, but since this book is written from the point of view of philosophy, we think that dogmatism is the most perfidious of intellectual vices. All in all, we subscribe to the Socratic injunction that one is an educated person to the extent one knows one's ignorance. Moreover, it is our conviction that the strengthening of the public sphere needs an open and non-dogmatic discussion of ideas about what Trump's surprising electoral victory means. If, as several of the contributors point out, the dangers of the present political landscape stem from our inability to rationally discuss the great issues of our time—that we are more comfortable arguing with the like-minded—we hope that this book will foster a dialogue across political divides that can improve the quality of American democracy.

Of course, this book cannot provide all the insights that the philosophers might bring to bear on contemporary politics, or even just Trump, even taken together with its companion volume. But like the proverbial exiled poet, we have launched this book like a message in a bottle thrown into the sea. We hope some fishermen in search of human messages will find it and read it. Perhaps it can help them to get their bearings amidst a troubled moment in the American political landscape.

NOTE

1. The term "liberal" is not used here in the typical contemporary American political sense, i.e., in opposition to postwar conservatism. We use the term "liberal" to refer to all those political philosophies and ideologies which place an emphasis on formal, legal freedom, and the constitutional orders which support it. Our use of the term does not entail any particular stance as to the proper role of government in regulation of business, about which our contributors disagree, i.e., some of them are liberal, some conservative, and some radical in the conventional terminology of American politics. Depending on context, "neoliberal" might refer to a general acceptance of free markets, which has dominated thinking worldwide since the 1980s, or it might refer to the specific position represented by the Clintons' reformist politics within the broad parameters of contemporary corporate capitalism.

Acknowledgments

A project like this—which we count as including its sister volume, *Trump and Political Philosophy: Patriotism, Cosmopolitanism and Civic Virtue*—necessarily generates different sorts of debts than a work consisting of a single argument authored by a single scholar. These are the debts of friendship, in the broad sense of the Greek word *philia*. We are indebted in three ways: institutionally, professionally, and personally.

First, we thank the organizations which facilitated this project: The Northeastern Political Science Association (NPSA), where we organized the first "Trump in the Face of Political Philosophy" panels that took place three days after the 2016 presidential election. We thank the NPSA also for the two roundtables based on essays in this book, one year later, and, more generally, as a forum where we met many of the contributors. The Association for Core Texts and Courses was also an excellent venue, where in the spring of 2017 we met a number of the contributors to this volume and quickly become friends.

In addition, Angel Jaramillo was able to work on this project thanks to a postdoctoral fellowship provided by Consejo Nacional de Ciencia y Tecnología (CONACYT, Mexico's equivalent of the National Science Foundation). He was able to work on this project as part of a postdoctoral position at the Coordinación de Estudios de Posgrado at Universidad Nacional Autónoma de México (UNAM). He wishes thus to thank the coordinator in the area of philosophy at that time, Leticia Flores Farfán. He acknowledges the support of the philosopher Josu Landa too.

Second, there are also numerous individuals who facilitated this project, by helping to foster the conversation that we hope these two books constitute. We owe particular thanks to Nathan Tarcov of the University of Chicago, Richard Velkley of Tulane University, Joshua Parens of the University of Dallas, William Kristol of The Weekly Standard, and Jeffrey Bernstein of the College of the Holy Cross. Although none contributed essays, each made suggestions for inclusions in the volume and generously put us in contact with scholars who did participate. Three others who did contribute essays—Susan Shell, Gladden Pappin and Catherine Zuckert—also helped us to identify scholars whose essays likewise grace this volume.

Above all, this project would have been impossible without the scholars who wrote essays for this book, and its sister volume. We believe their essays exhibit not only a very high quality of scholarship but also a seriousness about politics. More prosaically, they were patient with two editors who learned "on the job" how to manage an intellectual project with 37 contributors. Moreover, they were fine colleagues, responding to comments on drafts and providing materials in a prompt fashion. We thank them all.

We are of course grateful to the staff at Palgrave Macmillan, especially Michelle Chen and John Stegner who helped these novice co-editors through the process of turning a collection of essays into a finished manuscript. We are also highly appreciative of Palgrave's design for the striking cover designs. A thank-you is also due to Chris Robinson, no longer at Palgrave, who first suggested that we turn two academic conference panels into a book-length project.

Finally, we wish to thank our teachers. In the case of Marc Sable, these include, especially, Amy Kass, David Greenstone, Susanne Rudolph, David Smigelskis, and William Sewell, Jr. In the case of Angel Jaramillo, these include, particularly, Rafael Segovia, James Miller, Heinrich Meier, and Christopher Hitchens. Like the vast majority of human beings, our first teachers were our parents. We thank them, for helping us to become the people we are, and for their support, both emotional and material, which has enabled us both to become scholars and to bring this project to completion.

CONTENTS

NOTES ON CONTRIBUTORS

John Burt is Paul E. Prosswimmer Professor of American Literature at Brandeis University. He is the author of *Lincoln's Tragic Pragmatism* (2013), which interprets the Lincoln-Douglas Debates through the philosophy of Kant and Rawls. His *After the Southern Renascence* was in 1999 as volume 7 of the Cambridge History of American literature. He was awarded the John Simon Guggenheim Memorial Foundation Fellowship in 1997 for exceptionally productive scholarship in American Literature, in particular *Robert Penn Warren and American Idealism* (1988). He is also the editor of several volumes of Robert Penn Warren's poetry and the author of four volumes of his own.

Christopher Colmo is Professor of Political Science and former chair of the Department of Political Science at Dominican University, where he teaches courses on philosophy of law, Gandhi and the Western classics, Latin American political thought, women in political philosophy, and contemporary political thought. In 2015–2016 he was the President's Distinguished Service Professor at Dominican University. He is the author of *Breaking with Athens: Alfarabi as Founder* and has written in the *Review of Politics* and the *American Political Science Review*.

Kate Crehan is Professor of Anthropology (Emerita) at the City University of New York (CUNY) Graduate Center and College of Staten Island. She has conducted fieldwork in Zambia and Britain. She is the author of *The Fractured Community: Landscapes of Power and Gender in Rural Zambia* (1997); *Gramsci, Culture and Anthropology* (2002);

Community Art: An Anthropological Perspective (2011); and *Gramsci's Common Sense: Inequality and Its Narratives* (2016), and is the joint winner of the 2017 Sormani Prize.

Bernard J. Dobski is Chair and Associate Professor of Political Science at Assumption College in Worcester, Massachusetts, where he teaches courses on political philosophy, international relations, and american foreign policy. He is the co-editor of two volumes on Shakespeare (*Souls with Longing* and *Shakespeare and the Body Politic*), and has written essays, articles, and book reviews on Thucydides, Xenophon, Shakespeare, Mark Twain, liberal progressivism, and American foreign policy, in the *Review of Politics, POLIS, Interpretation, Philosophy and Literature, Society,* and *Review of Metaphysics.*

Murray Dry is Charles A. Dana Professor of Political Science at Middlebury College. He is the author of *Same-Sex Marriage and American Constitutionalism: A Study in Federalism, Separation of Powers, and Individual Rights* (2017) and *Civil Peace and the Quest for Truth: The First Amendment Freedoms in Political Philosophy and American Constitutionalism* (2004). He assisted Herbert Storing in his seven-volume edition of *The Complete Anti-Federalist* (1981) and selected the material for a one-volume abridged version, *The Anti-Federalist* (1985). He has also written extensively on the debates over ratification of the Constitution and various issues concerning American constitutional law.

George A. Dunn spent the past nine years as Lecturer in Philosophy and Religion at the Ningbo Institute of Technology, Zhejiang University, in China. He is currently with the Philosophy Department at Marian University in Indianapolis. His research interests include moral and political philosophy, classical Chinese philosophy, Leo Strauss, René Girard, and philosophy and popular culture. He has edited or co-edited six books on philosophy and popular culture, including *Sons of Anarchy and Philosophy* (2015) and *The Philosophy of Christopher Nolan* (2017), both co-edited with Jason Eberl. His current projects include books on Plato, Nietzsche, and Strauss; René Girard and the Western Philosophical Tradition; and Leo Strauss in China.

Angel Jaramillo Torres is currently a postdoctoral fellow at Universidad Nacional Autónoma de México (UNAM). He has been a journalist, essayist, editor, speechwriter, public servant, consultant, and academic. He holds a BA in international relations from El Colegio de México and an MA and PhD in political science from The New School for Social Research in New York, and was a DAAD fellow at the Ludwig-Maximilians-Universität München. He has taught at CUNY York College and City College and UNAM. He has worked for the Mexican government as a foreign policy analyst and speechwriter. His journalistic pieces have appeared in several outlets in Spanish and English. He is the author of *Leo Strauss on Nietzsche's Thrasymachean-Dionysian Socrates: Philosophy, Politics, Science, and Religion in the Modern Age* (2017).

Ashok Karra received his doctorate from the University of Dallas in December 2017. His dissertation, *Xenophon's Republic: Nobility, Self-Knowledge, and the Identity of the Philosopher*, wonders aloud about a strange miniature Xenophon presents of Socrates in the *Memorabilia*, where Socrates seems most competent to advise generals, politicians, and perhaps even to rule himself. Xenophon tempts his readers with the possibility that rule can be perfectly rational and useful before acknowledging that human reason may not serve political ends properly in the least. The purpose of this temptation, Karra argues, is to highlight the uniqueness and moral character of the philosophical life itself. Karra also maintains a blog, *Rethink*, (http://www.ashokkarra.com), devoted to close-reading poetry and highlighting philosophical or political issues of note.

Yu Jin Ko teaches English at Wellesley College and has written extensively on Shakespeare, with an emphasis on performance. His first book, *Mutability and Division on Shakespeare's Stage*, appeared in 2004. He has also co-edited a book collection that brings together essays from scholars and theater professionals: *Shakespeare's Sense of Character: On the Page and From the Stage*. His articles and reviews have continued to focus on Shakespeare in performance, both in the theater and on film. They include pieces like a review of *Twelfth Night* in Central Park featuring Anne Hathaway as well as an essay on a production of *Macbeth* by inmates of a correctional institution ("Macbeth Behind Bars"). More recently, he has moved into the area of Shakespeare in production across the globe, especially in the East. "The site of burial in two Korean hamlets" is his latest foray into this field.

Kenneth Masugi has enjoyed careers in academia and government. He is the co-author, editor, or co-editor of nine books on American politics including a forthcoming monograph on Tocqueville's *Democracy in America*. While directing programs at the Claremont Institute, he also served as the editor of its quarterly *Claremont Review of Books* in its early years. He is on the editorial board of two political science journals. Masugi has taught at several institutions, including the US Air Force Academy, where he was Olin Distinguished Visiting Professor; the Ashbrook Center of Ashland University; and the center for the Study of American Government at Johns Hopkins University. Masugi has been a speechwriter for two Cabinet members and a special assistant for Clarence Thomas, when he was Chairman of the Equal Employment Opportunity Commission. He is currently writing a book on the Declaration of Independence and the changing meaning of American citizenship.

Arthur Milikh is associate director of The Heritage Foundation's B. Kenneth Simon Center for Principles and Politics. He conducts research on America's founding principles, oversees the center's research portfolio, and gives talks on the tenets of the American political tradition to policy-makers, political leaders, and the public.

Patrick Lee Miller is Associate Professor of Philosophy at Duquesne University. He is the author of *Becoming God: Pure Reason in Early Greek Philosophy* (2012) and co-editor of *Introductory Readings in Ancient Greek and Roman Philosophy* (2015). His recent philosophical writing uses Platonism to address current problems such as gender, sexuality, child psychology, pedagogy, natural evolution, virtual reality, spirituality, indecision, honesty, and liberal government.

Feisal G. Mohamed is Professor of English and Renaissance Studies at CUNY Graduate Center. A past president of the Milton Society of America, his most recent books are *Milton and the Post-Secular Present: Ethics, Politics, Terrorism* (2011); *Milton's Modernities: Poetry, Philosophy, and History from the Seventeenth Century to the Present, co-edited with Patrick Fadely* (2017); and *A New Deal for the Humanities: Liberal Arts and the Future of Public Higher Education* (2016), co-edited with Gordon Hutner. In addition to scholarly journals, his work has appeared in *Dissent, The Huffington Post, The New York Times, The American Scholar*, and the website of The New Republic. At present, he is completing a book manuscript provisionally entitled *Sovereignty: Seventeenth-Century England and the Making of the Modern Political Imaginary*.

Gladden J. Pappin is Assistant Professor of Politics at the University of Dallas and is the deputy editor of *American Affairs*. He is also a permanent research fellow and senior adviser of the Center for Ethics and Culture at the University of Notre Dame. He received his AB (history) and PhD (government) from Harvard. He has written on the origins and criticism of modern politics, with particular attention to ecclesiastical politics and the question of technology. His articles and reviews appear in *American Affairs, History of Political Thought, Review of Metaphysics, Perspectives on Political Science, Comunicazioni sociali, Politics and Poetics, Modern Age, Intercollegiate Review, Claremont Review of Books, First Things*, and elsewhere.

Joseph Reisert is Harriet S. and George C. Wiswell, Jr., Associate Professor of American Constitutional Law in the Department of Government at Colby College. He is the author of *Jean-Jacques Rousseau: A Friend of Virtue* and is currently writing a book on *The General Will and Constitutional Democracy*.

Leslie G. Rubin taught political philosophy, American politics, constitutional law, and American political thought for 34 years at Kenyon College, at the University of Houston, and at Duquesne University. She was first exposed to Aristotle as a political science student at Dickinson College and wrote her dissertation at Boston College on the *Politics*. Since 2015, Rubin was an independent scholar working on the connections between Aristotle's political thinking and the writings of the founding generation of the United States, to be published as *America, Aristotle and the Politics of a Middle Class* (Baylor University Press, 2018). During most of the last quarter century, she was Coordinator, then Director, of the Society for Greek Political Thought, an international organization through which she kept in touch with studies of the wide variety of Greek political philosophers and poets.

Marc Benjamin Sable taught political science at Bethany College in West Virginia for ten years; since 2016, he has taught at Universidad de las Américas and Universidad Iberoamericana in Mexico City. He received his PhD from the University of Chicago in 1997 with specializations in comparative politics, American politics, and political theory. He was a 1993–1994 Fulbright grantee in Cairo, Egypt, and a 2014 NEH

Summer Institute Participant. His research has focused on Abraham Lincoln, American political thought, and Aristotle, and is currently in the final stages of a book manuscript entitled *Lincoln's Virtues and Aristotle's Ethics*. He has served at the Northeastern Political Science Association, as section coordinator for Continental Political Thought and Modern Political Thought, and on the General Council. In 2016–2017, he was a visiting researcher at the Institute for Philosophical Research of UNAM, where he has prepared a translation and analytic essay on Carlos de Sigüenza y Góngora's *Theater of Political Virtues*.

CHAPTER 1

Leadership, Statesmanship and Tyranny: The Character and Rhetoric of Trump

Angel Jaramillo Torres and Marc Benjamin Sable

This volume gathers together a set of essays which, like its companion volume, *Trump and Political Philosophy: Patriotism, Cosmopolitanism, and Civic Virtue*, seeks to make sense of contemporary politics through the works of many of the greatest political thinkers. Following a venerable tradition, we have arranged this volume chronologically, and grouped the essays into sections based on whether they discuss premodern, modern or postmodern thinkers. However, the reader has probably come with the primary intention of understanding Trump's rise in light of political philosophy, rather than seeking to use Trump to understand the history of political philosophy. This introduction, then, will lay out the philosophical disputes which underlie varying interpretations of Trump, with a focus on the broad theme of what counts as wholesome or pernicious leadership.

This collection discusses the ways that Trump exercises leadership for good or ill, and thus the extent to which he exhibits the qualities of either a statesman or a tyrant. Statesmanship is the way a political leader successfully deals with matters of government. Tyranny is government which

A. Jaramillo Torres (✉)
Universidad Nacional Autónoma de México, Mexico City, Mexico

M. B. Sable
Universidad Iberoamericana and Universidad de las Américas,
Mexico City, Mexico

© The Author(s) 2018   1
A. Jaramillo Torres, M. B. Sable (eds.), *Trump and Political Philosophy*,
https://doi.org/10.1007/978-3-319-74445-2_1

abuses its citizens and a perennial human possibility. Its actualization has troubled all the great political thinkers, who have imagined ways to avoid it. Because tyranny and statesmanship are types of leadership, and since political philosophy seeks the objective good, true leadership is the opposite of nihilism. In the best description, a true leader knows the why and wherefore of human actions, and good leadership is thus equivalent to statesmanship. In referring to Trump we are obviously referencing his character as a person and as political leader. We understand rhetoric here very broadly, as referring to his comportment and political style, since his significance stems as much from *how* he communicates and shapes the political discourse as *what* he communicates, i.e., his ideology or political views.

The authors of the essays included here do not view Trump and rhetoric through a single theoretical lens. Moreover, they take their bearings from political history as well as from political philosophy. The contemporary political predicament is probed from American, European, Middle Eastern, and Chinese traditions of political thought: The volume is thus wide in scope and ambitious in its approach. The essays, however, can be grouped under two broad categories: on the one hand, Trump's rhetoric and his demagogy and, on the other, his character and how it relates to democratic institutions.

A good place to frame the debates here is the typology in Joseph Reisert's essay, "Knave, Patriot, or Factionist," which deftly relates the question of Trump's character to his political craft. He delineates three possible interpretations of Trump. Roughly, these are (a) a selfish demagogue who seeks political power for personal advantage, (b) a skillful politician who utilizes rhetoric in defense of his country, and (c) a clever demagogue who manipulates the masses in order to impose his ideological agenda. On the first score, some have seen in Trump a man whose main purpose in life is to strengthen his own economic well-being, which includes his immediate family. Not only his rhetoric but also his biography seems to fit this characterization. In office he placed his daughter and her husband as chief advisors, at least temporarily. A self-centered man as a type has certainly been probed and discussed by ancient and modern philosophy. It is what we know today as the bourgeois. On the second score, Trump's defenders argue that his rhetoric appeals to that section of the citizenship that has not attended elite schools. It is a language that from the point of view of over-educated elites might seem irrational, but in fact is a bridge that allows underdogs to communicate with the leader. Both Trump and his supporters concur in the fact that the time has come for a national reawakening. On the final score, Trump's policies may constitute a kind of ideology. For those who are sanguine about Trump, this ideology takes its bearings from the American political experience. For the time being, Trumpism seems to be a practice in search of a theory.

CHARACTER AND LEADERSHIP

Small-mindedness, willfulness and greed are certainly among the traits which render one unfit for leadership, while a concern for the regime's stability, the defense of the masses and seriousness of purpose would define the statesman. George Dunn, Ashok Karra, Yu Jin Ko, and Murray Dry deploy these concepts to critique Trump, utilizing the thought of Confucius, Xenophon, Shakespeare, Hamilton and Lincoln, respectively. In effect, each condemns Trump as lacking the character of a decent political leader, and all conclude that he is driven by egoistic motives, i.e., a Rousseauian knave of one sort or another.

Christopher Colmo on Alfarabi, Gladden Pappin on Machiavelli, Arthur Milikh on the Federalist, and Feisal Mohamed on Carl Schmitt are all more focused on reading the relationship of the leader's character to the regime. Pappin and Milikh are more generous to Trump, inclined to see him as a patriot or at least as representing important value for the American people (in Milikh's case) or that of the working class against the elite (in Pappin's). They are inclined to view him as a patriot. By contrast, Mohamed's assessment is more critical; he views Trump as potentially taking advantage of expanded presidential powers to impose dominance by his political base. In short, as a Rousseauian factionist. Colmo is primarily interested in Trump's rise as a thought experiment on how Alfarabi would understand a regime totally without religious foundation, and what that would entail for political leadership, leaving the precise question of Trump's character open.

THE CHARACTER OF TRUMP

George Dunn's essay is the only in this collection devoted to a non-Western thinker (if we regard Alfarabi as Western). The question Dunn asks is simply what Confucius would have thought about Donald Trump. Not surprisingly the answer to this question is complex. Dunn offers a variety of reasons for why Confucius might have supported Trump, but also tells us why the iconic Chinese philosopher would take issue with the 45th president and his behavior. According to Dunn, both Confucius and Trump share conservatism as part of their personal constitution, for both live in times they consider corrupt and look back to a time they deem great. Unlike Trump, however, Confucius put great emphasis on the concept of culture (文, wén) as a way to overcome man's natural state, one of zero-sum conflict that makes all worse off. Culture was very significant for Confucius, as well as his followers Mengzu and Xunzi. According to Dunn, a philosopher in the Chinese tradition is, among other things, an expert of culture, which includes "all the practices that were regarded as the marks of a civilized human being." Confucius' notion of the ideal man or the gentleman (君子) sets high demands on political leaders. Dunn suggests that Confucius would not have regarded Trump as a gentleman, but rather as a "small man" (小人, xiǎorén). It is not fanciful to point out that Dunn's Confucius would have concurred with the moral judgment of Oscar Wilde, who made Lord Darlington quip that a cynic is "a man who knows the price of everything and the value of nothing."

The Athenian general, politician and political philosopher, Xenophon, belongs to the same axial age as Confucius, and surprisingly may help us better understand present-day American political figures. Karra's essay presents three portraits of political personalities by Xenophon: those of Glaucon, Meno, and Hiero. The author shows ignoble characteristics which the reader can use to evaluate contemporary political figures. In Karra's account, Xenophon shows Glaucon as "an extremely ignorant but extremely ambitious man", lacking the slightest idea of how to govern. Meno, on the other hand, appears as greedy and grasping, while Hiero is seen as a man who is deeply unsatisfied with his everyday life, despite reaching supreme power. In the first two cases, Socrates is presented as a man who educates ambitious young men in moderation. The reader cannot avoid thinking that Trump lacks Socratic education. In Karra's presentation of the third case, that of Hiero, Xenophon's Simonides appears as witness to the tyrant's life, a life made distasteful due to the excessive and base nature of his pleasures. Karra ends his essay suggesting that ignorance, greed, and intemperance—the vices he discusses in his Xenophontic portraits of ignobility—render a man unfit to govern. Behind this portrait looms the figure of Trump.

Taking his bearings from Stephen Greenblatt's *Invisible Bullets*, Ko analyzes the saga that begins with a rebellion against Richard II and ends with a rueful chorus anticipating the disastrous reign of Henry VI. Ko follows Henry V—the hero of the saga—as he spent his youthful years as Hal frequenting taverns in the company of Falstaff rather than attending the court of his father, King Henry IV. Drawing on the Foucaultian idea that power produces its own subversion, he investigates whether Trump can be said to have the traits of both the lord of misrule Falstaff, and the mischievous Hal. The 45th president is known for his abstinence, but as a young man he carried on with a score of Falstaffian characters, from whom he learned the mendacious arts, in the world of Tammany Hall politics, real estate chicanery and tabloid entertainment that was 1970s New York City. This was to Trump what the tavern and Falstaff were for young Hal. The presentation of the relationship of Hal and Falstaff demonstrates the extent to which an education in the toughness on the streets may be beneficial for a future leader. At the same time, Ko is not sanguine about the current state of American politics, as Trump's strange combination of Falstaff and Hal does not exhibit the virtues of the mature Henry V.

In "American Constitutionalism from Hamilton to Lincoln to Trump," Murray Dry explains how Washington and Hamilton developed in tandem the foreign and economic policy of America's first administration. Dry probes Hamilton's concerns regarding the danger of a man unfit for office reaching the Presidency. According to Dry, while Hamilton understood that the statement, "ambition counteracts ambition" could be used to paradoxically found a virtuous republic, Lincoln's actions and thought exhibited both prudence and civic virtue. Behind Dry's presentation stands the idea that America has been successful to the degree it has because it has combined the way of Hamilton and the way of Lincoln. The danger of Trump, points out Dry, is that Trump seems to behave in a manner which is both anti-Hamiltonian and anti-Lincolnian.

Trump's Character, Leadership and the American Regime

In "Trump, Alfarabi, and the Open Society," Christopher Colmo engages in a thought experiment imagining what the medieval philosopher Alfarabi, would have thought about the American republic, in general, and about Trump's style of governing, in particular. According to Colmo, Alfarabi would be struck by the possibility of a regime where the church and the state are separated into different spheres of influence, and freedom of speech is guaranteed by the constitution. As a student of kalam (defensive theology), Alfarabi would have tried to see whether the American regime might deserve to be defended. Colmo argues that Alfarabi might be the thinker who thought most profoundly about the possibility of a politics that does not need philosophy, or knowledge of objective truth. For Alfarabi there are "two kinds of rulers who do not need philosophy: the traditional king, who follows his predecessors, and the one 'who rules through a certain shrewdness and cunning that he learns from experience.'" The ruler who needs philosophy will take as his guide policies based on universals, while the ruler who does not need philosophy will learn only from experience. In the latter case, prudence and shrewdness replaced philosophy. Colmo seems to argue that Trump is a species of ruler who does not need philosophy because he possesses mere shrewdness. Although for Alfarabi prudence cannot be separated from shrewdness, Trump's "art of the deal" does away with the sphere of prudence entirely. (Following Aristotle, Alfarabi understood prudence to be the shrewd pursuit of one's ends, but the nature of those ends was justified by knowing them as objectively true or right.) Trump's rejection of universals might explain his preference for particulars as such. In this light one can understand his advocacy of economic nationalism at the expense of globalization. This is just one of the ways in which a medieval Islamic political philosopher can help us to understand present-day America.

In his essay "Machiavellian Politics, Modern Management and the Rise of Donald Trump," Gladden Pappin resorts to an important distinction in Machiavelli—the humors of the *grandi* and the *popolo*, the elites and the people—to explain the rise of Trump in modern commercial America. Pappin argues that although "Trump's election was portrayed in potentially apocalyptic terms," it took place within the constitutional framework. Pappin finds elective affinities between Machiavelli's notion of "managing" (*maneggiare*) and the concept of commercial "management." The modern turn—inspired by John Locke—from political managing to the commercial management of captains of industry "has arguably made the singular 'venting of the popular humor' more difficult." Pappin argues that, in the world of modern industrial management, Peter Drucker, "wittingly or unwittingly describes a world of activity suffused with Machiavelli's strategies, but modified in crucial ways. Those ways lie at the root of our current political problems." Although the scientific management of Drucker and Taylor promised an era of economic prosperity, it ended up chiefly benefitting the managerial classes while harming workers. The world described by Drucker is no longer functioning in modern America due to globalization and mechanization through robotics. These two phenomena have led the working class ("the popular humor") to become fragmented, but with the capacity "to be constituted as a whole". Donald Trump is seen by Pappin as a kind of modern-day Machiavellian prince, allied with the *popolo* against the modern *grandes*, namely, the managerial elites. With Trump, the American polity is returning to the Machiavellian world where the two political humors are again at odds.

Like Pappin's essay, Milikh's relates Trump's leadership to the nature of the modern regime, and like Colmo's essay (and Dry's, discussed above) he relates it to the particular nature of the American regime. However, while Dry focuses on the disjuncture between Trump and great figures in the American political tradition, Arthur Milikh argues there is a deep affinity between the founders and Trump, specifically the Hamiltonian project of fostering commerce to increase American national power. "Trump and the Federalist on National Greatness in a Commercial Republic" maintains that Trump won the 2016 presidential election in part due to his promise to "Make America Great Again", and that "the clearest articulation of national greatness is found in The Federalist." Milikh focuses on demonstrating that "for Publius commerce will serve as the means by which America will develop its [own] form of greatness". He argues that republican principles can only survive in a unified nation that is powerful enough to defend its sovereignty and independence from foreign encroachments. Publius' political thought advanced a new form of greatness that was not based on military control of other countries—as in Europe and the rest of the world—but founded upon competitive commercial exchange. According to Milikh, Trump proposes a new paradigm whereby the United States will shrewdly use all the tools at its disposal to gain an edge over other nations in the economic disputes of the future. Milikh maintains that Publius imagined a political regime of human rationality. "In this regard", argues Milikh, "America will be the first non-theocratic country, the reason for which it is the example of human nobility".

The subject of Feisal Mohamed's essay is Carl Schmitt, the German scholar who compellingly described the nature of politics as depending on the friend-enemy distinction. Just as the beautiful-ugly dichotomy is to esthetics, or the good and bad distinction to morality, so Schmitt claimed the friend-enemy dichotomy was the essence of politics. In his essay, Mohamed sets out to examine whether the Schmittian understanding of politics can be applied to Trump's measures, principally "the so-called Muslim ban" and his pardon of Arizona Sheriff Joe Arpaio, both of which have, for now, been stymied by the exercise of judicial review. For Mohamed the Trump administration has all the features of the "commissarial dictatorship", a situation that allows the executive power to decide whether the state finds itself in a state of exception. This allows a president to circumvent the rule of law. But Mohamed does not single out Trump for condemnation: When behaving like a dictator, he simply takes advantage of an American legal tradition that "rhymes well with the commissarial dictatorship that Schmitt finds in the Republican tradition". Ever since Hamilton described the need for an executive with "energy", argues Mohamed, the presidency has claimed "unilaterally to exercise force against external enemies". Mohamed ends his essay on a pessimistic note, for Trump might be only a prelude of what is to come: the victory of reactionary forces claiming sovereign decisionism for the sake of the *Volk*.

RHETORIC AND DEMAGOGY

Political philosophy has always been interested in investigating what makes a ruler capable of governing well. The essays by Patrick Lee Miller, Bernard Dobski, Leslie Rubin, John Burt, Kenneth Masugi, Joseph Reisert, Marc Sable, and Kate Crehan lay out different accounts of whether the 45th president has used the rhetoric of a statesman or sheer demagogy.

Patrick Lee Miller takes his bearings from Plato's portrait of philosophers, sophists, and tyrants to lay out a typology of truth. Miller points out that there are three ways of disregarding the truth, "with three correlative types of people." The philosopher is a seeker of truth and is always honest, even if he appears to be lying. The sophist, on the other hand, manipulates words for purposes other than seeking the truth: to become rich, famous, or more powerful. Sophistry is then the genus under which demagogy falls, a species defined by its political motive. Miller argues that when Trump had not yet reached power, he ignored the truth in the fashion of a generic sophist. This changed, however when he became president, for he began to lie with tyrannical purposes. For Miller, the tyrant seeks to exert his power by defining the truth. He is in the business of inventing an alternative reality where the truth becomes his will to power.

Bernard Dobski begins his essay by belittling "comparisons of Trump to the 'baddies' of the twentieth and twenty-first century" such as Hitler and Stalin. He argues that a better analogy is with the Athenian political leader, Cleon, primarily as presented by the political historian, Thucydides. Like Trump, Cleon was a "flatterer of the city demos". Drawing on an insight by Timothy Burns, Dobski claims that the most significant trait of Cleon is anger triggered by frustrated hopefulness.[1] Dobski backs his assertions by laying out a variety of historical examples taken from the *History of the Peloponnesian War* and probing the judgment of philosophers such as Aristotle. But Dobski doesn't engage in an all-out attack on Cleon, whose virtues allowed Athens to maintain its hegemony for a while. Against prevailing opinions about Thucydides' alleged realism, Dobski presents us with a more complicated portrait, one in which justice is given its due. He claims that Cleon's appeals to Athenian pride contain an implicit notion that Athens *deserves* to rule. Like Trump's "Make America Great Again" slogan, the grounds for this claim are never spelled out. Dobski finishes his essay by showing that Cleon's politics might be complemented by Pericles', whose rhetoric provided those grounds and whose policies were more self-controlled. He suggests that the 45th president might learn from Pericles' example.

Aristotle belongs to the next generation. Leslie Rubin's essay provides penetrating "observations on Aristotle's insights into the campaign for the presidency" in 2016. Her essay focuses on two Aristotelian political ideas. Firstly, she uses "the philosopher's understanding of demagogy" to shed light on the current moral predicament of American politics. Secondly, Aristotle's reflections on regime stability enable Rubin to set forth some remedies for the conditions that made possible the election of a demagogue in the 2016 presidential elections. She points out that demagogy can be a method of regime change. In particular, she warns us that tyranny typically begins when democracy descends into demagogy. In Rubin's opinion, Trump engages in textbook demagogy, fulfilling many of Aristotle's descriptions of the demagogue. The reader of Rubin's essay will find countless examples that show how Trump's actions conform to Aristotles' diagnoses. That this is the case makes one think that the philosopher's chief thoughts may truly be timeless. Hers is a cautionary tale of the dangers when a demagogue divides a polity into two, of enemies against friends. Her solution takes up an idea by Aristotle—to strengthen the middle class, for it educates "natural peacemakers". This could be accomplished, in part, by "understanding the political/moral role of education" and its impact in promoting the republican virtues of prudence and moderation.[2]

In his essay, Reisert eschews an all-out attack on Trump, finding reasons why Rousseau might have supported some of Trump's qualities and political inclinations. He reminds us that Rousseau's concept of the general will is chiefly thought to function only in a polity the size of eighteenth-century Geneva. Although Rousseau was in favor of direct democracy as the best way to make decisions in a city, he nevertheless reflected on the best way to select candidates for public office in representative democracies. Still, Reisert argues that, if Rousseau had his way, Trump would have never become president, due to his lack of experience and civic virtue. He is the product of the reality TV and social media era and "the decline of civic experience and civic virtue in the public." However, Reisert conceives a scenario where the opening of the highest office to political novices such as Trump might be beneficial to a polity suppurating with corruption. When it comes to Trump's policies, Reisert argues that Rousseau would not have been displeased by Trump's support of particularist patriotism and his criticism of cosmopolitanism. However, Reisert points out that Rousseau would have rejected Trump's embrace of "finance and commerce."

In "Lincoln, Moral Conflict, and Herrenvolk Democracy in the Age of Trump," John Burt argues that the mature Lincoln's political posture, taken after coming out of political retirement in 1854, as the slavery crisis reached its peak, provides a model for democratic rhetoric from which we can glean insights for the current era. According to Burt, Lincoln developed a strategy of dialog with those who "undermine the mores and norms upon which democratic culture depends" and those who "seem to have closed themselves for persuasion." Drawing on his previous work, *Lincoln's Tragic Pragmatism*, he points out that the rhetoric of many Trump supporters is "suicidally apodictic," because it is designed to close off an argument. Burt maintains that Trump's politics is a negation of two traits upon which the United States had historically fulfilled its democratic promise. Firstly, America has been a multicultural society with a common identity based not on common blood or religion, but on a commitment to the idea that all men are created equal. Secondly, America has been committed to "a world founded upon multilateral agreements ... to international institutions of collective security ruled by open covenants." The latter reflects democratic values because it treats relations between nations as requiring dialog and consent. He sees both the domestic commitment to equality and the foreign policy of international institutionalism as under attack by the Trump administration. For Burt, the option facing present-day America is either a return to Lincolnian rhetoric and actions founded on Kantian liberal politics that has consent and persuasion as its greatest values, or a Schmittian agonistic politics that bestows more importance to competition and zero-sum politics. The latter is, according to Burt, the hallmark of Trumpian politics. At stake is the very soul of the American

Republic. As a strategy for coping with opponents who seem to have closed themselves off from persuasion and thus from democratic culture, he recommends that we adopt two Lincolnian rhetorical strategies. First, that we construct an idealized version of opponents, and speak to that idealized opponent as if she were persuadable, asking for small concessions that "keep alive the possibility of a shared political life even in the face of a deep conflict." His second suggestion is to address the fears which we believe close the minds of our opponents. Both strategies were ultimately unsuccessful in breaking the death-spiral of apodictic argumentation by pro-slavery Southerners, but Burt points out that they did enable Lincoln to wage a bloody civil war without rancor and welcome them back into the national community afterwards.

Like Burt, Kenneth Masugi finds important analogies between Lincoln's era and the age of Trump, but his interpretation is the polar opposite: He claims that Trump embraces a Lincolnian call for citizens to embrace common citizenship that will strengthen a sense of patriotism. According to Masugi, Trump is like Lincoln, because he was able to make inroads against the establishment of the Republican Party, thus steering the party into a place closer to the interests of the people. Drawing on Aristotle's notion of political friendship (*politike philia*) in the *Nicomachean Ethics*, Masugi maintains that the tenth and 45th presidents "bring together citizens for all practical purposes of politics" based on the three Aristotelian types of friendship: utility, pleasure, and virtue. Masugi claims that the central theme of Lincoln's campaign was how to foster American nationalism and that Trump's attempt to make America great again is a means to "recovering the America of Lincoln and the founders." The two fundamental passions that Lincoln highlighted in his Dred Scott speech and in the Gettysburg address are self-interest and a sense of duty. Masugi goes out of his way to demonstrate through a discussion of key Trump speeches that the current president appeals to both interest and duty, thus embracing a Lincolnian politics. We leave for the reader to decide whether Burt's or Masugi's reading of Trump squares better with the character of Lincoln.

In "Charisma, Value and Political Vocation," Marc Sable applies Weberian conceptions of legitimacy, ethics and political vocation to make sense of the 2016 election. One can read this essay as a meditation on why rhetoric succeeds or fails. With regard to political legitimacy, Sable holds that, at the end of the day, the sources for Weber seem to be only two: traditional and charismatic legitimacy—although traditional legitimacy is in the end nothing more than institutionalized charisma. If this is the case, only charisma ultimately grounds political legitimacy. Sable thus suggests that the distinction Weber made in "Politics as Vocation" between the ethics of responsibility and the ethics of final ends may lack foundations, even as it can be used to critique all the major candidates of 2016. He argues that Hillary Clinton represented institutional charisma in crisis, while Trump represented a sheer personal charisma that succeeded among a great part of the electorate precisely because it challenged a neoliberal value system in which many had lost faith. In short, Clinton versus Trump: institutional versus personal charisma. According to Sable, Hillary Clinton's defeat is best explained by her failure to articulate the values of an American civic nationalism, such as individual freedom, social justice, popular democracy, and postracial equality.

In "The Common Sense of Donald J. Trump," Kate Crehan provides an arresting reading of Gramsci's prison books to explain Trump's populist appeal. She argues that Gramsci's understanding of the causes that led to the rise of fascism in the 1920s can shed light on the present-day American predicament. She focuses on Gramsci's concept of *senso commune*, which is "a taken-for-granted 'knowledge' to be found in every human community." A variegated phenomenon, *senso commune* can be regarded as the opposite of critical thinking. In the Anglo-Saxon tradition, argues Crehan, an appeal to common sense is seen as beneficial by politicians. In the 2016 presidential campaign, Trump successfully positioned himself as the candidate of common sense as opposed to the "elitist" Hillary Clinton. Trump brilliantly used his knowledge of the media to garner the sympathy of Tea Party supporters. Crehan concludes her essay by suggesting that a different appeal to *senso commune* may be necessary to "bring about social transformation" for the benefit of the "subaltern" classes. Only an alliance between the intellectuals and "those who are subordinated" will allow for the cultural victory of the progressive sector in America. Crehan sees in the Occupy Wall Street movement—"a mass of 'ordinary people'" with the effective slogan "We are the 99 percent"—a paradigm for future attempts to challenge populist conservatism in the Trump era.

Judging Trump

The editors believe that including viewpoints which defend—or at least explain sympathetically—Trump as a political leader, is necessary both to elevate the theoretical conversation and preserve the preconditions of democratic discourse. However, we also believe it is our duty, as scholars and as citizens, to make clear our own position on Trumpian leadership.

This introduction began by laying out three possible interpretations of Trump as a political leader: "knave, factionist, or patriot." Classical political thought, with its emphasis on virtue, typically presented tyranny as a function of the tyrant's base character. By contrast, modern and postmodern interpretations tend to emphasize the tyrant's willful imposition of political goals contrary to the common good. We believe that Trump has a tyrannical soul, in both senses, and that he vacillates between knave and factionist. First, judging his personal character, we cannot overlook his intemperance and injustice. In the *Republic*, Socrates describes the tyrant as a person enslaved to his appetites, carnal or pecuniary, incapable of self-control. The evidence of both in Trump seems to us overwhelming. This personal corruption, we think, is reflected in a second tyrannical quality: His demagogy treats all inconvenient facts—let alone arguments—as mere obstacles to the fulfillment of his appetites for fame, wealth and power. While this has ancient antecedents, postmodern skepticism makes this problem all the more profound. Admittedly all rhetoric treats persuasion, not truth, as its end, but tyranny occurs when leaders do so shamelessly in order to impose their will. Shame in the face of truth is what separates decent from indecent leaders, be they ancient demagogues or modern ideologues. It is fortunate that Trump's excessive appetites and his "will to power" seem to be in conflict, i.e., that his personal desire for approval and wealth renders his nihilistic demagogy in pursuit of his agenda less effective, i.e., undermines his capacity to suborn political opposition. Those who would treat Trump as a decent leader do so because they believe he defends America—or rather a vision held by their section of it. In a word, we think him neither statesman nor true patriot, but a factionist whose primary nature as a knave makes him less dangerous.[3]

Granted, it is easier to condemn Trump's leadership when one rejects his policies. Certainly, if Trumpism—and not just some particular policy articulated by Trump—is objectively right, in aggregate, then we might label him not a factional ideologue but a normal democratic politician engaged in a new sort of rhetoric. The claim of Trump's apologists seems to be that he defends the true American national interest against grave threats and advocates for those whose rights have been neglected. On the contrary, however, we believe that his policies are, to borrow Madison's telling phrase, "contrary to the rights of other citizens, or to the permanent and aggregate interests of the community." Still, we do believe that it is possible to distinguish gross demagogy from decent rhetoric, by the very fact that his discourse makes rational discussion of the issues fundamentally more difficult. By treating every debate as a conflict between friends and enemies, in which both the true and the desirable is judged according to whether it advances his agenda, he educates the American people to disregard reason itself, and he encourages blind partisanship. If statecraft is soulcraft, Trump teaches the vice of nihilism by example. His rise is then equally an effect of civic corruption and its reinforcement.

Finally, although partisan factors have limited public opposition from within Trump's own party, we take some solace from the fact that his most extreme threats to *constitutional* norms—threats to fire the Special Counsel, upend voting protections, and bully the press—have provoked effective opposition and generally achieved little. This indicates to us that the American republic is not as corrupted as his staunchest defenders believe. But for a discussion of the degree to which civic virtue is still present in the American public today, we recommend that our readers turn to the companion volume.

Notes

1. His argument thus runs parallel with Ericka Tucker's Spinozistic analysis of the shift from Obama to Trump, which can be found in the companion volume.
2. She elaborates on this argument in *America, Aristotle, and the Politics of a Middle Class* (Waco, Texas: Baylor University Press, 2018).
3. We would also observe that in these two volumes, not one contributor dares to state explicitly that Trump is a statesman—even when they offer full-throated endorsement of Trump's policies or defend his political rhetoric.

References

Burt, John. *Lincoln's Tragic Pragmatism: Lincoln, Douglas, and Moral Conflict.* 1st ed. Cambridge, MA: Belknap Press, 2013.

Rubin, Leslie. *America, Aristotle, and the Politics of a Middle Class.* Waco, TX: Baylor University Press, 2018.

PART I

Ancient and Medieval Political Thought

CHAPTER 2

Truth, Trump, Tyranny:
Plato and the Sophists in an Era
of 'Alternative Facts'

Patrick Lee Miller

What is Trump's attitude to truth? In the era that he is quickly defining, what is yours? Do you tell the truth, even when it's difficult, or are you comfortable with lying, especially when it's to your advantage? Those are the two attitudes commonly distinguished when we consider someone's relationship to truth. The truth-teller thinks the truth to be something or other, and says what he thinks it to be, even in the face of adversity. Like the truth-teller, the liar thinks the truth to be something or other, but unlike him she says the opposite of what she thinks it to be in order to deceive. So much is familiar. But there are three other attitudes to the truth, with three correlative types of people. They are less often recognized than the first two, but they are far more relevant to our assessment of Trump and his era. In brief, these three attitudes are those of the philosopher, the sophist, and the tyrant.

The philosopher is not only a truth-teller but also a truth-seeker. She is honest in the fullest sense. The mere truth-teller is not. He reports the truth as it appears to him, but makes little or no effort to discover the real

P. L. Miller (✉)
Duquesne University, Pittsburgh, PA, USA

© The Author(s) 2018
A. Jaramillo Torres, M. B. Sable (eds.), *Trump and Political Philosophy*,
https://doi.org/10.1007/978-3-319-74445-2_2

17

truth when this differs from immediate appearances. Sophocles' Oedipus, for example, tells the truth of his life as it appears to him—he abandoned home to save his parents, consulted an oracle for guidance, killed a man who threatened him, solved a riddle to save a city, and married its grateful queen. He is not a liar. But neither is he a truth-seeker. After all, he did not flee home to save his parents, as it turns out, but went toward them with a congenital grievance. He visited an oracle, yes, but only to pervert its prophetic warning and thereby fulfill it. He killed not just any man, nor did he do it in self-defense; in a fit of road-rage, he slew his own father and all of his attendants. He brilliantly solved the riddle about Man, sure, but he could not see how it applied to one particular man: himself. Finally, he married a queen who also happened to be his own mother. How could he not have noticed?

That Oedipus cannot seek the truth is his tragic flaw.[1] This flaw so dominates his character that even when he seems to seek the truth about himself, his search is no search, but instead a distraction, a way of hiding— above all from himself—the fact that he's not really searching. This is because he doesn't want to know the truth as it really is; the search is too difficult and the destination too painful. But isn't that the case with most truths that matter? You don't have to have suffered Oedipus's abuse or have committed his crimes to hide from some truths about your life. Whatever your particular trials, if the world is as terrible a place as Sophocles and the other Greek tragedians knew it to be, you will always have reason to cloak yourself in comforting illusions. This universal problem is what the Oedipus story dramatizes. The truth-teller who nonetheless tries at all costs to avoid the painful truth is compelled by hard fate, and only after causing much grief, to become an honest man, a philosopher.

PHILOSOPHY AND SOPHISTRY

The "philo-sopher," as Plato defines him, is a lover (*philos*) of wisdom (*sophia*).[2] It is impossible, he adds, for a lover of wisdom to be a lover of falsehood (486d). As such, he cannot rest content with how things appear. Appearances depart from reality, and he longs to learn how things really are. "So, right from childhood," this "genuine lover of learning must strive above all for truth of every kind" (485d). Telling the truth will be a tool of that striving, but it is far from sufficient to reach the goal: knowing the truth. The philosopher "does not linger over each of the many things that are believed to be," the popular opinions, the conventional wisdom, the received dogmas that satisfy mere truth-tellers (490a–b). He keeps going until he reaches the object of his love. "Once he has drawn near to it, has intercourse with what really is, and has begotten understanding and truth," writes Plato, "he knows, truly lives, is nourished, and—at that point, but not before—is relieved from his labor pains" (490b). Far more is involved in the philosopher's attitude to truth than admitting that he chopped down a cherry tree.

What about those who are content with conventional wisdom? Plato calls them "philo-doxers," lovers of opinion, belief, or dogma. They can be truth-tellers, so long as they assume convention to be true. Think of the faithful Catholic who loves her Church, accepts its beliefs as true, and follows them accordingly, without ever having made her own investigation. Contrast her with the embittered priest who no longer cares whether the Church is right, but still enjoys the influence he wields over his parishioners through his fluency in its beliefs. Here is a fourth attitude to truth, that of the grifter or confidence man. He doesn't care about truth and falsity. He uses his mind and his words not to investigate the truth, or even to report what it seems to be, but to get what he wants. Truth is for suckers. Harry Frankfurt called this attitude *bullshit* in an essay he wrote under that title three decades ago. A canny publisher recognized an audience for the distinction between lying and bullshitting during the junior Bush years and put out the same essay as a little book.[3] Frankfurt had his fifteen minutes of fame on Jon Stewart's show and then faded from public awareness. His distinction lives on, but it was never really his in the first place.

Plato first drew it to identify the danger of the Sophists. These were famous men who traveled the Greek world selling their power with words. Words are always potent tools, but more so in democratic societies such as classical Athens, where political office can be acquired by making speeches. When you can manipulate words, you can sway crowds. The Sophists became rich, and in a few cases powerful, by promising to make their customers masters of words. As Plato shows, their expertise was a facility with *bullshit*, in Frankfurt's sense. The Sophist knows how to say what it takes to win—a court case, a business deal, a democratic election. He doesn't care whether what he says is true or false; that's irrelevant. After a while, in fact, he stops paying any attention to the truth. Thinking about it becomes a distraction from his purpose. Life is a contest, whether for money, fame, or power; words are the tools for winning it.

Plato's analysis of *bullshit* goes deeper than Frankfurt's, however, because it shows how this attitude to truth, when it becomes the attitude of educators, presages political decline. The Sophist "teaches nothing other than the convictions the masses hold when they are assembled together, and this he calls wisdom" (493a). He learns these convictions the way a tamer learns "the passions and appetites of a huge, strong beast that he is rearing," but because he cares only about making the beast do his bidding, he doesn't care whether these passions and appetites are good or bad, just or unjust. "He uses all these terms in conformity with the great beast's beliefs," Plato concludes, "calling the things it enjoys good and the things that anger it bad" (493c). Such disregard for truth, such deference to popular views, such peddling of bullshit, characterized Trump's long campaign for the presidency.

This is the man who first flirted with a campaign in 2011 by calling into question the citizenship of a sitting president. Not even the grudging publication of a birth certificate would silence his conspiratorial objections. Did he really doubt Obama's citizenship? It didn't matter: his followers did, and this was the passion he was exploiting for his own purposes. He spoke in conformity with the great beast's beliefs. Was there ever any hope of setting the record straight with either him or these followers? Not unless the distinction between the true and the false mattered to them. Eventually it became clear that it didn't. Too many falsehoods followed, and they came too fast, so that only devoted journalists could keep up: among the Arab population of New Jersey, "thousands and thousands of people were cheering" as the Twin Towers fell; Ted Cruz's father colluded with Lee Oswald in the Kennedy assassination; and so on. To discredit these claims one after the other became overwhelming. After a while, it seemed pointless even to point them out.[4]

It was shocking at first. Remember? Before Trump, we had not seen it done so often or so brazenly in American politics. Previous candidates had been liars, to be sure, and some had been confidence men—but none so openly, so successfully. Trump's contempt for the truth was not hurting his candidacy; on the contrary, it seemed to be helping him. The spectacle of Trump's campaign in 2016 was the explosion onto the national scene of some new attitude to truth. By all accounts, Trump has never used words for investigating the world, coming to understand it, and then communicating this understanding with others. To state the obvious: he is not a philosopher. What then is he? What is his attitude to truth? The answer is complex because he and his attitude have changed—more or less as Plato predicted—with his acquisition of power.

Before he became president of the United States, he was a con-man, a grifter, using words like pieces on a board, moving them for one purpose: winning. "Lying is second nature to him," says Tony Schwartz, ghost-writer of *The Art of the Deal* (1986), which Trump began his campaign in 2015 by falsely claiming he wrote himself. "More than anyone I have ever met," Schwartz adds, "Trump has the ability to convince himself that whatever he is saying at any given moment is true, or sort of true, or at least *ought* to be true."[5] This ability has helped him aggrandize himself—whether with money, in his many years as a businessman; fame, in his dozen years on reality TV; or with power, during his campaign for the presidency. Because most people are constrained to some extent by the truth—even liars pay attention to it in order to say the opposite—Trump's ability "gave him a strange advantage." Schwartz invented a term for this ability and reports that Trump loved it: "truthful hyperbole." In Frankfurt's idiom, it's called bullshit; in Plato's, sophistry.

The first generation of Sophists arrived in Athens and advertised their expertise in the art of persuasion, rhetoric. There were no mass media then, but their advertisements were at least as persuasive. Gorgias entered the court of public opinion, as we call it nowadays, taking as his client the villain of the Trojan War, the face that sailed a thousand ships, Helen. Against universal condemnation, he argued that she was innocent.[6] Either she had been abducted forcefully by Paris or she went willingly. If she had been forced, it wasn't her fault. Nor was it her fault if she had gone willingly. For what made her willing? If it was Love, this was either an affliction of the soul or an irresistible god. If she had been persuaded by Paris's words, this too would have been irresistible in its own way. "Speech is a powerful lord," he declaimed, "which by means of the finest and most invisible body effects the divinest works." Gorgias was exploiting the newest scientific jargon, with all its prestige, to argue that speech was the flow of little atoms from the mouth of the speaker into the ears and souls of the audience. A clever speaker would manipulate words, the effluences of atoms from his mouth, in such a way that they would strike the souls of the audience as forcefully as the grip of a god or a rapist.

Gorgias did not appeal to atomism because it was true—he didn't care what was true, anymore than he cared what was false—but because it helped him win customers. He played a confidence-game, and he won. With the appearance of an exhaustive argument, rich with the learning of science and religion, Gorgias became rich himself. Indeed, he became a celebrity abroad and a powerful man in his native Sicily. With a speech that claimed speech could force people to do the bidding of the speaker, Gorgias got people to give him their money, their attention, and their political offices. He was the ancient equivalent of the business guru who gets rich traveling from town to town offering expensive seminars that promise to teach you how to get rich. Then, as now, the ambitious and gullible flocked to hear Gorgias and Protagoras, hoping to learn this trick. But what exactly was it?

Whenever he had the opportunity, Plato's Socrates would ask the Sophists about their expertise. "I'd like to find out from the man," says Socrates of Gorgias, "what his craft can accomplish, and what it is that he both makes claims about and teaches."[7] Was it knowledge? If not, then what was it and why would anyone pay so much for anything less? If it was knowledge, what was it knowledge of? The truth? How could it be? Gorgias wrote speeches that were heedless of the truth. Socrates asked him whether his art of persuasion was "the one that results in being convinced without knowing or the one that results in knowing" (454e). Gorgias admits that he specialized in conviction without knowing the truth.

For his part, Protagoras wrote openly that there was no such thing as truth: "Human being is the measure of all things, of things that are, that they are, and of things that are not, that they are not."[8] Sophists seem to have assumed this Protagorean relativism—according to which human being, especially when it is gathered in groups, determines what is real and what is not—yet they also advertised themselves as *experts*, wise men, *sophistēs*. Don't experts know how things really are, that is, the truth? (*Theaetetus* 161c–162a) Protagoras insisted that he did "not deny the existence of both wisdom and wise men" (166d). But they are not wise because they know some objective truth—the sort supposedly made possible by a reality beyond appearances—because there is no such thing. "The man whom I call wise," he says instead, "is the man who can change the appearances—the man who in any case where bad things both appear and are for one of us, works a change and makes good things appear and be for him" (166d).

The physician, for example, is an expert in bodies, whereas the rest of us are not. Between sickness and health, he is able "to make a change from the one state to the other, because the other state is *better*" (167a). He is able to do this reliably because symptoms and treatments appear to him in a way they do not to the rest of us. But his success does not require the existence of any truth, although Protagoras concedes that "the things which appear to him are what some people, who are still at a primitive stage, call 'true'" (167b). When he compares the appearances of this expert to those of us who do not know, his sophisticated, relativist position "is that the one kind are *better* than the others, but in no way *truer*" (167b). By replacing the notion of truer with the notion of better—the notion of truth, in short, with the notion of good—Protagoras thinks he can preserve a role for experts while avoiding the distinction between appearance and reality. "Human being" can remain "the measure of all things," yet he can also remain the sort of wise man worthy of a hefty fee (167d).

But Protagoras's response works only when there is agreement, as in his example of health, about what is better. To nearly everyone, health appears better than sickness. Few would wish to contest this appearance and dispute that, in reality, health is not better than sickness. Were anyone to do so, however, Protagoras would have to grant that the physician who is able to exchange sick appearances for healthy ones only *seems* an expert to the majority. This concession may seem trivial, inasmuch as the vast majority deem health better than illness without qualification. Perhaps only a philosopher will object that in some circumstances it is better to be sick than healthy (during a military draft, e.g., for an unjust war).[9] But the concession seems far from trivial when there is a heated, painful, even violent dispute about the appearances of goodness. Yet this is often the case in politics.

Is it good to deport eleven million undocumented immigrants? Is it good to freeze the immigration of all Muslims? Is it good for police to return to racial profiling? Trump said these were good during his campaign. His supporters obviously agreed. Would you? Was it good to appoint another strict constructionist to the Supreme Court? Was it good to withdraw from the Paris Climate Accord? Was it good to withdraw from the Trans-Pacific Partnership? These were among the most dramatic moves of the early months of the Trump presidency. Do you agree with his supporters that they have indeed been good? If not, what response could Protagoras offer you here? None. You have your notion of the good, Trump and his supporters have theirs. There is nothing else to say, because there is no independent truth to which you can appeal. For them, there is only power. For you, there is only resistance.

TYRANNY AND TRUTH

Take something that everyone knows to be false and insist that it is true (or *vice versa*). If you are powerless—or at least relatively so, as Trump was the year he championed the "birther" conspiracy theory—you will be mocked and ostracized, as Trump was by President Obama at the 2011 White House Correspondents' dinner.[10] But if you become powerful—as Trump did upon winning the Republican nomination, and more so the presidency—you will achieve very different results. Most will still recognize the difference between true and false, privately, but your audacity will have drawn a clear line around yourself, testing the public allegiance of everyone.

Regarding your power, many will step immediately inside this circle with hopes of reward for doing so or fears of punishment for not doing so. More will do so over time as you consolidate your power. But you will remember those who did so early, especially when they defend your most manifest falsehoods; they have proven that they acknowledge (at least publicly) no truth independent of your will. These are the perfect subjects that your tyrannical attitude to truth is creating. Kellyanne Conway's phrase "alternative facts" was the candid admission of someone who jumped early into Trump's circle and tenaciously defended its illusions as reality. Of course, that was her job as his campaign manager, strategist, and counselor.

More revealing were the conversions of Republican leaders, who eventually supported Trump as president, despite denouncing him before his nomination and election as a "phony," a "con artist," or "unfit for the presidency." Those who persisted in their dissent, by contrast, implicitly declared themselves his implacable enemies. No further rational discussion was possible between those on opposite sides of the line Trump had drawn around himself. Communal reasoning presupposes an independent truth. We who acknowledge such a thing may disagree about this or that, but at least we are aiming for the same target: the independent truth, whatever it turns out to be. When someone removes the target, however, when the tyrant has spoken his "truth," you are either with him or against him.

This attitude became increasingly clear after the election, although there had been signs of it beforehand. It is easy to forget that in the final weeks of his campaign Trump wouldn't commit to accepting its results. The election was rigged, he claimed, *against* him! Now that evidence of Russian meddling *on his behalf* has come to light, the irony is rich. But Trump shows as little regard for irony as for evidence. Evidence is for losers. Trump clarified his meaning at a rally two days later: he would accept the results of the election *so long as he won*. It was a perverse relief to hear him say openly what some had suspected him of thinking all along. The goal had never been justice or truth, which require respecting laws and evidence. The goal had always been power. If laws and evidence became obstacles to winning it, well, greatness has a cost. And if greatness—understood as power—is the goal, no cost would be too high. The tyrant's attitude to truth, like his attitude to justice, makes both the creatures of his will and power.

This attitude became more evident after his election, as we should have expected from a grifter who can now convert his will immediately into "truth" through tweets, and into "justice" through executive orders. Had Trump remained merely a con-man, after all, he would have dropped the narrative of electoral fraud after he had won. Why bother? Yet he kept claiming—again without any evidence, even against the testimony of every expert—that millions of illegal immigrants had given Clinton her victory in the popular vote. Could vanity be his only motive? If so, why would he also claim, without evidence and against all the experts, that Trump Tower had been bugged by the Obama administration? He was not merely inventing a self-aggrandizing narrative, regardless of the truth; he was demonstrating his power over the "truth" of the experts: the professors, the intelligence agencies, anyone who claimed independence from his created "reality." He exhibited this power most distinctly in May of 2017 by appointing a commission to "investigate" electoral fraud. Its purpose, however, was to "prove" that there had been.

"It's not just that both Putin and Trump lie," wrote Masha Gessen prophetically during the transition period, "it is that they lie in the same way for the same purpose: blatantly, to assert power over truth itself."[11] She became familiar with this tyrannical attitude to truth while living under Putin, before she fled to the United States to escape the increasing repression of his regime.[12] "By denying known and provable facts," she added more specifically, "Mr. Trump exercises his ever-growing power over the public sphere."[13] This exercise became more explicit after his inauguration. Trump claimed that the sun had shone when he delivered his address to the biggest crowds in history. In fact, as footage showed, the assembled dignitaries covered themselves from the rain as he began to speak; in fact, as aerial photographs also showed, Trump's crowds were noticeably smaller than Obama's. Why would he lie about something demonstrably false? Why would his press secretary choose to defend his patent lie?

These were the questions of incredulous journalists, but they were imprecise, for this was not lying (the attempt to deceive). Neither was it sophistry (an indifference to the truth). Instead, it was tyrannical control over the "truth." Trump was demonstrating his power over those who could produce archival photos and television footage, believing their diligence would set the record straight. These people, the mainstream media, he called "the enemy of the people." No one should have been surprised by this media strategy of President Trump; it merely enhanced the media strategy of his campaign. Before the election, he repeatedly threatened serious news organizations with lawsuits, banned their reporters from his rallies, and promised to restrict their journalistic freedom when he became president. With that power achieved, he drew a line around himself: the media could assent to obvious falsehoods, and step within the circle (with whatever immediate benefits this submission promised, such as press credentials to the White House, which were extended to the conspiracy site *InfoWars*), or testify to the truth, remain outside the circle, and risk professional consequences (for example, being called "fake news," as Trump called the *New York Times* and the *Washington Post*).

Within a week of his inauguration, Trump announced his "Muslim ban" and presented the judiciary with a similar choice: step inside or remain without. This time, moreover, the line he drew around himself represented the tyrannical attitude to justice as well as to truth. When James L. Robart—a judge who had been appointed by George W. Bush and confirmed unanimously by the Senate—granted a restraining order against the ban, Trump immediately responded by Twitter that Robart was a "so-called judge." Evidently he will not be the next nominee to the Supreme Court. The message to the rest of the judiciary was clear enough: anyone who resists Trump's orders is not really a judge and should expect humiliation. The function of a real judge, conversely, is to cover the president's will with a veneer of justice. "The powers of the president," added Trump-adviser Stephen Miller, "will not be questioned."

TYRANNY AND TRUMP

Trump's attitudes to justice and truth are hallmarks of a tyrant, the sort of leader who locks up his political opponents. "By leveling the usual false charges and bringing people into court," writes Plato of the tyrant, "he commits murder" (565e). Trump hasn't committed judicial murder, but one of the persistent chants of his campaign rallies was "Lock her up!" He has not kept that promise—not yet anyway—despite saying during the second debate with Clinton that if he were in charge of the law she would be in jail. When Obama was in charge of the law, the summer before the election, the F.B.I. investigation of her handling of a private email server concluded without an indictment. Then the F.B.I. director, James Comey, opened it again eleven days before the election—earning Trump's praise for his "guts"—only to close it a second time two days before the election, when his new avenue of investigation proved to be a dead-end.

Once he was in charge of the law, Trump did not pursue Clinton further, nor did he long remain an admirer of Comey, for the F.B.I. director had also been conducting a silent investigation of the Trump campaign's connections to Russia. According to Comey's May, 2017 testimony before the Senate Intelligence Committee, President Trump invited him to the Oval Office, dismissed everyone else from the room, including his immediate superior, the Attorney General, and expressed a "hope" that the case against Trump's disgraced former National Security Adviser (Michael Flynn) would be dropped. Flynn had lied not only about income from Russian sources but also about a phone conversation he had had with the Russian ambassador during the transition. Comey deflected the request by saying only that Flynn was "a good guy." Comey also testified that President Trump had earlier invited him to a private dinner in the White House residence, where he twice sought a pledge of loyalty. After demurring, the closest Comey could come to that pledge was a promise of "honest loyalty," an awkward compromise that clearly did not satisfy the president.

To Comey, on one hand, the purpose of an investigation was to find the truth. To Trump, on the other, it was obedience to his will. Thus, when Comey could not promise that fealty, when he stood outside the line Trump had drawn around himself, the president simply fired him. Contradicting the implausible initial rationale—that Comey had improperly conducted the investigation of Clinton—Trump admitted on national television that he had taken this action because of Comey's handling of the Russia investigation. Indeed, when a Russian delegation visited him in the White House, Trump admitted that he "faced great pressure because of Russia," but that he had relieved it by firing Comey, who was "crazy, a real nut job."

A special counsel (Robert S. Mueller III) was then appointed to direct the investigation Comey had to surrender when he was fired. Until this point in his career, Mueller's support has been bipartisan and his integrity has been undisputed. That will surely change as he exerts increasing legal pressure on Trump and his inner circle. For as his purview inevitably broadens, Mueller is now investigating whether the president obstructed justice with the firing, a charge that is hard to deny even with facts already in the public record, never mind those which lie hidden in classified documents and the memories of the principals. Trump has claimed that Comey is lying, although he has provided no plausible motive or counter-narrative of the relevant meetings. So far, then, it's the word of one man (Comey) who has devoted his life to finding the truth and pursuing justice, without any evidence that he has lied or acted unjustly, against the word of another man (Trump) who has devoted his life to winning money, fame, and power, sometimes by lying, sometimes by sophistry, and lately by exercising a tyrannical power over "truth."

For months, Trump's supporters agreed with the president that this was a "witch-hunt," that obstruction of justice was the only charge to be leveled in the absence of any evidence of collusion between the Trump campaign and Russia. But that protest has proven hollow. Donald Trump Jr. has since revealed a meeting that he and two other leaders of the Trump campaign (Paul Manafort and Jared Kushner) had with Russians connected with the Kremlin. Chief among them was Natalia Veselnitskaya, a lawyer who campaigned for the repeal of the Magnitsky Act, which the Kremlin has always despised because it froze the American assets of corrupt Russian oligarchs. Trump Jr. was tantalized with information that would "incriminate" Hilary Clinton, "official documents" obtained by "the Crown prosecutor of Russia." In the email correspondence he himself disclosed to the public, Trump Jr. replied: "I love it."

How could Trump Sr. not have learned of this prospect, as well as this meeting, especially when his "joking" invitation to Russian hackers to find Clinton's emails came that very week? Like several other meetings Trump associates took with Russians during both the campaign and transition, these ones tried to keep the whole thing secret. Then, after their efforts failed, they lied about the meeting's purpose and failed to mention other participants. Such revelations, occurring in such a way, augured others, and every month since has brought new ones. Now we know, for instance, that Donald Trump Jr. was in a long correspondence with Wikileaks, who received from Russian agencies the hacked emails of the Democratic National Committee's leadership.[14] The coincidence between some of these communications and some of his father's tweets and speeches is suspicious, to say the least.

Mueller is investigating many threads in this tangled web, and has already indicted Manafort and his assistant on multiple charges, including conspiracy against the United States. However this investigation unfolds, then, a showdown over its results is already inevitable. So far, many of Trump's usual supporters have proudly stepped within his circle, while his longtime critics remain conspicuously outside. At the moment of writing, it is impossible to predict what will happen. With every new revelation, there are more rumors that Trump hopes to fire Mueller. If he does, as Nixon fired Archibald Cox, the special prosecutor into the Watergate burglary, there will be a constitutional crisis, for the president will be putting himself above the law.

If Mueller is allowed to finish his investigation and there are indictments against the president or his inner circle, as appears likely, there will be the same sort of crisis. Trump has boasted of "complete power to pardon," extending not only to his inner circle, but perhaps even to himself. In either event, those who must decide where to stand in such a crisis will no longer be merely the experts—professors, journalists, intelligence officials, judges, and prosecutors—but instead the representatives of the American people. At that point, as Archibald Cox said after he was fired, "whether ours shall continue to be a government of laws and not of men is now for Congress and ultimately the American people." What might happen during such a showdown is impossible to determine. Cox's words apply as much to our times as they did to his: the president's fate will depend on his popularity as a leader.

"It is clear that when a tyrant arises," Plato writes, "the position of popular leader is the sole root from which he springs" (565d). When common people feel that the system is rigged against them, that the levers of their ostensibly democratic government are being pulled by secret elites, they promote a demagogue who promises to "drain the swamp."[15] Because that was never really his intent, however, he must distract their attention with political theater (e.g., Scaramucci) and scapegoats (e.g., transgender people in the military). When minor distractions fail, though, he must create a major one (North Korea or Iran?). "His primary concern," as his supporters entertain second thoughts, "is to be constantly stirring up some war or other, so that the people will need a leader" (566e). War or no, those supporters will eventually recognize that he is not accomplishing the purpose for which they empowered him.

Rather than "shaking things up," as promised, he is merely aggrandizing and protecting himself. "They did not father him and establish him in power," Plato imagines them protesting, "so that, when he had become strong, they would be enslaved to their own slave." No, they empowered him "so that, with him as their popular leader, they would get free of the rule of the rich and the so-called fine and good people in the city" (569a). At that point, but not until then, they ask him to leave. Everyday Americans will likely have to decide at some point whether Trump has committed impeachable offenses. Beyond all the procedural questions that will be disputed by their representatives, they will ultimately have to decide whether or not they are getting what they wanted when they elected him.

They will also have to decide whether his tyrannical attitude is going to be the new American way. Of his many pernicious contributions to American politics, most dangerous has been to give this attitude, which has always been present in the United States, its first American presidency. What does this contribution portend? Again, to anticipate the actions of Trump in power we need only remember candidate Trump. Dissenters at his campaign rallies were beaten, but rather than repudiating the violence, Trump encouraged it. In the Russia of Putin, whom Trump has often praised as a strong leader, dissenters, like the journalists who report their dissent, are killed. Why not? "Once he takes over a docile mob," Plato adds, "he does not restrain himself from shedding a fellow citizen's blood" (565e). When asked about Putin's assassinations of journalists and dissidents, candidate Trump replied, "I think our country does a lot of killing, too." Asked the same question in the first month of his presidency, Trump's reply was the same: "We have a lot of killers. Well, you think our country is so innocent?"

The tyrannical attitude must eventually become violent. As we have seen, this attitude acknowledges no independent standard of truth or justice by which to mediate any reasonable discussion with opponents. They cannot be persuaded, so they must be forced. At first the targets will be those who have remained conspicuously outside the circle. Examples will be made of them, so that those who straddle the line will be intimidated into submission. But as the tyrant grows more imperious, as the realities he cannot control exact their indifferent revenge, he must constrict his circle with ever more preposterous demands. Those who were once within it, therefore, will find themselves on the outside (e.g., Rex Tillerson). So, dissidents will be eliminated first, but supporters will follow unless they are willing to pledge unquestioning loyalty. "Honest loyalty" will not be enough. It never was. "The ones who are bravest," writes Plato, "speak freely to him and to each other, criticizing what is happening." But it does not end any better for his brave supporters, than it did for his initial enemies: "the tyrant will have to do away with them all" (567b).

NOTES

1. See Miller 2007.
2. See *Republic* 474b–487a. All quotations of Plato are from *Republic*, unless otherwise stated. All quotations of *Republic* are from Reeve 2004.
3. Frankfurt 2005.
4. Murphy 2016.
5. Mayer 2016.
6. *Encomium of Helen*, in Reeve and Miller 2015: 36–38.
7. Plato, *Gorgias* 447c. All quotations of Plato's dialogs, apart from *Republic*, are from Cooper 1997.
8. Protagoras fragment DK 80B1, in Reeve and Miller 2015: 35.
9. Plato raises this problem about health and other apparent goods at *Meno* 87e6–88a1. Whether or not they are really good requires wisdom, which alone, therefore, is really good. See also *Republic* 6.491b–c.
10. Coppins 2016.
11. Gessen 2016a.
12. Her superb account of this regime and its rise is now available in Gessen 2017.
13. Gessen 2016b.
14. Ioffe 2017.
15. Sullivan 2016.

REFERENCES

Cooper, J. *Plato: Complete Works*. Indianapolis: Hackett Publishing, 1997.

Coppins, M. *How the Haters and Losers Lost*. Buzzfeed, 2016. Accessed 17 July 2017, https://www.buzzfeed.com/mckaycoppins/how-the-haters-made-trump?utm_term=.pa2Wknz6Q#.dmBYdK03y.

Frankfurt, H. *On Bullshit*. Princeton: Princeton University Press, 2005.

Gessen, M. The Putin Paradigm. *New York Review of Books*, 2016a. Accessed 13 December 2016. http://www.nybooks.com/daily/2016/12/13/putin-paradigm-how-trump-will-rule/.

———. Arguing the Truth with Trump and Putin. *New York Times*, 2016b. Accessed 17 December 2016. https://www.nytimes.com/2016/12/17/opinion/sunday/arguing-the-truth-with-trump-and-putin.html?_r=0.

———. *The Future is History: How Totalitarianism Reclaimed Russia*. Riverhead Books, 2017.

Ioffe, J. The Secret Correspondence Between Donald Trump Jr. and Wikileaks. *The Atlantic*, 2017. Accessed 13 November 2017. https://www.theatlantic.com/politics/archive/2017/11/the-secret-correspondence-between-donald-trump-jr-and-wikileaks/545738/.

Mayer, J. Donald Trump's Ghostwriter Tells All. *New Yorker*, 2016. Accessed 25 July 2016. http://www.newyorker.com/magazine/2016/07/25/donald-trumps-ghostwriter-tells-all.

Miller, P.L. "Oedipus Rex Revisited." *Modern Psychoanalysis* 31, no. 2, 2007: 229–50.

Murphy, T. How Donald Trump Became Conspiracy Theorist in Chief. *Mother Jones*, November/December, 2016. http://www.motherjones.com/politics/2016/10/trump-infowars-alex-jones-clinton-conspiracy-theories/.

Reeve, C.D.C. *Plato: Republic*. Indianapolis: Hackett Publishing, 2004.

Reeve, C.D.C., and P.L. Miller. *Introductory Readings in Ancient Greek and Roman Philosophy*. Indianapolis: Hackett Publishing, 2015.

Sullivan, A. America Has Never Been so Ripe for Tyranny. *New York Magazine*, 2016. Accessed 1 May 2016. http://nymag.com/daily/intelligencer/2016/04/america-tyranny-donald-trump.html.

CHAPTER 3

Portraits of Ignobility: The Political Thought of Xenophon, and Donald Trump

Ashok Karra

All serious political thought rests on moral judgment, and Xenophon's is no exception. The typical path into his conception of political life rests on comparing three figures he depicts in his corpus: Cyrus the Great, the perfect political man; Socrates, the philosopher *par excellence*; Xenophon himself. That path traces the highest concern, how one ought to live. What follows assumes that the current presidential administration of the United States of America is a product of a desire for regime change by a number of people.[1] It therefore traces another concern, not attempting to compare President Trump to Cyrus the Great, Socrates, or Xenophon, but wishing to establish something no less important but not as grand as the typical path. The president, not known for his largesse before his turn to leadership, displays several well-known defects despite his elevation to power. One can see similar personal problems to his concerning goal-setting, love of money, and attitude in the following portraits Xenophon presents.[2] In Glaucon, Xenophon presents an extremely ignorant but extremely ambitious man. With Meno, Xenophon does not spare any words condemning his greed. And regarding Hiero, Xenophon dares to show the everydayness of tyranny. These three figures do not compare as much as complement each other, as Xenophon's portrait of each sheds

A. Karra (✉)
University of Dallas, Irving, TX, USA

© The Author(s) 2018
A. Jaramillo Torres, M. B. Sable (eds.), *Trump and Political Philosophy*,
https://doi.org/10.1007/978-3-319-74445-2_3

light on opinions silently held which may overturn decency and lawfulness. To be sure, one might think decency and lawfulness at times are employed as excuses for much greater evils. My primary concern below is to simply bring the opinions silently held to the surface, to show the fly the way out of the fly-bottle.

GLAUCON: *MEMORABILIA* III.6

Xenophon's Glaucon occupies a specific place in his corpus. At first glance, it does not appear to be a particularly strange place. He appears in the *Memorabilia* in a series of chapters meant to illustrate that Socrates "benefited those who yearned for noble things by making them attentive to what they yearned for."[3] Socrates moderates Glaucon, showing him that his ambition reached far beyond his knowledge or competence. However, Leo Strauss notes that this same series has the character of an ascent.[4] In earlier chapters, Socrates talks to nameless interlocutors; in later chapters, he does the same with named ones.[5] Similarly, earlier discussions about what a ruler should do or know give way to questions about the utility of virtue, finally culminating in a discussion with Pericles, son of the great Pericles, about whether a return to virtue would be beneficial to Athens.[6] So it is very strange, then, that Glaucon follows Pericles: "From the height of Perikles we descend without any visible preparation to the folly of a youth whose longing for the noble things was blind ambition."[7]

The placement suggests that Xenophon's introduction of Glaucon has a higher purpose than showing how Socrates moderated him. Still, Xenophon does not undersell the story itself. He presents Glaucon as nearly impossible to deal with, and Socrates as a singular hero, providing a service neither family nor the city could:

> When Glaucon, the son of Ariston, attempted to make a public address out of a desire to preside over the city although he was not yet twenty years old, none of his other relatives or friends was able to stop him from being dragged from the speaker's stand and making himself ridiculous. But Socrates, who was well intentioned toward him for the sake of Charmides, the son of Glaucon, and for the sake of Plato, stopped him all by himself.[8]

Glaucon wanted to lead the city, and so he went to speak and was pulled off the speaker's stand. Xenophon makes him sound utterly pathetic even while touting Socrates' skill in getting him to change his behavior. Is

Glaucon someone incapable of gaining rulership over Athens? This is certainly a dangerous possibility to discount. Socrates' achievement does not appear trivial or redundant. His capability, much less the eventual result, impresses no less than Plato, as the *Republic* attests.

What impresses Glaucon most are the "resplendent rewards" for ruling.[9] Socrates uses these to enrapture him and keep him listening. If he could rule Athens, he would be able to get whatever he desires and benefit his friends; make his father's house great; enlarge the fatherland; earn fame in the city, then Greece, then even among the barbarians. Everyone would gaze at him, as if he were an object of wonder.[10] Glaucon sees the nobility of rule in its beautiful rewards, the experience it creates for him: "When he heard these things, Glaucon was exalted and remained [in Socrates' presence] with pleasure."[11] However, as seen below, learning to rule, or actually demonstrating that he can rule well, do not have the same weight for him. Quietly, Xenophon hints that there are some—perhaps many—who do not hold knowledge of how to rule or experience in ruling to be noble. This would be an opinion akin to the notion that once one gets into Harvard, one has already overcome the highest difficulty.

Of course, whether or not knowing how to rule or actually ruling competently are simply noble is an open question. Socrates asks Glaucon to tell him and the audience present where he will "begin to do good deeds for the city."[12] Glaucon stays silent, seemingly unsure where to begin. Socrates begins feeding him suggestions. Glaucon affirms he wants to make the city richer, but has not paid any attention to the city's revenues:

> Socrates said, "Just as you would attempt to make a friend richer if you wished to enlarge his household, will you also try to make the city richer?"
>
> "Certainly," he [Glaucon] said.
>
> "Would it be richer, then, if its revenues increased?"
>
> "It's plausible, at any rate," he said.
>
> "Tell, then, the sources and amounts of the city's revenues at present," he said. "For it is clear that you have examined this so that if any of them are in a deficient state you may bring them to full capacity, and if some are being passed over you may provide them in addition."
>
> "But, by Zeus," said Glaucon, "these things I have not examined."[13]

Pressed on whether he has an opinion on the city's expenditures, he again confesses his ignorance.[14] He does hold that one can make the city richer by means of conquest and plunder, e.g. "take the oil." However, when

further questioned about the relative military power of Athens compared
to its enemies, he is forced into a corner once again.[15]

Glaucon seems irredeemably silly. Pericles in the chapter before seems
noble partly because he has a vision of a virtuous Athens and is willing to
ask Socrates about it. (It does not hurt that historically he helped the
Athenians win a battle and was punished by his own city for his competence.)[16] He openly wonders "how we [Pericles and Socrates] might turn
them [the Athenians] toward passionately loving again their ancient virtue, fame, and happiness."[17] He wants the Athenians to have "likeness of
mind" while "working together to one another's advantage," for he particularly deplores the "enmity and hatred" the citizens have for each
other.[18] However, what exact expertise does Pericles have? When Socrates
says he must have inherited much from his "father's store of generalship,"
Pericles says he has much to learn.[19] It would be a mistake, then, to conclude that any actual knowledge or experience Pericles has of rule is noble.
What makes Pericles noble is his desire to rule well, to be a beautiful ruler
for a beautiful city. Glaucon is not so far from Pericles in this respect. One
might say there is a thin line between nobility and ignobility, and that I
will certainly grant. But it does look like Xenophon has a radical question
in mind when he places Pericles and Glaucon side-by-side. If nobility is
ultimately dependent upon one's conception of the beautiful, then is the
only thing making rule or the willingness to rule noble its engagement of
the beautiful? If this is the case, then the qualities which make one an
effective leader are only coincidentally linked to the noble as popularly
held.

If this is the case, then it is no wonder that Glaucon, in addition to
knowing nothing of the budget or Athens' military power, fails to adequately defend his position regarding the guarding of the land, professes
knowing nothing about the decrease in production from the silver mines,
and has given no thought to Athens' grain supply.[20] Regarding the last,
Socrates speaks of what Glaucon calls a "huge task," but one we recognize
as manageable if one delegates, pays attention to numbers from shipments
and surveys, and has some idea of what has worked or not worked in the
past:

> [Socrates said:] "I know that you [Glaucon] have not neglected, but you
> have examined for what length of time the food that comes from the land is
> capable of continually sustaining the city, and how much in addition is
> needed annually, so that the city may never come to be in need of this with

you unawares, but, knowing it, you would be able to come to the city's aid and save it by advising about its necessities."

"You speak of a huge task," said Glaucon, "if one will have to attend to these sorts of things as well."[21]

One might detect in Glaucon's tone a dismissal of Socrates, as if Socrates were joking. Indeed, one aspect of the Socratic rhetoric directed at Glaucon is making a given task seem as complicated and difficult as it can be in order to dissuade him from seeking power immediately. However, cities do manage to feed people and anticipate shortfalls. Armies make sure every man is provided for. The information and expertise for this matter exists, and some familiarity with how policy of this sort works is not unreasonable to demand of a politician, especially one eager to lead a city in wartime.

Glaucon knows leadership is held in high esteem, but he does not understand leadership as having anything to do with defending the land, having funds, or feeding one's people. One might interject and say that the people of Athens dragged him from the speaker's stand for precisely these reasons. But all communities, in all times and places, have been vulnerable to demagogues. It is more likely they were angered because Glaucon appeared ludicrous and ignoble more than he lacked knowledge, a desire to learn, or experience.

Typically, one opposes what is noble to what is shameful. However, since nobility does not entail any specific claim to knowledge, the very concept of nobility can become an attack on those who know or have expertise. Nobility inflates hopes in order to inspire service to the city—serve the city well, and it will give you honor and remember you honorably. The combination of a lack of knowledge and inflated hopes can become a willful ignorance, an ignorance immune to shame. Glaucon, for his part, backs down. Socrates tells him that if he truly wants to rule, he should start by managing a household. History has no record of Glaucon, tyrant of Athens, for Glaucon demonstrates shame. He recognizes that he is being made fun of late in the conversation, and Socrates' final remarks to him concern his handling of his own reputation.[22] Socrates would not speak of a good reputation unless it was something important to Glaucon.

It does seem that a number of people could double-down on a most shameful notion, thinking they serve noble ends. Often, they will cast their enemies as ignoble or subhuman, justifying their actions not by demonstrating virtue or aiming for a specific goal, but by attacking those they feel deserve resentment. Glaucon does not descend into this monstrousness, but Xenophon follows the chapter we have discussed with one featuring his uncle, Charmides, who thought his right to rule was clear and distinct because the Athenian *demos* was only worthy of contempt by him.[23]

One wonders where true nobility lies. Pericles' desire to serve the city well and promote virtue is certainly noble, but it is a noble desire. Glaucon's moderation, however belated, is not ignoble. What of Socrates? He asks Glaucon sharp questions about matters of government, questions that to merely articulate involve a level of knowledge an exceptional citizen might have and only a few politicians. It does not matter that Socrates probably does not know the answers to his own questions. He can use them to moderate others, which is no small task. His knowledge ties into his communication skills, which are exceptional. His sense of priority regarding budgets, the military, defense, money, and food tailors itself to the situation but is perfectly accessible to many. It makes him the sort of person any government could use in a leading position, if he were not its leader simply. Xenophon does not directly call Socrates' knowledge noble. If Socrates led or ruled, it is not clear that would immediately be noble in Xenophon's thought. Pericles' willingness to serve and sacrifice puts him on the path to nobility; Socrates' knowledge and ability do not entail this same willingness, even though he moderated Glaucon.

True nobility hints at something larger than the city itself. The city can collapse into inhuman monstrousness, turn men into the most savage, lawless animals. This collapse is larger than the city or a number of political phenomena, though it can be directly caused by either. In a like manner, we note that there is shame, a desire for a good reputation, which also transcends the city. Glaucon's silliness almost obscures the fact that he understands this—he does wish, after all, to be admired even by barbarians. In an earlier chapter of the *Memorabilia*, Socrates told a nameless interlocutor that speech not only reinforced the nobility of existing law, but also discovered other noble things, and provided conversation which could be considered noble itself:

> Or haven't you pondered the fact that it is through speech that we learned all the things that we have learned are most noble according to law, things by means of which we understand how to live; and that if someone learns any other noble thing, he learns it through speech, and that those best at

teaching use speech the most, and that those who have the most understanding of the most serious things converse most nobly?[24]

A great lawlessness and ignobility can hide within some uses of the law.
Socrates' question not so thinly veils a progression in defense of speech
and reason, not so much law. Through speech used well, one learns what
is noble in law, how to properly live, as other noble things can be found
that reinforce and illuminate that which is noble in law. Moreover, to
know, to try to know, is to go beyond the particularities of one's time and
place and find things that many more, given their "understanding of the
most serious things," can consider noble. The danger of nobility as willful
ignorance is not to be underestimated: it can and will strangle philosophy's ability to defend itself. It cannot win, given time, but the damage it
causes for actual people should not be discounted. Crucial to love of wisdom is a radical embrace of chance, of diversity, which anger and artificial
unity reject out of fear and hatred: "Socrates remarks that illness turned
his companion Theages to philosophy, and in his own case the *dai-
monion*—whatever made Socrates unlike anyone else—had the same
effect, but he did not know of another who experienced the same consequences he did."[25]

MENO: *ANABASIS* II.6.21–7

To say the least, Meno appears difficult in the Platonic dialog named after
him. "Can you tell me, Socrates, whether virtue is something teachable?"
are his first words to Socrates, the first words of the dialog.[26] Socrates
immediately responds with a quietly devastating explanation of why this
question is even being asked. Once Thessaly, where Meno is from, had a
good reputation for horsemanship and wealth. Now, perhaps, they should
be "admired for wisdom," as Gorgias' time teaching rhetoric in the city
has established a habit in quite a few of the men. They, like Meno, will
answer "fearlessly and magnificently" whenever asked anything; they think
they know, and thus will answer any question from any Greek. Socrates
says his part of the world does not have such wisdom, and that he himself
has no idea whether virtue is teachable, for he does not even know "what
that thing virtue itself is."[27]

Meno, maybe sensing that he will be denied a rhetorical demonstration,
asks Socrates if he would like it reported in Thessaly that he does not know
what virtue is. Socrates fires back that this is fine, as he himself not only

does not know what virtue is, but also has never met anyone else who did know. Meno expresses alarm at this, as Gorgias visited Athens recently, and thus begins the dialog in earnest.[28]

From this opening episode we encounter quite a bit to consider about Meno. A pupil of Gorgias, he has somewhat of an intellectual side. He may want to display his rhetorical skill; he may have some concerns inspired by Gorgias. It is hard to say his concerns are earnest when he expresses much more interest in an answer to whether virtue is teachable than with having a robust conception of virtue himself.[29] Either way, he has a certain pride in what he has been taught, and his impudence is extreme. Does he desire rhetorical combat with Socrates, of all people, thinking he can win? At times, he sounds unashamed to provoke it.[30] Ultimately, he proves immoderate and immature, but the reader of Plato's dialog does not directly encounter someone completely mercenary. There are overtones of this, to be sure. Meno says the virtue of a man is "easy" to tell, declaring early in the dialog: "this is the virtue of a man: to be sufficient to carry on the affairs of the city and while carrying them on to do well by his friends and harm to his enemies and to take care that he not suffer any such thing himself."[31] Meno's provisional opinion of virtue holds it as political capability, the helping of friends and harming of enemies, with an added, potentially immoral twist: the virtuous man ought not to suffer any harm himself. If one assumes in addition that the virtuous man will try to obtain what is good for himself, then with regard to the previous section of this paper, gone is the shame which moderated Glaucon, much less the self-sacrifice which Pericles wanted Athenians to practice and which he himself performed.

Throughout Plato's dialog, Meno shows an eagerness to get what is best for himself, but does demonstrate a willingness to commit to nobility if it grants the good.[32] Meno neither endorses tyranny, nor proclaims a life of hedonism to be the best, nor angrily or violently rejects Socrates' philosophic rhetoric. A serious reader of Plato's dialog might come away with the impression that Meno tries to learn, despite being distracted and frustrated, collapsing into his worst tendencies because of the limits of human wisdom and convention.

Of course, another sort of reader might feel Meno is unteachable, incapable of learning virtue, and someone who should never have been given the rhetorical tools and power to act on his worst desires. Would Xenophon be such a reader? The *Anabasis* displays righteous anger regarding Meno's deeds: he attempted to betray the army with which he fought to its enemies in order to secure the favor of the Persian king. Through his fraud, all the generals of that army were killed, including Meno himself. Xenophon is unsparing in summarizing his life: "Meno the Thessalian was clear in his desire to be exceedingly wealthy, in his desire to rule so as to get hold of more, and in his desire to be honored so that he might gain greater profit."[33]

Plato's Meno demonstrates quite a bit of selfishness, but Xenophon emphasizes his greed to incredible extremes. Could it have been the case that Meno panicked when trapped in a foreign country, as he was surrounded by hostile Persians with only a group of mercenaries for protection? Xenophon acts as if panic does not exist, that he went to the Persian king motivated only by greed: "he wanted to be a friend to those with the greatest power so that he might not pay a penalty for his injustices."[34] The portrait Xenophon develops starts to become more realistic when he describes Meno as having been consumed by immoral tactics. Meno thought he could get what he wanted quickest through "perjury and lying and deception," seeing "simplicity and truthfulness" as "foolishness." He plotted against those he called his friends, as they would be less on their guard than his enemies. He was scared of those like him, the "perjurers and unjust," as they would be "well armed," but held that the "pious" and truthful lacked manliness.[35]

Still, this does not quite convince. Xenophon says "Meno prided himself on the capacity to deceive, on the concocting of lies, on the mockery of friends." "Mockery of friends" stands out: Meno is a complete exaggeration. Defined neither by acquisition nor an art of acquiring, he is simply everything faithless wrapped into one man, a man who features prominently in a story about a mercenary army which intended to overthrow a legitimate ruler. We are told he held those who were not "scoundrels" to be "uneducated," used slander to advance himself, and procured obedience by sharing in the wrongs of his soldiers. He wanted honor and attention "because he showed that he had the power and willingness to commit the greatest injustices." Xenophon concludes with this notice: "he counted it as a benefaction done, whenever someone broke with him, that in using him he hadn't destroyed him."[36]

There are those like Meno, even those far more monstrous than this depiction. But it is hard to imagine anyone who conforms strictly to the singularity Xenophon presents. The worst tyrants must help their friends in a recognizable way, not just inspire fear through ruthlessness. Great villains dress their evil in moral guises. Racists say they are preserving tradition; confidence men think they must take advantage of others, or be taken advantage of.[37] Moreover, ignorance and carelessness typically create situations where bad ideas and bad behavior spiral out of control, causing terrible harm.

Why does Xenophon advance such a horrible portrait of Meno, aside from his obvious (and perfectly reasonable) dislike of the man? If the *Anabasis*, styled in certain ways after the *Odyssey*, follows epic convention, one can make this suggestion: truth comes in ugly guises. Just as Thersites in the *Iliad* is exactly right about Agamemnon's awful leadership, Meno's exaggerated mercenary qualities reflect the truth of the army Xenophon will eventually command.[38] This is an army with which Xenophon himself hopes to found a city, one whose men he will be accused of caring for too much. No one is utterly faithless, looking to manipulate others all the time, unless one is pathological. But there are situations where people feel continually compelled to break faith, as the basis for trust is broken to begin with. A band of mercenaries brought to a foreign land in bad faith, one which attempts to overthrow the lawful king and is continually threatened with destruction, is probably more prone to creating people like Meno than Xenophon cares to depict. One can reason that problematic societies and situations create problematic people, that fraternity, virtue, and reason are not enough to contain vice. This is not a pleasant thought for one eager to hear the tale of the Ten Thousand, how Greek virtue preserved Greek men in the most critical moment. A romantic conception of the fatherland demands romantic villains. Indeed, one prone to see Meno as simply the worst of all human beings on account of his faithlessness would be prone to see his supposed punishment by the Persian king as just. Xenophon reports that it is said Meno, unlike the other generals, was not merely executed but tortured for a year by no less than the Persian King, who of course benefited from Meno's crime.[39]

HIERO: *HIERO*, 1ST CHAPTER

Hiero, tyrant of Syracuse, is asked by the poet Simonides how being a despot and a private citizen compare. What "joys and sorrows" attend each?[40] Right away, Hiero senses a potential threat in the question, and asks Simonides, a private citizen, to tell him what happens in a private citizen's life before he elaborates on any differences. Simonides takes full advantage of Hiero's mistrust. Instead of asking directly whether having power creates additional thrills or concerns, Simonides says "sights affect private citizens with pleasure and pain through the eyes, sounds through the ears, smells through the nostrils, meat and drink through the mouth, carnal appetites—of course we all know how."[41] Hiero wants to know whether Simonides is a threat, and thus must engage a treatise in miniature about how the senses shape pleasure and pain. Simonides even goes so far to wonder how pleasure and pain are affected by physical inputs and moral conceptions, musing at one point how a loss of consciousness could be pleasurable.[42]

Hiero expresses brief relief after Simonides' statement: a despot cannot possibly differ from a citizen in these respects! Simonides immediately counters, demonstrating command of the conversation. A despot has access to a much larger number of pleasures and far fewer pains than a private citizen. Hiero panics and promises to show the exact opposite. He argues that a despot cannot experience as much pleasure as a private citizen through sight, since he cannot travel to see shows and spectacles where he likes for fear of being killed abroad or displaced at home. He can only get a select number of people to come to him, and he must overpay. Simonides pretends to concede this, mildly countering that at least in hearing, the despot experiences great pleasures. He hears only praise, no abuse. Hiero says flatly that many conceal their evil thoughts through such praise and have every incentive to flatter. Simonides' response is remarkable: "...I agree with you entirely, Hiero, praise from the freest is sweetest."[43]

Unfortunately, if Simonides is a true lover of freedom, he does not reveal his stance immediately. Hiero relates that he gets no pleasure from banquets as his table is filled with plenty every day; as a result, his appetite is "jaded and pampered." The mockery Hiero's argument makes of moderation would be laughable if it did not flimsily paper over the deadliest of truths: tyrants are often able to perversely build from moral principle. Their shamelessness is not entirely opposed by moral stricture, but in curious ways is supported by it. Hiero's moral failure in his lack of moderation can dissuade threats to his rule. It impresses those who like tales of fame and fortune, it dissuades the more virtuous from raising a hand against him, as they feel they are better regardless. Some might even think Hiero more human on account of his hypocrisy.[44]

Simonides does not bother to fight with Hiero over this issue, instead merely asking if the tyrant's full table is much better than cheaply or barely eating, and saying that the rich scents a tyrant adorns himself with are much better for others than the awful smells of eating badly. Hiero ultimately looks ludicrous in this exchange, and Simonides' stated concerns—the health of citizens, the use of a full table and luxurious scents to impress those invited—imply an understanding of Hiero as one who weakens the citizenry at large so he can cultivate powerful friends to secure his rule.[45]

Simonides finally catches Hiero while discussing sexual pleasure. Hiero says that unless he marries a foreigner of high standing, he must marry someone beneath him, and thus receive no pleasure. Then he outrageously asserts that he has no passion for young men, for passion cannot arise when one gets whatever he wants. Simonides nearly erupts in laughter: Hiero's pursuit of one particular boy was well-known. Hiero attempts to explain his behavior and instead shows a major principle underlying the tyrant's logic: "For to take from an enemy against his will is, I think, the greatest of all pleasures, but favours from a loved one are very pleasant, I fancy, only when he consents." Hiero's insatiable *eros*, directed toward a most beautiful boy, leads him to desire his consent. But that same intensity with which he desires to benefit a beloved is matched by his desire to harm enemies.[46]

The first chapter of Xenophon's *Hiero* presents a man of limited intellectual ability, governed by fear, exercising incredible power despite repeated humiliation in conversation. Hiero sees, hears, smells, tastes and touches many things which pleasure him. The power the tyrant wields does not merely stem from his command over armies and fleets, or his exploitation of political division, or a people's need for security. It receives countenance from the opinion that the life of a tyrant is infinitely preferable to a private, moral life. It is a lack of nerve and opportunity which keeps many in check; they ordinarily convince themselves that tyranny is not something they want. But if they could take it, or desired to take it enough, they would try. Otherwise Hiero would not worry when Simonides asks his question; the comedic tone of the chapter helps conceal that underlying it is the logic driving tragedy. "Tragedy [is] … an essentially popular form of literature: there are equal portions in it of satisfaction and distress, for we take open delight in the fated fall of him whom we secretly desire to be."[47]

The opinion that a tyrannical life is pleasurable and to be desired has its root in the notion of justice as helping friends and harming enemies. The tyrant's home is truly his castle, and his notion of home is one where friends are benefited maximally and enemies are cast into the darkness, where they will weep and gnash their teeth. Tyranny, one can provisionally say, takes "help friends and harm enemies" as a principle of justice to an extreme. The most helpful thing for friends, especially against enemies, is a strong leader who brings his backers all the benefits he can while ruthlessly damaging those opposed. Freedom is not a serious consideration, which leads to the abandonment of any sense of justice itself. Political life, where one can rule and be ruled in turn, ceases to be conceivable for many. Tyranny enables a crude notion of utility which in turn reinforces that tyranny itself.

CONCLUSION: ON CLASSICAL POLITICAL PHILOSOPHY

Can we not thus see a critique of how ignorance, greed and intemperance render a person unfit for rule? Is there not evidence that consideration of these vices applies to President Trump? In our brief look at a few figures from Xenophon, a larger set of problems has become visible. First, the president exercises rule, bringing out problematic thoughts, speech, and action not only from those who support him, but those who feel justified by the climate created. Second, as someone so defective lacks any sense of self-control, yet has been elevated to extraordinary heights, one must wonder what sort of society created him. Purportedly, the United States of America has a very well-educated citizenry, and many who support the president and his party not only have the means, but are partial to notions of education that emphasize tradition. One might even imagine those of the president's party being apt to quote Xenophon if he were mentioned on any of the broadcast networks fueling their sense of the present.

There is more to say, for any given nation must of necessity only partially engage more erudite matters. Xenophon's mode of writing—e.g. placing people, themes, and ideas in peculiar order, indulging in rhetoric that purposely undoes itself, hiding tragedy inside comedy—lends itself to a particular reading of the history of political thought. That reading, as spoken of today: once, people who knew better hid subtle, dark, difficult truths about grave matters such as religion, the ability of people to rule themselves, and the limits of science from those who would posit dogma where there were questions. Some might say that particular reading of the history of political thought has itself become a dogma, used to create an ideological conformity in the name of high standards as opposed to understanding the world in which one actually lives.

Natural right and esoteric writing do constitute the heart of classical political philosophy. I have reached two tentative conclusions about how these things interact in Xenophon. First, there is no way to divorce Xenophon's political thought from the question of what sort of people a given regime will create. It is no accident that Glaucon is inspired by a noble vision that knows nearly no bounds, or that Hiero really is trapped within his decadence. Second, Xenophon's subtle, dark, difficult truths cannot become dogma unless crudely read out of context. That context is always questionable, always variable, despite the fact some readings are firmer than others. The reason for the questionability and variability is that Xenophon, even with strong opinions, wonders aloud to his readers about the world he has experienced. Is Glaucon, who was ignorant and was shamed, better than Alcibiades, who, knowing and unabashed, did as he pleased? Is Meno's spirit, terrible and murderous as it is, the true spirit of Cyrus' expedition? Is Hiero some sort of joke, or what free people must recognize in themselves so as to overcome? There are no easy answers to these questions, for different parts of Xenophon's corpus illuminate different parts at different times. Once, a free writer wrote for a free people that they may learn. I have my doubts as to where that learning is happening nowadays.

NOTES

1. The notion that the American people voted for "regime change" in the 2016 presidential election was originally voiced for this author by Roosevelt Montás of Columbia University. Also see Marc Sable, "Charisma, Value and Political Vocation: Max Weber on the 2016 US Election," [pp.]
2. The president's difficulty setting and following through with goals more than likely connects to a sense of entitlement. See Ta-Nehisi Coates, "The First White President," *The Atlantic*, October 2017. On this note, the president's disregard for the dignity of women is pure entitlement. See Clare Foran, "Trump's Victory Sends a Disturbing Message About Sexual Assault," *The Atlantic*, Nov. 9, 2016. The president's love of money perhaps makes itself most manifest in his willingness to embrace business plans which may exploit others for money. See Rick Perlstein, "I Thought I Understood the American Right. Trump Proved Me Wrong," *The New York Times Magazine*, April 11, 2017. Finally, the president's attitude has been well-documented as bullying, domineering, and tyrannical. His daughter Ivanka attests to this unknowingly in an anecdote from her childhood. See the opening of Hannah Seligson, "Is Ivanka for Real?" *The Huffington Post*, September 7, 2016, accessed at http://highline.huffingtonpost.com/articles/en/is-ivanka-for-real/ on October 28, 2017.

3. Xenophon, *Memorabilia* III.1.1. All references to the *Memorabilia* are from Amy Bonnette's translation, unless otherwise stated: Xenophon, *Memorabilia*, trans. Amy L. Bonnette (Ithaca: Cornell University Press, 1994).

   "Noble" is *kalon*, which can mean either "noble" or "beautiful." Xenophon's chapter on Glaucon focuses on political matters, which usually implies nobility (e.g. being a gentleman, noble and good; able to rule; able to serve the city). However, Glaucon listens to Socrates speak about complex political issues because of a most beautiful vision Socrates paints for him of his reputation (*Memorabilia* III.6.2).

4. Leo Strauss, *Xenophon's Socrates* (South Bend: St. Augustine's Press, 1998). 56.

5. Carol McNamara, "Socratic Politics in Xenophon's *Memorabilia*," *Polis* 26, no. 2 (2009). 233.

6. One may be curious about what a return to virtue, or a return to political origins, for the United States of America looks like. The typical argument, one in vogue with the president's party, is that a reduction in administration and regulation by the government should yield a smaller government, one that looks like it is directly produced by the Constitution itself, protective of individual liberties. One notes the complete absence of the most powerful, resonating line of the Declaration of Independence, i.e. "all men are created equal."

7. Strauss, *Xenophon's Socrates* 69.

8. *Memorabilia* III.6.1.

9. Strauss, *Xenophon's Socrates* 69.

10. *Memorabilia* III.6.2; Strauss, *Xenophon's Socrates* 70.

11. Ibid., III.6.3.

12. Ibid.

13. Ibid., III.6.4–5.

14. Ibid., III.6.6.

15. Ibid., III.6.7–10.

16. Xenophon, *Hellenica* I.7.

17. *Memorabilia* III.5.7.

18. Ibid., III.5.16–17.

19. Ibid., III.5.22–24.

20. Ibid., III.6.10–13.

21. Ibid., III.6.13.

22. Ibid., III.6.12; III.6.16–18.

23. Ibid., III.7.5–8. Charmides ultimately aided the Thirty Tyrants, becoming one of the Ten who ruled in the Piraeus.

24. Ibid., III.3.11.

25. Seth Benardete, "Freedom: Grace and Necessity" in *Freedom and the Human Person*, ed. Richard Velkley (Washington, DC: CUA Press, 2007). 264.
26. Plato, *Meno*, 70a. References to the *Meno* that follow are from Robert Bartlett's translation. Robert C. Bartlett, *Plato: "Protagoras" and "Meno"* (Ithaca: Cornell, 2004). This volume also contains scholarly apparatus which will be cited in author, page number format below.
27. Ibid., 70a–71b.
28. Ibid., 71c.
29. Bartlett, 139 argues that Meno's first questions to Socrates show an "urgent desire to know the answer" and some "prior reflection." Bartlett does not seem to think Meno is eager to demonstrate his rhetorical skill.
30. I have in mind the aforementioned 71c, where Meno could be said to threaten Socrates with ruining his reputation in Thessaly, and the famous "Meno's Paradox," 80a–b, where Meno tells Socrates that he could be carried off to jail because of the confusion he causes. At least to me, these demonstrate an impudence which could very easily get a reaction from anyone else.
31. *Meno*, 71e.
32. Bartlett, 143.
33. Xenophon, *Anabasis* II.6.21. Bartlett, 154 has a translation of Xenophon's *Anabasis of Cyrus*, II.6.21–27. References to this text that follow are from this page.
34. Ibid.
35. Ibid., II.6.22–25.
36. Ibid., II.6.26–27.
37. Since the 2016 election, there has been a surge in white nationalist activism and violence. As of this writing, candidates have called for Confederate symbols to remain on public land in states such as Ohio and Montana, states that were not part of the Confederacy. If the United States of America depends in some way on equality among mankind being a truth or a proposition, then it follows of necessity that white nationalism, as of this writing a potential majority faction, is an existential threat to the regime as conceived in 1776.

The president's views on race are well-documented. However, the links between his faithlessness, white grievance, and his rise to power have primarily been documented by minority voices. One cannot recommend too much Ta-Nehisi Coates' essay "The First White President." From that essay: "…whereas his forebears carried whiteness like an ancestral talisman, Trump cracked the glowing amulet open, releasing its eldritch energies. The repercussions are striking: Trump is the first president to have served in no public capacity before ascending to his perch. But more telling,

Trump is also the first president to have publicly affirmed that his daughter is a "piece of ass." The mind seizes trying to imagine a black man extolling the virtues of sexual assault on tape ("When you're a star, they let you do it"), fending off multiple accusations of such assaults, immersed in multiple lawsuits for allegedly fraudulent business dealings, exhorting his followers to violence, and then strolling into the White House. But that is the point of white supremacy—to ensure that that which all others achieve with maximal effort, white people (particularly white men) achieve with minimal qualification."

38. Homer, *Iliad* II.218–275; Seth Benardete, *The Rhetoric of Morality and Philosophy* (Chicago: University of Chicago, 2009). 101.
39. Leo Strauss, "Xenophon's Anabasis," in *Interpretation* 4, No. 3 (Spring 1975). 120–121.
40. Xenophon, *Hiero* I.2.
41. Ibid., I.4.
42. Ibid., I.5–6.
43. Ibid., I.7–16.
44. Ibid., I.17–23.
45. Ibid., I.17–26.
46. Ibid., I.26–38.
47. Benardete, *Freedom: Grace and Necessity* 265.

REFERENCES

Bartlett, Robert C. *Plato: "Protagoras" and "Meno"*. Ithaca: Cornell, 2004.
Benardete, Seth. "Freedom: Grace and Necessity" in *Freedom and the Human Person*, ed. Richard Velkley. Washington, DC: CUA Press, 2007, 1–12.
McNamara, Carol. "Socratic Politics in Xenophon's *Memorabilia*." *Polis* 26, no. 2, 2009: 223–245.
Strauss, Leo. "Xenophon's Anabasis." *Interpretation* 4, no. 3, 1975: 117–147.
———. *Xenophon's Socrates*. South Bend: St. Augustine's Press, 1998.
Xenophon. *Memorabilia*. Translated by Amy L. Bonnette. Ithaca: Cornell University Press, 1994.

CHAPTER 4

Demagogy and the Decline of Middle-Class Republicanism: Aristotle on the Trump Phenomenon

Leslie G. Rubin

The most, though by no means the only, inflammatory aspect of the 2016 elections was Donald Trump's candidacy. These observations on Aristotle's insights into the campaign for the presidency are divided in two parts: First, the Philosopher's understanding of demagogy and its relation to contemporary American politics, then his advice to a republic similar to the one America's was intended to be on remedies to the regime to avoid a reprise of the upheaval of this election. That advice—to strengthen the middle class—focuses on Aristotle's surprising praise of the virtues that most people can aspire to practice.

The Demagogue

Aristotle tried to pin down the phenomenon of demagogy. Given the way he uses the term, it seems clear that it was thrown around in politics rather loosely in his day—as it still is. The term was used to describe—and to condemn—Donald Trump.[1] Is Trump a demagogue in Aristotle's sense of

L. G. Rubin (✉)
Independent Scholar, Pittsburgh, PA, USA

© The Author(s) 2018
A. Jaramillo Torres, M. B. Sable (eds.), *Trump and Political Philosophy*,
https://doi.org/10.1007/978-3-319-74445-2_4

51

the term? There are at least five ways Aristotle talks about popular leaders (*demagogoi*) in the *Politics*. Some are fairly objectively descriptive, others more normative. His comments on the popular leader bring to light aspects of current political campaigning and suggest warnings for democratic republics such America's.

In the sense that *demagogia* is a method of regime change, in which a single (wealthy) oligarch manages to take over power from an entrenched group of oligarchs by leveraging the force of the many against the few,[2] Trump used a demagogic strategy. He tried to convince less-privileged groups (the out-of-work and underemployed,[3] Hispanics,[4] African-Americans[5]) that he, unlike all the other privileged people who campaigned for their votes, was the one who cared about and could fix their problems. Aristotle seems fully aware of the irony of this demagogic trope (V.10.1311a9–19).

It would be hard to associate Trump with the "popular leader" Pericles, whose demagogy consisted, according to Aristotle, of "cut[ting] back the council of the Areopagus … [and] establish[ing] pay for the courts," that is, he made Solon's democratic regime allowing the poor to sit on juries into a more democratic system by paying them for jury service and by reducing the influence of the oligarchs (II.12.1274a6–11). The wealthy and highly esteemed Pericles used his political power to change the rules to favor the poor—demagogy, again, in an objective sense. It would not be a pejorative use of the term, if used by a partisan of democracy. The changes Trump claimed he would implement do not involve an understanding of the structure of American democracy and a strategy to change *the institutions* to favor the many. Trump's demands, *e.g.*, for a strong border wall and more favorable trade deals, are policy results appealing to those who feel that they are not getting a fair share of the benefits the government distributes. Trump did not propose a way to make American political *institutions* friendlier to those who feel neglected. That would require a sustained attention to the Constitution and laws by which American politics works—matters Trump ignored during his campaign or denounced (as "rigged"). It will be interesting to see whether his advisors and administrators persuade him to work within the Constitution or to try to make changes in it to benefit the working classes. (By the way, Pericles, though suspicious in Aristotle's eyes

(II.12.1274a11–15), *did* make some serious strides in the direction of making Athens "great." How 'bout that Acropolis!)

A more critical analysis of demagogy occurs in *Politics*, Book IV, when Aristotle is distinguishing types of democracy. In most types, "the law rules" and what makes the regime democratic is that the poorer citizens participate in choosing who takes office. The more democratic, the greater the portion of the multitude eligible to vote and to hold office. In the most extreme form of democracy, however, a radical change takes place: "the multitude has authority and not the law. This comes about when decrees rather than law are authoritative, and this happens on account of the popular leaders [*demagogoi*]" (IV.4.1292a4–11).

Insofar as Trump made promises to "make America great again" by his own actions and claimed *his leadership alone* can accomplish this task,[6] his vision of American democracy "working" is having a leader who makes things happen—who does not wait upon the institutions of the republic to effect change through legal processes. Of course, Trump cannot be blamed for this attitude. Presidents and other political "leaders" over the last century have been striving for such an authority. President Obama carried further than those before him the strategy of getting around the law-making process with his pen and his phone, but he is far from the first to do so. The executive-heavy understanding of the workings of the national government has been pushing in the direction of this connotation of demagogy for a long while, which is why Trump could plausibly blame past presidents for the messes he claims only he can clean up.[7]

Aristotle proceeds to argue that, as the most extreme form of democracy, this demagogy is tyranny (IV.4.1292a11–28). Aristotle is far from an alarmist, but he is sending a warning about trusting a "popular leader" and he would include Hillary Clinton and most candidates for the presidency in recent decades along with Trump. In the typical progression Aristotle outlines, the many bestow upon "their favorite" authority beyond the law and expect that he (or she) will rule through decrees (executive orders) or actions (administrative rule-making) of which the people approve; the demagogue's power increases as he or she exercises it, because once the people have chosen their leader, they *want to believe* they have made the right choice; this chosen person can "safely" be above the law, because he or she will do what the people want. As Aristotle puts it, the demagogues "become great through the people's having authority in all matters, and *through having authority themselves over the opinion of the people*, since the multitude is persuaded by them."[8] This lawlessness, the tendency to grant above-the-law status to the favorite, is precisely the paradigm of governance Americans saw in this election year: Trump followers dismissing all accusations against his character, business dealings, past behavior as trumped up irrelevancies and Clinton followers clinging to the FBI's decision not to prosecute and ignoring the questionable relationship between the Clinton Foundation and the State Department, her "extreme carelessness" with classified documents, and the "misstatements" in her testimony before Congress.[9] The dangers of factional conflict (*stasis*) are magnified when democracy descends into demagogy—the actions of the demagogic leader become the de facto principles of the party he or she comes to embody once he gathers a sufficient following.[10]

In a pattern akin to Trump's turn against the members of his party in government who did not endorse his candidacy (or failed to endorse him enthusiastically), Aristotle says the next step of a typical demagogue is to "bring accusations against certain persons holding offices and assert that the people should judge; the invitation is gladly accepted and all the offices are thus overthrown" (IV.4.1292a28–31). Trump's denunciations not only of the opposite party's candidates, but also of the members of the party he chose to join and insisted he should "lead," indicate an understanding of the office of president as monarchy—the end goal of a demagogue. Any House or Senate candidates who gained or kept their seats by endorsing him through thick and thin have schooled their colleagues in the long-range danger of demagogy—no one's opinions remain his/her own when one is following a demagogue.[11] Trump may have managed to damage the careers of many politicians—tarring some with disloyalty to their party and others with cowardice in failing to stand up to his insults. During the transition, he rehabilitated some of those he had previously denounced—surely they will be hesitant to criticize him again.

Executive predominance is not a new mindset in the presidency, but this case is more extreme, in that Trump did not even seem to care whether Congress would be controlled by his own or the opposite party. His immediate predecessors *should* have served as a cautionary example concerning what can and cannot be accomplished when the American tripartite government is polarized along party lines, but it seems rather to have served as a challenge to Trump's self-image. He assumed that the force of his will and his businessman's negotiating skills would prevail in ways that

President Obama could not manage. His belligerence toward the Senate Majority Leader and the Speaker of the House suggested he expected to bully them to accept his actions uncritically. That mindset is behind the attitude of an Aristotelian demagogue who pulls all power into his own hands and encourages all other officials to be stripped of authority.

These Aristotelian observations on the phenomenon of democracy descending into tyranny suggest one institutional change that would make a demagogue less likely to succeed either in winning the presidency or, that barrier failing, in accomplishing dangerous aims: return the presidency to its status as one among the three coordinate powers of the national government. The New Deal reorganization of the executive branch and all of its successor attempts have been the background for increasing both the range of executive ambitions and the size of the bureaucracy. Once the agencies are there, they must be used (or they will lose their funding for next year). The ever-widening use of executive agreements reduces the Senate's capacity to moderate the president's international activity. The rediscovery and increased use of the signing statement elevate the president's interpretation of a new law above that of Congress when it is challenged in court, placing the executive above both of the other "equal" branches. The use of executive orders not only to specify the manner of implementing duly-made law, but of announcing that the law will not be enforced in significant categories, makes the legislature quite impotent in controlling the actions of government. If the president were not understood as capable of fixing every perceived problem with his pen and his phone, perhaps the voters would not expect unreasonable results and would not reject candidates with moderate platforms in favor of those who flatter them with unworkable promises while denigrating other authorities' capacities to "get things done."

One characteristic of Trump's campaign creates an interesting twist on another of Aristotle's points, the demagogue as flatterer: Aristotle sees the popular leader as achieving power not by reasoned speech about the just and the unjust, the good and the bad (the definition of politics), but by flattering the people (IV.4.1292a15–28; V.11.1313b33–14a5). Trump's flattery takes this form: I may have the portfolio of a rich person, but I will use the attributes that put me at the top to help you little people who deserve to be treated better than the current 'elite' treats you (Cf. Trump University.). Trump flattered those he expected to vote for him, but he also expects to be flattered—any criticism is dismissed, not discussed and refuted, by attaching a demeaning epithet to the critic.[12]

In Book V, Aristotle warns that as democracy declines into demagogy, the "notables" or the respectable (the rest of the rich, well-born, well-educated who have kept silent under democratic rule) tend to revolt. Demagogic democracy does not last because it stirs up rebellion among those (with some resources at their disposal) who feel targeted by the powers that be, for instance, when the demagogue makes the rich "yield up their properties for redivision" (V.5.1304b20–05a7, also VI.5.1320a5–16). As long as a democracy remains basically law-governed, the elite can find some protection. When Trump claimed that he knows all the ways the wealthy legally avoid paying taxes and take advantage of the bankruptcy laws (because he uses them) and then that he would plug all those loopholes, he was effectively promising to take much more from the rich than the IRS is taking now. To be fair, without identifying themselves with the privileged, Bernie Sanders and Jill Stein relied on this demagogic trope as well, or as Aristotle puts it, "sometimes [demagogues] slander the wealthy in order to be in a position to confiscate their goods."[13] All of these candidates' tactics would come under the modern expression "inciting class war"—just the danger Aristotle warns against. In any case, demagogy creates a delicate balancing challenge.

After eight chapters of discussion of the causes of revolution in all types of regimes, including the rise of a demagogue, Aristotle summarizes:

> Hence the lawgiver and expert in politics should not be ignorant of which of the characteristically popular things preserve democracy *and which destroy it* … For neither [democracy nor oligarchy] can exist and last without the well off and the multitude … Popular leaders [demagogues] err in democracies where the multitude has authority over the laws: by always fighting with the well off they make the city two cities, yet they should do the opposite, and always be held to be spokesmen for the well off.[14]

As a number of Aristotle's mentions of demagogues suggest, the political atmosphere in a city and the citizens' expectations of their government are as important for explaining their rise as the institutional structures of the democracy or the personal characteristics and campaign strategies of a rising popular leader. A citizen of a democracy or a democratic republic must above all resist the temptation to place the will of the people over the rule of law, as Trump in effect promised.[15] In a law-governed community, such promises should be unacceptable in a public forum. Such temptations appear, Aristotle argues, when the community becomes socio-economically imbalanced; the regime that puts the majority in charge must be peopled by a large and influential middling class.

THE MIDDLE-CLASS REPUBLIC

Aristotle argues that a troubled democracy would be wise to make reforms in institutions and citizenship rules to move away from the extreme form of democracy and toward a middle-class polity or republic (*politeia*) (V.9.1309b19–10a36). An examination of Aristotle's account of such a regime challenges Americans to think about the state of their democratic republic in light of the desire among some vocal Trump supporters to "burn it all down," among Clinton supporters to overlook in their candidate behavior that would get other people indicted, and among Sanders supporters to imitate European socialism.

Aristotle's *Politics* presents the polity based upon the middling element as the best political regime. Like that of the United States, this regime balances institutions and electoral procedures that favor the majority with institutions that tend to favor the elite and it requires a large, politically-dominant class occupying the middle of the economic scale. Much commentary upon the 2016 election involves two interrelated perceptions (1) that the middle class has lost its political influence, perhaps is even disappearing altogether, and (2) that "the system" (electoral, financial, social/political) is "rigged" to favor the insiders against the outsiders and the rich against the less rich. Aristotle's analysis and defense of the middle-class republic helps us to see new dimensions in the electoral contest and insights into the causes of the middle class' decline. The key problems include a rhetorical failure that leads to a misunderstanding of the political/moral role of education and a failure to appreciate the virtues of a republic (as opposed to pure democracy[16]) and the virtues of the middling citizen.

REPUBLICAN POLITICS IN DECLINE

Aristotle distinguishes democracy's types according to the character of the majority's way of life. The first, most stable democracy, earlier described as the one "based on equality" between the poor and the rich, where all free people may participate according to law, is where "the multitude of farmers predominates..." (IV.4.1291b31–38; 6.1292b26–34). Even in this most law-governed, pastoral democracy, Aristotle advises the legislator to "add those of the middling sort to the dominant element in the regime" (IV.11.1296a22–96b1). When one extreme appears to be gaining excessive authority, the middle class can side with the less powerful party to restore a balance: "neither will want to be the slaves of the other, and if they seek a regime in which they will have more in common, they will find none other than this." The middling person arbitrates between the extremes. Better than a law-governed democracy (or oligarchy), a polity or republic is the more stable regime, because it mixes election procedures and laws between those that favor the rich and those that favor the poor. A republic that contains a large middle class (for Aristotle, the "best regime" and way of life for "most cities and most human beings") maintains that mixture even more effectively (*Politics* IV.11.1295a25–26). The democrats may see the resulting regime as favoring the wealthy and the oligarchs as favoring the poor, but neither can plausibly claim that a revolution would likely make things better for them.

Insofar as twenty-first century America has tended toward political polarization, creating an atmosphere in which demonizing political opponents prevents deliberation and compromise, we have fallen into the trap Aristotle warns about. If the votes of the middle class were seen to predominate in an election year and large swaths of middle-class voters were not derided as thoughtless religionists clinging to their guns or deplorable racists, but also not as envious of government benefits or hopelessly ill-informed and therefore closed to persuasion, more public rhetoric and public policy would be directed toward satisfying those Aristotle identifies as natural peacemakers. It was once taken for granted among election-watchers that much of the middle class (and certainly much of the voting public) occupied "the middle-of-the-road," and therefore that, after primaries and conventions of those with less center-line opinions had determined the nominees of the parties, the general election would settle down to enunciating policies amenable to the middle and aligning candidates' characters with a broadly moderate moral consensus. The middle class behaved as political animals to some moderate extent, attending to the state of their neighborhoods, towns, and states, and acquiring a working knowledge of the advantageous and the disadvantageous, the just and the unjust, so that they could exert political, not merely economic, influence as a moderating force. Although Aristotle approves of the middle class' need to attend to private affairs and therefore not to spend *lots* of energy on public matters, he does expect them to nurture a moderate ambition to serve the community, to rule in turn as well as to be ruled in the manner of a free person.

A Long-Term Failure to Support Middle-Class Virtue

Thomas Jefferson famously argued that "the natural aristocracy ... [is] the most precious gift of nature for the instruction, the trusts, and government of society."[17] With the abolition of the entail and free public schools available to the children of the working class, Virginia (and, by extension, all American states) would be able to "rake geniusses from the rubbish" and turn the rubbish into literate citizens who have so well absorbed the lessons of history as to vote those "geniusses," once they have received a full liberal education (and not the merely wealthy or ambitious) into political office. Over two centuries later, we have no primogeniture and we have free education available to most everyone in the country. Every year a larger proportion of students attend college. And yet, with approximately 176 **million** people eligible to run for president in 2016,[18] the primary system and the major parties' activists raked from the basket of deplorables Donald Trump and Hillary Clinton! Both were multimillionaires, one who started from a legacy of multi-millions and proudly gained and lost multiple fortunes in his life of conspicuous acquisition, and one who claims to have acquired this level of wealth, starting from being "dead broke," over sixteen years of public/philanthropic service. At any rate, neither was chosen for the talents and virtues Jefferson expected a solid education would inculcate and develop. American voters showed through the primaries and the general election that they did not recognize, or at least did not care to thwart, naked ambition; the electorate failed to select the truly talented and virtuous and reject the merely wealthy, as Jefferson expected they would, once enlightened to the low tricks of past politicians.

Despite hitting a home run (in the very long game of establishing a republic in the new United States) with his draft of the Declaration of Independence, Jefferson was not always right. His well-intentioned education scheme is one of the roots of the American urge to put the best and the brightest in charge of the biggest and thorniest problems we face collectively, and therefore, to bestow much political influence upon them. Of course, it is a tempting strategy. In some sense, the entire educational system we live in today, however imperfectly implemented, is a product of his vision of fostering a "natural aristocracy" or what we call "meritocracy." Barack Obama, Bill Clinton, and Hillary Clinton are examples of what promotion (despite humble origins in two cases) on the basis of academic achievement, without much attention to moral virtue, can produce: very influential professional politicians. The popularity of Donald Trump is perhaps an inevitable, though surely unintended, consequence of that scheme by way of the backlash it stimulates.[19] A significant segment of the voting populace followed Trump's lead in denouncing the results of the policies produced by the political "elites." "What!" the highly educated (clinging to their offices and striving ever upward) exclaim, "Should we wish to be governed by the worst and the stupidest?" Well, of course not, but what is the alternative? Aristotle's *Politics* anticipates just this problem. I don't know whether he has a workable solution, but he articulates the problem in such a way as to suggest that the current version of Jeffersonian meritocracy cannot solve it.

The middle books of the *Politics* describe and defend the polity based upon the middle element, the regime I call Aristotle's republic. It is the most stable and the most just regime "for most cities and most human beings" (IV.11.1295a25–26). Its treatment of all citizens as free and equal is consistent with Aristotle's argument that the human being is naturally political, so it is a just regime and that justice supports its stability. The stability, in turn, encourages its citizens to view the regime as just, that is, to maintain that stability.

Aristotle gives extended attention to virtue in the *Nicomachean Ethics*. Some might say that, for a man who lauded moderation, he goes on a bit too long about it. Every *thing* has a virtue—it consists in performing its function in the best way. The *Ethics* devotes an entire book to justice, speaks at some length about courage and moderation, and later looks closely at the intellectual virtue of prudence or the wisdom most active in politics. Each of these virtues practiced to its full extent is well beyond the capacities of most people. The truly virtuous, the noble and good person, always acts for the sake of the noble, for the right reason, at the right time, and to the right extent. To do so requires correct training from a young age, practice under the eye of virtuous elders, and possession of the right equipment—both physical and financial. The only honor one seeks is from those at least as virtuous as himself (a small club), not from the many. He must keep this up until he dies—only then can he declare his life happy, and happiness is the point of human life. Not many people could ever live like this gentleman.

In the *Politics*, in contrast, Aristotle praises the republic of the middling element as the best regime for most human beings. It is not merely the most practicable city given human imperfection, however. It is the best *political* regime—the best organization within which human beings practice being the political animals they are by nature. It is the most stable political order: it is the one in which it is least likely that any major part will wish to cause a revolution, because in no other regime would their interests be better served without sparking troubling opposition. It is the most just regime because it distributes honor as if the citizens were all capable of living freely, *i.e.*, of making decisions for themselves.

The polity/republic is labeled a good regime. Like kingship and aristocracy, it must, therefore, reward virtue. Aristotle first labels its characteristic virtue "military" (III.7.1279a38–b5). The problem with Jefferson's plan to put the natural aristocracy in governing office in a democratic republic comes to light when Aristotle lists the further virtues that the middle class practices and holds in esteem in its republic: middling citizens (1) hold "a **middling possession**" of "the goods of fortune," so they are self-controlled rather than self-indulgent, (2) are **"ready to obey reason"** (neither arrogant nor malicious), which means not likely to commit "acts of injustice," (3) are **willing and able to rule and be ruled in turn**, the definition of political life (neither tyrannical nor slavish), (4) are "equal and similar" to others in the city, therefore **friendly toward the other elements** in the city (not polarized), and (5) are **self-reliant** (neither envious nor envied) (*Politics* IV.11.1295b1–34). These qualities he associates with "the mean," the key to the virtues of the *Ethics*. Now, every Nicomachean virtue is a mean on a continuum of actions from too little to too much. It is, however, the extreme of virtue, the most correct action, when it is exactly in the middle—true courage (*andreia*, literally manliness) is neither pusillanimity, nor recklessness, but exactly the most manly way to act (*Nicomachean Ethics* II.8–9; III.6). None of the virtues associated with the middle class is the result of such life-long striving for perfection. These virtues are associated with the mean in an entirely different way: they are the "mean that is capable of being attained by each sort of individual" (*Politics* IV.11. 1295a35–40). The excellence of these qualities comes out when Aristotle looks at the community dominated by the middling: it is not subject to polarization because the middling citizens support themselves and serve as natural arbitrators. The best citizens are not the most highly educated, the most talented, nor the most exquisitely virtuous—all of these types could well become arrogant or be the objects of envy; they would not commonly be the friendliest to those who were not of their class or social set.

The current political climate in America is often characterized as polarized—if not precisely the rich versus the poor, then the advocates of rights-based liberalism versus the advocates of progressivism. Those parties are distinguished most commonly by their *economic* stances—for and against free-market capitalism, for and against the extension of government power over the distribution of resources and over formerly private decisions. Significant elites (the wealthy, the well-educated, the policy wonks, the permanent bureaucrats) operate at one or the other of these poles. One explanation for the surge in popular support for Trump, as well as Sanders, Stein, and Johnson for that matter, is that they claim to want to help the ordinary American and to combat the entrenched elites, however defined. These candidates claimed not to represent either of the two warring factions (however much their policy positions resemble those of one side or the other), but rather to know how to break the log-jam of bipolar politics and provide benefits to the less-wealthy, the less-well-educated, the person who has more important things to do in private life than study the latest statistics on poverty, crime, or healthcare, and (for the Green Party) to save the environment for the whole world in the process.

In short, the middle-class got a lot of rhetorical attention during this seemingly-interminable election cycle in the form of proposed tax increases on the rich, more support for family leave and childcare, free or heavily-subsidized higher education. After the election, will the middle class be able to perform a moderating role in American politics that Aristotle suggests it should? Aristotle would have some advice for those who want to rebalance America in favor of the middle class (which seems to have come to mean making middle-class buying power available to more people on their way to gaining a more-than-middle-class income): the *real* reason you want a large middle class is not their paychecks, not their tax payments, not even their spending to boost the economy. You want a large middle class because you want a citizen body characterized by satisfaction with a middling income, reasonable law-obedience, moderate public ambition, friendliness toward all fellow citizens, and self-reliance. Aristotle speaks of the middling as neither rich nor poor, but also not "overly handsome," not "overly strong," not "overly well-born," not "overly weak," not "overly dishonorable," neither having too many nor too few friends (Woe to Facebook!), neither desiring a luxurious lifestyle nor being resented by those with less income (IV.11). To get such a citizen body, Aristotle is willing to *suggest* that the middling ways of life and middling virtues are somehow connected with the great Nicomachean virtues, though the connections are rather tenuous.[20] The middle-class citizen controls his appetites—he doesn't make them dissipate altogether. Aristotle does not make the following declaration in his own name, but he also makes no qualification of it: "Many things are best for the middling; I would be of the middling sort in the city" (IV.11.1295b34).

Aristotle thus produces propaganda of a sort. For the sake of peaceful stability, opinion leaders should speak *very highly* of the most peaceful and stable citizens. The middle-class citizen should be conscious of living an *admirable* life and fulfilling a *crucial social role* right where he is. The surrounding culture should not be constantly pulling him toward the acquisition of luxury or excess, in the form of either stimuli to consumption or disparagement of homely satisfactions. Those privileged to have a fancier education should not remind those who do not that they are not PhDs in public policy, sociology, or "science." Perhaps Jefferson might have rephrased his project to rake "geniusses from the rubbish," but the public school movement in the United States should also not have changed to orient its students toward academic performance to the exclusion of character formation.[21] In a social milieu dominated by the middle class, the more wealthy would be ashamed to use their wealth to live in luxury and to get ever more wealth; as a nation, the community should not strive only for an ever-increasing GDP (see also *Politics*, I.8–11). The privileged and well-provided-for are free to pursue their own understanding of the good life in private,[22] but must learn to check their privilege in public. A moderate middle class *confident in the value of its virtues* would not object to a rich person's wealth *per se*, but would be appalled at a political candidate accumulating great wealth during a lifetime of "public service" and "philanthropy" or flaunting his wealth—even more so at one whose net worth is founded on no more than the market value of his name.

Aristotle, who appreciates aristocracy in principle, models what middle-class propaganda might look like while showing why it is necessary. Stability is arguably the goal of any city (hence all of *Politics* V) and the virtues that produce it become admirable by association. In turn, the practice and appreciation of those virtues produce an admirable republic. Self-control in the citizens and a society that values self-control produce self-control in the government (contrasted with the Athenian democracy's imperialist foreign policy, for instance); reasonable people choose the reasonable to hold political office and take their turn when they are called upon themselves. Self-reliance in the citizens and a society that values self-reliance produce a modest public policy; if the vast majority of the populace works to support itself and its own, there is much less need for ever broader government policies. Frugality in the citizens and the representatives they choose will translate into manageable tax bills.[23]

What Aristotle does not say here, but does imply[24] is that a community that strives for the highest human excellence will fail. The middle class needs to be able to feel satisfaction in its accomplishments and to practice its middling virtues self-confidently in order to make the republic, the best political regime, possible. Managing to support oneself and one's family in modest comfort, being friendly to fellow citizens whether of the same or a different class, not envying the wealthy nor being envied by a class barred from attaining a modest competence, understanding the viewpoints of the rich and the poor so as to be able to balance their rightful demands—these are the virtues that should receive rewards in political life.

Interestingly these are the virtues that were highly praised in the writings of America's founding generation,[25] but they are generally today given the toxic label "bourgeois" and are considered at best to be boring, at worst inauthentic. Donald Trump's claim to the presidency is a reflection—and an unflattering one—of contemporary mores: the popular culture honors the financially successful, celebrates the celebrated, teaches children that they can be whatever they want to be, so a grand old party with a venerable history of standing for republican liberty and equality chooses as its presidential candidate a rich celebrity who claims to want to be president.[26] Since education, like middle-class status, has been reduced in most people's minds to its economic value,[27] Trump can make claims to be smarter than all current political leaders the world over and be believed, simply because he has a large fortune.[28] His supreme self-esteem, despite the many failings his opponents have loudly identified, could be a product of the current idea that education has no moral content, meant to make one capable of living a happy life practicing attainable virtues, but rather is meant to bolster one's self-image and make one richer than his or her parents (and Trump's parents were, apparently, fairly rich).

By the testimonies of supporters talking to "the media," part of Trump's support was kindled by his unrefined way of speaking (pulling no punches, speaking unqualifiedly of American—and his own—greatness, attacking political correctness and other sacred cows of the intelligentsia) among those of the somewhat old-fashioned middle class. It seems that his supporters wish their common-sense reasonableness, their modest ambitions, their love of their families and communities were appreciated more and the elites' technical knowledge and extensive resumes of highly-paid "public service," coupled with disdain for unabashed patriots in fly-over country, were appreciated less. To avoid a repeat of 2016s upheaval, the nation's natural aristocrats of talent (if not of virtue), of which there are surely *some*, should be put to work on the technical solutions to problems that the whole society can understand, but they should also be very careful not to despise the contributions of those of more ordinary talents. If a self-confident middling element practicing modest virtues were to make a larger political footprint, *i.e.*, setting the tone for the nation's mores and acceptable political discourse, it would be much less likely that either a political neophyte whose proudest accomplishments are his mutually reinforcing celebrity and "huge" net worth or a former secretary of state who spent her entire tenure in that office hiding her e-mails not from real or potential national adversaries, but from her boss and from the American people, would have had a chance of winning the majority of electoral votes.

Aristotle says the best, most stable and just, republic is a rare phenomenon, but not unattainable. One needs a large middle class and he did not know how to create one. The rise of merchants and burghers, the industrial revolution, and the freeing of markets produced a growing middle class and happily these economic advancements coincided with political liberalization to produce a republic in America (and a few other nations) ruled by persons of some but not great wealth. The American founding generation was aware that the likely economic prosperity that America's vast resources and hard-working people would generate could be a threat to the homely virtues that they saw practiced among the yeoman farmers, the rising professional men, the artisans and "mechanics," and the merchants who greased the wheels of exchange. Without undermining the breadth of prosperity that liberal capitalism has generated, Aristotle and the American founding generation would seek in the twenty-first century to put training in the middling virtues back into the public education curricula, and perhaps to dethrone intellectual achievement as the only goal of a good citizen, in favor of training all for self-supporting work appropriate to their various talents and supportive of their virtues. Further, they would offer their examples of the rhetorical task to influence the culture to appreciate the intrinsic and extrinsic value of those virtues. Ever-growing GDP cannot be flogged as the whole goal of American society. If the middle class were not only a more accessible, but also seen as a more attractive place to live, the temptations of luxury would be reduced and the envy of the very wealthy and the accompanying political rage against "the 1 percent" could dissipate. The citizens of a republic perceived as just and stable are much less likely to find a demagogue appealing or to feel a desperate desire so to vote as to bring down the whole system.

NOTES

1. Megan Garber, *The Atlantic*, December 10, 2015, cites several uses of this descriptor for Trump at an early stage in the nominating process at http://www.theatlantic.com/entertainment/archive/2015/12/what-we-talk-about-when-we-talk-about-demagogues/419514. Her explanation of Aristotle's view of demagogy is superficial at best.
2. *Politics* V.6.1305b23–25, 29–34; 10.1310b12–31. All references to the *Politics* use *Aristotle's* Politics, trans. Carnes Lord, 2nd ed. (Chicago: University of Chicago Press, 2013).
3. "The hardworking people [Hillary Clinton] calls deplorable are the most admirable people I know: they are cops and soldiers, teachers and firefighters, young and old, moms and dads, blacks, whites and Latinos—but above everything else, they are all American. They love their families, they love their country, and they want a better future.
   These are the forgotten men and women of America. People who work hard but don't have a voice.
   I am running to be their voice, and to fight to bring prosperity to every part of this country." Donald Trump, Speech on the American Economic Plan, September 15, 2016 as quoted by Tessa Berenson, *Time*, September 15, 2016 at http://time.com/4495507/donald-trump-economy-speech-transcript.
4. "'I'll take jobs back from China,' he went on. 'I'll take jobs back from Japan. Hispanics are going to get those jobs, and they're going to love Trump, and they already do.' … 'I think I'll win the Hispanic vote,' he

concluded, insisting that the Hispanic community was not insulted by his comments." Heather Saul, *The Independent*, July 24, 2015 at http://www.independent.co.uk/news/people/donald-trump-declares-the-hispanics-love-me-they-were-chanting-for-me-after-being-met-by-protesters-10412777.html.

5. "On Fox News' *MediaBuzz* today, Howard Kurtz asked Trump about appealing to minorities. Trump said he'll do great with African-Americans, Hispanics, and Asians. 'The African-Americans love me,' he said, 'because they know I'm gonna bring back jobs.' And then Trump claimed, 'They're gonna like me better than they like Obama. The truth is Obama has done nothing for them.'" Josh Feldman, *Mediaite*, January 24, 2016 at http://www.mediaite.com/tv/trump-black-people-will-like-me-more-than-they-like-obama.

6. "Donald Trump told a divided Republican Party on Thursday he will be the 'voice' for frustrated Americans who have been let down by government and the 'elites' who run it. 'Nobody knows the system better than me, which is why I alone can fix it,' Trump told a fired-up crowd of backers..." David Jackson, *USA Today*, July 22, 2016 at http://www.usatoday.com/story/news/politics/elections/2016/07/21/donald-trump-republican-convention-acceptance-speech/87385658.

7. Trump argued that the United States is in decline under the Obama administration, citing a litany of grim statistics about crime and violence, terrorism and national security, and the rising number of Americans who have stopped looking for work.

   Election opponent Hillary Clinton and other Democrats are to blame for many of the nation's ills, Trump said, and 'the problems we face now—poverty and violence at home, war and destruction abroad—will last only as long as we continue relying on the same politicians who created them in the first place.' ...Citing the recent spate of police killings and terrorism, the businessman who has never held public office promised that 'the crime and violence that today afflicts our nation will soon, and I mean very soon, come to an end.'" Ibid.

8. *Politics* IV.4.1292a26–28, emphasis added. Compare Woodrow Wilson's view of presidential rhetoric as taking the incoherent desires of the people, formulating them into policy programs that they can understand and then teaching them that that is what they wanted all along. (Woodrow Wilson, "Cabinet Government in the United States," *International Review* VII (August 1879)) And of course, there is Teddy Roosevelt's president as "steward of the people" using a "bully pulpit."

9. Although the FBI did not find evidence that Clinton or her colleagues *intended* to violate laws, Comey chastised Clinton's actions as "extremely careless." "There is evidence that they were extremely careless in their

handling of very sensitive, highly classified information." Meghan Keneally, ABC News, July 5, 2016 at http://abc30.com/news/fbi-recommends-no-charges-be-filed-against-clinton/1414041.

"Although there is evidence of potential violations of the statutes regarding the handling of classified information, our judgment is that no reasonable prosecutor would bring such a case." James Comey, July 5, 2016, FBI National Press Office Release at https://www.fbi.gov/news/pressrel/press-releases/statement-by-fbi-director-james-b-comey-on-the-investigation-of-secretary-hillary-clinton2019s-use-of-a-personal-e-mail-system.

See also Rep. Gowdy's questioning of Comey in the House Oversight Committee: Steve Guest, *The Daily Caller*, July 7, 2016, at http://daily-caller.com/2016/07/07/comey-confirms-hillary-clinton-lied-to-the-public-about-her-emails-video/#ixzz4OlvsZcmO.

10. See *Politics* V. 5, in which Aristotle argues that the most common cause of the downfall of democracies into factional conflict is demagogy, such as the tactic of stirring up enmity between the rich and the poor. A similar tactic in twenty-first century democracy is called identity politics and may involve dividing the populace along other lines, such as "race," ethnicity, or sexual identity, though wealth/privilege and its lack always lurk beneath the surface. When the political landscape is divided into equally powerful warring factions with "nothing or very little in the middle," the regime is about to "change," i.e., undergo a revolution (*Politics* V.4.1304a40–b4). Compare Federalist 10: "The smaller the society, the fewer probably will be the distinct parties and interests composing it; the fewer the distinct parties and interests, the more frequently will a majority be found of the same party and the smaller the number of individuals composing a majority, and the smaller the compass within which they are placed, the more easily will they concert and execute their plans of oppression." (Alexander Hamilton, John Jay, and James Madison, *The Federalist*, ed. Robert Scigliano (New York: Modern Library, 2000)), 10.60.

11. http://www.politico.com/story/2016/12/donald-trump-congress-republicans-232800.

12. Trump revealed his own character, especially during the primaries, when he seemed to believe that everyone who criticized him was a would-be competing demagogue appealing to the many by trying to bring Trump down, thus his/her unflattering opinion of Trump must be thrust beyond the pale of acceptable opinion, rather than answered with a reasoned argument. Again, Trump is hardly alone in this tactic but his sensitivity to any negative evaluation, his tendency to chase and maul every potential slight, places the inverse-flattery element of his campaign in high relief.

The impact of Twitter and other "social" (really asocial, if not anti-social) media on this election has been noted. (http://www.cio.com/article/3137513/social-networking/twitters-impact-on-2016-presidential-election-is-unmistakable.html; http://www.theatlantic.com/technology/archive/2016/11/election-bots/506072; http://www.govtech.com/social/2016-Presidential-Election-Circus-Is-Social-Media-the-Cause.html, among lots of others.) More interesting would be an exploration of the political atmosphere in which citizens/voters and candidates find 140 characters sufficient to change someone's mind. And if changing minds is not the goal, as it probably is not, but rather to signal one's virtue and the other's disgrace, Aristotle might suggest that an examination of the seriousness of our ethics is in order.

Moreover, the rhetorical strategy of stirring up anger against the opposition may be effective in some cases (Aristotle, *The Rhetoric and the Poetics of Aristotle*, W. Rhys Roberts, trans., Edward P. J. Corbett, ed. (New York: Modern Library, 1954, II.2.1378a32–36, b14–16, 23–32, 38–79b3, 27–30; 1416a3–7)), but it potentially creates a counter-productive backlash: Trump's emphasis on examples of law-breaking by illegal immigrants was countered by shouts of racism and xenophobia that successfully consolidated a large opposition coalition; Clinton's dismissal of a significant segment of the populace as deplorable racists and homophobes stirred up the ire of "undecided" voters and those Trump supporters who were neither. By the way, Aristotle explains the magnitude of the anger felt and expressed by Clinton supporters after Trump's election at 1379a22–24: "We are angered if we happen to be expecting a contrary result: for a quite unexpected evil is especially painful…"

13. Clinton publicly criticized the super-rich and privately salved their fears, likely in order to avoid the revolt of the oligarchs that Aristotle predicts. https://wikileaks.org/podesta-emails/emailid/927.

14. *Politics* V.9.1309b35–10a7, emphasis added. In his inaugural address, Trump spoke of his task as governing for the sake of all Americans, regardless of party. Jefferson did so as well, after a very "divisive" campaign. If it is a banality of American inaugurations, it may rest upon the truth Aristotle insists upon: that a political regime cannot survive if those wishing it to continue do not vastly outnumber those who wish the opposite (*Politics* IV.12).

15. "During Thursday night's debate on Fox News, Trump reaffirmed his willingness to target the families of terrorists and supported the use of waterboarding, implying a willingness to use torture. 'We should go for waterboarding and we should go tougher than waterboarding,' he said.

"But in a statement Friday, Trump said that he understands 'that the United States is bound by laws and treaties' and that he would 'not order our military or other officials to violate those laws and will seek their advice on such matters.' He added, 'I will not order a military officer to disobey the law. It is clear that as president I will be bound by laws just like all Americans and I will meet those responsibilities.'" Ryan Browne and Nicole Gaouette, CNN Politics, March 4, 2016 at http://www.cnn.com/2016/03/04/politics/donald-trump-reverses-on-torture.

The later statement obviously was made after various military leaders expressed shock and his advisors alerted him to the incendiary rhetoric he had been using. The electorate was left free to decide which sentiments would guide Trump once he became Commander in Chief.

"Donald Trump's latest threat against the media came Friday at a rally in Texas. Once elected president, Trump promised, he will 'open up' federal libel laws to make it easier to sue news outlets like The Washington Post and New York Times..." reports Callum Borchers, February 26, 2016, in The Washington *Post* at https://www.washingtonpost.com/news/the-fix/wp/2016/02/26/donald-trump-vows-to-open-up-libel-laws-to-make-suing-the-media-easier-heres-how-he-could-do-it. Borchers reassures his fellow "horrified" journalists that Trump can't change the libel laws on his own, *unless,* of course, he can get the Supreme Court to overturn *Times* v. *Sullivan*. Again the electorate was left to wonder what a President Trump would do to politicize the judiciary further during his term. That the Court is seen as the next best thing to Congress for changing the law is yet another sign of the trend away from a law-governed republic.

16. As Publius distinguishes them in Federalist 10 (Hamilton et al. [2000], 10.58–9).

17. Thomas Jefferson to John Adams, 28 Oct. 1813 (http://founders.archives.gov/documents/Jefferson/03-06-02-0446). He goes on: "it would have been inconsistent in creation to have formed man for the social state, and not to have provided virtue and wisdom enough to manage the concerns of the society. May we not even say that that form of government is the best which provides the most effectually for a pure selection of these natural *aristoi* into the offices of government?" And would we be equally justified in suggesting that the deplorable rubbish be content to be despised by the geniusses? Jefferson's education plan proposes to make those who are not up to a university education but who performed tolerably well through the secondary levels of schooling the schoolmasters of the next generation. The system both promotes the most talented and virtuous and inculcates respect for them among those who do not advance, because it teaches virtue and hones talent and then selects the more virtuous and talented for more teaching and honing. It seems unlikely that such a system

would inculcate respect in the natural *aristoi* for those left behind, despite the equality of their rights and their voting power.

18. Counting all citizens over 35 not incarcerated and not on active military duty. I did not ask to examine the length of residence in the U.S. nor the "naturalness" of the citizenship, which would reduce this number somewhat. I thank Edward A. Rubin for this calculation.

19. Closer to Jefferson's lifetime, Andrew Jackson used his presidency to advance a similar backlash—one that birthed the spoils system of filling executive branch offices with party loyalists rather than administrators chosen for their competence and virtue: "There are, perhaps, few men who can for any great length of time enjoy office and power without being more or less under the influence of feelings unfavorable to the faithful discharge of their public duties. Their integrity may be proof against improper considerations immediately addressed to themselves, but they are apt to acquire a habit of looking with indifference upon the public interests and of tolerating conduct from which an unpracticed man would revolt." Andrew Jackson: "First Annual Message," December 8, 1829. Online by Gerhard Peters and John T. Woolley, *The American Presidency Project*. http://www.presidency.ucsb.edu/ws/?pid=29471.

20. *Nicomachean Ethics* VII.1–10. The truly moderate person does not even feel a desire to indulge to excess, while the middle-class citizen is temperate and frugal out of a habit instilled by a middling income and a need to support himself and his family.

21. Others of the founding generation argued for more emphasis on training the youth in trades and professions, both to make them productive members of society and to foster virtues such as frugality, self-reliance, and self-control. See, for instance, Robert Coram's and Noah Webster's educational schemes.

22. Jefferson, following Aristotle and many others, assumes the good life has a strong moral component. His natural aristocrats are supposed to be those "endowed with genius *and* virtue" and they are promoted in his proposed publicly-funded schools on the basis of both qualities.

23. Benjamin Franklin's "Information to Those Who Would Remove to America," 1782, though playfully written, makes interesting connections between middle-class income and politically salutary virtues:

> The almost general Mediocrity of Fortune that prevails in America obliging its People to follow some Business for subsistence, those Vices, that arise usually from Idleness, are in a great measure prevented. Industry and constant Employment are great preservatives of the Morals and Virtue of a Nation. Hence bad Examples to Youth are more rare in America, which must be a comfortable Consideration to Parents. To this may be truly added, that serious Religion, under its various

Denominations, is not only tolerated, but respected and practised. Atheism is unknown there; Infidelity rare and secret; so that persons may live to a great Age in that Country, without having their Piety shocked by meeting with either an Atheist or an Infidel. And the Divine Being seems to have manifested his Approbation of the mutual Forbearance and Kindness with which the different Sects treat each other, by the remarkable Prosperity with which He has been pleased to favour the whole Country. (http://press-pubs.uchicago.edu/founders/documents/v1ch15s27.html)

Cf. Melancton Smith's socio-economic analysis of middle-class virtue at the New York Ratifying Convention, 1788, in the midst of his Anti-Federalist argument that the House needs to be larger so that it cannot be filled exclusively with lawyers and wealthy men:

Those in middling circumstances, have less temptation—they are inclined by habit and the company with whom they associate, to set bounds to their passions and appetites—if this is not sufficient, the want of means to gratify them will be a restraint—they are obliged to employ their time in their respective callings—hence the substantial yeomanry of the country are more temperate, of better morals and less ambition than the great. The latter do not feel for the poor and middling class; the reasons are obvious—they are not obliged to use the pains and labour to procure property as the other.—They feel not the inconveniences arising from the payment of small sums. The great consider themselves above the common people—entitled to more respect—do not associate with them—they fancy themselves to have a right of pre-eminence in every thing. (http://press-pubs.uchicago.edu/founders/documents/v1ch13s37.html)

24. Also strongly suggested in *Politics* II.6, 8–10, through the critiques of Plato's *Laws*, Sparta, Crete, and Carthage.
25. In addition to Franklin's (rather ironic) and Smith's (likely more sincere) encomia to the middling state, a wide array of famous and not so famous writers at the time of the founding praised the virtues practiced by the neither rich nor poor: John Adams, Charles Pinckney, John Dickinson, James Wilson, Noah Webster, Jeremiah Atwater, and Robert Coram, to name a few.
26. Consider Yuval Levin's wise analysis of contemporary American culture in *The Fractured Republic* (New York: Basic Books, 2016), especially pp. 39, 55, and 73. My argument might diverge from his on this point, introducing his analysis of the need for upward mobility for the poor: "Wealth is not a social problem, but poverty is" (124). The poor must indeed to be able to rise into the middle class, but the middle class should not be

primarily in the business of trying to rise out of the middle class, but rather of reaping the rewards of self-reliance and self-restraint. Money is not the root of all evil, but the love of it just might be.

27. The Huffington Post (November 2, 2016) collects various current opinions on the "value of a higher education," all of which analyze its financial benefits at http://www.huffingtonpost.com/news/value-of-college-education. See also Jennifer Barrett, CNBC, June 19, 2015, at http://www.cnbc.com/2015/06/19/is-a-college-degree-overvalued.html. Even a site called "Education Corner," when adding "other benefits" to the financial ones, produces a list that boils down to social prestige and a higher standard of living: http://www.educationcorner.com/value-of-a-college-degree.html. Contrast this view with that of Benjamin Rush, Noah Webster, and the "Foreign Spectator," Nicholas Collin, at the time of the founding. For further development of arguments showing the parallels between Aristotle and the founders on the middle class and its virtues, see my *America, Aristotle, and the Politics of a Middle Class* (Waco, Texas: Baylor University Press, 2018).

28. An interesting further development in this election: This reduction of the value of education to its monetary benefits results also in the notion expounded by Trump's competitors that the less fortunate can "get a foothold" in the middle class and, by extension, become able to climb higher on the economic ladder if the government makes a college education free for all without regard, as Jefferson once insisted, to talents or virtue.

References

Aristotle. *The Rhetoric and the Poetics of Aristotle*. Trans. W. Rhys Roberts, ed. Edward P.J. Corbett. New York: Modern Library, 1954.

———. *Aristotle's Politics*. Trans. Carnes Lord, 2nd ed. Chicago: University of Chicago Press, 2013.

Hamilton, Alexander, John Jay, and James Madison. *The Federalist*, ed. Robert Scigliano. New York: Modern Library, 2000.

Kurland, Philip B., and Ralph Lerner. *The Founders' Constitution*, 2000. http://press-pubs.uchicago.edu/founders/. Accessed 30 November 2017.

Levin, Yuval. *The Fractured Republic*. New York: Basic Books, 2016.

Rubin, Leslie G. *America, Aristotle, and the Politics of a Middle Class*. Waco, TX: Baylor University Press, 2018.

CHAPTER 5

Democracy, Demagogues, and Political Wisdom: Understanding Trump in the Wake of Thucydides' *History*

Bernard J. Dobski

"Athenian" Trump, "American" Cleon

Critics of President Donald J. Trump tend to illuminate their analyses of our chief executive with comparisons to the "baddies" of the twentieth and twenty-first centuries. These analogies call upon men like Hitler, Stalin, Kim Jong Un, Chavez, and Peron—those tyrants, fascists, strongmen, "caudillos," and authoritarians whom we all love to hate.[1] Such comparisons may be gratifying to those who make them, but in the end they are too facile to help us understand Trump, if only because he lacks the ideological fervor animating the most murderous thugs of the modern world. Trump does not want to remake man in pursuit of some utopian project. Nor does he seek to impose on the world a systematic solution to the problems facing mankind, resorting to the terror, torture, and tyranny that such impossible abstractions require. On the contrary, Trump, in some of his more public statements on behalf of national sovereignty, candidly denounces those calls for "citizens of the globe" to set aside their particular national loyalties and embrace a rootless cosmopolitanism. American advantage, not airy abstraction, is Trump's calling card.

B. J. Dobski (✉)
Assumption College, Worcester, MA, USA

© The Author(s) 2018
A. Jaramillo Torres, M. B. Sable (eds.), *Trump and Political Philosophy*,
https://doi.org/10.1007/978-3-319-74445-2_5

But Trump's more articulate defenses of national sovereignty often get muddled by the nativistic tones of his outbursts on social media and at political rallies. "Make America Great Again" may be an effective political slogan, but without a standard to judge the greatness of our aspirations, one independent of our particular national interests, we drift further and further from the universal ethos informing our nation's founding documents. The exhortation to American greatness thus remains unmoored and unleavened by a reference to anything noble or exalted. A tribalistic and soul-flattening reduction of the good to one's own emerges from the thoughtless jingoism of "my country, right or wrong." And while the effort to recover the dignity of this more traditional form of patriotism might explain part of Trump's appeal, such a recovery proceeds apart from that larger moral order in which the goodness, or greatness, of our "parts" can be rationally grasped and defended. Without cognition of that larger order, we could never actually *know* if we have made America great again, leaving Trump's most popular political imperative unfulfilled and unfulfillable.

Trump's effort to restore dignity to the particular hearkens to a time before ideological politics, long before the architects of the Enlightenment retrained political thought to conceive political solutions solely in universal terms. The appeal of Trump therefore lies in something deeper, older, in an aspect of our humanity best captured by works of classical political thought. For this reason, one can find more apt comparisons to our president in portraits of pre-modern political life. Among the pantheon of demagogues and dictators of the classical world, few offer a more tempting comparison with our 45th president than Cleon, an Athenian politician from the fifth century BCE.[2] While we can sketch a partial portrait of this demagogue from the works of Plutarch and Aristophanes,[3] we get a more complete picture of Cleon's political career from the *History* of Thucydides.[4]

As Thucydides reports, Cleon came to political power in Athens in 429 BCE as a leader and flatterer of the city's *demos*, or "The People". His political ascendance came at a critical moment for the city. Two years into what would be a twenty-seven year war with Sparta and her Peloponnesian allies, Athens suffered a potentially debilitating blow: Pericles, the visionary of Athens' maritime empire, the steward of her foreign policy, and the undisputed leader of the city, died from the plague then ravaging the city. Eager to reap for himself the glory that his predecessor had won for Athens, Cleon courted the favor of the Athenian *demos*. In doing so, he effectively wrested leadership of Athens from his main rival, the conservative, pious, and overly cautious general, Nicias (the original "low-energy" pol). Because of his popular support, Cleon predominated in Athenian politics until his death on the battlefield outside the city of Amphipolis in 422 BCE. Though his tenure was marked by no small political achievements, Cleon's rule was a failure, and not merely because of his untimely death.

In his eulogy of Pericles (II.65), Thucydides notes that the Athenians deviated from Pericles' counsel to wait out the Spartans, tend to their own navy, and attempt no new conquests. Instead, they allowed "private ambitions and private interests, in matters quite apparently quite foreign to the war, to lead them into projects unjust both to themselves and to their allies—projects whose success could only conduce to the honor and advantage of private persons, and whose failure entailed certain disaster on the country in the war" (II.65.7). While Pericles possessed the foresight, moderation, and reputation for integrity that allowed him to encourage or contradict the passions of his fellow citizens, his successors were more "on a level with each other, and each grasping at supremacy, they ended by committing even the conduct of state affairs to the whims of the multitude" producing a "host of blunders" (II.65.10–11). Because Cleon lacked the virtues and public spiritedness that distinguished his more celebrated predecessor, the example set by his own self-interested rule helped erode his fellow citizens' attachments to the public good, sowing the seeds for Athens' eventual defeat in this war. No less a judge than Aristotle appears to confirm this view. In his *Athenian Constitution*, Aristotle declares that Cleon "more than anyone else, seems to have been the cause of the corruption of the democracy by his wild undertakings".[5] How so?

According to Thucydides' portrait of this demagogue, Cleon bullied his opponents, attacked the public use of reason to serve the common good, used political power to persecute his critics, and was known for his "towering moral indignation and its accompanying boastfulness, bloodthirstiness, calumnies, lies, pretense, theft of the deeds of others, and cowardice".[6] Cleon also articulated a view of politics, both foreign and domestic, as a game characterized by winners and losers. In his speech during the Mytilinean Debate, Cleon frankly states that Athens' empire is a despotism (III.37.2), one whose origins lies in her superior power over her subjects. Because winning and losing is a zero-sum game, any effort by her subjects to achieve political liberation can portend nothing less than the destruction of Athens herself. Of course, Cleon decries the Athenian practice of treating public speech like an athletic competition, where rivals look to their own interests in competing with each other for public influence. But he advances this otherwise public-spirited argument for *his* sake; he wants to prevent the Athenian assembly from overturning its earlier decision to back *his* proposal to kill all the adult males of the city of Mytilene. Cleon is an "athlete" who loathes rivalry and who views contestation as an affront to his superiority. Those he has defeated are losers who should remain so.

The similarities between Trump and Cleon become even stronger when one considers that Cleon, like President Trump, was especially well-known for his vulgar speech. To this end, Aristotle writes that Cleon "was the first to use unseemly shouting and coarse abuse on the *bema* and to harangue the people with his cloak girt up about him, whereas all his predecessors had spoken decently and in order".[7] And though not as wealthy as "the Donald," Cleon nevertheless possessed a considerable fortune relative to his fellow Athenians, one that contributed to his sway among the demos and which he owed to his *father's* success as a tanner. While the dramatists of fifth century Athens did not want for risible material, Cleon nonetheless remained a favorite target of poets like Aristophanes, appearing in his comedies for derision long after the demagogue died. Thucydides himself reserves a special distinction for Cleon: he is the only figure in the entire *History* to be openly mocked (IV.28.5). Over the last two centuries, it would be hard to think of a political figure of such significance who is as easy a target for comic ridicule as Donald Trump.

A study of the rise, rule, and fall of Cleon in democratic Athens should therefore teach us about not only the virtues and vices of President Trump, but of the democracy that elected him. Thucydides' presentation of Cleon, and especially the anger at the heart of his demagogy, illuminates the political psychology behind democratic Athens' empire and indicates why the rhetoric of Pericles, Cleon's illustrious predecessor, offers a better model for a White House caught between the Scylla of nativism and the Charybdis of cosmopolitanism.

TRUMP AND THUCYDIDEAN REALISM

Drawing a link between Trump and Thucydides is hardly novel. Revelations that the Trump White House had been briefed by Harvard Professor Graham Allison, author of the *Thucydides's Trap*,[8] and that members of his inner circle were devotees of Thucydides' masterpiece spawned numerous columns and essays all trying to show how the "power politics" allegedly advocated by the *History*'s author would influence America's foreign policy.[9] But Thucydides advances no such teaching in his own name. It is true that many of the Athenians in the *History* advocate a form of *realpolitik*, or what scholars call the "Athenian thesis." This view holds that, in relations between states (as well as between men and the gods), it is might that makes right; "the strong do what they can and the weak suffer what they must" while justice only pertains "among equals in power" (V.89). But Thucydides nowhere states that he shares their views. His silence on this score should inspire his fans in the Oval Office to approach his text with greater caution.

If we resist the temptation to identify Thucydides with some of the actors of his work, then we can see that the thrust of the *History* actually trends against the realist view. Take for example, the speeches of the Athenian envoys at Melos (V.85–112). Long held to be the expositors of *realpolitik* in Thucydides' work, these men ultimately concede that honor and justice do not result from contests between equals, as they originally claim (V.89). Instead, as they state to the Melians near the end of their exchange, honor and justice come from courting danger, greater risks presumably promising greater honor and justice to be won (V.107). And by contrasting themselves favorably with the risk-averse Spartans, who merely pursue what is expedient, the Athenians at Melos indirectly indicate that they are concerned with an imperium that is honorable and just—hence risk-taking—and thus not simply self-interested.

In this way, these Athenians recall their fellow envoys at Sparta, who defended their claim to imperial rule in part on their superiority to compulsion (i.e., they rule more leniently than their power allows them to, I.76.2–3). According to these earlier advocates of the "Athenian thesis," Athens' rule over others owes itself not to her superior power but to her superior worthiness. The view that "might makes right," so often a part of Athenian justifications for their empire, thus gets complicated by the fact that many of the arguments advanced in service of this realist view end up supporting the opposite position, namely that "*right* makes might."

Of course, to think that right is or should be the means by which one gains political dominion over others is to presuppose a world ordered toward justice. It is to think, or at least to hope, that the world is governed by powers or principles that are essentially benevolent insofar as they reward one's selflessness—understood here as a superiority to the compulsion to rule others as harshly as one's power will allow—with a superior claim to rule over others. Like the Greek Olympians who wrestled nude in order to display their natural greatness (I.6), the Athenians understand their superior worth, made evident both in what they do and in what they say, to give them a just claim to domination or sovereignty over others. The just *claim* to power trumps its mere possession; power by itself is not enough. It is for this reason that the Athenians at Melos insist on pushing such a misguided rhetorical strategy, one that requires the admittedly pious Melians to accept an impious view of the gods and man. They thus deploy a shocking frankness with their allies in the belief that by disclosing (what they think to be) their true motives in ruling as they do, they will make their superior worth manifest to others and thereby win their voluntary submission.

While the free acceptance of Athenian mastery by her subjects would surely serve the interests of her imperial rule, the candor by which her citizens advance these claims most certainly does not; the envoys' honesty is self-defeating, making their insistence on its use puzzling for those who would see them as shrewd Machiavellian plotters. Thucydides reinforces the humanity underlying the envoys' honesty at Melos by noting, almost in passing, that the eventual slaughter of the Melians gets carried out by a different contingent of Athenians, under a different general no less, *months after* the original envoys returned to Athens (V.114.2, 116.3). Whatever one might say about the harsh statements made by these envoys, their arguments need not eventuate in mass murder. Such bloody deeds belong to a different political register.

Thucydides indicates his distance from the power-politics of the "Athenian thesis," and thus his affinity for his narrative's subtle critique of that view, in his comments about the destruction of the small town of Mycalessus. This defenseless hamlet, distinguished chiefly by the presence of a large school for boys, was sacked by Thracian mercenaries on their return home from Athens. Having just sent a massive and sumptuously outfitted armada to Sicily, Athens declined the use of these mercenaries on the grounds that she lacked sufficient funds. Angered at the loss of these monies, the mercenaries, on their way back to Thrace, fell upon a weak Mycalessus and tried to slaughter everything within it: men, women, children, even beasts of burden. The strong doing what they can indeed! Of the pointless assault on Mycalessus, Thucydides says that *no misfortune* suffered during this war was greater, especially since its particular fate was so unexpected and terrible (VII.29). That Thucydides should single out this act of destruction as the greatest misfortune in a war that knew no shortage of bloody deeds shows just how far removed he is from the "power-politics" commonly attributed to him. Against his "lament" over Mycalessus (VII.30.3), one should set his assessment of Cleon as "the most violent man in Athens" (III.36), an all-too-fitting description for a man who called for the desolation of Mytilene (III.36.6), Scione (IV.122), and Torone (V.3.4).

Thucydides' negative judgment against Cleon should not prevent us from studying his career seriously. After all, Thucydides dedicates his life's work, a work whose insights into "the clear truth" about human nature make it a "possession for all time," to a war whose greatness consisted in its violent suffering (I.23). Indeed, Thucydides himself tells us that war is a "violent teacher" (III.82.2).[10] If war is a violent teacher that teaches through violence, then a study of the most violent man in Athens should promise to shed light on the scope and limitations of the vulgar realism that so many casually attribute to Thucydides himself and which so many claim characterizes Donald Trump. While Cleon's anger distinguishes him from the more generous advocates of the "Athenian thesis", it neverthe-less reflects a fundamentally moral outlook on the world shared by virtu-ally all advocates of Athenian imperium. It is precisely such a moral perspective that Pericles' rhetoric both cultivates and manages.

THE ANGER OF CLEON

In his chapter "Anger in Thucydides and Aristophanes: the Case of Cleon," Tim Burns argues that Cleon's violence is born from a frustrated hopefulness.[11] Like the envoys at Sparta and Melos, Cleon is animated by the beliefs that Athens has a just claim to her imperial domain, one rooted in her superior power, and that the world is ultimately ordered so as to uphold the claims of justice against the forces that would deny it. But whereas the envoys appear to think that the mere disclosure of Athens' superior claim to rule others sufficient to its realization, and so like Alcibiades limit themselves to speeches, Cleon dismisses moral suasion in favor of violence. In his first reported speech in the *History*, Cleon urges the Athenians to kill all the adult males of Mytilene and to sell the women and children of this rebellious city into slavery.

Mytilene was a city in the heart of Athens' maritime empire, an ally of Athens, and had enjoyed considerable freedom under Athens' imperial sway; unlike other subjects of the empire, the Mytilineans didn't have to pay taxes to Athens (III.36.2). Nevertheless, this city plotted with Sparta, upon whom the success of her enterprise depended, to free herself from

Athens' power and thereby introduce Athens' enemies into the heart of her maritime empire. Because Spartan military support failed to materialize in time, the rebellion at Mytilene was put down by Athens (III.28). In a fit of rage at this unprovoked revolt, the members of the Athenian assembly passed Cleon's terrible decree only to find themselves reconsidering this decision twenty-four hours later. In an extraordinary move, the Athenians called a second assembly in as many days to redeliberate (III.36.4).[12]

In response to this sharp deviation from custom, Cleon tried to rekindle the Athenians' original outrage (III.37–40). He reminded his audience that the Mytilineans' rebellion was unprovoked, that it sought to undermine Athens' empire, and that it, because so clearly unjust, would have required nothing less than the destruction of Athens. Mytilene clearly deserves punishment. But if one is to mete out justice to the wicked, argues Cleon, then one must not wait. The longer one waits to get revenge, the less angry one will be when he does punish; as a result the unjust will suffer less for the harm they inflicted, making them more likely to commit such crimes in the future. Cleon's understanding of the nature of human transgressions thus suggests that harsh punishments are not only just, but that they also deter crime. As Burns points out, implicit in this view is the unacknowledged belief that harsher punishments will help prevent *all* transgressions in the future. Cleon's criminology believes that the world allows injustice to be completely eliminated. This is why he rails against the dangers of compassion, pleasurable speeches, and reasonableness (III.40). Compassion and reasonableness should be reserved for those who can reciprocate them, not those who will of necessity remain our enemies.

Of course, Cleon does not ground his position in justice alone. He concedes that even if it is unjust for Athens to rule over her fellow Greeks (he earlier calls her empire a tyranny), it is still necessary that she fight to preserve her dominion. Failure to do so will profoundly harm her interests. Given that Cleon provides no defense of Athenian justice, no argument as to why she has a superior moral claim to rule her fellow Greeks, it is not altogether surprising to see that Cleon should also provide a particularistic defense of "one's own": Athenians should defend Athenian empire because it is theirs. It is as simple as that. Thus by severely punishing the injustice of the Mytilineans, the Athenians will deter future attempts at rebellion by their allies and secure both justice and self-interest.

Fortunately for the Mytilineans, Cleon's bid here is defeated by Diodotus (III.42–48). In his only appearance in the *History*, this citizen, whose name means "gift of Zeus", urges the Athenians not to give in to anger. Instead, he counsels them to consider their self-interest, not justice, and adopt a more lenient path by killing only those deemed most guilty. While Cleon thinks harsher punishments will deter future crimes, Diodotus argues that harsher punishments will only encourage those who rebel from Athens to hold out until the very end. And since punishments such as Cleon advises are to be carried out against the whole of the rebellious city, this policy will force the blameless to join the cause of the guilty out of a concern for self-preservation. The result will be prolonged sieges whose reduction will come at greater cost to an Athens that can only hope to recover ruined cities for its efforts. By contrast, Diodotus urges the Athenians to punish as few as possible, even if it means letting some of the guilty escape punishment, and to keep their allies under close surveillance so that they can extinguish rebellions before they flare-up. This more lenient response holds out the possibility of conditional surrender and manages to keep "The People" in these subject cities well-disposed toward Athens.

But the strongest arguments advanced by Diodotus are leveled against Cleon's criminology. According to Diodotus, humans are passionate and needy creatures compelled by their passions and needs to pursue the goods they believe will satisfy them. Under the influence of hope and erotic longing, men will be compelled to transgress what laws, written and unwritten, forbid. Driven on by their erotic desires, they will defy the threat of even the harshest punishments in the hopes of securing those goods, like freedom and empire, that they take to be the greatest. It is thus foolish to think that Athens will secure her imperial interests by the bloody sentence Cleon would impose on the Mytilineans and it is unjust to punish men for what they are compelled to do.

The humanity of Diodotus succeeds in defeating the anger of Cleon but only because he undermines the moral freedom on which such anger rests. For if men are compelled to act as they do, then their actions are not free and without that freedom the anger of Cleon becomes groundless. But in requiring such freedom, Cleon must also presuppose a world that allows wrong-doing to take place; he must accept a world in which it is possible for humans to err about the good and for the unjust to refuse to recognize or submit to the superior justice of cities like Athens. Moral freedom implies the possibility of moral error and injustice which, for the morally upright, requires correction, and hence the rational instruction of the unjust consistent with their freedom as moral agents. But Cleon offers only violence in support of the law. Because he insists on violently punishing transgressors, Cleon tacitly concedes the shortcomings of his own hopes about the world even as he refuses to acknowledge what such insistence—the very fact that he *must* insist—implies about his wish to eliminate injustice forever.

The anger that blinds Cleon from recognizing what his disappointed hopes mean for him is not simply a failure of reason. It is a moral failing. Cleon's anger stems from a refusal to face what he fears to be true about both justice and the world that he hoped would protect it. His anger is thus a kind of cowardice, one that issues in an irrational defiance of all of those obstacles that stand in the way of him realizing his deepest hopes. This is why, despite his reputation for anger and violence, he cowardly refuses Nicias' offer of his generalship, a move designed to shame Cleon into making good on his reckless boasts (IV.28.1–3). It is why he delays his assault on Brasidas' outmanned Spartan forces at Amphipolis, even though Cleon's force enjoys superior numbers (V.6). And it is why he retreats from the field of battle, a move that leads to his death, the deaths of many of his soldiers, and the failure to recapture Amphipolis (V.10.3–9). Such battlefield cowardice is the reverse side of his hope in a world that eliminates injustice. A truly just world would provide him protection, rule over others, and the wholeness he so desperately craves. Cleon fears that the world denies us such justice and thus denies us the immortality for which we most hope. Such fears account for the angry and shriveled nativism behind his defense of Athenian empire.

The Virtues of Cleon?

Given the similarities between Cleon and Trump, it might be tempting, on the basis of the preceding analysis, to condemn and dismiss those who support such men as merely rabble, a "basket of deplorables" angry at a world that refuses to support their superstitions and narrow self-interests. Conversely, it might be tempting to embrace the enlightened compassion of Diodotus' universal wisdom, especially given its "proximity" to the urbane progressivism of contemporary liberal America. But such temptations lead us amiss. It is not simply ignorance or a narrowness of soul that draws "The People" to support such impulsive and violent men, but an irrational demand for perfect justice in this world, the same moral impulse at work in the more humane adherents of the "Athenian thesis". If the study of Cleon's character illuminates that of Trump, then we might conclude that the president's apparent impetuosity is the consequence not of a pathological narcissism but of outrageous moral demands made on both his fellow citizens and the international order.

Needless to say, such demands, born from excessive hopefulness, would benefit from a more honest reflection on what it is those who make it seek from others when they allow indignation to rule their souls. This reflection is made possible in the immediate context by Diodotus, whose speech highlights an aspect of the human soul to which Cleon and his kind are blind, namely the power of eros. If eros represents the soul's longing for transcendence, for liberation from a world beset with evils, for a good that completely satisfies one's deepest needs, then in Thucydides' *History*, the embodiment of erotic longing is certainly not Cleon, but Alcibiades, the ward of Pericles, the student of Socrates, and arguably the greatest political talent in Athens at the end of the fifth century. But the turn to Alcibiades as an alternative or antidote to Cleon must itself be cautioned by an awareness that the eros he embodies inspired the Athenians to attempt the conquest of Sicily, a campaign whose disastrous results nearly doomed Athens. And this campaign failed not only for reasons practical and strategic, but because it was animated by the impossible hope that in conquering Sicily Athens could secure for herself and her citizens all the goods they would ever need, providing her with, in effect, an apotheosis (VI.24). As Alcibiades later confessed, the conquest of Sicily, though itself "yuuuge", was to be only one step toward a much larger imperium, one whose logic knew no borders (VI.90). With its mad self-forgetting of particular limits, needs, and concerns, such universal empire comes to sight as a classical version of the global humanitarianism which Trump so loudly criticizes. In seeking a remedy to Cleon's narrow particularism, we must therefore be careful to avoid indulging the opposite extreme. This is another way of saying that while Cleon has many vices, he also has virtues that Pericles' rhetoric preserves. Before turning to that rhetoric, let us consider Cleon's specific virtues.

A partial rehabilitation of Cleon might begin by noting that he is not stupid. Given the massive change of heart that occasioned the second Athenian assembly on the fate of Mytilene, Cleon's narrow loss to Diodotus testifies to his effectiveness as a speaker. After all, he managed to reignite the moral outrage of those Athenians whose humane second-thoughts began to weaken their murderous resolve. Diodotus may be wiser, but Cleon is more persuasive. And while his manner of speech is crude and violent, it is not artless; its "many ... embellishments" reflect the influence of the sophist Gorgias, the renowned teacher of rhetoric.[13]

Cleon's rhetorical skills best come to light in his response to the Spartan appeal for the release of the 400 Spartiates the Athenians had trapped on the island of Sphacteria. Using the Spartans' plea for leniency against them, Cleon claims that if the Spartans are to get back the 400 men they lost due to chance, then the Athenians, on that same basis, should get back the three cities they lost in the first Peloponnesian War (ca. 446 BCE; IV.21.3).[14] This rhetorical gambit nearly works. Had his subsequent angry denunciation of the Spartans not bungled his rhetorical success here, Athens could have ended the war after ten years as the undisputed imperial master of the Greek Mediterranean.

One should also not ignore the role Cleon plays in Athens' eventual capture of the Spartan troops on Sphacteria, arguably the greatest Athenian triumph of the entire war. Of course, the true cause of this victory lay in the genius and foresight of Demosthenes. But it is Cleon's braggadocio that fires Athenian interest in sending a "fresh expedition" to Pylos when the original campaign lags (IV.27.4). His boastfulness also inspires Nicias' surrender of his command. And it is Cleon's inexperience as general that empowers Demosthenes to carry out as he sees fit his carefully calibrated plans at Pylos. Without Cleon's outrageous claim that "it would be easy, if they had men for generals, to sail with a force and take those in the island" (IV.27.5) or his mad promise to capture the Spartiates within twenty days (IV.28.4), Nicias would not have offered up his generalship. Nor would the Athenians have clamored for Cleon to make good on his boasts. And Demosthenes would have lacked the specific troops he requested. In other words, as impressive as Demosthenes' military brilliance is, Thucydides' narrative suggests that intelligence by itself is not sufficient to bring Sparta to her knees. To translate that brilliance into power requires a capacity for shameless hyperbole that Cleon possesses in spades.

Finally, while Diodotus' victory in the Mytilinean debate represents the triumph of human decency, his victory comes at the expense of the moral freedom that makes healthy political life possible. For if Diodotus is right, if people are truly compelled by their erotic hopes to act as they do, then they lack the freedom required for moral agency, making all transgressions excusable. The just punishment of wrong-doers is therefore impossible. Furthermore, the consistent application of Diodotus' argument would not only exonerate the rebellious Mytilineans. It would also excuse the Athenian decision to wipe out this allied city since they too were doing what they thought was best for themselves, their ignorance in this case excused by their erotic hopefulness. By contrast, Cleon's argument, which issues in a brutality that dismisses compassion, provides a basis on which one could uphold the law and order necessary for civilized political life.

It seems then that both in speech and deed the example of Cleon reminds both his fellow citizens and the readers of Thucydides' text of the importance of our particular and exclusive attachments to our particular, exclusive communities and of the harshness often required to preserve them. The robust defense of political justice in this world requires an account of its goodness that does not enervate those passions that make us deeply committed to one another. Diodotus may illuminate for us what is universally true about human beings, but because he abstracts from the concerns expressed by individuals, be they cities or citizens, for their own particular goods, his speech risks severing the ties that both bind individuals to one another and fuel their common enterprises.

One is compelled to wonder if, according to Thucydides, free politics—that is, a politics capable of robustly defending itself—requires the anger, fear, irrational hopefulness, and denigration of public reason that Cleon seems to embody and call for. Though Thucydides' thoughtful and sober humanity would exclude Cleon's brutal example, we should also recall that it was xenophobic Sparta, and not culturally vibrant Athens, that won the war. In his speech to the Spartans before the war, the Spartan king Archidamus emphasizes that his regime's civic and martial virtues are made possible by his citizens' unhesitating obedience, born from a refusal to "look over", or to try to be wiser than, the laws (I.84). And, as Thucydides indicates, Sparta's famed virtue of moderation, so important to the freedom and stability of her regime, was both required and made possible by her massive, indigenous slave population (VIII.24.4; VIII.40.2). The suggestion that powerful and free political communities must depress the impulse to seek a rational account of their good offers political cover for the more nativistic possibilities inherent in President Trump's sometimes angry calls to make America "first" or "great again."

Fortunately, this is not Thucydides' last word on the subject. In the rhetoric of Pericles, Thucydides provides us with an appeal to those elevating aspirations fueling Athenian empire, aspirations that refine Cleon's particularism without also ignoring the legitimate concerns of political bodies for their individual goods. Thucydides' presentation of a rhetorical regime that corrects both a vulgar nativism, such as one sees in much of Trump's support, and a rootless cosmopolitanism, like the progressivism that Trump criticizes, preserves the conditions necessary both for exercising political judgment and for recovering political wisdom.

TRUMP AND PERICLES

Because a thorough treatment of Pericles' rhetoric exceeds the scope of the present effort, these concluding comments outline the kind of political speech most suitable to a regime dedicated to the actualization of universal principles for its particular citizens. Despite their differences in tone and context, the three speeches of Pericles recorded by Thucydides share a common theme: they address the concerns of both Athens and its citizens for self-sufficiency and wholeness and the ability of empire to satisfy them. This is especially the case in his Funeral Oration (II.35–46). There, amidst his praise of an imperial city whose material prosperity is the envy of the Greek world, Pericles calls upon his fellow citizens to become lovers of the city (and its power). According to Pericles, Athenians should become lovers (*erastai*) of their powerful city because that particular, powerful city provides them the immortal glory presumed to satisfy their deepest and most powerful longings. Glorious service to the cause of Athens is the path by which the particular, individual citizen gains the immortal renown that promises to makes him whole.

But this famous speech, long read as *the* classic statement on patriotism, actually inverts the traditional relationship between citizen and city, part and whole, by making the city the instrument—the "highway"—of its most daring citizens' eros. Despite this, Pericles' rhetoric does not thereby liberate the particular individual to do just anything to secure his own happiness. According to the implicit understanding of Pericles' speech, our nature as human beings, and the hierarchy of goods dictated by such a nature (at the top of which presumably sits imperial glory), governs and limits the effort to satisfy our longings. As with his other speeches, the Funeral Oration's case for the political satisfaction of our longings depends on an understanding of what is good for humans by nature.

Because its promises of self-sufficiency are so appealing, Pericles' rhetoric invites its audience to take seriously the notion of a nature that stands outside of themselves; such openness thus requires that one reject the older, more nativistic identification of the good with one's own. Pericles' celebration of empire would not in principle prohibit Spartans, Thebans, or even Persians from enjoying those goods generated by the particularly Athenian approach to mastery. This modification of the concern for one's own good that such a rejection entails has many consequences, among which is the possibility of reflection on or deliberation about what constitutes our good and how we can best secure it for ourselves. For if the good is not identical with our own, then we are forced to wonder what it in fact is and to go in search for it. These questions become even sharper and more pressing in light of Thucydides' problematic presentation of Pericles. To wit: if, as Pericles suggests, the city is to the citizen as the world is to Athens, then his speech is best read *not* as a patriotic call to selfless sacrifice, but as an invitation to global tyranny. And nobody offers immortal glory for this.

The point of Thucydides' portrait of Pericles is not to endorse his political vision or to tempt his readers to pursue his particular policies. Under the influence of Thucydides' text, the White House should not embrace Periclean dreams of imperial glory. America is not Athens and it should not try to become like her for reasons too obvious to mention. The point is that by presenting Pericles' rhetoric as he does, Thucydides inspires readers to take seriously the possibility of a good independent of what is "their own", only then to show them the problems with the particular account of that good provided by Pericles. The frustrated hopes that result from such a problematic portrait are precisely what Thucydides seeks to refine in and through his *History*. Because he clearly rejects the example offered by Cleon, such refinement and guidance must move in the direction of greater reflection and deliberation. It must consist in weakening the angry demand that the world accommodate our own particular and impossible hopes for perfect justice and immortality. For Trump, the moderation made possible by such wisdom means reforming his tendency to understand the world solely in terms of American national interests and encouraging him to recognize the legitimate, if limited, roles played by other parts, domestic and foreign, in the wholes to which they all belong.

The domestic import of such abstractions can be seen, once again, by reflecting on the example of Pericles. It is precisely an awareness of the roles played by contentious parts of Athens' community, and reflection on how best to order those parts in the name of civic unity, that allows Pericles to manage effectively the rivalries between oligarchic and democratic factions in Athens. One could thus contrast Pericles' awareness of the dangers posed to Athens by her dispossessed oligarchic knights and his effective deployment of them during the plague, with the catastrophic failure of an erotically disposed Athens to include sufficient cavalry on their massive campaign to Sicily. Pericles succeeded where the Sicilian-mad democracy failed because he, unlike they, understood that Athens was not a seamless, unified democratic whole. He knew that achieving even a semblance of civic unity required constant conjugation of the city's factions.

That Pericles did not always succeed in such efforts testifies to the danger-ous allure of imperial glory, with its temptation to confuse the interests of the part for the good of the whole. Such failures throw into specific relief the fragile success achieved by the rule of the Five Thousand, *the* Athenian regime that Thucydides praises most highly (VIII.97.2).

Thucydides praises this mixed regime as he does because it effectively conjugated the various, contentious parts of the city in its bid to revive an Athens nearly crushed by the war. The Five Thousand could only achieve the limited success it did if it recognized the city's dependence on its parts and if those parts understood the limited nature of their competing claims to rule over each other. For President Trump and his partisans, attaining such wisdom does not mean foregoing a robust defense of American national interest. But it does mean gaining a deeper appreciation of the genuinely human good at stake in the success of American principles. And it means developing a taste for the limited nature of all moral claims to rule. One may well wonder if such "Periclean" taste and appreciation are possible in an America that elects Donald Trump to its highest office. However this might be, cultivating the proper moral posture necessary for that appreciation and taste belongs to those most fully committed to mak-ing America great, even if such appreciation should come from reading the ancient *History* of "Thucydides an Athenian" (I.1).

NOTES

1. A simple Google search for "Trump" and any one of these twentieth cen-tury monsters will produce a litany of columns, editorials, blogs, and tweets over the last two years that are just too lengthy to list here.
2. One of the few to make this comparison is Harvey Mansfield, "The Vulgar manliness of Donald Trump", August 14, 2017, https://www.commentary-magazine.com/articles/vulgar-manliness-donald-trump/. One should also see David Clifton, "Make Athens Great Again!", http://www.thecrimson.com/article/2017/3/1/clifton-make-athens-great/; Kevin Morell, "Before There Was Trump There Was Cleon", http://whchronicle.com/before-there-was-trump-there-was-cleon/; and Elizabeth Markovits, "Trump 'tells it like it is'. That's not necessarily a good thing for democracy", https://www.washingtonpost.com/news/monkey-cage/wp/2016/03/04/trump-tells-it-like-it-is-thats-not-necessarily-a-good-thing-for-democracy/.
3. See Plutarch's *Lives* of "Pericles" and "Nicias" and Aristophanes' *Knights, Wasps,* and *Frogs.*

4. Thucydides' work has no official title. I follow convention in referring to it as the History. All references to Thucydides' History are in standard book, chapter, and, where relevant, sentence, form. For the sake of readability, I use translations of Thucydides' Greek from *The Landmark Thucydides: A Comprehensive Guide to The Peloponnesian War*, edited by Robert B. Strassler (Free Press: New York, 1994).
5. Aristotle, *The Athenian Constitution*, trans. Frederic G. Kenyon (London: G. Bell, 1914), para. 28.
6. Timothy W. Burns, "Anger in Thucydides and Aristophanes: The Case of Cleon," in *The Political Theory of Aristophanes: Explorations in Poetic Wisdom*, ed. by Jeremy Mhire and Bryan-Paul Frost (Albany: SUNY Press, 2014), 233.
7. Aristotle, *Athenian Constitution*, para. 28.
8. The complete title is *Destined for War: Can America and China Escape Thucydides's Trap?* (New York: Houghton Mifflin Harcourt, 2017).
9. Simon Caterson, "Donald Trump and Thucydides' Trap—A Lesson or a Lure?", www.dailyreview.com.au/donald-trump-in-thucydides-trap-a-lesson-or-a-lure/61759/; Michael Crowely, "Why the White House is Reading Greek History", www.politico.com/magazine/story/2017/06/21/why-the-white-house-is-reading-greek-history-215287; Chris Mackie, "The Donald Trump of Ancient Athens", August 9th, 2016, www.latrobe.edu.au/news/articles/2016/release/the-donald-trump-of-ancient-athens; Osita Nwanevu, "Steve Bannon Boasts About His Love of Thucydides for All the Wrong Reasons", www.slate.com/blogs/the_slatest/2017/06/21/steve_bannon likes_thucydides_for_all_the_wrong_reasons.html; Daniel Drezner, "The good, the bad, and the ugly aspects of Thucydides in the Trump administration", www.washingtonpost.com/news/posteverything/wp/2017/06/22/the-good-the-bad-and-the-ugly-aspects-of-thucydides-in-the-trump-administration/; www.keeptalkinggreece.com/2017/06/22/trump-thucydides-trap/; Graham Allison, "The Thucydides Trap", foreignpolicy.com/2017/06/09/the-thucydides-trap/; Chris Mackie, "Can we learn from Thucydides' writings on the Trump of ancient Athens?", https://theconversation.com/can-we-learn-from-thucydides-writings-on-the-trump-of-ancient-athens-63391; Jeva Lange, "The Trump administration is obsessed with a 2500 year-old Greek war", theweek.com/speedreads/707352/trump-administration-obsessed-2500 yearold-greek-war; Peter Jones, "What Thucydides would have thought of Donald Trump", www.spectator.co.uk/2016/11/what-thucydides-would-have-thought-of-donald-trump/; Jessica Evans, "Revise and Resist: Donald Trump and Thucydidean Masculinity, One Year Later", https://eidolon.pub/revise-and-resist.

10. The reckless handling of Thucydides perpetrated by so many of the authors cited above has resulted in what one columnist has called "the summer of misreading Thucydides." I concur, if for slightly different reasons. See Kori Schake, "The Summer of Misreading Thucydides", www.theatlantic.com/international/archive/2017/07/the-summer-of-misreading-thucydides/533859/.

11. Burns, "Anger," 239. This entire section is particularly indebted to the analyses of Cleon offered by Burns in "Anger" and by Clifford Orwin's classic *The Humanity of Thucydides* (Princeton: Princeton University Press, 1994).

12. Meetings of the Athenian assembly were customarily held in the Pnyx only once every ten days.

13. Jan Blits, *Telling, Turning Moments in the Classical World* (Lanhma, Maryland: Lexington Books, 2011), 94. For Cleon's Gorgic "embellishments" see 104, n. 25.

14. Edith Foster, "Aristophanes' Cleon and Post-Peloponnesian War Athenians: Denunciations in Thucydides," *Histos* Supplement 6 (2017) 129–52.

References

Allison, Graham. *Destined for War: Can America and China Escape Thucydides's Trap?* New York: Houghton Mifflin Harcourt, 2017.

Aristotle. *The Athenian Constitution.* Translated by Frederic G. Kenyon. London: G. Bell, 1914.

Blits, Jan. *Telling, Turning Moments in the Classical World.* Lanham, MD: Lexington Books, 2011.

Burns, Timothy. "Anger in Thucydides and Aristophanes: The Case of Cleon." In *The Political Theory of Aristophanes: Explorations in Poetic Wisdom,* edited by Jeremy Mhire and Bryan-Paul Frost. Albany: SUNY Press, 2014.

Dobski, Bernard J. "The Enduring Necessity of Periclean Politics." *POLIS: The Journal for Ancient Greek Political Thought* 34, no. 1, 2017: 62–93.

Foster, Edith. "Aristophanes' Cleon and Post-Peloponnesian War Athenians: Denunciations in Thucydides." *Histos* 6, 2017: 129–52.

Orwin, Clifford. *The Humanity of Thucydides.* Princeton: Princeton University Press, 1994.

Schake, Kori. "The Summer of Misreading Thucydides." *The Atlantic Monthly,* 2017, July. www.theatlantic.com/international/archive/2017/07/the-summer-of-misreading-thucydides/533859/.

Thucydides. *The Landmark Thucydides: A Comprehensive Guide to the Peloponnesian War,* edited by Robert B. Strassler and translated by John Marincola. New York: Free Press, 1994.

CHAPTER 6

The Strongman, the Small Man, and the Gentleman: Confucius and Donald Trump

George A. Dunn

The Chinese philosopher Confucius (551–497 BCE)—孔子 (Kǒngzǐ) in Chinese—was born in the state of Lu during the sixth century BCE. His era was one that some might say resembles our own, since it was marked by both political turmoil and what Confucius diagnosed as a state of acute moral decline. The political and moral disorders of his society had a common source, he believed, in the collapse of the authority once exercised by the Zhou[1] dynasty, the exhaustion of which had triggered the dissolution of the Chinese polity into a collection of warring feudal states competing for political hegemony. His proposed remedy for these disorders wasn't to lay down a blueprint for a new social order, but rather to return to the 道 (dào) or the way of the early Zhou rulers, whose institutions, rituals, and other practices he regarded as exemplary.

His claim "to transmit rather than innovate" and to "trust in and love the ancient ways"[2] would seem to place Confucius solidly in the conservative, even perhaps reactionary, camp. Just as Donald Trump's slogan "Make American Great Again" evokes a mythic past in which America

G. A. Dunn (✉)
Ningbo Institute of Technology, Zhejiang University, Zhejiang Sheng, China

© The Author(s) 2018
A. Jaramillo Torres, M. B. Sable (eds.), *Trump and Political Philosophy*,
https://doi.org/10.1007/978-3-319-74445-2_6

prospered because our values were sound and the right sort of leaders were at the helm, so too Confucius outlined a way to "Make China Great Again" by reversing the corruption that he believed had seeped into Chinese society due to its neglect of the ways of the Zhou. To many of his supporters, Trump offers hope that the American way of life as they have idealized it can be rescued from all those deviant forces and newfangled ideas that they believe have knocked it off the rails. Just so, the followers of Confucius saw in him the embodiment of a nobler way of life whose goodness was certified by its antiquity but whose future was imperiled by modern forces of corruption.

Given that both Confucius and Trump look to the past for a model of how address present problems and future challenges, we might wonder how Confucius would regard the phenomenon of Donald Trump. Would Confucius support Donald Trump? To arrive at an answer, we'll need first to consider several sub-questions: Could Confucius support Donald Trump's campaign platform? What would Confucius think of Donald Trump's conduct in office? And how would Confucius judge the man himself, his moral character? As we'll see, this last question is decisive from a Confucian point of view. To anticipate our conclusion, there are indeed a few reasons to think that Confucius might endorse certain aspects of the Trump platform, but many more reasons to conclude that he definitely would not support Donald Trump.

CONFUCIAN CONSERVATISM

On its face, the agenda of the Republican Party has much in common with the perennial themes of the Confucian tradition, which also stresses strong families, promotes personal responsibility, and urges rulers to trim government expenditures, keep taxes low, and in general govern with a light hand. The Confucian tradition has also shown a marked preference for a relatively closed and homogeneous society. What holds society together is 文 (wén), which we could translate as "culture," concerning which Confucius was a recognized expert. Anticipating some of the insights of modern anthropology, he recognized that human beings enter life relatively unformed and so require 文 (wén) or culture to give their lives shape and even to help them become fully human. But whereas today we like to celebrate the rainbow diversity of *cultures* in the plural, for Confucius there was only one 文 (wén) that counted, the 文 (wén) of the early Zhou dynasty, containing all the paradigms of proper conduct, as well as the traditions of poetry, music, and dance through which the sensibilities and worldview of the Zhou rulers were passed down. Believing that the renewal of Chinese civilization depended on deploying the unique power of the Zhou 文 (wén) to shape the moral character of the Chinese people and ensure the right ordering of society, Confucius would not have been a fan of multiculturalism. Neither are many of Donald Trump's supporters.

Yet, while teaching that Chinese culture as preserved in the rituals, music, poetry, and practices of the early Zhou was superior to the known alternatives, Confucius did not believe that there was anything special about the Chinese as an ethnicity. The *Analects*, a collection of Confucian sayings and anecdotes, report that he was once so thoroughly discouraged by his failure to find a local ruler receptive to his teachings that he announced a plan to give up the search and depart for the barbarian regions to the east. When asked by a disciple how he could bear to live among these uncouth tribes, he replied, "If a gentleman [君子, jūnzǐ] were to dwell among them, what uncouthness would there be?"[3] Clearly, he believed that the moral influence of the gentleman could civilize even these rude barbarians, who would become as good as Chinese if they were to embrace Chinese culture. In this regard, he was not unlike those American conservatives who, while not opposing immigration per se, insist that immigrants assimilate completely, shedding every last vestige of their former cultural identity in order to become American tip-to-toe.[4] However, Confucius would think it even better if we all were to become culturally Chinese, a prospect that most Trump supporters would probably regard with horror. In any case, Confucius would certainly have no tolerance for the racism that seems to motivate some Trump supporters, which may even be encouraged by some of the president's own statements.

Confucius believed that it was one of the responsibilities of the state and its ruler to uphold 文 (wén) and the traditional customs associated with it. Confucius, like many of our own social conservatives, didn't place the high premium on personal freedom that is the hallmark of modern liberalism, believing instead that it was the business of the state to promote virtuous conduct rather than to secure individual liberty. And, in his mind, it was the traditional practices of a culture, sometimes known as its 礼 (lǐ) or rituals, that served as a school for virtue. For many American conservatives, the importance of America's distinctive traditions is bound up with their belief that America is a Christian nation, whose founding fathers were guided by providence in establishing the American regime.

Similarly, Confucius associated the authority of the 道 (dào) of the Zhou dynasty with 天命 (tiānmìng), the Mandate of Heaven, the providential power that testified to the virtue of the Zhou by placing them on the throne. And just as some American conservatives believe that America's declining standing in the world reflects God's disapproval of our abandonment of the God-fearing traditions (such as saying "Merry Christmas") that made America great, so too Confucianism held that 天 (tiān) or Heaven would withdraw its support from a dynasty when too much moral corruption had seeped in, resulting in its inevitable collapse and replacement.

THE SMALL MAN AND THE GENTLEMAN

It would be remiss not to mention that Confucius also shared the troubling habit of some socially conservative Republicans of occasionally uttering remarks about women that many find difficult to hear as anything other than misogynistic, regardless of how they might have been intended. For example, he is reported to have said, "Women and servants [小人, xiǎo rén, literally "small man (or men)," which can mean someone of either low social status or low character, depending on the context] are particularly hard to manage: if you are too familiar with them, they grow insolent, but if you are too distant they grow resentful."[5] This jarring comparison reflects Confucius' highly traditional view of social roles in the family, wherein wives are subservient to their husbands and thus comparable to servants. The apparent misogyny strikes a sour note for modern readers, though his statement arguably makes a valid point about the twin dangers over-familiarity and aloofness when managing subordinates. In any case, the idea that men ought to assume a leadership role in the family is one to which many of the social conservatives in the Republican Party would assent. Both contemporary social conservatives and Confucians value traditional gender roles, seeing them as a source of social order and stability. Yet Confucius would be horrorstruck at the idea of any man, let alone a prospective ruler, acting as though his status or rank granted him the license to "grab [women] by the pussy" or to make crude and demeaning remarks about them. As for Trump's notorious reputation as womanizer, it's noteworthy that Confucius resigned in protest from his post as Minister of Justice in the state of Lu after the local Duke began neglecting his duties to indulge himself with 80 dancing girls who had been sent to him as a gift from the ruler of the neighboring state of Qi. Confucius was not impressed with those who put their wealth and power in the service of sexual conquest.

But, though Confucius was what we would today call a social conservative, some of his other views would put him on the left side of the aisle, such as his belief that rulers should ensure that wealth didn't simply pile up in the vaults of the elites but was dispersed among the people, so that no one would be ground down by poverty. While many of today's conservatives oppose wealth redistribution, believing that it rewards laziness, destroys the incentive to work hard, and robs its recipients of their pride, some of the leading voices in the Confucian tradition have argued that the state must guarantee an adequate livelihood to everyone precisely as part of its responsibility to promote virtue. After all, it's difficult to become virtuous while struggling to survive extreme poverty or even just acute economic insecurity. "Only a noble [a gentleman or 君子 (jūnzǐ)] is capable of having a constant heart while lacking a constant livelihood," observed the philosopher Mengzi (孟子) (372–289 BCE), a successor to Confucius whose importance to that tradition is second only to Confucius himself. "For this reason, an enlightened ruler must regulate the people's livelihood to ensure that it is sufficient, on the one hand, to serve their fathers and mothers, and on the other hand, to nurture their wives and children. [...] Only then do they rush toward the good, and thus the people follow the ruler easily."[6] The truly noble person may be able to withstand the morally corrupting effects of poverty and resist the temptations of crime, but most hearts are not so stalwart. That's why any government serious about encouraging virtue must first ensure that the people's basic needs are met. Would Confucius have favored contemporary entitlement programs like Social Security and Medicare? Would he have opposed the dismantling of the Affordable Care Act? Would he have supported replacing it with a single payer system? Perhaps so, in which case a Confucian politics, which weds traditionalism on social issues with protections for the most vulnerable members of society, might be very appealing to some of Donald Trump's socially conservative but pro-entitlement working class supporters.

In short, Confucius might be sympathetic to many aspects of the Republican platform—and especially those parts that reflect Trumpian populism—since he shared many values with those who identify themselves today as social conservatives. That would not be enough to win his support for Donald Trump, however. For Confucius, one of the most important responsibilities of a ruler is to be the sort of person whom others can admire and emulate, to be, in short, a gentleman or 君子 (jūn zǐ)—a term that originally referred to someone of noble birth, but which in the Confucian corpus came to mean anyone whose dispositions and conduct make him worthy of occupying a high social station, even if Heaven has seen fit to place in lowly circumstances. If the health of society depends on the vigor of its unified culture or 文 (wén) that the gentleman or 君子 (jūnzǐ) embodies and upholds, then a non-gentleman in high office is a recipe for disaster. The opposite of a gentleman is a 小人 (xiǎo rén), which, as we noted above, can designate someone of either low social status or deficient moral character. Literal translated, the 小人 (xiǎorén) is a "small man," an individual who lacks refinement and is consumed by petty concerns, whose moral defects render him unfit to occupy any high ranks in society. When Donald Trump stood on the GOP debate stage and bragged about the size of his genitals, he was, from a Confucian point of view, revealing himself to be extremely small in every respect that matters.[7]

Confucius would be dismayed to hear the American conservative Michael Anton (hiding behind his nom de plume Publius Decius Mus) declare in the *Claremont Review of Books* that "Trump's vulgarity is a god-send" rather than disqualification.[8] From a Confucian perspective, a ruler who flouts gentlemanly etiquette to make a vulgar display of himself is the very opposite of heaven-sent, since Heaven or 天 (tiān) had only ruin in store for rulers who openly defy what we might call "ritual correctness." On first blush, this view might strike us as superstitious nonsense, as though Heaven were some anthropomorphic deity with an eccentric fixation on enforcing good manners. But Confucius' view was much more sophisticated than it might seem on first blush. Though 天 (tiān) was originally the name of the high god of the Zhou dynasty, within the Confucian tradition 天 (tiān) came to be synonymous with the natural order as a whole. Within a couple centuries of Confucius' death, the Confucian philosopher Xunzi (荀子) (310–235 BCE) had completely depersonalized 天 (tiān), equating it with the fixed context of natural causality to which individuals and societies must adapt if they're to live well.[9] Since human beings can flourish within this natural order only with the aid of culture, Heaven (天, tiān) could never deliver us through a ruler whose public conduct made a mockery of that culture. Paradoxical as it may sound, Confucius underscores the importance of ritual, etiquette, and all things conventional precisely because he understands some very important facts about our nature.

THE PHILOSOPHY OF CULTURE

In his own day, Confucius was known as a 儒 (rú), a word that we now translate as "scholar," and his school of thought was 儒家 (rújiā), the scholar's school.[10] A 儒 (rú) was an expert on 文 (wén) and all of the practices that were regarded as the marks of a civilized human being, such as archery, calligraphy, music, and chariot racing. But, above all, the 儒 (rú) was an authority on 礼 (lǐ).[11] Often translated as "ritual" 礼 (lǐ) encompassed a broad range of practices and behaviors handed down by tradition to be performed in a socially-prescribed and often highly formalized manner. 礼 (lǐ) included much of what we would now place under the heading of morality, but it also included social etiquette, religious ceremonies, political protocols, and much more—in short, all of the things that govern the conduct of a refined human being who has a proper respect for tradition. The chief part of Confucius' recipe for making China great again was to restore the 礼 (lǐ) of the early Zhou dynasty, believing that this set of practices and their accompanying moral sensibility were ideally suited to foster the social harmony that was sorely lacking in his day.

Every culture has some sort of 礼 (lǐ), some set of ritualized practices that structure the common life of people within that society. In addition to religious rituals like baptism, bar mitzvahs, and formal prayers, there are innumerable rituals with detailed scripts that we perform to mark ostensibly secular occasions, such as the enthronement of a monarch, the inauguration of a president, or the opening of a football game. There are also well-defined protocols that govern the conduct of a press conference or a meeting of heads of state, as well as many other less explicitly formalized but nonetheless well-understood rules that we expect a refined—or even just minimally civilized—person to follow. These include rules prescribing how we should greet our friends, dress for a wedding, an office party, or a funeral, speak to those in authority, give and receive gifts, queue up to enter a concert hall, request that someone pass the salt, and on and on. Confucius believed that the 礼 (lǐ) of the early Zhou dynasty was exemplary in every respect, but he probably would concede that almost any 礼 (lǐ), any ritualized ordering of the social world, is better than none. As the authors of a book on ritual observe, "Ritual is the ornament of life."[12] It brings order and grace, even beauty, to our social interactions. But ritual is more than just ornamentation. It plays a vital role in enabling social life to run smoothly, setting expectations that render our interactions more predictable and avert possible sources of conflict.

However, in the West we often think of ritual as a mere window dressing that adheres to the surface of life or, worse still, as a sleepwalking conformity to calcified routines. In the modern West, ritual and formal etiquette have often come to be associated with insincerity, a set of artificial filters and inhibitors that impede an open and honest presentation of the self. We admire the person who "tells it like it is," even—or maybe even especially—when the telling is accompanied by a kind of artlessness that certifies its total lack of pretense. Trump's flagrant disregard of the established protocols that govern how a candidate for president or an actual holder of that office ought to behave is a *HUGE* source of his appeal in some quarters, welcomed by many as a refreshing departure from the usual pretentions and affectations of political life. If he offends elite sensibilities, that's just shows how much he values honesty and sincerity over being politically correct. While Confucius' preoccupation with ritual might seem to consign him to the mere surface of social life, Trump presents himself as someone who cuts right through the bullshit, casting aside the social niceties to "present the facts plainly and honestly [because] we cannot afford to be so politically correct anymore."[13] However, just as there are precious few actual facts in Trump's boisterous displays of "sincerity," there's actually more to the Confucian teaching on ritual than appears at first glance. To understanding the importance of ritual, let's take a detour to examine one of our most commonplace social practices: the handshake.

WHAT'S IN A HANDSHAKE?

Among the many unconventional things for which Donald Trump is known are his aggressive, inappropriate, and (let's face it) downright weird handshakes. Of all the egregious things that Trump has done, delivering a hard yank and a patronizing pat to the hand of Japanese Prime Minister Shinzo Abe or some other head of state may seem like a relatively minor breach of etiquette, but it's highly telling from a Confucian point of view. As it turns out, handshakes offer an excellent way of illustrating the importance of 礼 (lǐ), since they are a highly stylized social ritual that when performed properly function to smooth social relations and enable us to establish cordial relationships. More than just a coordinated movement of our limbs, a handshake is a ritualized gesture intended to communicate good will in way that would be cumbersome and probably even less persuasive if we had to do so in words invented anew for each new occasion of greeting. There are implicit rules governing the occasions for which handshakes are offered, the appropriate duration of the handshake, and the amount of force that should be applied. But these aren't rules to be applied robotically—one might grasp the hand of a close friend more tightly and shake it more vigorously than one would a frail elderly woman to whom one is being introduced for the first time. Performing the ritual properly is a matter of discernment. One needs to be socially adept enough to recognize and respond to the particularities of each situation, tailoring one's performance to the needs of the occasion. No one is born knowing how to shake hands, but with practice and habituation it becomes second nature, so that the action can be performed effortlessly and gracefully, without having to think about when to extend the hand, when to withdraw it, or how hard to squeeze.

As we are being trained in the proper performance of this gesture of goodwill toward others, the same warm disposition is being cultivated in us, accustoming us to feel the friendliness that the gesture communicates to others. More than just communicating good will, the handshake, when properly performed, actually helps to bring a state of concord into being, so that we are strangers somewhat less after shaking hands than we were before. That's why the gesture of shaking hands is in some sense false if not accompanied by the appropriate disposition. As Confucius said regarding a very different sort of ritual (sacrificing to the spirits of one's ancestors), "If I am not fully present at the sacrifice [that is, if I display insufficient reverence], it is as if I did not sacrifice at all."[14] Absent the proper attitude, the ritual becomes an empty formality. The importance of ritual or 礼 (lǐ), not only for training us in right behavior but also for inculcating in us the right dispositions, explains why Confucius could define 仁 (rén)—the consummate human virtue—as "restraining yourself and returning to the rites [礼, lǐ]."[15]

Like any ceremony, a handshake can be bungled, with disruptive and even occasionally disastrous social consequences. The bungling of a ritual can result from it being performed insincerely or incompetently or even from a deliberate decision to deviate from the script. Donald Trump's numerous handshake malfunctions could be variously interpreted in each of these ways. In general, though, Trump tends to use handshakes as an occasion to assert dominance, pulling the recipient in close, throwing in a couple of pats, and taking too long to finish. Herbert Fingarette, in his book *Confucius: The Secular as the Sacred*, describes the practice of shaking hands as a cooperative ceremony expressing mutual respect and trust. "We shake hands," he writes, "not by my pulling your hand up and down or your pulling mine, but by spontaneous and cooperative action."[16] But the Trump handshake is precisely the opposite of what Fingarette describes, not a gesture of cooperation that signals mutual respect, but a power play that forces the other into a kind of submission. If the aim of the ritual when properly performed is to enact a sort of concord between the two parties, then Trump's manner of shaking hands accomplishes just the opposite, initiating a contest that, even it doesn't exactly signal malice, at least introduces awkwardness and strain into the relationship.

Bungling the ritual is tantamount to bungling the relationship to which the ritual gives formal expression. And since, for Confucius, one of the chief aims of politics is to foster social harmony, it is important that the ruler understand the rituals that maintain concord in society and perform them properly, not only in order to establish harmony among those with whom he has direct dealings but, just as importantly, to set the right tone for society as a whole, since others will tend to follow his example. All of the big and little rituals through which we perform our common life— raising your hand when you want to speak in class, adopting an appropriately solemn manner at funerals, standing when the judge enters the courtroom, offering introductions when two friends meet, not using familiar forms of address when speaking to superiors unless invited to do so—are all ways that we signal respect and treat each other with dignity, rather than as things to be manipulated for our own ends. Rituals can also serve as ways to express our loyalty to the groups to which we belong and to train us in the dispositions that sustain that loyalty. The controversy over NFL players kneeling during the National Anthem as a protest against police violence against African-Americans is essentially about the importance of a certain ritual as a demonstration of patriotism. Despite Trump's ritual ineptitude in many other areas, his insistence on the necessity of proper ritual performance on the part of these NFL players is one instance where Confucius might conceivably concede that Trump got it right. On the other hand, Confucius also stressed the importance of being flexible in one's performance of rituals and sensitive to the surrounding circumstances, exhibiting a willingness to endorse certain departures from traditional or customary practices when there was a sufficiently good reason.[17] It could be argued that "taking the knee" is not so much a matter of bungling or disrespecting the ritual as it is modifying it to take present realities into account, incorporating a ritualized expression of mourning for the country's moral failings into this civic rite of patriotism. Be that as it may, Confucius would certainly be struck by the incongruity of a serial bungler of ritual performances lecturing others on the ritual propriety.

Decorum, Coercion, and Social Order

An exhaustive list of Trump's many social faux pas could easily fill a book. He loutishly gushed to Brigitte Trogneux, the wife of French president Emmanuel Macron, about how much he admired her "great shape." He displayed an appalling lack of solemnity by describing his visit to Yad Vashem, Israel's Holocaust memorial, as "so amazing" in the site's guest book. He left his own wife Melania trailing awkwardly behind as he marched down the steps of Air Force One without her, a move most observers interpreted as a sign of disrespect. And he drove his golf cart on the putting green of his New Jersey golf club, in flagrant violation of golf etiquette. What all these breaches of decorum have in common is a gross failure to appreciate just what sort of behavior was required in that particular situation, how one is supposed to act, feel, and express oneself in such a context. Such actions are disconcerting in part because they leave observers uncertain about how to act or feel in response. They interrupt the smooth flow of social interaction and open the door to social friction, misunderstandings, and conflicts. The Confucian emphasis on ritual thus comes to light as more than just the quaint preoccupation of an ancient traditionalist, but rather as the product of deep philosophical reflection on the nature and needs of society.

But, from the Confucian perspective, properly performed ritual does more than just establish us in a harmonious relationship to others. It also has the power to transform us, not only collectively but as individuals as well—and it's in considering how this occurs that we encounter some of Confucianism's deepest philosophical reflections on the nature of human beings and society. Confucius compared the work of self-cultivation through which one becomes a gentlemen to the lapidary arts, to the cutting and polishing of ivory and the carving and grinding of jade, arduous but delicate processes through which initially rough raw materials are shaped into something beautiful.[18] This metaphor combines a rather unflattering view of human nature in its original state with a highly optimistic view of what human nature can become if worked upon properly. It was one of Confucius' successors, the philosopher Xunzi, who most fully explored the role of 礼 (lǐ) in this process.

The starting point for Xunzi is the originally boundless nature of human desire, the absence of any natural limits on the human appetite for profit and pleasure, and our natural animosity toward those who thwart us in our efforts to satisfy those desires. Consequently, our default state is to be 小人 (xiǎorén), taking this term in its moral sense.[19] However, if everyone were simply to follow his or her natural inclinations, the world would be beset with violence and disorder. In fact, the world would be very much as it appears in the speeches of Donald Trump—a violent place where cities are "war zones" and criminals are "roaming free to threaten peaceful citizens," where "we have to fight so viciously and violently because we're dealing with violent people."[20] Believing himself to inhabit such a dangerous world, Trump puts his faith in the power of massive retaliation to keep him and the country he now leads safe. "They hit me and I hit them back harder" is his maxim.[21] We saw this code of vengeance in practice when he campaigned for president, when every little slight, real or imagined, was answered with the most vicious insults (such as accusing Megan Kelley of being in state of menstruation-caused distemper), a practice that has persisted even after he became president (as in, for example, his vicious Twitter attack on Mika Brzezinski, involving another slur that made mention of blood). The word "bloody" sums up Donald Trump's worldview very well, but it also describes the world that Xunzi believed human beings inhabited before the introduction of 礼 (lǐ).

Xunzi imagines that the ancient kings, whom he depicts as sages, looked upon this disordered human condition and "viewed this chaos with revulsion." As a remedy, they created 礼 (lǐ), the rituals and rules of social interaction, in order to raise us from our natural state of violent disorder into a peaceful, prosperous, orderly society based on cooperation, one in which the distribution of social rank would be according to individual merit. The key to this social transformation, according to Xunzi, lay in the power of 礼 (lǐ) "to cultivate and shape people's desires,"[22] which he compares to the difficult but eminently worthwhile process of bending a tough piece of wood against its natural resistance to craft from it something beautiful and useful. The sage-kings, moved by a kind of esthetic revulsion, invented an entire way of life with the ambitious aim of effecting a thoroughgoing transformation of the human personality—thoughts, imagination, habits, sensibilities, and desires—and ushering in a beautiful and harmonious order. Through the lifelong practice of 礼 (lǐ), our desires and emotions are educated and we develop the habit of expressing them in the right way, in the right measure, and on the right occasions, and thus become civilized human beings.

For Confucius, rulers have a special responsibility to uphold 礼 (lǐ), since they will invariably be looked to as models. The sine qua non of a good ruler is to conduct himself in a manner befitting the dignity of his office, which in the American context imposes an obligation on the president to act, for want of a better word, presidential. Unfortunately, there's no clear-cut definition of what it means to act presidential. The nature of presidential decorum seems to belong to that category of things about which we say that we just know it when we see it. Yet there does seem to be considerable consensus that, whatever it may be, it's rarely seen in Donald Trump, so rarely in fact that commentators tend to marvel and gush on those occasions, such as his first State of the Union address, when he doesn't say or do something cringe-worthy. But however elusive the concept of acting presidential may be, it means at a bare minimum to conduct oneself with class, another hard to define concept that nonetheless plainly excludes such things as unnecessarily inflammatory language, incessant boasting, "locker room" talk, ranting and raving at press conferences, and initiating a Twitter feud with Arnold Schwarzenegger.

From a Confucian perspective, it is incumbent that the ruler conduct himself at all times with the utmost dignity and decorum, exhibiting the most conscientious 礼 (lǐ), in recognition of the grave responsibility that comes with an office in which one's every word and gesture sends a message to one's subjects or, in the case of the American president, to the world. Moreover, it is through properly performed ritual and the decorum that respect for the social order is instilled in the people, minimizing the need for the sort of violence that Donald Trump deems necessary to maintain order. "If those above love ritual [礼 (lǐ)]," Confucius is reported to have said, "then the common people will be easy to manage."[23] But without the respect fostered by 礼 (lǐ), the ruler has no choice but to resort to coercive measures to maintain his power. For Confucius, the ideal is to rule through wúwéi, 无为, a term that literally means "doing nothing," but might be more felicitously translated as "not forcing." "Was not Shun one who ruled by means of wu-wei?" asked Confucius, referring to one of the fabled kings of old, celebrated as an exemplary sage who ruled during a time of exceptional peace and harmony. "What did he do? He made himself reverent and took his [ritual] position facing South, that is all."[24] No doubt this account wildly exaggerates the power of ritual, but it reflects Confucius' conviction that a social order governed by transformative power of ritual is, from a Confucian point of view, the only alternative to the regime of violence.

PROMISES, PROMISES

King Shun may have been able to govern merely by adopting a ritually correct posture as he sat facing South, but a modern president requires considerably more in terms of a governing agenda. Confucius himself was light on policy proposals, merely advising rulers to "be respectful in your handing of affairs and display trustworthiness; be frugal in your expenditures and cherish others; and employ the common people only at the proper times."[25] They should also, somehow or other, enrich the populace while keeping taxes low. When it comes to the nuts-and-bolts of running a state, however, the advice offered by Confucius rarely rises above the level of platitudes. In this respect, at least, he had something in common with candidate Trump, who during his campaign for president presented very little in terms of genuinely workable policy proposals, apart from his dubious pronouncements on immigration, some of which he subsequently walked back. If Hilary Clinton ran as a policy wonk, Trump came across as a pure showman, indifferent to the impracticality of his proposals as long as they played well with his audience. In place of policy substance, he offered mostly empty bravado about how he would be "the greatest jobs president God ever created," replace the Affordable Care Act with "something terrific"—"great health care at a fraction of the cost"—implement some unspecified plan to "knock the shit out of" ISIS, compel people to say Merry Christmas again, and accomplish countless other wonders on his checklist of castles in the air. Needless to say, he has yet to deliver on these promises. How serious he was about keeping even his most vague promises is an open question, since, as he confided to The New York Times editorial board, "Everything is negotiable." And given that Trump once held very different positions than he professes to hold now on issues such as abortion, taxes, guns, health care, and even Hilary Clinton (whom he once called "a terrific woman"), the bottom line is that during the campaign no one could predict with confidence what Donald Trump would do as president. It's likely that he didn't even know, since he seemed eager at one point to outsource the job of making policy to one of his prospective VP candidates, John Kasich. Even now he remains full of surprises. It has been suggested that his thinking is so unformed and his mind is so pliable that it's often the last person with the opportunity to speak with him who actually ends up setting the policy.

Even after he was elected, there was considerable speculation about the extent to which Trump's chief strategist Steve Bannon was not only crafting the administration's overall vision of the world but also actually guiding specific policy decisions. Now that Bannon is gone, it is becoming unmistakably clear that Trump has no actual plan to make America great again and only the dimmest idea of what renewed American greatness would look like. He has continued his campaign strategy of making vague promises, laced with empty braggadocio, assuring the public that more details with be forthcoming at a later date, typically in a few weeks. In early February of 2017, he declared to a group of airline executives, "We're going to be announcing something I would say over the next two or three weeks that will be phenomenal in terms of tax and developing our aviation infrastructure."[26] After this huge fanfare, eleven weeks passed before the Trump administration finally issued its still vague one-page tax plan, which differed little from the vague one-page tax plan that his campaign had issued in September of the previous year. In late April, Trump promised that in two or three weeks he would be unveiling his infrastructure plan: "We've got the plan largely completed and we'll be filing over the next two or three weeks—maybe sooner."[27] Months later, he has yet to introduce the promised infrastructure legislation to Congress, thus proving one Confucius' dicta about the dangers of boasting: "If you are shameless in what you propose, you may then find it difficult to put your words into practice."[28] Adorning vaguely defined outcomes with superlatives like "phenomenal," "tremendous," and "fantastic" is no substitute for facing the difficult challenges of transforming promises into policy, though it does afford him the opportunity to claim premature credit for accomplishments that have not yet materialized and perhaps never will. Confucius would take these empty boasts as simply more evidence that Trump is not a gentleman, for a "gentleman is ashamed to have his words exceed his actions."[29]

"You're Fired!"

In one respect, however, Trump's professed view of leadership does have something in common with the Confucian approach, though, as with much about Trump, there is considerable discrepancy between what he says and what he does. On the campaign trail, Trump frequently painted a picture of a government based on an aristocracy of talent, presided over by someone whose track record in business proved his ability to recognize and promote those with the most outstanding aptitude for their jobs. His campaign for president often highlighted his supposedly exceptional skills as a CEO who knew how to run a tight ship and get things done, a highly misleading impression as it has turned out. He seemed to envision his presidency as a grander version of his reality TV show *The Apprentice*, with himself surrounded by a retinue of extremely bright courtiers brimming with ideas and serving—or being fired—at his pleasure. "I'll hire the best people," he promised. However, for someone whose TV persona was a man with a great knack for good hiring decisions, he has been alarmingly remiss in filling top-level government posts. Nine months into his term, hundreds of executive branch positions requiring Senate confirmation remained vacant. On the other hand, he does still seem to relish exercising the prerogative to fire or aggressively elbow out anyone who displeases him, as Sebastian Gorka, Steve Bannon, Anthony Scaramucci, Reince Priebus, Sean Spicer, James Comey, and many others can testify.

In any event, hiring the best is precisely what Confucius would have advised Donald Trump to do—hire them and then to let them do their jobs. However, those exceptional people with whom Trump promised to staff the government have often turned out to be mediocre at best. Moreover, even when the people close to him have given him sound advice, he far too often disregards or even undercuts it. Disregarding the advice of his national security team, he omitted from his Brussels' speech to our NATO allies an affirmation of Article 5 of the NATO agreement, which commits the U.S. to come to their aid if they are attacked, an apparently impulsive decision that has seriously strained our relationship with Germany and other NATO countries. And after his Justice Department labored to put the best face possible on Trump's ill-conceived Muslim travel ban, modifying it and offering a rationale for it that Justice Department lawyers hoped would overcome the legal objections that had persuaded the courts to block the implementation of an earlier version, Trump, again apparently acting on impulse, undermined their efforts with a series of early morning tweets denouncing their "watered-down, political correct version" of the travel ban.[30] There's no shortage of other examples that could be given, all of which illustrate Trump's violation of one of the most basic Confucian strictures concerning governing well: "Let the lord be a true lord, the ministers true ministers."[31] As this passage implies, the roles of ruler and minister are distinct, with the smooth functioning of the government depending on each performing his allotted task without stepping on the other's toes or attempting to usurp the other's prerogatives. Trump's routine disregard of these boundaries offers yet more evidence that 礼 (lǐ)—specifically those aspects that deal with the protocols of governing—plays little if any role in the president's character.

In addition to being Personnel Officer in Chief, Trump suggested that his most unique contribution to the governing enterprise would be his allegedly unparalleled mastery of the Art of the Deal, which he promised to deploy on behalf of American workers to wrangle better trade agreements from China, lower prices from pharmaceutical companies, and even a wall from Mexico. As usual, the reality has fallen far short of the hype. Tyrants like Vladimir Putin and King Salman of Saudi Arabia have milked the master negotiator's inexperience, gullibility, and susceptibility to flattery for all its worth, while the prospects of Mexico paying for Trump's wall are even dimmer now than they were when he first proposed it. And then there's the way he's lashed out at staunch allies like Australia, in a contentious phone call with the prime minister, and South Korea, in a series of incendiary tweets, while alienating our European allies as much with his boorish, gaffe-prone manner as with his policy choices. Clearly, Trump's poor performance as a negotiator and "deal maker" can be attributed in large measure to his flawed understanding of 礼 (lǐ) or perhaps just his open disdain for it.

His real talent seems to be not so much the Art of the Deal but the huckster's Art of the Sales Pitch, through which he was able to persuade a large block of voters that his purported expertise as a businessman— through which he claims to have amassed his personal fortune—could be put to work to restore the fortunes of the country as a whole. By his own admission, his business acumen consists in part in having shrewdly "taken advantage of the laws of this country," the bankruptcy laws in particular, a shrewdness he has promised to employ on behalf of downtrodden Americans.[32] He has boasted of being "very greedy," which is considered a vice in every moral tradition, not just Confucianism, while incredibly suggesting that somehow he can put that vice to work for good of the country as a whole.[33] The sources of wealth that his greed has tapped are not fully known to the public, however, since he refuses to release his tax returns. That his supposed talent at making money would impress many voters is understandable from a Confucian perspective, since the small man, the 小人 (xiǎorén), is easily dazzled by displays of wealth. However, with respect to wealth and status, Confucius issues this warning: "Wealth and social eminence are things that all people desire, and yet unless they are acquired in the proper way I will not abide them. Poverty and disgrace are things that all people hate, and yet unless they are avoided in the proper way I will not despise them."[34] Confucius would take Trump's excessive love of wealth and his ruthlessness in obtaining the finery that money can buy as evidence of the coarseness of his soul and his unfitness for the office that he now holds. What Trump lacks above all, from a Confucian perspective, is the sine qua non of the good ruler—virtue.

The Virtuous Ruler

Confucius put the accent on the character of the ruler and his ability to recognize and promote competent and virtuous ministers, rather than on specific acts of legislation. In fact, from his perspective, the less legislation the better, since one byproduct of laws is to encourage people to seek clever ways to get around them or to work them to their personal advantage, as Trump apparently has done with the tax code and with laws of eminent domain and bankruptcy. Unlike most modern political theorists, Confucius favored the rule of virtue rather than the rule of law. Trump has been criticized for his lack of respect for—or even understanding of—the United States Constitution with its system of checks and balances, which is not surprising given his background as the head of a family business in which he exercised the imperious authority of a paterfamilias, without having to answer to either investors or a board of directors. But Confucius would have been equally impatient with the complicated fetters imposed by the separation of powers and he too looked to the patriarchal family for his model of how the state should be run. However, it's crucial to have a proper understanding of what exactly Confucius believes the duties of both father and ruler to be. The ruler, like the head of a household, is responsible not only to see to the welfare of those under his charge but also, as we have already noted, to exhibit the sort of moral conduct that other can take as a model. The wise ruler, the sage-king, rules best when there is nothing to tie his hands but his own virtue or, to use the Confucian term, his 德 (dé).[35]

The term 德 (dé) is usually translated as "virtue" but it has nuances of meaning that go beyond what is ordinarily denoted by the English word. Like "virtue," 德 (dé) as used by Confucius refers to a moral quality but it also signifies a mysterious inner potency or personal charisma that exercises an almost preternatural sway over those who fall within its compass, changing their hearts and minds for the better. "One who rules through the power of Virtue [德, dé]," reports Confucius, "is analogous to the Pole Star: it simply remains in its place and receives the homage of the myriad lesser stars."[36] To borrow a term associated with the literary theorist and social critic René Girard, the 德 (dé) of the ruler works as a kind of "good mimesis" that inspires others to take him as a model and to emulate his noble qualities. In a famous passage, Confucius likens the 德 (dé) of the noble individual, the gentleman or 君子 (jūnzǐ), to the wind, while the small man or 小人 (xiǎorén), the man of more humble social station or weak moral character, is compared to the grass: "when the wind moves over the grass, the grass is sure to bend."[37] Although Confucius describes 德 (dé) as an almost magical force, the underlying idea is that the political leaders set the tone for the rest of the society, for better or worse.

In modern society, we often look to celebrities—entertainers, actors, sports figures, even reality TV stars—as models of what we should desire, how we should speak and act, and what constitutes a good life. In Confucius' day—and no doubt to great extent in our day as well—the political leaders were the models that everyone aspired to emulate, since they were the most visible and prominent members of society. Consequently, when an official asked Confucius what could be done about the alarming number of robbers in his state, Confucius replied, "If you could just get rid of your own excessive desires, the people would not steal even if you rewarded them for it."[38] By coveting luxury items for himself, this official was infecting the people with his own desire for opulence and, whether intending to or not, encouraging them to value money more than virtue and to act outside the law in order to satisfy the desire that their ruler had implanted in the them. Similarly, by exhibiting vulgarity and hostility, engaging in petty squabbles, scorning the norms of civil discourse, acting from spite and vengeance, and, above all, stoking the anger of the public in order to scapegoat vulnerable segments of the American polity, Donald Trump infects the entire body politic with these vices. An early harvest of the poison he's sown was seen in Charlottesville, Virginia in August, 2017. It would be reasonable to expect more of the same as Trump continues to model the sort of conduct that creates division rather than harmony. By contrast, the positive force of 德 (dé) is the mimetic charisma of the truly\ the gentleman, whose kindness and rectitude Confucius hoped might have a cascading effect that could affect a moral revival in society at large. Through the power of his 德 (dé), the virtuous ruler brings about a degree and depth of social harmony that could never be accomplished by mere acts of legislation. Therefore, the primary responsibility of the ruler, besides attending to the material well-being of his people, is to cultivate and display his charismatic 德 (dé).

There's no doubt that Trump also packs a potent charismatic charge. When the mighty gusts sally from his mouth at rallies, the assembled grass dutifully bends. But while he may possess something resembling 德 (dé), it's certainly not what Confucius would call the 德 (dé) of a gentleman, for reasons that are too numerous—and far too obvious—to repeat. But one reason in particular warrants mention. What distinguishes the gentleman from the small man [小人, xiǎorén], according to Confucius, is that "the gentleman understands rightness, whereas the petty person understands profit."[39] Stated differently, the gentleman is motivated by the intrinsic satisfactions of moral excellence rather than external rewards, like wealth, sex, and acclaim. He seeks opportunities for public service not out of a desire for luxury or accolades, fortune or fame, but in order to exercise his virtue to its fullest capacity. Admittedly, such a perfect gentleman is rare. Indeed, Confucius is reported to have said, "I have yet to meet a man who loves Virtue as much as he loves female beauty."[40] Needless to say, the person he sought most definitely will not be found currently residing on the top floor of Trump Tower, at Mar-a-Lago, or in the Oval Office. And, for Confucius, the fact that the current resident of those suits is such a small and petty man, such a 小人 (xiǎorén), is likely to have dire consequences not only for the operation of the government but for the moral health of the society, as we are already witnessing.

With the mind of a monarch, but the moral disposition of a small man or 小人 (xiǎorén), Donald Trump has much more in common with those sixth century rulers whose unbridled ambition, avarice, and disdain for decorum had thrown China into political turmoil than with the sage-king whom Confucius imagined as its salvation. Confucius laid the responsibility for the moral corruption of the small man squarely on the doorstep of those rulers and the poor example they set. He also believed that without the moral force of 德 (dé), a ruler would be compelled to fall back on coercive measures in order to maintain order, his methods necessarily as draconian as the people had become incorrigible. The alternative to non-coercive rule through moral virtue is rule by naked force. So it's not surprising that Donald Trump has on occasion endorsed or even incited the unlawful use of violence, inviting his supporters to physically abuse protesters at his rallies and, more recently, suggesting that it would be okay for police officers to rough up suspects. Neither is it surprising that the era of warring states in China was brought to a close with the ascendency of a brutal strongman, the ruthless Qin Shi Huang, the First Emperor, who managed to unite China but ruled without pity. There are indications that Trump would be pleased to play the strongman role in American politics, which is yet another reason why Confucius would not support Donald Trump.[41]

NOTES

1. Pronounced like the name "Joe."
2. Confucius, *Analects: With Selections from Traditional Commentaries*, trans. Edward Slingerland (Indianapolis: Hackett Publishing, 2003), Section 7.1, p. 64.
3. *Analects*, Section 9.14, p. 91.
4. Of course, the tricky problem is to define exactly what American cultural identity is.
5. Ibid., Section 17.25, p. 211.
6. *Mengzi: With Selections from Traditional Commentaries*, trans. Bryan W. Van Norden (Indianapolis: Hackett Publishing Company, 2008), pp. 14–15.
7. This boast was his response to a taunt from his opponent Marco Rubio, who had insinuated that Trump's small hands might be a clue to the size of his penis. Trump is reportedly very sensitive about the size of his hands. In *Vanity Fair* last year, Graydon Carter recalls Trump's extremely childish response to Carter's description of him in print as a "short-fingered vulgarian": "To this day, I receive the occasional envelope from Trump. There is always a photo of him—generally a tear sheet from a magazine. On all of them he has circled his hand in gold Sharpie in a valiant effort to highlight the length of his fingers." ...
8. Michael Anton [Publius Decius Mus], "The Flight 93 Election," *Claremont Review of Books*, September 15, 2016, http://www.claremont.org/crb/basicpage/the-flight-93-election/.
9. Whether this understanding of 天 (tiān) extends back to Confucius is a matter of controversy, but it's certainly not something we can rule out.
10. 家, which here designates a school of thought, can also mean home or family. That the character for "family" can represent a group of thinkers bound together by the kinship of ideas perhaps indicates something about the centrality of family in Chinese culture, its place as the exemplary social institution.
11. In Confucius' day, 礼 was written 禮. The traditional 禮 became 礼 when the Chinese government introduced "simplified" Chinese in the 1950s. In Taiwan and many Chinese diasporic communities, the traditional characters are still preferred. Today, the word 礼 most often refers simply to good manners or etiquette.
12. Adam B. Seligman, Robert P. Weller, Michael J. Puett, and Bennett Simon, *Ritual and Its Consequences: An Essay on the Limits of Sincerity* (Oxford: Oxford University Press, 2008), p. 121.
13. Trump's address to the Republican National Convention, July 21, 2016.
14. *Analects*, Section 3.12, p. 22.

15. Ibid., Section 12.1, p. 125.
16. Herbert Fingarette, *Confucius: The Secular as Sacred* (New York: Harper & Row, 1972), p. 9.
17. Consider *Analects* 9.3, p. 87.
18. Ibid., p. 6.
19. In contrast to Xunzi's rather dim view of human nature, his near contemporary Mengzi held that human nature contained the seeds of goodness in the form of innately pro-social inclinations and sentiments such as sympathy, which, if properly cultivated, could be nurtured into mature virtue. It's likely that there's some truth to both views, as recent developments in evolutionary psychology have shown how evolution could have fostered competing tendencies toward both selfishness and social cooperation.
20. Paul Waldman, "Trump's response to terrorism is both weak and barbaric," *Washington Post*, June 29, 2016, https://www.washingtonpost.com/blogs/plum-line/wp/2016/06/29/trumps-response-to-terrorism-is-both-weak-and-barbaric/.
21. Dan Merica, "Trump's love of getting even comes to Washington," *CNN*, May 30, 2017 http://edition.cnn.com/2017/03/31/politics/donald-trump-getting-even-washington/index.html.
22. *Xunzi Books 17–32: A Translation & Study of the Complete Works*, trans. John Knoblock (Stanford: Stanford University Press, 1994), p. 55.
23. *Analects*, Section 14.41, p. 171.
24. Ibid., Section 15.5, p. 175.
25. Ibid., Section 1.5, p. 2.
26. David Morgan, "Trump vows 'phenomenal' tax plan, offers no details," *Reuters*, February 9, 2017, https://www.reuters.com/article/us-usa-trump-taxes/trump-vows-phenomenal-tax-announcement-offers-no-details-idUSKBN15O2AY.
27. Eugene Scott, "Trump: Infrastructure plan largely completed, coming in 2–3 weeks," *CNN*, May 1, 2017, http://www.cnn.com/2017/05/01/politics/donald-trump-infrastructure-plan/index.html.
28. *Analects*, Section 14.20, p. 162.
29. Ibid., Section 14.27, p. 165.
30. Donald J. Trump @realDonaldTrump, 2:59 PM–5 Jun 2017.
31. *Analects*, Section 12.11, p. 130.
32. Hunter Walker and Colin Campbell, "Fox News moderator confronts Trump: How can we trust you after 4 bankruptcies?" *Business Insider*, August 6, 2015, http://www.businessinsider.com/donald-trump-i-have-never-gone-bankrupt-2015-8.
33. Bradford Richardson, "Trump: I'm very greedy," *The Hill*, January 20, 2016, http://thehill.com/blogs/ballot-box/gop-primaries/265335-trump-im-very-greedy.
34. *Analects*, Section 4.5, p. 31.

35. Pronounced *duh*, with a rising tone, as in "Duh! Thank you, Captain Obvious."
36. Ibid., Section 2.1, p. 8.
37. Ibid., Section 12.19, p. 134.
38. Ibid., Section 12.18, p. 133.
39. Ibid., Section 4.16, p. 35.
40. Ibid., Section 9.18. p. 94 (Some translate the last word of this sentence as "sex," rather than "female beauty.")
41. Thanks are owed to Angel Jarimillo, Kevin Corn, and especially Jonathan Evans, whose comments and suggestions helped to make this a better chapter than it would have been otherwise.

REFERENCES

Anton, Michael [Publius Decius Mus]. "The Flight 93 Election." *Claremont Review of Books*, 2016, September 15. http://www.claremont.org/crb/basicpage/the-flight-93-election/.

Confucius. *Analects: With Selections from Traditional Commentaries*. Translated by Edward Slingerland. Indianapolis: Hackett Publishing, 2003.

Fingarette, Herbert. *Confucius: The Secular as Sacred*. New York: Harper & Row, 1972.

Mengzi. *Mengzi: With Selections from Traditional Commentaries*. Translated by Bryan W. Van Norden. Indianapolis: Hackett Publishing Company, 2008.

Merica, Dan. "Trump's Love of Getting Even Comes to Washington." *CNN*, 2017, May 30. http://edition.cnn.com/2017/03/31/politics/donald-trump-getting-even-washington/index.html.

Richardson, Bradford. "Trump: I'm Very Greedy." *The Hill*, January 20, 2016. http://thehill.com/blogs/ballot-box/gop-primaries/265335-trump-im-very-greedy.

Seligman, Adam B., Robert P. Weller, Michael J. Puett, and Bennett Simon. *Ritual and Its Consequences: An Essay on the Limits of Sincerity*. Oxford: Oxford University Press, 2008.

Trump, Donald J. @realDonaldTrump, 2:59 PM–5 June, 2017.

Waldman, Paul. "Trump's Response to Terrorism Is Both Weak and Barbaric," *Washington Post*, June 29, 2016. https://www.washingtonpost.com/blogs/plum-line/wp/2016/06/29/trumps-response-to-terrorism-is-both-weak-and-barbaric/?utm_term=.6dbef64578ec.

Walker, Hunter, and Colin Campbell. "Fox News Moderator Confronts Trump: How Can We Trust You After 4 Bankruptcies?" *Business Insider*, August 6, 2015. http://www.businessinsider.com/donald-trump-i-have-never-gone-bankrupt-2015-8.

Xunzi. *Xunzi Books 17–32: A Translation & Study of the Complete Works*. Translated by John Knoblock. Stanford: Stanford University Press, 1994.

CHAPTER 7

Trump, Alfarabi, and the Open Society

Christopher Colmo

The election campaign of 2016 was certainly hard-fought. In trying to bring together Trump and political philosophy, we must not behave as the candidates sometimes behaved, with anger and indignation, even righteous indignation. Mr. Trump, both as candidate and as president, prides himself on hitting back and hitting back hard. Perhaps it is only to be expected that the president would in some ways behave as the candidate behaved. In his *Attainment of Happiness* (sec. 36), Alfarabi suggests that human beings will always do what is easiest for them. This does not mean that they will take the easy path; they may very well take a very hard path if that is what is easiest for them. They may take the most angry or spirited path.

Of course, one of the most striking things about the campaign of 2016 was that one of the candidates of a major party for president of the United States was a woman. The difference between Alfarabi (870–950) and twenty-first century America is brought into focus if we ask how Alfarabi might have reflected on this event. Now as far as I know, Alfarabi never speaks of the gender of the ruler, and this is true even when he is speaking of Plato and Plato's *Republic*, where the possibility of women as both philosophers and rulers is explicitly discussed. It is hard to know what to make of his silence. Perhaps he simply rejected the possibility that a woman

C. Colmo (✉)
Dominican University, River Forest, IL, USA

© The Author(s) 2018
A. Jaramillo Torres, M. B. Sable (eds.), *Trump and Political Philosophy*,
https://doi.org/10.1007/978-3-319-74445-2_7

could rule or, at any rate, that a woman could be a good ruler. We know that Averroes, in Muslim Spain, was well acquainted with Alfarabi, indeed influenced by him, and yet in writing of Plato's *Republic*, Averroes goes out of his way to point out that in restricting women to the rearing of children one wastes the energy of half of the population. He specifically mentions the contribution that women might make to the economy (Averroes, *Epitome of Plato's Republic*, First Treatise, 53–54). It is hard to know whether Alfarabi would be sympathetic to Averroes' point of view.

If we turn to some of the issues of the campaign, trying to see them through Alfarabi's eyes raises some interesting questions. Would Alfarabi, as a Muslim, be simply appalled by candidate Trump's calls to restrict the flow of Muslims into the United States? Would he have seen the "extreme vetting" to which Mr. Trump sometimes referred as a violation of human rights? What would he have thought of the wall that Mr. Trump promised during the campaign to build between the United States and Mexico? How do these questions appear if we try to see them through Alfarabi's eyes? Would he see these as the policies of a good regime?

Of course, Alfarabi might turn the tables on us and try to see these questions through our eyes. That is to say, he might ask what kind of regime America has and how well the policies mentioned cohere with that regime. Alfarabi might read the Constitution of the United States and see that it is not a religious document. The possibility of a political community which was not a religious community might be a new thought to him. We can return to this question later. In trying to understand us as we understand ourselves, Alfarabi might have seen two of the most characteristic features of our regime as being freedom of speech and the separation of church and state. It is hard to know what he might think about our claim to a right of freedom of speech; he says nothing about the possibility of such a right and the caution he exercises in his own writing does not indicate that he sees freedom of speech as a wise or prudent idea. And while Alfarabi says a great deal about politics and religion, he does not frame his thinking on this issue in terms of a separation of religion and politics. To the contrary, he seems to see religion as a form of politics. For exactly this reason, he might be struck by the novelty of their separation. That novelty might encourage him to agree with Garry Wills' recent claim that separation of church and state is the "one entirely innovative element in the Constitution."[1]

If we continue with the thought experiment of trying to have Alfarabi understand us as we understand ourselves, he might well see the attempt by the government to single out people by religion as in conflict with one of the fundamental features of our regime. We can, of course, only speculate on this, just as we can only speculate on how Alfarabi might have seen Mr. Trump's attempts to ridicule other Republican candidates during the primaries. Would Alfarabi have seen these attempts as an exercise of freedom of speech, or would he have seen them as an attempt to shut down freedom of speech?

I have tried to suggest that Alfarabi as a student of our regime might have seen at least two features of Mr. Trump's campaign as being in tension with the fundamental principles of the regime in which he sought to rule. As a student of *kalam*, understood as the rhetorical defense of the law, Alfarabi would certainly have been interested in understanding the fundamental principles or basic law of our regime.[2] He would have acknowledged that any regime must defend its own fundamental principle. It is a different question altogether what Alfarabi might have thought of the fundamental principles of our regime.

Let me set aside for the moment, what Alfarabi might have thought about the theory and practice of freedom of speech in the United States' regime. His own often invoked distinction, in the *Book of Religion*, for example, between opinion and action might actually lend some support to independence of opinion and even of speech. However that might be, let us consider instead how he might have seen the attempt to separate politics and religion or the attempt to render religion a merely private affair. Certainly if Alfarabi took his bearings by the regimes of his own time, in tenth century Baghdad or Damascus, he would have seen regimes that did not at all separate politics and religion. Indeed, religion pervades every aspect of political life, so much so that one might even be surprised to find a separate word for religion. One could easily find support for this view in the fact that Muslim authors speak not of religion but of *sharia* or of the law. To borrow for a moment the language of Eric Voegelin, one might think of the Islamic world of Alfarabi's time as a compact society, one that had not differentiated or separated out the notion of religion as separate from the life of the community.[3] If one makes this imaginative leap, then it is, in fact, surprising to see that Alfarabi does develop a concept of religion, though he does this not primarily through a contrast between religion and the political community, but rather through a contrast between religion and philosophy.

Let us retrace our steps. Assuming that Alfarabi identified separation of church and state as a crucial part of the United States as regime, how would he go about defending that regime? Could Alfarabi provide a *kalam* not only for the general idea of law but for American law in particular? Would the defense of this principle be rooted first of all in the separation of religion and philosophy, as it was for Spinoza (*Theological-Political Treatise*, Chap. 14)? Or would Alfarabi see the separation of religion from philosophy and of politics from religion as a crucial flaw in any regime? Does Alfarabi open a way to Spinoza, or does he show us the folly of that path?

A defense of the separation of politics and religion, if it were deep enough, might become a reflection on the nature of politics. It would be a philosophic reflection. But does candidate Trump, now President Trump, need such reflection? Does President Trump have any need of philosophy? If not, what does he need? Does he need a certain shrewdness? Is he best served by the art of the deal? But where did President Trump acquire the art of the deal? He himself seems to think that he acquired this art from experience and, in particular, from his experience in business.

The philosopher known to me who has made the most emphatic reference to a kind of political rule that does not need philosophy at all is Alfarabi. If we wanted to explore the theme of Trump and political philosophy, it might be useful to see what Alfarabi has to say about politics that does not at all need philosophy. This discussion can eventually lead us to consider what it might mean for a society to be open to philosophy and what the limits of such openness might be. How might openness to philosophy relate to openness to religious or cultural diversity? Do these two kinds of openness belong together, or are they necessarily apart?

Alfarabi actually writes about two kinds of rulers who do not need philosophy at all. One is the traditional king, the king who simply follows in the footsteps of his predecessors. The other one rules through a certain shrewdness and cunning that he learns from experience and through observing the experience of others (*Book of Religion* sec. 18). We cannot help but be reminded of the distinction Machiavelli makes between a hereditary prince and a new prince. According to Alfarabi, neither the traditional ruler nor the shrewd ruler has any need of philosophy.

Aristotle also describes a shrewd ruler who can get what he wants through cunning, but he distinguishes between the shrewd man and the prudent man (*Nicomachean Ethics* 1144b). The prudent man can also devise means to an end depending on the circumstances. Why then does Aristotle distinguish between the prudent man and the clever or shrewd man? Prudence is always directed at a good end. Alfarabi explains that "what the Ancients call prudence" has to do with determining particular actions under particular circumstances. He does not explicitly say, as Aristotle does, that the action must be good. Instead, Alfarabi indicates that there are universals that the king knows, but that these by themselves are not enough. One must also know the particulars, and this comes only from long experience. The shrewd man, who is not above cunning and deceit, also knows from experience how to achieve the end he seeks. Alfarabi does not draw out the difference between shrewdness and prudence in the way that Aristotle explicitly does. Perhaps the most cautious thing one could say is that Alfarabi does not understand shrewdness by contrast with prudence. In his account, it is easier to see the similarity than to see the difference between the two. Philosophy leads us to the universals of an art; the ruler who does not need philosophy is in no need of those universals. Instead, he can rely on the political art that he has learned from long experience and from long observation of the experience of others. The prudent man is distinguished from the shrewd man not by his goodness but by the prudent man's reliance on universal rules. Unfortunately, the examples Alfarabi gives of the application of universal rules to particular cases are all drawn from medicine, not politics. We are left wondering if either the prudent man or the shrewd man has any need of universal rules.

If we return from these murky waters to the election campaign of 2016, we see that both candidates tried to argue that they were better qualified for office because of their experience. Mrs. Clinton could point to her years in the Senate and as Secretary of State. Mr. Trump frequently cited his experience as a successful business man. Whether experience in business translates into skill in politics is one important question that is put to the test by Mr. Trump's presidency. But Mr. Trump was certainly telling the truth when he relied during his campaign on experience as evidence of his competence rather than on his knowledge of what Alfarabi would call the universals of philosophy.

The passage I have pointed out (*Book of Religion* sec. 18) in which Alfarabi eschews the need for philosophy in accomplishing a properly political end is not the one commonly thought to be representative of Alfarabi's thinking. More often, he is described as the founder of a philosophic school, for example, the founder of Islamic Neoplatonism.[4] Scholars present Alfarabi as an eclectic transmitter of a system he did not create but received from various predecessors, especially Aristotle and Plotinus and, to a lesser extent, Plato. One thing that Alfarabi takes over from Plato is the notion of a philosopher-king, although in the writings of Alfarabi, the philosopher-king is now dressed in Islamic garb, so that he is not the philosopher-king but the philosopher-prophet (*Attainment of Happiness* sec. 58). Does the philosopher-prophet bring together the universalism of philosophy and the universalism of Islam? Mr. Trump seems more inclined to the particular than to the universal.

In *Politico* in January of 2016, Thomas Wright identified three features of Trump's politics. Trump's admiration for strong leaders like those of Russia and China is coupled with a sense that free trade works to the disadvantage of the United States and that American military alliances often involve us in the defense of those who do not pay for their own security. Wright makes a good case that one could find similar ideas, at least with respect to trade and alliances, in the thinking of the mid-twentieth century Republican leader, Senator Robert Taft. "Trump seeks nothing less than ending the U.S.-led liberal order and freeing America from its international commitments," Wright explains. In other words, one way to see the Trump campaign is in terms of a kind of particularism or nationalism in opposition to the liberal internationalism that has dominated American policy since World War II.

Alfarabi could be pointed to as Trump's antithesis, combining the universalism of philosophy and the universalism of Islam. Alfarabi's universalism may have an even deeper root in the attempt to accommodate the human longing for certainty, for a ground—a ground that was threatened not by religion but rather by the inquisitive impulse of philosophy itself. We can only speculate on the universalism of Islam. Alfarabi himself suggests to us the thought that the universalism of religion is an imitation of the universalism of philosophy. At least he says that for the Ancients religion is an imitation of philosophy (*Attainment of Happiness* sec. 55). He also says that philosophy and religion are similar (*Book of Religion* sec. 5). Of course, the universalism of Islam is compatible with and perhaps even leads to the idea of *jihad* or struggle or holy war. What is somewhat surprising is to see that Alfarabi, on philosophic grounds, anticipates that the virtuous city will make war in order to spread the virtuous way of life and the virtuous religion.

Scholars have debated how seriously to take Alfarabi's assertions about just war, but in this essay I do not plan to go down that path.[5] It is rather the universalism of philosophy as it affects politics that I want to examine. Here we run into an immediate problem. Alfarabi speaks of the virtuous city and the virtuous religion in the plural, virtuous cities and virtuous religions (*Political Regime* sec. 90). There are virtuous cities and virtuous nations and virtuous religions but these are all particular cities and nations and religions. This would seem in tension with, if not a denial of, the universalism of Islam, but it is also a rejection of the universalism of philosophy. Plato and Aristotle sought the best regime, the best always and everywhere. Alfarabi seeks the virtuous cities and virtuous nations. What is the relation between these two philosophic projects? Are they simply the same project?

What is a virtuous city, and how can there be many of them? As Alfarabi argues in the opening pages of his *Principles of the Opinions of the People of the Virtuous City* (ch. 1, sec. 2), the perfection of a species or class is one. Let me suggest two ways that one could look at Alfarabi's writings about the virtuous city. One is to see Alfarabi's political philosophy as a continuation or repetition of the quest for the best regime initiated by Plato and Aristotle. Seen in this light, no existing regime is the best regime. Plato makes it very clear that the best regime is open to philosophy. But philosophy is not primarily concerned with doing good to friends and harm to enemies. If philosophy could not benefit everyone, at least it would harm no one (*Republic* 335d). Alfarabi goes farther than this when he says that Plato aims at the happiness of all mankind (*Philosophy of Plato* sec. 22). This is what Plato called for.

Perhaps Alfarabi simply repeats and owns what he sees as Plato's call for universal happiness, an extravagant philanthropy open to all mankind. Another plausible interpretation seems possible however. Does every city and every nation see itself as the virtuous city or the virtuous nation, the one that seeks for its citizens the ultimate happiness? True, these cities and their rulers might pursue what Alfarabi calls an ignorant good—wealth or conquest or even survival and other necessary goods—but does any city or ruler understand itself as pursuing an ignorant good? Can any city survive if its ruler and its citizens see it as being merely the cave? The ignorance of the ignorant city consists precisely in this, that it mistakes mere political goods and political happiness for ultimate happiness. Every city sees itself as the virtuous city. In this sense, every city and every ruler is what Alfarabi calls the errant city and the errant ruler. The errant city and the errant ruler pursue one of the ignorant goods while believing that they pursue the ultimate happiness of the virtuous city (*Book of Religion* sec. 1). Is this the essence of the political? Alfarabi does not rule out the possibility that the ruler of an errant city might propagate this error as a conscious ruse in support of the legitimacy of his rule and the stability of his government.

And so in the taxonomy of regimes that Alfarabi offers at the beginning of the *Book of Religion* (sec. 1) there are four kinds of rulers: the virtuous ruler, the ignorant ruler, the errant ruler, and the deceptive ruler.

Every city and every nation sees itself as the virtuous city, the one that is open to the ultimate happiness and pursues the ultimate happiness. The fact that the people of the virtuous city may be in error does not lessen the opposition they see between the virtue of their city and the ignorance of others. From this perspective, it is easy to see how Alfarabi arrived at the thought that there is more than one virtuous city and nation, for there are many forms of error and many errant cities and nations, each of which sees itself as the virtuous city.

Can Alfarabi's political science shed any light on the 2016 American election campaign? Perhaps only by contrast. Alfarabi's virtuous city is a closed society, a religious community that understands itself in contrast to other religious communities. The United States is not at all a religious community, but rather an open society whose fundamental principle is the separation of church and state. America's founding documents promise its citizens not the ultimate happiness but only the pursuit of happiness in whatever way they each may understand happiness. But for just this reason America sees itself as the city on a hill, a kind of chosen people pursuing the American Dream. If Alfarabi is right in thinking that every city sees itself as the virtuous city, then we are right in thinking that America and Americans also see their nation as the virtuous city or virtuous nation, even if of a kind that Alfarabi, perhaps, never imagined. This is why Americans are open to exhortations to patriotism, to nationalism, to making America Great again. But in Alfarabi's analysis (such is our hypothesis) the virtuous city is also the errant city. Every city and nation sees itself as something more than it is—be it the idea that is France, or China as the Middle Kingdom, or Great Russian nationalism, or America as the indispensable nation. The errant city is the virtuous city, and this delusion is essential to its political health.

A concrete example may be helpful here. President George W. Bush insisted that we were not trying to impose our way of life on the Afghan people; we were simply defending basic human rights that all people share. No irony was intended. In the eyes of President Bush, America is a virtuous city; only in the eyes of another virtuous city do we seem to be errant. President Bush's notion of American virtue makes it difficult for him to see it in opposition to the virtue of others. Without any help from philosophy or from political science, candidate Trump was able to exploit this paradox of the American regime: even a regime whose goal is openness can be called upon to put America First. The open society can be rallied in opposition to other societies whose virtue is not openness, at least not openness in the sense of religious diversity. There are different kinds of openness, each of which appears closed from another perspective.

I began by trying to imagine how Alfarabi might see the fundamental premise of the American regime, and I suggested that he might see the separation of church and state, politics and religion as the fundamental feature of our regime. Certainly for Alfarabi, who treated every regime of which he had knowledge as a religious community of some kind, the attempt to separate politics and religion would be a striking feature of the American regime. Whether Alfarabi thought that a regime based on the separation of the theological from the political question was possible, whether it would work in practice, is an open question. Certainly the successful candidacy of President Trump highlights the way in which even a society which sees its virtue in openness of a certain kind can be rallied to close itself off, to seek the goods of the regime first for itself.

I have been assuming that Alfarabi never imagined an open society, but I have also said this is only an assumption. His *Book of Religion* treats all of the different kinds of regimes—those devoted to wealth or war or honor—within the confines of the virtuous city, which is itself a religious community sharing common opinions and actions. But there is one kind of regime conspicuously not mentioned in the *Book of Religion* and that is democracy or the regime devoted to freedom. It is not the case that Alfarabi does not mention democracy because he never thought of democracy, since he describes a democratic regime devoted to freedom in a book called *Political Regime* (secs. 113–117). Alfarabi's silence about democracy in the *Book of Religion* raises the possibility that he envisioned a kind of regime that was not properly described as a religious community.

We as a people can safely say that the United States was not conceived of by its founders as a religious community. Other changes in our history—the abolition of slavery, the decline of federalism, the rise of the New Deal—did not test the fundamental principle of separation of politics and religion. Candidate Trump did not openly challenge that principle but he did question it and that question was shown to have wide appeal. In his speech in Warsaw (July 6, 2017), President Trump did explicitly raise the question whether or not Western civilization has the will to survive.[6] It remains to be seen whether by Western Civilization President Trump meant to assert that Western Civilization is essentially Christian Civilization. If one were, indeed, to reach this conclusion, would the president be showing that the West had the will to survive, or would he be giving up on the religious neutrality that has been considered essential to the modern West and especially to the United States?

NOTES

1. Garry Wills, "Child of the Enlightenment," *New York Times Magazine*, July 2, 2017.
2. For *kalam* as a defense of the law, see Ralph Lerner, *Revolutions Revisited: Two Faces of the Politics of Enlightenment* (Chapel Hill: University of North Caroline Press, 1994), 61. Note that Lerner here treats *kalam* as defending the law rather than defending, for example, philosophy.
3. For the language of compactness and differentiation, see Eric Voegelin, *Order and History*, volume I, *Israel and Revelation* (Baton Rouge: Louisiana State University Press, 1956), 84.
4. For example, Majid Fakhry, *Al-Farabi: Founder of Islamic Neoplatonism* (Oxford: One World, 2002).
5. For the just war debate see Joshua Parens, *An Islamic Philosophy of Virtuous Religions: Introducing Alfarabi* (Albany: State University of New York, 2006) and Michael J. Sweeney, "Philosophy and Jihad: Al-Farabi on Compulsion to Happiness," *Review of Metaphysics*, 60: 3, March 2007, 543–72. Note the plural in Parens' title. Also of interest, John Kelsay, *Arguing the Just War in Islam* (Cambridge: Harvard University Press, 2007).
6. "The fundamental question of our time is whether the West has the will to survive." Warsaw Speech, July 6, 2017.

REFERENCES

Alfarabi. *Attainment of Happiness.* In Alfarabi, *Philosophy of Plato and Aristotle.* Translated by Muhsin Mahdi. Ithaca: Cornell University Press, 1962a, 2001.
———. *Philosophy of Plato.* In Alfarabi, *Philosophy of Plato and Aristotle.* Translated by Muhsin Mahdi. Ithaca: Cornell University Press, 1962b, 2001.
———. *Principles of the Opinions of the People of the Virtuous City.* In Al-Farabi, On the Perfect State. Translated by Richard Walzer. Oxford: Oxford University Press, 1985. Reprinted by Great Books of the Islamic World, Inc., 1998.
———. *Book of Religion.* In Alfarabi, *Political Writings: "Selected Aphorisms" and Other Texts.* Translated by Charles Butterworth. Ithaca: Cornell University Press, 2001.

————. *Political Regime*. In Alfarabi, *Political Writings*, Vol. II: "Political Regime" and "Summary of Plato's Laws." Translated by Charles Butterworth. Ithaca: Cornell University Press, 2015.

Aristotle. *Nicomachean Ethics*. Translated by Joe Sachs. Newburyport, MA: Focus Publishing, 2002.

Fakhry, Majid. *Al-Farabi: Founder of Islamic Neoplatonism*. Oxford: Oneworld, 2002.

Kelsay, John. *Arguing the Just War in Islam*. Cambridge: Harvard University Press, 2007.

Lerner, Ralph. *Revolutions Revisited: Two Faces of the Politics of Enlightenment*. Chapel Hill: University of North Caroline Press, 1994.

Parens, Joshua. *An Islamic Philosophy of Virtuous Religions: Introducing Alfarabi*. Albany: State University of New York Press, 2006.

Spinoza, Benedict. *Theological-Political Treatise*. Translated by Martin D. Yaffe. Newburyport, MA: Focus Publishing, 2004.

Trump, Donald. Speech in Poland, 2017, July 6. http://www.nbcnews.com/politics/donald-trump/here-s-full-text-donald-trump-s-speech-poland-n780046.

Voegelin, Eric. *Order and History*. Vol. I: *Israel and Revelation*. Baton Rouge: Louisiana State University Press, 1956.

Wills, Garry. "Child of the Enlightenment." In *An Annotated Constitution, New York Times Magazine*, July 2, 2017.

Wright, Thomas. "Trump's 19th Century Foreign Policy." *Politico*, January 20, 2016. https://www.politico.com/magazine/story/2016/01/donald-trump-foreign-policy-213546.

PART II

Modern and Liberal Thought

CHAPTER 8

Machiavellian Politics, Modern Management and the Rise of Donald Trump

Gladden J. Pappin

More than any American presidential election in recent memory, the 2016 election showed what the venting of the popular humor looks like. Donald Trump ran an explicitly "populist" campaign, shunning common fund-raising channels and picking a fight with the media that he portrayed as self-interested and distant from popular concern. He scheduled frequent, large campaign events designed to rally those whose interests he said had been excluded from national economic and political life. Like most instances in which the popular humor is vented in modern politics, Trump's election was portrayed in potentially apocalyptic terms.[1] Yet it occurred within a constitutional framework designed to allow periodic changes while preserving its fundamental features.

The first political philosopher to thematize "venting" (*sfogare*) the popular humor, and to thematize the political humors themselves, was Machiavelli. Alongside his frequent discussions of the political humors Machiavelli also introduced a new way of considering how to address, balance or govern such humors—through the concept of "managing" (*maneggiare*) the humors. For a variety of other reasons that cannot be traced directly to Machiavelli, "management" itself has become a primary theme of commercial life and thus also of modern society itself. The

G. J. Pappin (✉)
University of Dallas, Irving, TX, USA

© The Author(s) 2018
A. Jaramillo Torres, M. B. Sable (eds.), *Trump and Political Philosophy*,
https://doi.org/10.1007/978-3-319-74445-2_8

131

connection between Machiavelli's introduction of "managing" the political humors and our broad social and commercial recurrence to "management" is, however, not accidental. Machiavelli used "managing" to
describe the actions of princes, political rulers, captains and conspirators;
he did not speak of "management." But from Machiavelli's time to ours,
the scope of action available to would-be "managers"—princes or captains
with lesser ambitions than strong political rule—has widened considerably.
The economic and political institutions of liberalism have grown, especially in the wake of Locke's outlining of them, to integrate the projects of
ambitious men into "project management."

As we shall see, the most important writers on "management" in an
explicitly commercial context—writers such as Frederick Winslow Taylor
and Peter Drucker—faced many of the same phenomena that Machiavelli
did, and addressed many of the same features of the popular humor that
required governing and direction. But the widening space of activity
granted to those of a "princely" humor—the captains of industry, the
innovators and the ambitious in every sector—has arguably made the singular "venting of the popular humor" more difficult. Management has
become a more universal phenomenon—in many respects a fundamental
phenomenon for understanding the contemporary world. By diffusing the
princely impulse, the modern commercial world inspired by Locke largely
succeeded in avoiding internal tumult over matters of religion. The discontent that became embodied in Trump's campaign, and which has
appeared elsewhere in the Western world, stems from the lesser-noticed—
but no less important—way that "management" has frustrated the popular humor in attempting to satisfy it.

THE ORIGINS OF MACHIAVELLIAN MANAGEMENT

In both his *Prince* and his *Discourses on Livy* Machiavelli offers a new analysis of the constituent elements of politics, replacing the classical distinction between the few and the many with a division on the basis of two
humors. In his chapter "Of the Civil Principality" in *The Prince*, Machiavelli
asserts that "in every city these two diverse humors are found, which arises
from this: that the people desire neither to be commanded nor oppressed
by the great, and the great desire to command and oppress the people."[2]
He introduces the same distinction in the chapter of his *Discourses on Livy*
criticizing the critics of the Roman Republic's disunion between the plebs
and the Senate: "They do not consider that in every republic there are two

diverse humors, that of the people and that of the great, and that all the laws that are made in favor of freedom arise from their disunion. ... I say that every city ought to have its modes with which the people can vent its ambition, and especially those cities that wish to avail themselves of the people in important things."[3] The republican context of the *Discourses* prompts Machiavelli to emphasize that the disunion of the two humors allows a republic's freedom. But he also introduces the division of humors as an explanation, in addition to "fortune and the military," of the "causes of the Roman Empire." And as he explains in the more forthright context of *The Prince*, the venting of popular ambition often entails the directing of that ambition toward outlets that actually increase the power of those the people criticize. Principality (such as the Roman Empire was), can come about "when the great see they cannot resist the people, [and so] they begin to give reputation to one of themselves, and they make him prince so that they can vent their appetite under his shadow."[4]

In both these contexts Machiavelli introduces the concept of managing (*maneggiare*) the political situations caused by the presence of these humors. In the scenario just mentioned, Machiavelli shows principality emerging as a strategic choice among the great, to allow one of their own to exploit popular discontent and thus vent the popular appetite. The prince who comes to power in such a scenario faces the difficulty of reconciling his dependence on the great who empowered him with his need to control them. Such a prince "finds himself prince with many around him who appear to be his equals, and because of this he can neither command them nor manage them to suit himself."[5] Managing other apparent equals falls short of commanding them, but it would be difficult to command those of a princely temperament, especially when one has depended on them for one's rise. Rather than speaking of managing the people, though, Machiavelli speaks of satisfying them, "since the great want to oppress and the people want not to be oppressed."[6] Satisfying the great's desire to oppress would involve "injury," but the popular humor is more easily satisfied. Managing the great "to suit himself," the prince would not control them directly but would govern the outcome of their actions. The people do not have a temperament that needs "managing," but in satisfying it the prince likewise obtains a satisfactory outcome without directly governing popular actions. Satisfying and venting the popular humor is also the necessity that Machiavelli describes in the corresponding chapter of the *Discourses* describing the two humors.

Before returning to the *Discourses* in greater depth, let us consider the complications Machiavelli adds to the politics of management in *The Prince*. Machiavelli uses the term *maneggiare* to describe a prince's stance toward any other political situation that requires carefully and strategically balancing its various aspects in order to achieve a particular outcome. Hence Machiavelli describes the introduction of new orders, the culminating ambition of the prince Machiavelli advises, by noting that "nothing is … more dangerous to manage."[7] Of all the princely ambitions, introducing new orders requires the most difficult and dangerous management of many aspects, including the temperaments of the many as well as the great. Louis XII would have succeeded in his ambitions in Italy "if in managing other things he had not made some error."[8] Likewise Cesare Borgia took a risky turn in using mercenary soldiers that he had difficulty "managing," and eventually eliminated them.[9] At times Machiavelli equates managing with the task of governing itself, such as when he speaks of someone who has "fortified his town well, and has managed the other governing of his subjects."[10] But Machiavelli never speaks of managing subjects directly. Here, for example, his discussion of "manag[ing] the other governing of his subjects" may involve using the great in such a way that the people are satisfied. A prince's subjects would include the great, and he would manage all the political and legal procedures that make up governing them. So, too, when Machiavelli speaks of the danger of divisions in cities, he notes that divisions are only useful in peacetime as an element of political management. "For in a vigorous principality," Machiavelli says, "such divisions are never permitted, because they bring profit only in time of peace, as subjects can be managed more easily through them; but when war comes, such an order shows its own fallaciousness."[11] Though Machiavelli advises against fostering such divisions (notably, the division between the Guelf and Ghibelline sects), it is the divisions which a prince would manage, and his subjects through them indirectly. Those at the head of such divisions would likely be not from among the people but rather from among the great. In these cases too, then, what a prince manages are his operations as well as the ambitions of the great. The people, by contrast, are satisfied.

Machiavelli introduces managing in the *Discourses* in explaining the impossibility of the golden mean. As in *The Prince*, managing emerges as the necessary strategy for governing the different humors among men. The enmities between the people and the Senate kept Rome free and contributed to building Rome's empire, but not without discord and tumult at home. If Rome had pursued harmony among its citizens by excluding the people from warfare or by excluding any foreigners from gaining Roman citizenship, those options would have left Rome weak. Thus Machiavelli observes the following:

> In all human things he who examines well sees this: that one inconvenience can never be suppressed without another's cropping up. Therefore, if you wish to make a people numerous and armed so as to be able to make a great empire, you make it of such a quality that you cannot then manage it in your mode; if you maintain it either small or unarmed so as to be able to manage it, then if you acquire dominion you cannot hold it or it becomes so cowardly that you are the prey of whoever assaults you. And so, in every decision of ours, we should consider where are the fewer inconveniences and take that for the best policy, because nothing entirely clean and entirely without suspicion is ever found.[12]

Managing replaces the pursuit of the best in the classical sense. As Machiavelli presents it, managing is a necessarily imperfect practice. Both the political goals he names—keeping a small city or maintaining a great empire—involve risks to management. Obtaining an empire means greater difficulty in managing it "in your mode," while keeping a city small makes managing the city's defense against assault a nearly impossible task.

Though Machiavelli in *The Prince* does not use "managing" to describe a prince's use of virtues and vices, his account makes substantially the same point. Learning "to be able not to be good, and to use this and not use it according to necessity," is like managing the virtues and vices according as they are necessary. Hence in the *Discourses*, Machiavelli describes Pope Julius II's temperament and modes of proceeding in just these terms. Since he always acted "with impetuosity and fury," he happened to be successful only because that mode corresponded with the times. "But if other times had come that had demanded other counsel," Machiavelli says, "of necessity he would have been ruined, for he would not have changed either mode or order in managing himself."[13] Politically, Machiavelli suggests that the central element of management concerns its need to create new structures through which to address new necessities. Rome followed that path, but the Florence of his own day, he laments, "has gone on managing itself" by still relying on old orders rather than creating new ones.[14] Both politically and personally, then, management emerges from the impossibility of choosing and sticking to a mean—either to some particular virtue or to virtue itself as a mean. Republics must either accept the inconveniences that come from seeking empire, and manage accordingly, or attempt to manage domestic tensions without recourse to empire-building. So, too, Machiavelli speaks of managing battles and the elements of war (bk. 2, chap. 16, pars. 1–2, pp. 160, 162), of the impossibility of "manag[ing] great things in small spaces" (bk. 2, chap. 17, par. 2, p. 164), and of the imprudence of "harshly manag[ing] their citizens" (bk. 2, chap. 24, par. 2, p. 186). Management prudently orders things in relation to an end, but on the basis of knowing that the mean is impossible.

Machiavelli speaks of managing most frequently (ten times), however, in his lengthy chapter on conspiracies in the *Discourses*. Prudent management is necessary in carrying off conspiracies, which encounter danger "in managing them, in executing them, and after they are executed."[15] But the close association of management and conspiracy also suggests that conspiracy is of the essence of management itself. It is thus in his chapter on conspiracies that Machiavelli expands from speaking of managing the great or managing necessities in politics and warfare to speaking of "managing [an] enterprise" as a whole.[16] Any enterprise that requires sophisticated planning and calculation to obtain a result through the use (or exploitation) of men's humors, temperaments, tendencies and likely behavior involves management. While concealment is essential to the specific tasks of conspiring, managing as a whole involves directing the parts of an enterprise so that a conclusion is obtained without the full awareness of those managed. Earlier in the *Discourses* Machiavelli describes things that are "managed and seen," "the entire knowledge of [which] is not in any part concealed from you," but whose results are evident.[17] As Machiavelli has suggested by distinguishing between a conspiracy's management and its execution, the conspiracy is organized in secret before completing its designs in a specific set of acts. The sort of management involved in conspiracies differs from management in ruling in this respect. A new prince may in fact be one who has conspired against his fatherland, as Machiavelli suggests. "In managing" such conspiracies, Machiavelli says, "there are not many dangers because a citizen can order himself for power without making his mind and his plan manifest to anyone." Few such conspiracies "were crushed in their managing," Machiavelli concludes, but rather were either successes or failures in their execution.[18]

We may summarize Machiavelli's account of managing in the following way. Managing is an activity of overseeing the different parts of an enterprise in order to bring it to a successful conclusion or to make possible its continued advance. The enterprises in question are above all ruling, making war and conspiring. The different parts of enterprises include those whose actions are either necessary to carry it out or necessarily present for some other reason, such as those occupying official positions in a government one directs. Ruling and making war involve ongoing sorts of managing, as political actions may build on one another (such as the growth of the Roman Empire) rather than reaching a specific conclusion; conspiracies, by contrast, distinguish their stage of management from the stage of execution, at which the conspiracy becomes visible in specific actions. Managing in political activities is done by those with a humor inclined toward rule, and includes managing the two humors as they appear in political life. Since the great who are also inclined toward rule scheme continually, managing them is an artful task requiring the advice of Machiavelli's *Prince* and *Discourses*. Since the people have simpler desires, managing them politically means finding ways to satisfy them, and to manage the ambitions of their leaders. Management begins from the realization that the best course of action is not always available, and that political choices must be made in view of ever-shifting necessities. Management is to Machiavelli's virtue as prudence is to Aristotle's virtues. It guides the strategic use of one's own human qualities and seeks to produce the best outcomes through the strategic use of others' tendencies, as well. Above all, though management is not the same as conspiracy, it is not "seen," though it may be detected or divined.

THE INDUSTRIAL TRANSFORMATION OF MODERN MANAGEMENT

Machiavelli's concept of management contributes to understanding the rise of populist leaders by outlining something that, after subsequent transformations, became a crucial element in the life of industrially advanced countries. This subsequent transformation does not make Machiavelli's thought irrelevant, but makes it necessary to consider those transformations before using Machiavelli to analyze the contemporary situation directly. The political humors whose existence Machiavelli proclaimed have been managed not only by statesmen but by other political philosophers, as well. The favor Locke gave to the "Industrious and Rational" over the "Fancy or Covetousness of the Quarrelsom and Contentious" eventually directed the activity of many ambitious young men toward conquest in business rather than the contentious worlds of civil or ecclesiastical politics.[19]

Though the softening effects of commercial activity were already attested by the likes of David Hume and Adam Smith, it was not till after the Industrial Revolution's transformation of economic life away from agriculture that widespread participation in commercial activity marked society in the way that Locke expected. As long after the Industrial Revolution as 1888, the British jurist (and later ambassador to the United States) James Bryce wrote his *American Commonwealth* and pointed to this very phenomenon in a chapter rather condescendingly entitled "Why Great Men Are Not Chosen Presidents." "One [reason]," he remarked, "is that the proportion of first-rate ability drawn into politics is smaller in America than in most European countries." In Europe, he said, "the total quantity of talent devoted to parliamentary or administrative work is far larger, relatively to the population, than in America," where by contrast "much of the best ability, both for thought and for action, for planning and for executing, rushes into a field which is comparatively narrow in Europe, the business of developing the material resources of the country."[20] That rush of human activity into business has made the phenomenon of enterprise a much wider one than Machiavelli discussed explicitly. And, by turns, business has become the realm of human activity in which managing has become necessary.

The triumph of management was first described by Peter Drucker, especially in his 1954 book *The Practice of Management*.[21] And while Drucker might seem to be an uneven pairing with a philosopher of Machiavelli's rank, it is because management became a universal and thus broadly accessible phenomenon that it could be so readily described. Drucker was in fact keenly aware of the shifts that had occurred in the role played by management over time. After spending his childhood in Austria (b. 1909) and passing his first professional years in Germany and England, Drucker taught politics and philosophy at Bennington College in Vermont from 1942 to 1949 before eventually becoming professor of management at the Claremont Graduate University (d. 2005). In his famous 1974 work *Management: Tasks, Responsibilities, Practices*, he consciously distanced the structure of contemporary business from the priority of politics in prior eras. "We still use as political and social model," Drucker lamented, "what the great thinkers of the late sixteenth and seventeenth centuries, Bodin, Locke, Hume, and Harrington, codified: the society which knows no power centers and no autonomous institution, save only one central government. Reality has long outgrown this model—but it is still the only one we have."[22] In 1967, some years after Drucker's 1954 work, the cottage industry of applying Machiavelli to analyzing business practices began with the publication of Anthony Jay's *Management and Machiavelli: An Inquiry into the Politics of Corporate Life*.[23] After Jay's work, books applying Machiavelli to every element of modern business become too many to count, though scholars such as Michael Jackson and Damian Grace of the University of Sydney have recently done so.[24]

Drucker looked upon Jay's book wryly, and with good reason. "The comparison of management, whether in business, in the university, the government agency, or in the hospital, with a true 'government,' which is done so entertainingly in *Management & Machiavelli*, is," Drucker wrote, "half-truth. The managements of modern social institutions (including the government agency that administers, e.g., a post office) are not 'governments.' Their job is functional rather than political. ... Their command is over resources allocated to a specific and limited, though vital, task."[25] Rather than attempting to apply Machiavelli straightforwardly to the understanding of modern business practices, throughout his works Drucker outlines the contemporary characteristics of management. By doing so he clarifies the changed situation of management since Machiavelli first developed it in the context of political strategy. In spite of Drucker's distancing of contemporary management from Machiavellian politics, he wittingly or unwittingly describes a world of activity suffused with Machiavellian strategies, but modified in crucial ways. Those ways lie at the root of our current political problems.

"The manager," writes Drucker in the first sentence of his seminal 1954 work *The Practice of Management*, "is the dynamic, life-giving element in every business."[26] This description almost suffices to make the manager the equivalent of those with Machiavelli's princely humor: those who desire to rule imprint a particular form on political life, and managers do the same in the context of business. Management, says Drucker, "expresses basic beliefs of modern Western society," such as "the belief in the possibility of controlling man's livelihood through systematic organization of economic resources."[27] Here the phenomenon of management reflects the attitude Machiavelli encouraged in Chap. 25 of *The Prince*, asserting our governing of worldly things over their being governed by fortune.

This rather high-flying ambition to control "man's livelihood" is embodied in what Drucker calls the organ of management within business enterprises. In business enterprises and only there—not in politics—can the phenomenon of management really be found, for only business enterprises aim directly at "economic performance." Hence management "must always, in every decision and action, put economic performance first."[28] Though Drucker never looks to Machiavelli for an account of management's features, his description of it reflects other telltale "Machiavellian" characteristics such as adaptability. "For management," he writes, "has to *manage*. And managing is not just passive, adaptive behavior; it means taking action to make the desired results come to pass."[29] In this respect the management described by Drucker shares with Machiavelli's account of *maneggiare* the use of foresight and adaptation to bring about the realization of a goal. Simply adapting is not enough: managing "implies responsibility for attempting to shape the economic environment, for planning, initiating and carrying through changes in that economic environment, for constantly pushing back the limitations of economic circumstances on the enterprise's freedom of action."[30]

If Drucker's account of management shared with Machiavelli only his enterprising spirit and argument for adaptation, it would fall short of including Machiavelli's concern for the two distinct humors. But Drucker, again as one simply describing contemporary business strategy and not intentionally applying "Machiavellian" categories, follows this path, too: "Management's second function is therefore to make a productive enterprise out of human and material resources. Concretely this is the function of managing managers."[31] The purpose of managing managers is "to make resources productive by making an enterprise out of them."[32] "The final function of management," he adds, "is to manage workers and work."[33] Machiavelli had carefully spoken of the need to manage those of a princely humor while satisfying those of a popular humor. Since managers are likely to be those with spirits ambitious for economic gain, they have to be managed. Eventually, however, what managers manage is the business enterprise itself, composed in part of managers and in part of workers. To be sure, at one level Drucker wishes to widen the set of jobs within companies that are taken to be managerial in spirit. But he distinguishes sharply between the managerial spirit and the spirit of work. When "we speak of 'organization,'" he says, "what we mean is the organization of managers and of their functions; neither brick and mortar nor rank-and-file workers have any place in the organization structure."[34] As if his equation of workers with brick and mortar were not clear enough, he admits that his rule "implies consideration of the human being as a resource—that is, as something having peculiar psychological properties, abilities and limitations that require the same amount of engineering attention as the properties of any other resource, e. g., copper."[35] But since human beings also have, "unlike any other resource, personality, citizenship, control over whether they work, how much and well," and thus require "motivation, participation, satisfaction, incentives and rewards, leadership, status and function," Drucker asserts that *they must be satisfied* through work and job and within the enterprise" (my emphasis).[36]

Though Drucker later rejects the use of Machiavelli by other analysts of modern business, his direct approach to describing business brings him precisely to the point that we drew from Machiavelli earlier: managers must be managed, workers must be satisfied. This basic similarity with Machiavelli's analysis of management, however, serves to bring out the key difference. In universalizing the phenomenon of management in business enterprise, management's need to "satisfy" the people or workers changes its character decisively. While Machiavelli certainly rejected the classical conception of the human good, nevertheless "the people" were constituted as a political entity. Their satisfaction would keep principalities calm, but an ambitious principality or republic could allow tension between the great and the people to fuel the people's participation in warfare and the building of empire. Modern political government "constitutionalized" the elements of Machiavelli's system, as Harvey Mansfield has argued, adopting Machiavelli's executive into the modern system of checks and balances, and including popular participation in the form of representation.[37] The people in Machiavelli's account still had a way of contributing to a common good in the form of the republic's continuation. Further, as we saw, the planning phase of Machiavelli's management also occurred out of sight of those whom it managed.

The operation of this principle on the level of the business corporation is very different. Indeed, its difference is what led Drucker to absolve Machiavelli of any responsibility for business management, and to impugn writers who would apply Machiavellian categories too closely to the business corporation. But when businesses began to adopt the tenets of management in the late nineteenth century (a beginning which Drucker judged was completed by the 1950s), the main area in which "the people" encountered "management" was not in their experience of political life but rather in the vast number of business enterprises in which they made their livelihoods. As Drucker argues, management effectively replaced the position of capital in the old relationships between capital and labor. In its original intention, the purpose of management was to make human workers more productive, thus leading to more profitable businesses as well as higher wages and better working conditions for workers. This view led Frederick Winslow Taylor (1856–1915) to formulate his *Principles of Scientific Management* (1911) as something mutually beneficial for workers and management. "The principal object of management," he wrote to begin that treatise, "should be to secure the maximum prosperity for the employer, coupled with the maximum prosperity for each employé."[38] Such a transformation would come about through the application of scientific understanding to each task of the productive process, from determining the proper intervals at which human beings should work and rest, to determining the scientifically optimal sequence of movements to carry out mechanical tasks. Even in Taylor's "scientific" resolution of the tensions between workmen and managers he recognized that a human sense of unfairness would persist. Some, he said, would "complain because under scientific management the workman, when he is shown how to do twice as much work as he formerly did, is not paid twice his former wages."[39] But Taylor felt that the "rights of the people" as a whole demanded products of higher quality and cheaper, and that their presence justified his development of managerial relations.[40]

By the time of Drucker's *The Practice of Management*, the problem had changed but not abated. "There is no greater danger to a free economy," he wrote, "than the hostility of employees toward profit."[41] Management of workers itself had changed considerably, however, and was to change further under Drucker's guidance. The theme he advocated, in words that he described as "a manifesto," was "Human Organization for Peak Performance." "By proclaiming peak performance to be the goal—rather than happiness or satisfaction—it asserts," he explained, "that we have to go beyond Human Relations. By stressing human organization, it asserts that we have to go beyond traditional Scientific Management."[42] Remarkable or even shocking as these statements may be, Drucker was quick to add, as he always was, that pursuing an "integrated" production environment would ultimately be more satisfying for workers as well. But since economic performance is the goal of management, the human benefits of more integrally organized methods of production are only incidental to the superior goal of economic performance.

In a discussion of IBM's growth story and its success in maintaining stable employment during the Great Depression, Drucker points to two elements of management's success that have lately become more problematic.[43] IBM was able to stay afloat and continue employing its workers because of its awareness that the function of business was to create new customers (i.e., new markets) continually and because IBM consciously intended to maintain full employment to the best of its ability. In the years following the boom in postwar American growth, American companies internalized the urgency of finding new markets and, having in many cases reached their saturation point in American markets, went abroad seeking to open foreign markets to American goods. But the second principle that IBM held—the importance of stable employment—has fallen by the wayside as American companies have become more nimble and choosier in the pursuit of economic performance. The instability in many parts of the American workforce has come about in part because of American companies' success in innovating as well as in providing goods to American consumers that have been produced more cheaply elsewhere. Drucker's early hopefulness about the importance of stable employment has thus not been borne out. Likewise, although American companies have been spared much of the sort of internal discontent and strikes that rocked business during labor's heyday, a general feeling of frustration and malaise has remained in large portions of the American workforce—particularly in parts of the country that have struggled to keep up economically with America's most successful cities. It is this frustration which has bubbled up, not primarily within the context of companies, but in politics.

Donald Trump and the Return of Machiavelli's Political Humors

The modern practice of corporate management, I have argued, reflected themes from the account of managing political humors first articulated by Machiavelli. The new management became a phenomenon of the increasingly ubiquitous business corporation and, in the view of those who articulated it, became distinctive of business itself rather than politics. This universalizing of management has been, however, also a process of fragmenting. The development of liberal politics sought to insulate politics from violently partisan disputes and direct the ambitious toward beneficial economic activity. These men became the "managers" of modern corporations. And just as "the great" from Machiavelli's political world formed many combinations in the pursuit of their ambitions, so too the modern company has given room to the ambitious to launch specific enterprises. But in this scheme "the people"—those who desired not to be ruled, and whom Machiavelli urged princes to satisfy—became fragmented by their being grouped into these many enterprises of the great.

Unlike in the political enterprises that Machiavelli described, ambitious businessmen are not placing themselves at the head of the people as a whole. Instead they have generally followed Drucker's advice and pursued "human organization for peak performance"—that is, for the purpose of their business enterprises. The people have become the workers. Most importantly, the practice of management has become ever more developed to get higher levels of production out of individual workers. Machiavelli's management focused squarely on arranging the great (including those who might be popular leaders) and satisfying the people; the main active role that the people could play was in warfare. But modern management turns workers into a resource that, in the respects Drucker outlined, is a resource like any other—but with additional complications resulting from the character of human nature.

The political doctrines that have become characteristic of Western regimes in recent decades all assume the fundamental soundness of the managerial paradigm.[44] In particular, they have assumed that "the people" should not be and do not need to be constituted as a whole.

It is this assumption that the electoral success of leaders such as Donald Trump has challenged. If the popular humor can be "managed" through business enterprises it can make, as the effects of liberal capitalism have shown, dramatic advances in human productivity. And in periods when the relationship between management and workers is at ease, the segregation of workers into different corporations has not been judged something bad: the years of increasing American domestic productivity after World War II were also years of fervent patriotism. But businesses have now become more effective at increasing productivity without maintaining stable employment—indeed, even with shifts toward more temporary and contract workers. Meanwhile, managers have expanded their operations far beyond the territorial limits of their own countries. In many industries (though certainly not all) they maintain their profits through foreign corporate development outside of any sense of obligation to their fellow citizens. The inequality among workers, and between workers and management, has thus returned as a source of friction.

The election of Donald Trump shows that we have partly returned to the situation described by Machiavelli, in which one from among "the great" can make a play for political power on the basis of a direct appeal to the people. Trump used nostalgia for a more unified or solidaristic

American past to appeal especially to workers who felt that the current state of the economy had left them behind. Accordingly, as Machiavelli would put it, "the people, when they see they cannot resist the great, give reputation to one, and make him prince so as to be defended with his authority."[45] More than any American president in recent memory, Trump exudes this sense of strength exercised on behalf of "the people." His repeated assertions that the election would be "rigged" (if he lost) built up and played upon the popular sense that "the great" were using stratagems that were unavailable to "the people."

This popular sense that the economy has been managed not to popular benefit is nothing other than the sense that managerialism has gone wrong. Taylor's scientific management and Drucker's managerial practice are both the possessions of those who manage. The managed must be "satisfied" by the results of economic performance arranged by the managers. Trump changed the political status of contemporary management by impugning it directly. To be sure, the modern marketplace has suffered many downturns, corrections and depressions over the years. But as Wolfgang Streeck pointed out in his 2016 book *How Will Capitalism End?*, the current economic situation of the Western world combines economic stagnation, rising inequality and rising indebtedness to an unprecedented degree.[46]

When the theorists of modern business practices introduced and spoke openly of scientific management and managerial science, they were confident that management would contribute to solving the "social question" that had plagued production in the late nineteenth century. So long as business enterprises were growing and successful, and contributed something recognizably good to the countries of which they were a part ("What's good for GM is good for America"), this system held. But when the economic situation is one of stagnation combined with rising inequality and rising debt, "the people" have less reason to remain satisfied through the business enterprises of which they are a part, and more reason to turn to a popular leader who would satisfy them politically. Donald Trump will not be the last such aspirant to the platform of popular leader. But he is the first to seize it on the political height of the American presidency, and to shift politics, at least for the moment, toward a situation that Machiavelli would recognize and that the promoters of modern capitalism had attempted to avoid.

NOTES

1. David Frum, "How to Build an Autocracy," *Atlantic* 319, no. 2 (March 2017): 48–59.
2. Niccolò Machiavelli, *The Prince*, trans. Harvey C. Mansfield, 2nd ed. (Chicago: University of Chicago Press, 1998), chap. 9, p. 39.
3. Niccolò Machiavelli, *Discourses on Livy*, trans. Harvey C. Mansfield and Nathan Tarcov (Chicago: University of Chicago Press, 1996), bk. 1, chap. 4, pp. 16–17.
4. Machiavelli, *The Prince*, chap. 9, p. 39.
5. Ibid.
6. Ibid.
7. Ibid., chap. 6, p. 23.
8. Ibid., chap. 3, p. 13.
9. Ibid., chap. 13, p. 55.
10. Ibid., chap. 10, p. 43.
11. Ibid., chap. 20, p. 85.
12. Machiavelli, *Discourses*, bk. 1, chap. 6, par. 3, pp. 21–22.
13. Ibid., bk. 3, chap. 9, par. 3, p. 240.
14. Ibid., bk. 1, chap. 49, par. 2, p. 101.
15. Ibid., bk. 3, chap. 6, par. 2, p. 220.
16. Ibid., bk. 3, chap. 6, par. 3, p. 222.
17. Ibid., bk. 2, pref., par. 1, p. 123.
18. Ibid., bk. 3, chap. 6, par. 19, pp. 232–33.
19. John Locke, *Second Treatise of Government*, in *Two Treatises of Government*, ed. Peter Laslett, student edn. (Cambridge: Cambridge University Press, 1988), chap. 5, par. 34, p. 291.
20. James Bryce, *The American Commonwealth*, 3 vols. (London: Macmillan, 1888), 1:100–1.
21. Peter Drucker, *The Practice of Management* (New York: Harper and Row, 1954).
22. Peter Drucker, *Management: Tasks, Responsibilities, Practices* (New York: Harper and Row, 1974), 5.
23. Anthony Jay, *Management and Machiavelli: An Inquiry into the Politics of Corporate Life* (New York: Holt, Reinhart and Winston, 1967).
24. See their essay critical of the application of Machiavelli to business practices: Michael Jackson and Damian Grace, "Machiavelli's Echo in Management," *Management and Organizational History* 8, no. 4 (2013): 400–14. A similar approach, tracking the effect of particular Machiavellian strategies on modern business, is Ernest Alan Buttery and Ewa Maria Richter, "On Machiavellian Management," *Leadership and Organization Development Journal* 24, no. 8 (2003): 426–35. See also, among others,

Phil Harris, Andrew Lock and Patricia Rees, eds., *Machiavelli, Marketing and Management* (London: Routledge, 2000); Michael Macaulay and Alan Lawton, "Misunderstanding Machiavelli in Management: Metaphor, Analogy and Historical Method," *Philosophy of Management* 3, no. 3 (2003): 17–30; Peter J. Galie and Christopher Bopst, "Machiavelli and Modern Business: Realist Thought in Contemporary Corporate Manuals," *Journal of Business Ethics* 65 (2006): 235–50.
25. Peter Drucker, *The Age of Discontinuity: Guidelines to Our Changing Society* (New York: Harper and Row, 1969), 208.
26. Drucker, *The Practice of Management*, 3.
27. Ibid., 4.
28. Ibid., 7.
29. Ibid., 11.
30. Ibid.
31. Ibid., 12.
32. Ibid., 14.
33. Ibid.
34. Ibid., 13.
35. Ibid., 14.
36. Ibid.
37. Harvey C. Mansfield, *Taming the Prince: The Ambivalence of Modern Executive Power* (New York: Free Press, 1989).
38. Frederick Winslow Taylor, *The Principles of Scientific Management* (New York: Harper, 1913), 9.
39. Ibid., 135.
40. Ibid., 136.
41. Drucker, *Practice*, 315.
42. Ibid., 289.
43. Ibid., 255–61.
44. See Julius Krein, "James Burnham's Managerial Elite," *American Affairs* 1, no. 1 (Spring 2017): 126–51.
45. Machiavelli, *The Prince*, chap. 9, p. 39.
46. Wolfgang Streeck, *How Will Capitalism End?: Essays on a Failing System* (London: Verso, 2016).

References

Bryce, James. *The American Commonwealth*. 3 vols. London: Macmillan, 1888.
Buttery, Ernest Alan, and Ewa Maria Richter. "On Machiavellian Management." *Leadership and Organization Development Journal* 24, no. 8, 2003: 426–35.
Drucker, Peter. *The Practice of Management*. New York: Harper and Row, 1954.

————. *The Age of Discontinuity: Guidelines to Our Changing Society*. New York: Harper and Row, 1969.

————. *Management: Tasks, Responsibilities, Practices*. New York: Harper and Row, 1974.

Frum, David. "How to Build an Autocracy." *Atlantic* 319, no. 2, 2017, March: 48–59.

Galie, Peter J., and Christopher Bopst. "Machiavelli and Modern Business: Realist Thought in Contemporary Corporate Manuals." *Journal of Business Ethics* 65, 2006: 235–50.

Harris, Phil, Andrew Lock, and Patricia Rees, eds. *Machiavelli, Marketing and Management*. London: Routledge, 2000.

Jackson, Michael, and Damian Grace. "Machiavelli's Echo in Management." *Management and Organizational History* 8, no. 4, 2013: 400–14.

Jay, Anthony. *Management and Machiavelli: An Inquiry into the Politics of Corporate Life*. New York: Holt, Reinhart and Winston, 1967.

Krein, Julius. "James Burnham's Managerial Elite." *American Affairs* 1, no. 1, 2017, Spring: 126–51.

Locke, John. Second Treatise of Government. In *Two Treatises of Government*, edited by Peter Laslett. Student edition. Cambridge: Cambridge University Press, 1988.

Macaulay, Michael, and Alan Lawton. "Misunderstanding Machiavelli in Management: Metaphor, Analogy and Historical Method." *Philosophy of Management* 3, no. 3, 2003: 17–30.

Machiavelli, Niccolò. *Discourses on Livy*. Translated by Harvey C. Mansfield and Nathan Tarcov. Chicago: University of Chicago Press, 1996.

————. *The Prince*. Translated by Harvey C. Mansfield. 2nd ed. Chicago: University of Chicago Press, 1998.

Mansfield, Harvey C. *Taming the Prince: The Ambivalence of Modern Executive Power*. New York: Free Press, 1989.

Streeck, Wolfgang. *How Will Capitalism End?: Essays on a Failing System*. London: Verso, 2016.

Taylor, Frederick Winslow. *The Principles of Scientific Management*. New York: Harper, 1913.

CHAPTER 9

Donald Trump: Shakespeare's Lord of Misrule

Yu Jin Ko

It is hard to think of a political phenomenon in the twenty-first century that has shaken, enraged and demoralized progressives more than the rise and election of Donald Trump. So few saw it coming because so few believed such an outrage could be possible. After all, the mainstream media seemed to reflect and channel the progressives' opposition with equally apoplectic ferocity and to participate in exposing the fraudulence of so many of Trump's claims. The realization that this widespread opposition proved ineffective has perhaps been the most disheartening aspect of Trump's election victory for progressives. And yet this failure has also been the most telling, though in ways that have not quite been fully digested. To understand more fully the relationship between Trump's rise and oppositional energies, one might turn to Shakespeare studies, which for over a generation—from at least the mid-1980s—has been consumed by a disconcerting insight borrowed from Foucault: that subversive opposition has a way of reinforcing Power.[1] Indeed, the so-called New Historicism in literary studies has largely focused on the various ways in which Power co-opts—or "contains"—subversion.[2] Ground zero of the New Historicism remains the history plays of Shakespeare, particularly the Henriad tetralogy (*Richard II, Henry IV*, Parts 1 & 2, *Henry V*). The plays seem to invite subversive skepticism by highlighting the fraudulence and Machiavellian calculation behind the workings of Power. And yet,

Y. J. Ko (✉)
Wellesley College, Wellesley, MA, USA

© The Author(s) 2018
A. Jaramillo Torres, M. B. Sable (eds.), *Trump and Political Philosophy*,
https://doi.org/10.1007/978-3-319-74445-2_9

149

somehow, as Henry V leads his outnumbered troops in battle against the French in the final play of the sequence, audiences (and readers) almost invariably get swept away by nationalistic passions ("We few, we happy few, we band of brothers").[3] My essay will explore the ways in which the history plays might illuminate how Donald Trump's improbable rise has been so crucially fueled by relentless subversive opposition. The essay will look in particular at how Trump combines the Machiavellian cunning of Prince Hal with the shameless but subversive egomania and excess of Falstaff to become a Lord of Misrule that feeds on opposition.

As a start we might recall the seminal essay by Stephen Greenblatt ("Invisible Bullets") that launched the thousand essays of New Historicism. However, a brief recap of the story that Shakespeare's Henriad tells, along with its reception history prior to Greenblatt, will help to contextualize Greenblatt's critical intervention. The historical saga begins (in *Richard II*) with a rebellion against King Richard II (1377–1399), who is traditionally considered a weak king and who is depicted in the play as something of a poet (if not also a philosopher) who is given to profligate ways and impulsive mismanagement. Richard is eventually deposed by his cousin Henry Bolingbroke, who orders Richard's murder in prison and takes the throne as Henry IV. Given the tremendous moral anxiety and opprobrium surrounding regicide, the usurpation delivers a tremendous shock to the political system, and as a result Henry IV struggles throughout his reign (1399–1413) with the issue of legitimacy and contends continuously (as depicted in the two parts of *Henry IV*) with various rebellions. Closer to home, he has to deal with his prodigal son Hal, who is shown, especially in the first part of *Henry IV*, to prefer the tavern to the court and the company of the aging, corpulent and gloriously (or grotesquely) epicurean Falstaff to noblemen and courtiers. However, Hal eventually reforms himself (or "redeems" himself, in the language of the play[4]) and, to the surprise of his father, leads the royal forces to a series of military victories over the rebels and his rivals. By the end of *Henry IV, Part 2*, the crown passes peacefully to Hal as his father Henry IV dies, and Hal becomes Henry V. Coincident with the transition to kingship (on the way, in fact, to the coronation), Hal renounces Falstaff publicly to complete his reformation from prodigal ne'er-do-well to monarch. Under the historical Henry V (1413–1422), England unexpectedly enjoyed a period of glory, though it was largely due to Henry's successful strategy of uniting rival factions by leading them on a military campaign to conquer France. The play *Henry V* dramatizes the military adventure that culminates in Henry's leading his outnumbered band of brothers to a stunning victory at Agincourt on St. Crispin's Day. The historical Henry V would die early, leaving the crown to his nine-month old heir and to new factions of rivals who would usher in the so-called Wars of the Roses. However, Shakespeare's play ends earlier in time and like a romantic comedy, as Henry successfully woos the defeated French King's daughter Katherine to be his wife and cements the union of England and France.

Although the critical response to the plays has never been uniform, it would be fair to say that from about the mid-nineteenth century to the mid-twentieth, the so-called Old Historicist interpretation was the most representative. Exemplified in scholars like E. M. W. Tillyard, the plays were said to dramatize the "education" of an ideal prince in near Bildungsroman-like fashion and to celebrate the apotheosis of royal power in Henry V's victory.[5] Falstaff, on the other hand, was understood to be the embodiment of Vice, whose rejection was necessary, in near Morality Play-like fashion, to completing the process of private and public matura-tion.[6] However, twentieth-century unease with nationalistic celebrations of power eventually took hold from sometime after the 1950s, leading to two broad trends. One, often reflecting the mantra "Always Historicize," tended to adopt the conclusions of the Old Historicists but subjected the conclusions to political critiques that tried to expose the workings of ideology behind Shakespeare's depictions of history.[7] The other trend (associated separately with both materialist critics and those who are some-times disparaged as "liberal humanists" by those critics) tended to empha-size how the plays themselves exposed the Machiavellian workings of power and thus challenged or undermined the movement toward jingois-tic celebration, or, often borrowing Mikhail Bakhtin's idea of the carni-valesque, how the plays locate radically subversive and oppositional energies in the plebian world of Falstaff and the tavern.[8]

It was into this critical mix that Stephen Greenblatt most memorably introduced the Foucauldian idea that power produces its own subversion as a mechanism of reproducing power. Greenblatt's essay duly notes that the Henriad plays continually expose "the lies" and "self-serving senti-ments" of the ruling powers and register "every nuance of ... [their] hypocrisy, ruthlessness, and bad faith."[9] Indeed, and perhaps most famously, 2 *Henry IV* shows the usurping King Henry IV on his death bed advising his son to distract the populace from domestic turmoil by launching a foreign war ("busy giddy minds/With foreign quarrels").[10] This extraordinary moment of ruthless calculation is further preceded by a scene of deceitful betrayal. At the battle of Gaultree Forest, Prince Hal's brother Prince John defeats the final faction of rebels through equivocation, or more simply, by deceiving them with false promises and lies. He asks the rebel leaders to "discharge" (4.2.61) their forces in exchange for the promise ("Upon my soul," 4.2.60) that their grievances will be "with speed redressed" (4.2.59). However, when the rebels disband their forces, they are immediately arrested and sent to "the block of death" (4.2.122) as Prince John quips that all he "promised" them was simply "redress of these ... grievances" (4.2.113) and nothing more. Bad faith is a family trait. When the action moves into *Henry V*, we see Henry V preparing for the very war his father advised him to undertake, and we further see his and his court's effort to justify the war by wringing contorted lawyerly arguments from ancient laws with hypocrisy so shameless and self-serving that it would make Donald Trump Senior and Junior proud. And yet, as previously noted and as attested by reactions to productions like Kenneth Branagh's film of the play, audiences seem inexorably drawn toward celebrating Henry's victory at Agincourt as a glorious achievement and a miraculous blessing. One might recall that in Branagh's film version, Henry's short order to sing "Non Nobis"—to acknowledge that glory is entirely God's since He "fought for us" (4.8.122)—becomes an extended musical sequence honoring the dead that serves as the emotional climax of the battle. Hence it is that Greenblatt concludes, "actions that should have the effect of radically undermining authority turn out to be the props of that authority" (53). More specifically, Greenblatt draws a link between "a poetics of power" and "a poetics of the theatre" (64): in the way that complexities and ambiguities "heighten the theatrical interest" (63) of a play, "the very doubts that Shakespeare raises serve not to rob the king of his charisma but to heighten it" (63). Put another way, especially in periods like Elizabethan England in which public performance (or "privileged visibility," 64) is integral to defining and sustaining power, the theatrical display of human failings, including the propensity for mendacity and fraudulence, can serve paradoxically to humanize and authenticate power. As Greenblatt himself writes, "the subversive doubts that the play continually awakens originate paradoxically in an effort to intensify the power of the king and his war" (63). It is not that Greenblatt disagrees with those who see subversion at work in Shakespeare's plays; he offers a different interpretation of the effect of subversion.

I would like to keep Greenblatt's model of strategic subversion in view in relation to Donald Trump, but with some crucial differences. Although

Greenblatt acknowledges that emotional reactions to Falstaff remain complicated, he still views Hals' rejection of Falstaff as principally serving "to verify Hal's claim that he has turned away his former self" (55). Hence, "the betrayal of friends does not subvert but rather sustains the moral authority and compelling glamour of power" (58). While there is no doubt truth to Greenblatt's assertions, I would first like to think about the ways in which Hal has incorporated or absorbed Falstaff's recklessly subversive energies as tools of power. Concomitantly, I would like to consider the various ways in which Donald Trump's electoral triumph (along with his continuing behavior as president) was enabled by his uncanny (and thoroughly repugnant) ability to deploy Falstaffian subversiveness with Hal-like calculation and cunning.

Scholars often talk about the three worlds in the two *Henry IV* plays: the worlds of the court, the tavern and the rebels. Viewed schematically, the tavern and rebel worlds pose a threat to the court as spaces of anti-establishment disorder and rebellion, or what the play calls "hurly-burly innovation" (*1 Henry IV*, 5.1.178). Falstaff, for instance, is routinely characterized as a Lord of Misrule, a figure from medieval and Elizabethan holiday customs who leads a period of topsy-turvy saturnalian disorder, riot and license.[11] This mock-king, however, does not simply usher in a saturnalian holiday of, as a contemporary document puts it, "heathenry, devilry, whoredom, drunkenness, pride and what not" (Barber 28).[12] As Mikhail Bakhtin has pointed out, such figures of carnivalesque misrule, in mocking and suspending formal ceremonials, "hierarchical rank, privileges, norms and prohibitions,"[13] release a populist energy that threatens to expose the "pretense" (22) that dignifies and authorizes everyday order, whether political, social or spiritual. Hence, Falstaff is often set in opposition to the legitimate ruler or sovereign. However, it is also a commonplace of criticism to note that the three worlds are fundamentally connected by a common action: stealing crowns.[14] Henry IV, the leader of the court, has of course stolen his crown from Richard II, which the rebels are trying to steal back; moreover, the first action that we see Falstaff and the taverners engaging in is a scheme of robbery in which they plan to steal "crowns" (*1 Henry IV*, 1.2.136) from travelers. All this is to say that, though the three worlds remain separate and in opposition in crucial ways, they are also porous and governed by a shared ethos. Each world is, for one, driven by a self-serving quest for power and advancement. A part of what distinguishes Hal is the clarity with which he recognizes this fact.

In particular, Hal recognizes that the quest for advancement generates a form of mendacity that is inseparable from distrust of the truths asserted by those from other worlds. For Hal, the trait of Falstaff that is both most endearing and infuriating is his capacity for the most outrageously transparent lies. From their first meeting (in *1 Henry IV*), Falstaff's lies come pouring out with disarming abandon and playful plenitude; though he has known nothing but gluttony and debauchery all his life, he says, "Thou hast done much harm upon me, Hal—God forgive thee for it! Before I knew thee, Hal, I knew nothing, and now am I, if a man should speak truly, little better than one of the wicked" (1.2.95–9). Falstaff's most memorable lies occur during the Gad's Hill caper (the above-mentioned robbery) after Hal, disguised as a thief in "buckram" (2.4.192) along with a confederate, robs Falstaff and his crew of the crowns that they had just robbed from travelers in a dark lane. Explaining how he was robbed of the money by inventing a story of being set upon by a multitude of thieves, Falstaff's lies become more outlandish, shameless and transparent. He begins by claiming that he was attacked by "fifty" (2.4.186) men, and then spins an elaborate tale in which the number of "rogues in buckram suits" (191–92) he claims to have killed grows in the telling from "two" to "four" to "seven" and then "eleven" (2.4.191, 195, 201, 217), which leads Hal to exclaim, "O monstrous! Eleven buckram men grown out of two!" (2.4.218–19). Then, when it is revealed to Falstaff that it was in fact Hal and a friend in disguise who attacked them, and that he fled like a coward without putting up a fight, Falstaff reverses course with egregious aplomb: "By the Lord, I knew ye as well as he that made ye. Why, hear ye, my masters. Was it for me to kill the heir apparent?" (2.4.268–70). Undeterred by reality, Falstaff is a master of inventing alternative facts to serve his needs.

Paradoxically, however, it is this very capacity for open falsehood—his capacity to generate skepticism about his own truthfulness—that authenticates Falstaff's status as someone beyond the standards of truth established by those in power and who therefore can expose the falsehoods of officialdom. No one in the entire Henriad provides a more subversive and devastating critique of the established rhetoric of war than Falstaff:

What is honor? A word. What is in that word honor? … Air—a trim reckoning! Who hath it? He that died a Wednesday. (*1 Henry IV*, 5.1.134–36)

It's hard to miss the power of his swipes at establishment authority when he points to the corpse of the nobleman Sir Walter Blunt and declares, "There's honor for you!" (5.3.32–3). And yet, at the same time, even as he exposes the hypocrisy and dishonorable ugliness of war, he is not beyond shamelessly profiting from exploiting the commercial opportunities created by a coercive and corrupt system of military recruitment. Given the power by Hal to enlist soldiers, Falstaff first calls up only those who have the financial means to buy out "their services" (4.2.23), leaving him eventually with only the most impoverished and wretched recruits ("slaves as ragged as Lazarus," 4.2.25). To add insult to injury, directly after his comment about Sir Walter Blunt above, he adds cavalierly, "I have led my rag-of-muffins where they are peppered. There's not three of my hundred and fifty left alive" (5.3.36–8). While such actions and words of course show Falstaff to be grotesquely immoral and remorselessly self-serving, they also reveal more powerfully the grotesqueries of war that officialdom depends on while ignoring. The self-exposing mendacity that places him beyond the standards of truth works hand in hand with a brazen disregard for the norms of decency that at once exposes the hypocritical indecency of the power establishment, while providing him a privileged and sheltered opportunity to profit from indecency.

In this light, we might say that Donald Trump is a self-subverting figure who undermines his credibility with transparently gross lies that paradoxically establish his authenticity as a subversive rebel outsider who will tell it like it is and shake things up from the inside. The preposterous distortions and grossly transparent lies that Trump has peddled, from before his presidential campaign to the early period of his presidency, are too numerous to list, though *The New York Times* and other publications have tried to catalog some of the more egregious ones. Beginning with the so-called birther claims about President Obama to his assertion that he saw thousands of Arabs in New Jersey celebrating the collapse of the twin towers on 9/11, and continuing with his claim that Mexico forcibly sends murderers and rapists to the US or that Ted Cruz's father was with Lee Harvey Oswald before Oswald assassinated President Kennedy, Trump's public assaults on the standards of truth paradoxically burnished his image among his followers as someone willing to dismantle the truth claims of the establishment. As a Falstaffian Lord of Misrule he acquired the legitimacy during his campaign to unmask the pretenses, for example, of political correctness among Washington insiders, the mainstream media and university intellectuals. It is of course true that many of Trump's lies and

distortions involve immigrants and foreigners of color and that his promise to make America great again is really a xenophobic effort to make
America white again. If Trump ever succeeds in building the wall along
the border with Mexico, it will indeed be built upon a deep foundation of
repellent lies. But Hillary Clinton and the Democrats had no chance during the campaign to win the argument about the wall, because walls and
fences—albeit porous and seemingly ineffective—already exist along the
border, financed over the years by both Republicans and Democrats
(including by Clinton and Obama when they were senators), while the
budget for border security increased by billions under the Obama administration. Indeed, the Obama administration had deported more undocumented immigrants (over three million) than the two previous
administrations (of Bill Clinton and George W. Bush) combined—in fact,
more than any president *ever*.[15] Hillary Clinton was of course Secretary of
State under Obama, and thus had a hand in shaping immigration policy.
Trump's promise to build the wall was certainly an exercise in nativist
bigotry, but it also exposed Clinton's slogan of "Stronger Together" as
something of a sham.

Along similar lines, Trump's long history of bankruptcies (Taj Mahal
and others), financial fraud (Trump University), and naked profiteering
(betting on the housing market crash of 2007–2008) also established him
among his followers as someone who has enviably and successfully
squeezed a rigged system for all its worth. Hence, though he promised to
cut back Wall Street regulations and continued to profit from financial
markets, he also possessed the Street credibility, as it were, to denounce
Wall Street financiers and hedge fund managers as scammers and paper
pushers "who get away with murder."[16] Hillary Clinton's attacks on
Trump's record of bankruptcies and law suits for fraud did not have nearly
the force of his horribly exaggerated charge that Clinton received over a
hundred million dollars in donations from Wall Street. After all, Clinton
did famously profit from speeches to Wall Street firms even as she styled
herself a protector of Main Street. Trump's shameless self-exposure as an
extravagantly successful gamer of a system that crushes the average person
is what empowers him to speak with populist irreverence and carnivalesque
offensiveness. Indeed, the same might be said of the release of the "Access
Hollywood" tape in which Trump is recorded as boasting about grabbing
women "by the pussy."[17] This did not turn out to be the scandal that
doomed Trump's campaign. Trump never apologized, but instead pointed
to the behavior of Hillary Clinton's husband while he was president,

making this an issue about Clintonian and establishment hypocrisy. And indeed, his approval among his core supporters arguably grew in intensity, as suggested by the woman who was pictured at a rally soon after the scandal broke wearing a t-shirt on which she drew an arrow pointing down to her crotch under the words, "Trump can grab my."[18]

It would be wrong, however, to think that Trump won the election by simply delivering a populist message to the equivalent of taverners in the American populace. First, in the general election, white women overall preferred Trump to Clinton by a margin of 53–43%.[19] More significantly, during the Republican primaries, Trump beat his rivals by large margins even among voters with college and post-graduate degrees, albeit by smaller margins than among those with only a high school degree.[20] That is to say, it was not only as a Falstaffian populist candidate that Trump succeeded. He was also Hal.

Hal's story in the Henriad is that of moving from his status as an outcast to the ultimate insider who assuages and reassures the court as he takes the reins of power. A part of what distinguishes Hal, however, is how much he absorbs Falstaff and strategically exploits the lessons he learns from him. The biggest lesson he learns is how to deploy theatrical falsehood. In both parts of *Henry IV*, the scenes between Hal and his father Henry are thick with volatile tension as Henry berates Hal for not only his "degenerate" (*1 Henry IV*, 3.2.128) ways, but also for his seemingly total lack of filial piety. In Part 1, for example, Henry calls Hal a "scourge" (3.2.7) sent by Heaven to punish him for his misdeeds, before adding that Hal is also his "nearest and dearest enemy" (3.2.123). In Part 2, the tension explodes when Henry, weakened by illness, lies down to sleep in his chamber and Hal, coming upon him and thinking him dead, takes the crown and leaves. Upon waking, Henry discovers what happened and summons Hal back to his chamber to unleash an embittered tirade:

> Thy life did manifest thou lov'dst me not,
> And thou wilt have me die assured of it.
> Thou hid'st a thousand daggers in thy thoughts,
> Which thou hast whetted on thy stony heart,
> To stab at half an hour of my life.
> What! Canst thou not forbear me half an hour?
> Then get thee gone and dig my grave thyself… (*2 Henry IV*, 4.5.104–10)

In response, Hal delivers a self-exculpatory oration filled with alternative facts that perfectly answers the dramatic needs of the moment:

> Coming to look on you, thinking you dead,
> And dead almost, my liege, to think you were,
> I spake unto this crown as having sense,
> And thus upbraided it: "The care on thee depending
> Hath fed upon the body of my father;
> Therefore thou best of gold are worst of gold..." (4.5.155–60)

No, that is not what he had said unto the crown, but the theatrical dexterity in the finely calibrated rhythms and antitheses can only be admired, as I believe his father does. That is, I believe the father recognizes at this moment that his prodigal son has the requisite Machiavellian streak and ruthless capacity for mendacious manipulation to be King. Indeed, what follows is a moving recognition scene of sorts in which the father acknowledges the "indirect crook'd ways" by which he acquired the crown and dispenses advice that includes the notorious strategy, "Be it thy course to busy giddy minds/With foreign quarrels" (4.5.184–85, 213–14). There is an element of *The Godfather* here, when the aging Don Corleone (Marlon Brando) advises his son Michael (Al Pacino) about how to conduct the family business after he has died.

Hal has, however, always been one step ahead of the game. In the cognate scene of the above in Part 1 of *Henry IV*, the father similarly dispenses advice to Hal, though about how to manage his public image. He warns Hal essentially about over-exposure ("being daily swallowed by men's eyes," 3.2.70), especially through "vile participation" (3.2.87), that is, by being so "lavish of [his] presence" in "vulgar company" (3.2.39–41). However, being so engulfed in that tavern company turns out to be part of a grand, calculated scheme in which Hal will dramatically betray and abandon that company to stage a public drama of reformation. Early in Part 1, directly after a scene of seemingly genuine and intimate camaraderie with Falstaff and his crew, Hal turns to the audience to deliver a shocking soliloquy:

> I know you all, and will awhile uphold
> The unyoked humor of your idleness.
> Yet herein will I imitate the sun,
> Who doth permit the base contagious clouds

To smother up his beauty from the world,
That, when he please again to be himself,
Being wanted, he may be more wond'red at
By breaking through the foul and ugly mists
Of vapors that did seem to strangle him. (1.2.199–207)

He will, in other words, cast off his "base contagious" company so that his "reformation" will "show more goodly" (1.2.217–8) because of the contrast with his checkered past. I believe that there is genuine affection, and even deep love, between Hal and Falstaff, but Hal understands how exploitative Falstaff is, as indicated by the frequency with which Falstaff repeats the phrase "when thou art king" (1.2.16–7) when talking about their future together. Hence, even deep friendship takes a back seat to Hal's ambition and becomes another mutually exploitative relationship that is pervasive in the political sphere where winning at all costs is primary.

I do not wish to push the analogy too far, but if one sees Hal in Trump, then Falstaff can also be seen in Steve Bannon, the head of Breitbart News and the purveyor of alt.right alternative facts (though given Bannon's own ambitions, one could also make the case that Trump is Bannon's Falstaff to Bannon's Hal). Bannon is of course a dangerous and poisonous racist who is arguably more responsible than anyone else living for perverting and degrading internet discourse. He, more than anyone else, has blurred the distinction between fake and real news and stoked the carnival of fake news that fueled the Trump movement. It appears that for Bannon deceit became a very public principle because he saw so much deceit in the world of mainstream media and politics. Bannon was thus indispensable to Trump's rise, but no one can truly be indispensable in Trump's court-like White House. Seven turbulent months into his presidency with little to show by way of legislative accomplishment, Trump of course dismissed Bannon from his position as a top White House advisor. Trump seems to have felt the need, especially with the military man John Kelly having recently been installed as new Chief of Staff, to restore—at least for the moment—some respectability and establishment seriousness to his administration. One might imagine Trump thinking that Bannon was, as Hal calls Falstaff when he rejects him in public, "the tutor and the feeder of [his] riots" (5.5.63) whose dismissal would resonate symbolically to the advantage of his administration.

In this light, disturbing as Trump's early tenure has already been, the prospect of what might come is truly frightening. Trump is a man in whom a riotous need for power and self-advancement has crowded out anything else, including principles. Hence, nothing is safe from self-serving Machiavellian calculation. We might recall here that the biggest boost to his ratings that Trump received occurred after he ordered the bombing of Syria in April of 2017. Trump does not need Henry IV to tell him that going to war is the simplest way to distract people from domestic discontent and create unity. Trump's many unhinged Tweets about the supposed threat that North Korea's nuclear ambitions pose to the US raise the chilling possibility that, to boost his political fortunes, Trump would start a war in Korea and risk the instant loss of millions of Korean lives in both North and South Korea. Here we might return to the original point about "contained" subversion in the Henriad. The plays (along with those in the so-called first tetralogy of *1, 2, 3 Henry VI* and *Richard III*) take pains to depict the horrors of war (and tyranny); along with actual battle scenes, we are also given descriptions of suffering. Such scenes might be said to subvert the public rhetoric of war. Yet, as with scenes that expose the lies, fraudulent motivations and deceptive justifications for war, the scenes that depict the human costs of war can have the effect of not undermining the war but ultimately honoring human suffering as well as battlefield heroism and thus serve to glorify war. This is the scariest part. Whatever Shakespeare's intentions may have been, his history plays ultimately show us how dangerous and destructive it can be when lies form the foundation of power.

NOTES

1. For a great introduction to this topic, see Geoffrey Galt Harpham, "Foucault and the New Historicism," *American Literary History* 3.2 (1991): 360–75.
2. Ibid., 372.
3. *Henry V*, John Russell Brown, ed. (New York: The Signet Classic Shakespeare, 1988a): 5.3.60. All further references to this play will be to this text.
4. *1 Henry IV, Part 1*, Maynard Mack, ed. (New York: The Signet Classic Shakespeare, 1988b): 3.2.132. All further references to this play will be to this text.

5. E.M.W. Tillyard, *Shakespeare's History Plays* (London: Chatto & Windus, 1944), 17–21.

6. In his comprehensive study of the Morality pattern, Bernard Spivack, for instance, asserts that Falstaff's "banishment and imprisonment are regular punishments for the Vice" (Shakespeare and the Allegory of Evil [New York: Columbia Univ. Press, 1958], 204).

7. See, for example, Jonathan Dollimore and Alan Sinfield, "History and ideology: the instance of *Henry V*," in John Drakakis, ed. *Alternative Shakespeares* (London and New York: Methuen, 1985): 206–27.

8. See, for example, Graham Holderness's Shakespeare's History (New York: St. Martin's Press, 1985), in which he suggests that the plays "affirm the reality of historical transformation, and imagine the infinite possibilities of change" (131). In this connection, see also Walter Cohen, "Political Criticism of Shakespeare," in Shakespeare Reproduced: The Text in Ideology and History, ed. Jean E. Howard and Marion F. O'Conner (New York and London: Methuen, 1987), in which he challenges the "leftist disillusionment" (36) seen in new historicist emphasis on the "triumph of containment" (35), and attempts to retrieve the ways in which the Henry IV plays can generate "subversive religious, social, and political ideologies" (36). See also Michael Bristol, *Carnival and Theater* (NY: Methuen, 1985).

9. "Invisible Bullets," in *Shakespearean Negotiations* (Berkeley and Los Angeles: University of California Press), 55–6.

10. *Henry IV, Part 2*, Norman Holland, ed. (New York: The Signet Classic Shakespeare, 1988c), 4.5.213–14. All further references to this play will be to this text.

11. See, for example, C. L. Barber, *Shakespeare's Festive Comedy* (Princeton: Princeton University Press, 1959), especially, "Rule and Misrule in *Henry IV*."

12. Phillip Stubbes, *Anatomie of Abuses ... in the Country of Ailgna* (London, 1583), 148. Quoted in Barber, *Shakespeare's Festive Comedy*, 28.

13. *Rabelais and His World*, Hélène Iswolsky, trans. (Bloomington: Indiana University Press, 1984), 10.

14. See, for instance, A. P. Rossiter, *Angel with Horns* (NY: Theatre Arts Books, 1961), 46.

15. See, for instance, Muzaffar Chishti, Sarah Pierce, and Jessica Bolter, "The Obama Record on Deportations: Deporter in Chief or Not?" Migration Policy Institute, January 26, 2017: http://www.migrationpolicy.org/article/obama-record-deportations-deporter-chief-or-not.

16. See Donna Borak and Henry Williams, "Where Trump Stands on Wall Street," *The Wall Street Journal*, November 9, 2016: http://graphics.wsj.com/elections/2016/where-trump-stands-on-wall-street/.

17. For a video of the conversation and a transcript, see "Transcript: Donald Trump's Taped Comments About Women," *The New York Times*, October 8, 2016: https://www.nytimes.com/2016/10/08/us/donald-trump-tape-transcript.html?mcubz=0.
18. For a picture, see: https://www.mediaite.com/online/people-are-losing-it-over-a-woman-whose-shirt-says-trump-can-grab-her-you-know/.
19. See   FiveThirtyEight: https://fivethirtyeight.com/features/clinton-couldnt-win-over-white-women/.
20. See Jeff Manza and Ned Crowley, "Working Class Hero? Interrogating the Social Bases of the Rise of Donald Trump," *The Forum* 15.1 (2017): 3–28.

References

Bakhtin, Mikhail. *Rabelais and His World*. Translated by Hélène Iswolsky. Bloomington: Indiana University Press, 1984.

Barber, C.L. *Shakespeare's Festive Comedy*. Princeton: Princeton University Press, 1959.

Bristol, Michael. *Carnival and Theater*. New York: Methuen, 1985.

Cohen, Graham. "Political Criticism of Shakespeare." In *Shakespeare Reproduced: The Text in Ideology and History*, eds. Jean E. Howard and Marion F. O'Conner. New York and London: Methuen, 1987.

Dollimore, Jonathan, and Alan Sinfield. "History and Ideology: The Instance of *Henry V*." In *Alternative Shakespeares*, ed. John Drakakis. London and New York: Methuen, 1985.

Greenblatt, Stephen. *Shakespearean Negotiations*. Berkeley and Los Angeles: University of California Press, 1988.

Harpham, Geoffrey Galt. "Foucault and the New Historicism." *American Literary History* 3, no. 2 (1991): 360–75.

Holderness, Graham. *Shakespeare's History*. New York: St. Martin's Press, 1985.

Manza, Jeff, and Ned Crowley. "Working Class Hero? Interrogating the Social Bases of the Rise of Donald Trump." *The Forum* 15, no. 1 (2017): 3–28.

Rossiter, A.P. *Angel with Horns*. New York: Theatre Arts Books, 1961.

Shakespeare, William. *Henry V*. Edited by John Russell Brown. New York: The Signet Classic Shakespeare, 1988a.

———. *1 Henry IV, Part 1*. Edited by Maynard Mack. New York: The Signet Classic Shakespeare, 1988b.

———. *Henry IV, Part 2*. Edited by Norman Holland. New York: The Signet Classic Shakespeare, 1988c.

Spivack, Bernard. *Shakespeare and the Allegory of Evil*. New York: Columbia University Press, 1958.

Tillyard, E.M.W. *Shakespeare's History Plays*. London: Chatto & Windus, 1944.

CHAPTER 10

Knave, Patriot, or Factionist: Three Rousseauian Hypotheses About the Election of President Trump

Joseph Reisert

Donald Trump personifies everything that Rousseau loathed and wanted to exclude from his ideal republic. In that republic, based on the principles of popular sovereignty and the rule of law, free and equal citizens would all have the right to vote on the nation's fundamental laws and to choose the public officials who would apply them. In that ideal republic, a broad and deep popular consensus would support the essential elements of the constitution, and the people would choose as public officials persons outstanding for their personal and civic virtue and for their demonstrated capacity to promote the public good.

Consider, then, what Rousseau might think of President Trump. The Genevan was famously critical of the rich, whom he characterized as "insolent and low, sensitive and delicate towards [themselves] alone," and he especially objected to their "ostentatious luxury" (E 345).[1] Trump is fabulously wealthy, notoriously thin-skinned, and his name a byword for gaudy excess. Rousseau disparaged cities as "the abyss of the human species" (E 59) and preached the virtues of rural life, having written that "one of the examples good men ought to give others" is the "rustic life" (E 474).

J. Reisert (✉)
Colby College, Waterville, ME, USA

© The Author(s) 2018
A. Jaramillo Torres, M. B. Sable (eds.), *Trump and Political Philosophy*,
https://doi.org/10.1007/978-3-319-74445-2_10

163

Trump is a New York real estate developer, who makes his home in Manhattan. Rousseau objected to gambling, "the fruit of avarice and boredom" (E 348); Trump put his name on Atlantic City casinos. Rousseau advocated chastity before and life-long faithfulness within marriage (E 324; see also J 292ff). Trump is twice divorced and has boasted in the most ungentlemanly terms of his sexual conquests and infidelities. Rousseau celebrated the strict integrity and austere virtue of Cato the Younger (PE 16, 25) and constantly expressed reverence for the rule of law (see e.g., LM 234, 260–1); Trump has been dogged by accusations of sharp dealing in his business enterprises and dishonesty in his public statements, and he has unsettled critics by his apparent disdain for the forms of law.

Nevertheless, Rousseau's political thought suggests three useful hypotheses to consider as possible explanations for Trump's ascent to the presidency. First is the *clever knave hypothesis*. Trump may be a "clever knave" and "insinuating talker" who took advantage both of the people's corruption and a fundamental weakness in our constitutional design—the absence of any institutional *cursus honorum*—to win the presidency (SC 4.1.3). According to this hypothesis, Trump's voters have been played for fools; they have mistaken the appearance of business success for the ability to govern in the public interest and allowed nostalgia for an imaginary past of American greatness to blind them to the many reasons to doubt that Trump's agenda or leadership will achieve what they hope.

Second, consider the *patriotism hypothesis*. The popularity of Trump's patriotic, "American greatness" agenda may vindicate Rousseau's empirical concern that cosmopolitan ideas would be unable to attract the passionate, ongoing support needed to sustain a viable polity; according to this hypothesis, Trump won the presidency by insisting—contrary to an important strand of contemporary, progressive thinking—that the government of the United States should primarily seek to advance the interests of citizens of the United States, rather than to act in some more impartial manner to promote global welfare. According to this view, Trump's voters are not fools at all; he spoke to and for the people who bristle at the phrase, "citizen of the world" but who proudly identify as citizens of the United States.

Third is the *partial society hypothesis*. Trump won as the candidate of a "faction," or a "partial society" (SC 2.3.3-4)—a response to, and an acceleration of a trend toward the dissolution of the United States of America into "two states in one" (SC 4.2.2). Rousseau used that expression to describe the condition of ancient Rome when it was divided between the Patrician and Plebeian orders, but it may be feared that the contemporary division between "Red America" and "Blue America" is emerging as equally fixed and equally acrimonious as that between Rome's class of hereditary nobles and its commoners. On this view, Trump's voters endorsed him not because they thought he would advance the interests of all Americans, but because he would fight for the "reds" against the "blues" in a zero-sum struggle to establish mastery over the other.

Before examining any of these hypotheses further, a fundamental objection must be addressed. It may be objected that any effort to examine contemporary American politics through a Rousseauian lens is fundamentally misguided. If the Jean-Jacques Rousseau we know from his writings would have detested Donald Trump, it is equally clear that the Genevan would have found much to condemn in contemporary America, which in obvious respects seems an unlikely place to interpret in light of Rousseau's political ideals. Rousseau stated explicitly that he could not see how the sovereignty of the people could be preserved except in a "very small" city (SC 3.15.12) where the citizens could assemble in person to show themselves to the government as sovereign; for that reason, he advocated only small states—ideally centered on a single city—rather than large ones, with vast territories and many population centers, such as the United States (SC 3.13.6). Hence he claims in the *Letters Written from the Mountain* that he took Geneva's constitution as "the model of political institutions" (LM 9:233). Moreover, Rousseau worried deeply about the politically corrupting consequences of economic inequality and therefore favored a simple and agrarian way of life, with substantially autarchic households and minimal commerce, as one sees in his *Plan for a Constitution for Corsica*. Finally, he frequently expressed deep pessimism about the prospects for freedom in the modern world, writing in the *Discourse on Inequality* that his philosophical history of humanity in that work should serve as a warning to "unhappy posterity" (DI 133) and observing in the *Social Contract* that, though barbarous peoples can "gain" freedom, civilized peoples that lose their freedom—as he thought France and England were soon to do—can never recover it (SC 2.8.4).

ROUSSEAU'S PRINCIPLES AND AMERICAN PRACTICE

Despite Rousseau's pessimism about the conditions under which his political ideals could be realized, there are nevertheless good reasons to think that modern constitutional and democratic states have to a large degree instantiated them. That claim will surely be controversial, but I have argued for it at length elsewhere.[2] Here, a summary of those arguments will have to suffice.

First, we must recognize that Rousseau presents his principles of political right as universal principles, applicable everywhere and for all time. In *Emile*, he explains that they establish the "standard" by which the "political [i.e., constitutional] laws of each country" are to be judged (E 458). These principles are derived, he writes in the *Social Contract*, "from the nature of things" and are "founded on reason" (SC 1.4.10). Likewise, he insists that the "real foundations of human society" are the same everywhere: civil right (*le droit civil*) is founded in the social contract that establishes "the Law and the right of property" (DI 125–26, 182; see also 173–74). Neither in the *Discourse on Inequality* nor in the *Social Contract* nor in the *Emile* does he present his theories about the origin and foundations of political societies as accounts that apply only to some especially well-constituted society. Instead, he states emphatically: "the social contract is the basis of every civil society" (E 460). Moreover, the terms of this social contract, Rousseau asserts, are "everywhere the same, everywhere tacitly admitted and recognized" (SC 1.6.5).

That is to say, Rousseau explicitly presents himself as trying to explain the normative logic underpinning the political societies he knew from history and experience—not only that of Geneva, but also of the Kingdom of France, and of the United Kingdom, the Republic of Venice, and of Republican and Imperial Rome, and all the rest. Of course not every state is a "political society"; some are despotisms, ruled by force alone (DI 185–86). But Rousseau clearly indicates that not all monarchies are despotisms: he presents Julius Caesar and Augustus as "genuine Monarchs", whose rule he pointedly contrasts with the "despotism of Tiberius" (SC 3.10.3, note). Nor does he ever suggest that the great states of Europe in his own day had been reduced to that dire condition, and there is good reason to think that this was a reasonable judgment, at least with respect to France, the state where Rousseau lived when he composed his major political works.[3]

Of course, *ancien régime* France fell far short of fully embodying Rousseau's normative principles. But the law to some extent reflected the people's settled notions of what the laws should be (and so to that extent could be said to express their general will), to some degree protected the basic rights of the people, and in some ways constrained the actions of the government. Clearly, it was no despotism. It was, we may say, an *imper-*

fectly constituted state—somewhere on a continuum between what we should call the *perfectly constituted state*, in which all of Rousseau's principles are fully instantiated, and despotism, where the government completely dominates the people by force, as a master rules slaves (DI 185–86; see also SC 3.10.10). Rousseau rarely speaks explicitly in the *Social Contract* about such imperfectly constituted states, but he indicates clearly that there exist degrees of corruption or imperfect constitution: In SC 4.1 he describes an imperfectly constituted state in which "the social knot [has begun] to loosen," which he contrasts with one that is "close to ruin," where "the social bond is broken in all hearts," and is therefore still less well constituted—but even this condition is not yet despotism, which represents for Rousseau the extreme end point at which the civil order breaks down and the state of nature is re-established (SC 4.1.4–5; DI 186).

What then are these universal principles of right? They can be found in the *Social Contract*, the work whose subtitle is *Principles of Political Right*. Rousseau does not provide a list, but I have argued that we can find seven principles, all familiar from the contemporary practice of liberal constitutionalism, in the *Contract*[4]:

1. *Popular sovereignty.* The people as a whole have the right to determine their own form of government, to enact the laws—which are to reflect the people's general will—and to elect the officials who will administer the laws (SC 2.1.1–2).

2. *Constitutional law.* The powers of the governing institutions are to be specified in a fundamental law that cannot be changed without the people's consent (SC 3.17.2, 3.18.7).

3. *Representative government.* The government is a body of officials distinct from the people and answerable to the people, responsible for translating the people's general will into specific actions (SC 3.1.6).

4. *The rule of law.* Public officials are forbidden from expanding their own powers beyond those granted them by the constitution, and they, like all other citizens, are obliged to follow the ordinary criminal and civil laws on the same terms as other citizens (SC 2.6.4–9).

5. *Periodic elections.* No government is fully legitimate if the holders of public office are not subject to periodic election by the people (SC 3.13.1–2, 3.18.5).

6. *Universal suffrage.* All citizens must have the right to vote (SC 4.1.7).[5]

7. *Equal basic rights.* The end of the state is the protection of freedom and civil equality (SC 2.11.1); such freedom is to be secured on terms that are equal for all (SC 2.4.5).

In the United States, the people are sovereign: the Constitution was issued in the name of "We the people of the United States" and derives its authority from a process of ratification that was both remarkably inclusive for its time and substantially independent of the nascent national government and of the existing state governments. The government—including not only the staffs of the administrative agencies, but also the public officials Rousseau would regard as magistrates, including the president and members of Congress—is answerable to the people. We have periodic, universal suffrage elections; we pride ourselves on our commitment to the rule of law and to the protection of equal rights for all.

Notwithstanding all the ways in which our political practice corresponds to the principles of political right developed in the *Social Contract*, Rousseau's critique of the use of representatives in the British Parliament seems to entail a fundamental rejection of modern forms of government, with representative legislatures (SC 3.15.5). If we read Rousseau carefully, however, we find that what he condemns so vehemently is the idea of parliamentary *sovereignty*; Rousseau's principles require that the powers of elected officials must be limited by some fundamental, constitutional law grounded in the general will of the people. Even so, his dictum that "any law which the People has not ratified in person is null" (SC 3.15.5) apparently stands as a sharp condemnation of contemporary practice. This maxim, however, stands in tension with the more flexible observation elsewhere in the *Contract* that the "commands of the chiefs" may be regarded as laws, if the people is "free to oppose them and does not do so." (SC 2.1.4). It should also be noted that much of the work of modern legislatures is executive in Rousseau's sense of the term—spending money, sharing in the conduct of foreign policy, translating constitutional mandates into acts regulating specific modes of conduct. Even so, it is clear that modern representative legislatures do not precisely embody Rousseau's institutional recommendations, but insofar as their strictly legislative powers are limited by fundamental constitutional principles reflecting the people's reasonably settled judgment and their legislative determinations are subject to revision (by subsequently elected legislatures), they may be seen as a reasonable, albeit imperfect, instantiation of his principles.

It is also widely believed that Rousseau's account of the general will demands a conception of social unity is incompatible with liberal, constitutional government. But that is not so. Recall that Rousseau introduces the idea of the social pact in order to explain "what makes it so that the state is one" (LM 231). That is, he introduces the idea of the social pact to articulate the conditions under which individuals should, and are in general, empirically likely to, feel and act like fellow-citizens. Although Rousseau's text makes the terms of the pact sound forbidding, they are simple enough: what makes a nation of citizens is the existence of many individuals who jointly and severally agree to obey the laws, in exchange for the guarantee of equal treatment under the laws and for an equal voice in making them (SC 1.6). That moral attitude of wholehearted citizenship is a general will; those who share in that general will are fellow-citizens. Moreover, Rousseau argues that the fundamental terms of the citizens' common life together—the laws—must also be willed generally by the citizens. That is, the law should reflect what "we the people" sincerely decide is good for all of us, collectively (SC 2.6.5).

To be sure, many people in the United States are alienated from the regime. But millions more do regard themselves as wholehearted citizens and willingly obey the laws, not out of fear of punishment, but out of a sense of duty. Given the immense complexity of modern life, it is doubtful whether even one person knows all the laws and administrative regulations under which we must all live. But the basic terms of our common life in society are not hard to understand: we must respect the rights of others and carry our fair share of the financial and other burdens of society, and in return we can expect our rights to be protected and to be aided by society when we are in great need. For all our political disagreements about matters of detail—what the tax rates should be, how social policies are to be designed, how best to protect the natural environment, and all the rest—there is broad and deep agreement on these basic terms.

A CLEVER KNAVE

Rousseau assumed that readers of the *Social Contract* would dismiss his republican ideal as unrealistic, assuming the people to be too foolish to vote wisely: "They laugh as they imagine all the nonsense of which a clever knave or an insinuating talker could persuade the people of Paris or London." What misleads such critics, he argues, is that "they see only states which are badly constituted.... They do not know that Cromwell would have been condemned to hard labor by the people of Berne, and the Duc de Beaufort to the reformatory by the Genevans" (SC 4.1.3). He argues that, in well-constituted states, the people can be trusted to vote on the laws and to elect "the most capable and the most upright among their fellow-citizens" to "govern the state" (DI 117). It would be difficult to maintain that President Trump is either the "most capable" public administrator or the "most upright" of Americans. Thus we are led to our first hypothesis: Perhaps Trump is a "clever knave" and "insinuating talker," who has duped the people into voting on the basis of something other than their best judgment about what would promote the common good. In light of Rousseau's suggestion that such persons could only come to power in a badly constituted state, we must consider also the possibility that our state is, indeed defective in some way, or that it has become so. (Note, too, that Cromwell and de Beaufort were both factional leaders in their respective nations' civil wars; we will consider the possibility that Trump may be the factional leader of "red" America as our third hypothesis, below.)

Rousseau says relatively little about the proper design of governmental institutions in the *Social Contract*, but he does insist that they will necessarily vary, according to circumstances (SC 3.3.7). Not surprisingly, he says almost nothing in that work about the institutions that should be used to select candidates for public offices. Presumably, he would favor institutions that enabled the people to select among a few candidates conspicuous for their "talents and virtue" (DI 120), while also assuring that the candidate selection process did not so restrict the people's choices as to render the government independent of the voters—something for which he pointedly criticizes the constitution of Geneva (LM 246). In the *Considerations on the Government of Poland*, however, Rousseau suggests one institutional mechanism for selecting candidates for public office. He proposes a system of "graduated promotions": only those who had faithfully performed all the duties of the lowest office would be eligible to stand as candidates for the next office in the sequence; only those who had performed well at the second rank would be eligible for the third; and so on (CGP 239–43). Rousseau argues that, where this institution is established, "no one, from the least individual to the foremost [official]," will see "any way of advancing but on the road of duty and public approbation" (CGP 252). At the apex of the *cursus honorum* Rousseau designed for Poland stands the office of the king, whom he envisions as a chief magistrate, much like the president of the United States.

If the American Constitution had imposed a strict *cursus honorum*, Donald Trump could not have been elected president, because he has never before held any public office, either civilian or military. Indeed, he is the first person to become president never to have held any prior office in the public sector. For most of the history of our republic, there was a strong, albeit unwritten, constitutional norm that one have previously served the public in some official capacity before becoming president. Minor party candidates have often had little or no prior experience in public office, but with few exceptions they have drawn negligible support. Major party candidates have generally had significant public-sector experience. In recent years, however, the electorate has looked increasingly favorably on "outsider" candidates for the presidency. To the extent that prior public service had been a constitutional norm, the Republican Party rejected it by nominating Trump, and a constitutional majority of voters confirmed that decision by electing him to the presidency. Why?

One hypothesis is that Trump indeed is a clever knave, who succeeded in fooling the voters into mistaking rudeness for courage, insult for integrity, vulgar splendor for magnificence, financial success for practical wisdom, and boasting for magnanimity. Perhaps, too, voters today are also poor judges of political virtue. Just as one must be at least moderately musical to distinguish the truly great performer from a merely competent one, so also must one have a degree of prudence and virtue to identify these traits in others. As our republic has grown larger, a smaller share of the public has ever held any local office; increasingly, we are compelled to leave the management of public affairs to others and so have no personal experience of the demands of public leadership. The difficulty of judgment is enormously compounded when ordinary citizens must judge the virtues of political candidates at a distance—by way of TV and Twitter. No wonder, then, that our candidates seem to have become ever more telegenic and media savvy. The election of a reality TV star with a mass Twitter following may then be the natural, if regrettable, outcome of the decline of civic experience and civic virtue in the public.

Another possibility is that Trump voters had good reason for abandoning the unwritten constitutional norm against electing inexperienced men to the highest public office in the land. One of Rousseau's great complaints in the *Letters Written from the Mountain* is that it doesn't matter who gets elected to lead the Republic of Geneva as First Syndic, because they all act on the same principles, and they do the same thing—which is to advance the interest of the ruling elite at the expense of the people (LM 246). The central, animating concern of Rousseau's whole political theory is the preservation of the people's sovereignty—its ability to make laws for itself and to choose magistrates, answerable to itself, who will serve its will—from the threat of usurpation by the government (SC 3 *passim*). Rousseau knew all too well that the natural tendency of ruling elites is to perpetuate themselves and to insulate their own power and position, even against the legitimate claims of the people they are nominally obligated to serve.

The increasing appeal of "outsider" candidates may well reflect the suspicion that our own government is beginning to succumb to this fate. On this theory, a vote for Trump was a calculated risk: yes, he's an "outsider" with no prior experience of public service and conspicuous for his brash disregard of the norms of political behavior—but some may have judged that only such a person would be willing and able to "drain the swamp." To the extent that this judgment is sound, the opening of the highest political office to political novices should be seen, not exactly as a step in the decline of the republic as an institutional adaptation to mitigate the effects of the increasing corruption of the republic (see SC 4.4.36).

Patriotism Versus Cosmopolitanism

Elections are not only about the character of the candidates but also about the substantive policies they advocate. Although Donald Trump the man exhibits few of the virtues Rousseau advised his readers to seek in political leaders, some of his key policy proposals correspond surprisingly well with Rousseau's political principles. Substantively, candidate Trump advocated an "American greatness" agenda that included three principal components: (1) Restricting immigration, and especially unlawful immigration, to protect the interests of those who are now American citizens; (2) Protectionism rather than free trade, with the aim of keeping or generating "good jobs" at home, rather than abroad; (3) Re-ordering US foreign policy around the promotion of American interests, narrowly or perhaps parochially understood. In short, and at the risk of considerably oversimplifying: Trump's substantive argument was that the American government has a special duty to promote the well-being of American citizens, and no duties at all to non-Americans. Corresponding to Trump's conception of government is a particular conception of patriotism: American citizens should take pride simply in being American; we should love our fellow-citizens and our country first, and strive to make it great or perhaps "great again," because we love it.

Trump's view of the purpose of government may be contrasted with a liberal, internationalist perspective according to which governments generally should be concerned with promoting the welfare of all, as close to impartially as possible. The accident of being born in one place rather than another is morally irrelevant: whatever rights and interests people have are common to all human beings as such. A government that too vigorously worked to advance the interests of its own nationals would, on this view, risk violating the demands of impartiality and justice. To the liberal internationalist, Trump's brand of patriotism is still more problematic. Trump's bitterest critics assume that his conception of "American" includes only white people, so that his ostensibly patriotic appeals are actually coded appeals to white supremacy. Even if they are not so intended, Trump's patriotism still represents a sharp departure from the cosmopolitanism of the liberal internationalist who aspires to be a "citizen of the world." If we truly acknowledge the equality of all persons, everywhere, we should not love our country more than others, simply because it is our own; the only valid ground of pride is what is good. To assert otherwise is chauvinistic at best and racist at worst—in short, deplorable.

Rousseau acknowledges the abstract truth of a moral universalism that regards "all men as children of the same God" and "brothers" in a "perfect society" (SC 4.8.20–2; see also LM 147–49). But he insists that the disinterested love of humanity cannot provide the foundations for a political society that would effectively protect people from oppression. The basic problem is that we are moved only by what happens to people we see and feel in some way close to ourselves; writes Rousseau, "the sentiment of humanity dissipates and weakens as it spreads to the whole earth" (PE 15). He continues: "interest and commiseration must in some way be constricted and compressed in order to be activated" (PE 15). What life in civil society demands of us is difficult and often contrary to our natural instincts: we must respect the rights of others, even to our own immediate disadvantage; we must embrace the impartiality demanded by law, rather than give preferences to our friends and kin. That is why Rousseau insists that we must be "denatured" to become citizens (E 40).

Rousseau's social contract specifies the conditions under which it is reasonable for one to subordinate one's personal interests and preferences to the demands of the law. Each citizen agrees, on his own account, to abide by the laws; all the members collectively undertake to protect the equal citizenship of each and every member, so that each citizen will enjoy the same scheme of basic rights as all the rest, including the rights of political participation (SC 1.7.1). Rousseau insists that all our legally-enforceable rights derive from the social contract, and that strictly speaking we have neither rights nor duties toward outsiders, who are not members of our particular political society (SC 1.8.1). Thus, for example, he argues that, with respect to our fellow citizens, our property rights are grounded in the social pact, but the territorial claims of the state rest on the rather more equivocal assertion of the "right of the first occupant" (SC 1.9.1–2). In like fashion, he insists that while any laws that "we the people" have wholeheartedly adopted must be just, there is no parallel guarantee that the laws of any one state will deal justly with the peoples of others. In short, Rousseau maintains that legal rights and duties are strictly correlative—and limited to citizens. It follows straightforwardly that the fundamental task of government is to promote the well-being of the citizens, and that governments have no duties to non-citizens.

Patriotism, Rousseau argues, provides the motive for citizens to obey the law. "Certain it is," he writes, "that the greatest marvels of virtue have been produced by … this gentle and lively sentiment which combines the force of *amour-propre* with all the beauty of virtue" (PE 30). The virtue he refers to here is the "conformity of the particular will to the general will," which is to say the willingness to obey the laws (PE 25). The patriotism Rousseau advocates cannot long be sustained by propaganda or coercion; people will truly love their country only when they see the advantages that citizenship confers. How will people love their country, Rousseau asks, if their country "is nothing more to them than it is to foreigners, and grants them only what it cannot refuse to anyone?" (PE 16). To inspire patriotic affection, the state must, at a minimum, protect the lives and liberties of the citizens (PE 17–19); additionally, it should "provide for the public needs" so that "plenty" is "so within [the citizens'] reach that, in order to acquire it, work is always necessary and never useless" (PE 23). Where the state secures the conditions for citizens to live well, there is every reason for the citizens to love their state. Note, finally, that a government that would inspire patriotism must not only establish the material conditions under which the citizens may flourish, the rulers must also respect the citizens' dignity, acknowledging their collective sovereignty. Thus Rousseau pointedly advises rulers to "respect [their] fellow citizens" (PE 19), to show the people "gratitude" and "esteem" for their political support and obedience (DI 120).

The similarities with Trump's campaign agenda are evident. On immigration, Trump favored ending policies that treat persons not lawfully present in the country with the same solicitude as citizens and lawful residents. "Building the wall" is the clearest possible embodiment of Trump's determination to prefer the interests of those already "in" to those of outsiders—foreigners—who would seek to improve their own life prospects by breaking our laws. On trade, Trump proposes to use the "art of the deal" to re-draw commercial treaties so that they will benefit Americans more than he thinks they have done in the past. In foreign policy, candidate Trump was very skeptical of American foreign commitments and insisted that he wants to use American power in ways that directly advance American interests. As we have seen, Rousseau thinks citizens can only be expected to love their country when their country and its government puts their interests first—that is, above the interests of outsiders. Hence the *patriotism hypothesis*: perhaps Trump's victory vindicates Rousseau's empirical concern that cosmopolitan universalism is, at best, too disinterested a commitment to motivate strong political attachment, or is at worst a mask for elite contempt for their neighbors and fellow-citizens (see E 39; compare GM 158).

None of the foregoing is to deny that important strands of Rousseau's thought suggest critiques of Trump's agenda. Most notably, Rousseau consistently expressed hostility to finance and commerce (see e.g., SC 3.15.2) and presented a simple, self-sufficient, rural, and agrarian way of life as ideal (most notably, in the *Constitutional Project for Corsica*). Likewise, he warns citizens against the desire for military greatness, on the grounds that wars provide a pretext, and a strong military the means, for the rulers to suppress the public freedom (PE 28–29). These are, however, primarily critiques of the modern American regime as such, which is a continent-spanning, urbanized, commercial republic, with powerful military forces and a global network of treaties and interests that have regularly embroiled our country in overseas conflicts.

The patriotism hypothesis presents a fairly optimistic interpretation of Trump's success and entails a relatively benign view of his supporters, who are—on this view—responding favorably, as should be expected given the reality of human nature, to the promise of treating citizens better than aliens. If these are Trump's principles, he should promote a "one nation" patriotism that clearly rejects any direct or indirect appeal to race and religion: he should work for the benefit of all those who are, by our laws, already citizens (or permanent residents), and he should make American national interests, rather than global welfare, the touchstone of his economic and foreign policies.

Two States in One

A more pessimistic interpretation of the present moment suggests that our country is becoming increasingly divided into two "partial societies"— Red (conservative, rural and small-town) America and Blue (progressive, big-city, coastal) America—as divided by interests, culture, and mores as the Patricians and Plebeians of ancient Rome. Those two orders, writes Rousseau, were "so to speak, two States in one," each relatively homogeneous, and each with its own interests and its own general will: the Plebeians wanted what was good for themselves, just as the Patricians sought the perpetuation of their own advantages (SC 4.2.2). As such "partial societies" grow in strength, Rousseau warns, the more difficult it is for the citizens to formulate and express a will that is general with respect to the body of all the citizens, rather than one that is general only with respect to their faction (SC 2.3.4).

The division between the two Americas does not map neatly onto the Plebeian/Patrician divide; Rome's Patricians were a hereditary caste of nobility, few in number, but wealthy and influential. Our divisions are cultural and matters of education and economic interest, and our two factions far more nearly equal in size. But the Red-Blue divide resembles the division Rousseau describes in one notable respect: just as "the people's plebiscites were always carried quietly and by a large majority," so also in this election we saw a huge number of "landslide" counties—where one or other candidate won by a considerable margin (SC 2.4.2). Thus we are led to our final possibility, the *partial society hypothesis*: perhaps Trump should be seen not as a patriotic, albeit deeply flawed man, but as a vicious factionist—the leader of Red America against Blue America, and thus our analog of Cromwell or the Duc de Beaufort (SC 4.1.3). Note that there are two ways Trump's presidency may deepen the divisions between the two Americas. He may prove himself in action to be a committed factionist—refusing to make any good faith effort to promote the interests of all, but instead seeking to advance the interests of the Reds against the Blues in a way that strengthens the power of the Red faction at the expense of a common, American identity. Or he may prove also, or instead, to be an unwitting factionist—which may be the case if the Blues turn so sharply against him and the "deplorable" people who voted for him that they increasingly think of themselves primarily as "Blue Americans" rather than simply as "Americans."

Political theory cannot tell us which of these hypotheses is true; indeed, all of them might be true, with respect to different actors. But political theory can provide us with some guidance, as we seek to understand this extraordinary time in the history of our republic.

NOTES

1. References to the works of Rousseau will appear parenthetically in the text. Page numbers are given except in the case of the *Social Contract*, for which citations indicate the book, chapter, and paragraph. The following abbreviations are used: CGP, "Considerations on the Government of Poland" in Jean-Jacques Rousseau, *The Social Contract and Other Later Political Writings*, ed. and trans. by Victor Gourevitch (New York: Cambridge University Press, 1997) [hereafter LPW]; DI, "Discourse on the Origin and Foundations of Inequality Among Men" in Jean-Jacques Rousseau, *The Discourses and Other Early Political Writings*, ed. and trans. by Victor Gourevitch (New York: Cambridge University Press, 1997); E, Jean-Jacques Rousseau, *Emile, or On Education*, trans. by Allan Bloom (New York: Basic Books, Inc., 1979); GM, "Geneva Manuscript" in Gourevitch, LPW; J, Jean-Jacques Rousseau, *Julie or the New Heloise*, trans. by Philip Stewart and Jean Vaché, *Collected Writings of Rousseau*, Vol. 6, series ed. by Roger Masters and Christopher Kelly (Hanover, NH: University Press of New England, 1997); LM, *Letters Written from the Mountain* in Jean-Jacques Rousseau, *Letter to Beaumont, Letters Written from the Mountain, and Related Writings*, ed. by Christopher Kelly and Eve Grace, trans. by Christopher Kelly and Judith R. Bush, *Collected Writings of Rousseau*, Vol. 9, series ed. by Roger Masters and Christopher Kelly (Hanover, NH: University Press of New England, 2001); PE, "Discourse on Political Economy" in Gourevitch, LPW; SC, *Of the Social Contract* in Gourevitch, LPW.
2. In my book manuscript, *The General Will and Constitutional Democracy*, forthcoming.
3. See, for example, Alexis de Tocqueville's account of the various constraints on the French monarchy under the ancien regime, *The Old Regime and the French Revolution*, trans. Stuart Gilbert (Garden City, NY: Anchor Doubleday Books, 1955), 116–18.
4. This enumeration is adapted from the introduction to *The General Will and Constitutional Democracy.*
5. Rousseau, of course, supported the exclusion of women from the franchise; his arguments for that conclusion do not persuade, and it is noteworthy that he made no reference to them in the *Social Contract.*

REFERENCES

Rousseau, Jean-Jacques. *Emile, or On Education*. Translated by Allan Bloom. New York: Basic Books, Inc., 1979.

——. *The Discourses and Other Early Political Writings*. Edited and Translated by Victor Gourevitch. New York: Cambridge University Press, 1997a.

——. *Julie or the New Heloise*. Translated by Philip Stewart and Jean Vaché. Vol. 6 of *The Collected Writings of Rousseau*, ed. Roger Masters and Christopher Kelly. Hanover, NH: University Press of New England, 1997b.

——. *The Social Contract and Other Later Political Writings*. Edited and Translated by Victor Gourevitch. New York: Cambridge University Press, 1997c.

——. *Letter to Beaumont, Letters Written from the Mountain, and Related Writings*. Edited by Christopher Kelly and Eve Grace and Translated by Christopher Kelly and Judith R. Bush. Vol. 9 of *The Collected Writings of Rousseau*, ed. Roger Masters and Christopher Kelly. Hanover, NH: University Press of New England, 2001.

Tocqueville, Alexis de. *The Old Regime and the French Revolution*. Translated by Stuart Gilbert. Garden City, NY: Doubleday Anchor Books, 1955.

CHAPTER 11

Trump and *The Federalist* on National Greatness in a Commercial Republic

Arthur Milikh

The success of Donald Trump's presidential campaign can be attributed in no small part to his promise to "Make America Great Again." This promise is more than a catchy campaign slogan—it invites us to think through Trump's analysis of the nation's health and to reflect on the meaning of greatness. In an American context, the clearest articulation of national greatness is found in *The Federalist*, the authors of which understood themselves to be founding a great nation. Publius considered deeply both the meaning of national greatness and its causes. Trump and Publius, as we will see, agree on certain critical points.[1]

For Publius, commerce serves as the means by which America will develop its peculiar form of greatness. Successful commerce, combined with naval power, in turn, is a means to achieving national sovereignty—the freeing of the nation insofar as possible from external compulsion and thereby securing its ability to choose for itself. Our republican principles require our form of national greatness. Both Publius and Trump understand that striving for national greatness is less a choice than a necessity, given the consequences of national weakness. Both Publius and Trump understand, moreover, that citizens must believe that they are part

A. Milikh (✉)
Arthur Milikh is the Associate Director of the B. Kenneth Simon Center for Principles and Politics at The Heritage Foundation, Washington D.C., USA

© The Author(s) 2018
A. Jaramillo Torres, M. B. Sable (eds.), *Trump and Political Philosophy*,
https://doi.org/10.1007/978-3-319-74445-2_11

179

of a nation worthy of their respect, which depends on pride in republican self-government. Since the space provided for this essay does not permit a comprehensive account of greatness as such for Publius, we will focus mainly on the means of obtaining it. But before, we should turn to the political landscape which Trump so deftly navigated, which accounted for the broad appeal of "Making America Great Again."

PROGRESSIVISM VERSUS REPUBLICANISM

For more than a generation, progressive doctrines alleging the moral illegitimacy of America on account of its irremediable bigotry, sexism, and xenophobia have sought to make citizens despise rather than to revere their nation.[2] While these doctrines had long existed in the academy, President Obama, for the first time, brought them into the White House and used the force of law to advance them.[3] To understand the popular appeal of Trump's promise to "Make America Great Again," we might reflect on these progressive doctrines from the *perspective of a citizen*. As we will see, these doctrines entail a paradoxical combination of determinism and boundless freedom, the combination of which is hostile to the self-respect necessary for citizens and for republican self-government.

Many progressives allege that deeply embedded, invisible superstructures—patriarchal, racial, xenophobic, classist—of American society so deform certain citizens' minds that even the well-meaning, not to mention the direct beneficiaries of these superstructures, are determined by them.[4] From a citizen's perspective, acceptance of these assertions requires some degree of self-loathing, accompanied by the view that the only noble course of action available is to reject these superstructures and to aspire to transform the country built upon them.[5] The high-minded must dutifully disassemble America's oppressive institutions—courts, families, churches, perhaps even the Constitution—until the aggrieved sound the bell of satisfaction. The lovable America, accordingly, is one that does not yet exist.

Gaining rational consent through persuasion for dismantling these institutions is presumably impossible because of the moral and intellectual deformities caused by these superstructures to their beneficiaries. Citizens must thus be ridiculed, intimidated, or even forced to reform themselves and these institutions. Again, from a citizens' perspective, these doctrines teach that almost nothing about their nation is lovable; that their pride cannot be attached to it, and that they cannot find their self-respect through it. This alleged structural determinism stands at odds with republican self-rule: A nation cannot be both great and determined by dehumanizing superstructures—for greatness, in the republican sense, implies anti-determinism, or the freedom to rule oneself.

If republican self-rule is dismissed as a political ideal, so too are its central components, one of which is national sovereignty. Accordingly, the public need not have authority, for instance, over whether it can control its borders. Partly for this reason, the question of immigration played such a central role in Trump's political ascent. As Trump pointed out on numerous occasions, "you either have a country or you don't." Citizens either have control over the fate of their nation as it is altered and ultimately transformed by immigration or, because citizens are determined by abstract superstructures which negate their authority and moral capacity to choose, the choice must be made on their behalf.

Moreover, fully securing this new understanding of liberty requires compelling fellow citizens, at first through the weight of public opinion, then through the force of the law, to not merely tolerate but to celebrate others' identity choices. To summarize with very broad strokes, the alternatives forced upon citizens within these progressive horizons point to either becoming a private, apolitical being, living for a private identity alone, or partaking in revolutionary passions which seek to transform or perhaps dissolve America's institutions. Within these horizons, little ground exists on which to base moderate human pride, nor is a place offered for a decent national reverence essential to citizenship. Trump's election perhaps proved the political improvidence of these doctrines: Rather than bringing about self-loathing in citizens which might begin a new progressive enlightenment, or which might at least compel the quiet acceptance of permanent progressive rule, they provoked spirited rebellion in citizens.

During Donald Trump's campaign, he articulated with some degree of clarity his understanding of American greatness and why he thinks the country must be made great *again*. In the domestic sphere, Trump seems to desire a reversal of the national self-hatred that is hostile to citizens' self-respect. Moreover, "draining the swamp," a prerequisite for making America great again, seems to broadly refer to a return of self-government: The swamp's inhabitants, on Trump's reading, care little about the lives of citizens, and their behavior demonstrated their willingness to sell out the nation's interests to the highest bidder (whether these bidders be foreign nations, multinationals, or interest groups). Trump won over blue-collar America, who sensed the selling out of their own interests by both parties, both of which had lost their sense of the nation. Shakespeare's Coriolanus thought he had nothing in common with the people; the people's rebellion against his harsh treatment caused the creation of the tribunes. Our political parties were supposed to be like tribunes in their representation of the people's interests, but they no longer are.

Moreover, contrary to the progressive teaching that America's power abroad tends to oppress and that an international brotherhood of harmony among nations may yet blossom, Trump saw great stakes competition between nations. "We are in a competition with the world, and I want America to win," he observed.[6] Specifically, on numerous occasions, Trump observed that China has successfully sought to slowly, almost silently, undermine America's interests through economic strategies, and that Iran has sought a nuclear weapon (essential for its imperial ambitions) while giving us the illusion that it is a treaty-abiding regime. Accordingly, our citizens "have lived through one international humiliation after another" under the Obama administration. As a consequence of this humiliation, "we can be assured that other nations will not treat America with respect," Trump observed.[7] While this may sound vulgar and combative to effete, excessively tame, and over-civilized spirits, many similar arguments are expressed in *The Federalist*, which can help us fill out Trump's broad outline, situate our thinking, and understand the stakes.

A New Form of Greatness

While some of *The Federalist's* political opponents opposed the notion of national greatness with varying degrees of vehemence, Publius is self-consciously founding a great nation.[8] Publius' new political science will create a new kind of power and thus a new understanding of greatness, which will set a new example for the world.[9] Publius' understanding of America's greatness should be contrasted with other forms of greatness. Europe, for instance, has achieved her imperial "greatness" "by her arms and by her negotiations, by force and by fraud."[10] Imperial greatness through military conquest and/or mercantilism is a political alternative still available today. While old Europe has declined, contemporary China, in its mercantilist colonization of parts of Africa, and its military policies in the South China Sea, demonstrates the durability of this alternative.[11]

National greatness is also in contradistinction to individual greatness, of the kind exemplified in ancient republics. The ancients misunderstood the principle of expanding the size of republics, what Publius calls "the enlargement of the orbit."[12] Small ancient republics bred great individuals motivated by their longing for honor and glory.[13] Rome, Publius observes, attained the "pinnacle of *human* greatness."[14] Cultivation of these passions led to "domestic faction and insurrection," circumstances which "could never promote the greatness or happiness of the people of America."[15] The modern republic, a conscious alternative to ancient republicanism, will to a lesser extent depend upon the "bright talents" and "exalted endowments" of individual men of antiquity.[16]

Individual greatness and imperial greatness are in contrast to Publius' own enterprise, that of "erecting one great American system."[17] The new union's structure will to a great degree subdue the individual passions animating ancient republics, or at least direct them away from politics. The union's structure will make such individuals less necessary. No doubt, Publius hopes to attract enlightened statesmen, future George Washingtons, to the highest posts of government. Nevertheless, America's republican institutions, rather than relying on the virtues of great individuals alone, will impose necessities upon these individuals so as to induce their service to the public.[18] Publius is aware that America will contain smaller men but greater politics. America's greatness will largely inhere in an enormous, very stable nation, which multiplies wealth through commerce. Our commercial spirit, in turn, will translate into military strength developed for the sake of national sovereignty and self-rule.

A COMMERCIAL REPUBLIC

Federalist 11 and 12 lay out most succinctly Publius' reflections on the commercial origins of America's greatness. Neither war nor conquest, but a "prosperous commerce is now perceived and acknowledged, by all enlightened statesmen, to be the most useful, as well as the most productive, source of national wealth." Commerce has thus become "a primary object of [enlightened statesmen's] *political* cares."[19] For Publius, the aim of commercial policy is not merely opulence and prosperity; it is to secure national independence and create the conditions to maintain it. Trump understood well that the main source of America's power should be first traced to its main source of wealth: "You have to be wealthy in order to be great," he repeated on many occasions.[20]

For Publius, obtaining national wealth requires the successful maintenance, not to say the liberation, of our "unequalled spirit of enterprise."[21] This unmeasurable, unquantifiable spirit, if properly ordered, becomes an "inexhaustible mine of national wealth," which should be nurtured and protected by the laws and by statesmen. This spirit is a "resource" to be used for the nation's happiness and security, a resource which will also be directed into the world.

This spirit is America's unique comparative advantage—our main source of competitiveness with other nations—and the means by which America's ways will conquer the hemisphere, if not the globe. There is no choice but to develop and rely upon this advantage, however, as other forms of national power are unavailable to America.[22] Not only is a warlike spirit contrary to the spirit of commerce and thereby absent in Americans, so too would imperial conquest undermine republican principles.[23] The spirit of enterprise occurs either to a greater degree or in a different form in America than it does in other nations because it is liberated from the opinions and laws that may restrain its development elsewhere. Unlike European nations of the time, America's spirit leads to the "mastery" of various branches of commerce, industry and science, rather than the mastery of peoples; the spirit of enterprise benefits citizens and the nation as a whole, not just monarchs.[24]

As experienced by "all orders of men" in America, commerce leads to the "pleasing reward" for their "toils." All men are free to acquire as these rewards will be protected by property rights and the government's power to secure (and thus enliven) the unequal acquisitive faculties of individuals.[25] This system leads to a great liberation of human energies, similar to the way modern natural science unlocks the energies of material nature to use natural forces to satisfy man's desires. For Publius, this liberation is not merely for private satisfaction and profit alone, as we often believe today, but for the sake of the nation as a whole. *Federalist* 12 reveals a part of how Publius hopes to enliven and reproduce this spirit. In considering its cause, however, we should heed Machiavelli's warning to avoid the error of "on the one hand admir[ing] this action" and "on the other condemn[ing] the principle cause of it."[26] The cause of our commercial spirit is "avarice," which Publius mentions twice in *Federalist* 12.

Publius reflects on the nature of avarice by contrasting its effects under circumstances of union and disunion. The "introduction and circulation of precious metals" and paper money, which remove the natural limit on spoilage, allow for hoarding, and enliven the desire for wealth.[27] Under circumstances of union, Publius connects avarice with the spirit of "enterprise," as the union makes this passion productive. America's domestic free-trade zone increases the "motion and vigour" of commerce by allowing this passion to satisfy itself while being channeled through a system of laws.[28] Moreover, under circumstances of union, avarice will be honored and encouraged, and will lead to great national projects that rouse citizens' pride and redound to them in profits. Publius' analysis implies that the passion itself is morally neutral and should be judged in terms of its effects.

In a state of disunion, however, avarice will not cohere with the interest of the whole. Indeed, America's geography is at once favorable to our enterprising spirit under union, and equally hostile to it under disunion. What seem like commercial advantages—easy geographic access between states, in addition to the similarity of our habits of character and our common language—would, without union, guide avarice toward illicit trade and black markets. Over time, this may culminate in a growing dissimilarity in character among the states, conflicts of interests and tensions, if not war. In disunion, "the adventurous stratagems of avarice" prevail over the spirit of enterprise.[29] The union is a form, ordering this and other passions in the structured arena in which they can productively satisfy themselves for the nation's benefit.

Furthermore, the enterprising spirit brings not only prosperity but national independence. Unfavorable consequences await nations who fail to develop it. Imperial Germany, for instance, in failing to cultivate this spirit neglects the development of lucrative natural resources and industries, the result of which means its emperor

has several times been compelled to owe obligations to the pecuniary succours of other nations, for the preservation of his essential interests; and is unable, upon the strength of his own resources, to sustain a long or continued war.[30]

An activated spirit of enterprise can overcome the seeming necessities that compel Germany. Through commerce, America will need not stake its interests or fate on the goodness or the arms of others.[31] When fully developed, this spirit may even lead to domination, and result in America dictating the terms to Europe, as we will see below. Trump's many uses of the phrase "it's time to declare our economic independence once again" denote a simplified though not inaccurate understanding of the cause of our power, especially in relation to adversaries like China.[32]

America's Commercial Spirit vis-à-vis Other Nations

But what especially "distinguishes the commercial character of America" is its "adventurous spirit." As mentioned above, this spirit leads to the "mastery" of industries, wealth, and sovereignty—but it also brings about "uneasy sensations" in competitor nations. This spirit causes both the perception and the fact of our "interference" in other nations' affairs. Foreign nations thus possess the "natural" desire to weaken America by intervening in our politics and commerce. Their jealousies, fears, ambitions, or perhaps good sense, will drive them to attempt to "restrain our growth." Europe wants to clip "the wings by which we might soar to a dangerous greatness."[33]

In openly or subtly acting against America, foreign nations act well or rationally from the point of view of their interests, something that Publius indicates America should do in turn, in its own particular way. Accordingly, the ever-present need to intervene, if only subtly, in other nation's spaces is a compulsion that America, too, is under. But our form of restraining foreign growth and ambitions is mixed, consisting partly of a new, less direct kind of power. The seeming softness of commercial power will not prevent it from culminating in America dictating "the terms of the connection between the old and the new world."[34]

Restraining foreign desires and ambitions is achieved in part through a navy that can "induc[e] an impracticability of success" in our adversaries. As David Epstein observes, "Neither the unthreatening weakness of disunion nor the formidable strength of union will make foreign powers complacent, but the latter will at least make them less sanguine about the prospect of gaining by war."[35] In acting upon the imagination and resolve of America's competitors, a navy is thus a partial source of control over foreign desires and ambitions. Moreover, a developed navy means that "a price would be set not only upon our friendship, but upon our neutrality."[36] This observation characterizes America's current situation: one wonders whether the nations surrounding China who are today friendly to America would continue to favor America if its military shrank, ceasing to credibly promise their security against China—or whether those nations would choose, under threat of the Chinese gun, to continue to trade with us if their choice was between commercial gain and Chinese military domination.

But America will restrain foreign desires through other, more tacit and long-term strategies as well. Publius presents America as being compelled by an "irresistible and unchangeable course of nature" to develop commercially, industrialize, and expand its enterprising spirit into the world.[37] America's commercial productivity will compel other nations, eventually a great portion of the world, to compete on our terms, commercially, a competition in which we have the advantage. The "regions of futurity" which Publius mentions but demurs from discussing imply his correct appraisal that the future belongs to enlightened commercial republics, which through their new power will alter other nations' self-understanding. In one of the most interesting passages in *The Federalist*, Publius draws our attention to yesteryear's allegedly "profound philosophers," such as Cornelius de Pauw (whom Publius cites), Count de Buffon, and the Abbe Raynal, who asserted European superiority based on racialist theories derived from an alleged science of natural history.[38] Their science "gravely asserted that all animals, and with them the human species, degenerate in America; that even dogs cease to bark, after having breathed a while in our atmosphere."[39] But the effectual truth of commercial power, truer than Europe's false sciences, Publius correctly predicted, will undermine over time through commercial competition the political justifications supporting the old world, exposing its boastfulness. Honor, it will be shown, belongs to humanity, not only to monarchs and aristocrats. When liberated and properly ordered by the "great American system," the powers derived from the human passions and their resulting fruits (industrial productivity, scientific progress, and innovation), will be demonstrated—not merely asserted—in the arena of the world. America's commercial power will thus "teach that assuming brother [Europe], moderation," democratizing them in the process.[40]

Publius presents commerce as a mild form of warfare in an industrialized world, even the first wave of American foreign policy. In competing with foreign nations, commercial power will continue to rid them of false sciences and "arrogant pretentions" upon which they make claims regarding their alleged greatness. Neither will the classic virtues of the yeoman farmer, proposed by Thomas Jefferson, find a firm place in this new world. By compelling other nations to compete on their terms, enlightened commercial republics will undo the hold of old-world pieties over minds—or these pieties will be modified to fit new commercial conditions, as their relative weakness comes to be felt through engagement with commerce and science. Today, one observes this taking place in many nations throughout the world that have been forced to abandon their ancestral orders and attempt, by whatever means available, though often with little success, to compete commercially. For these many reasons, the preservation of America's commercial spirit is of the highest long-term priority to this day.

PASSIVITY VERSUS ACTIVITY

Just as America is compelled by certain necessities, so too must foreign nations exploit America's weaknesses. These competitors will attempt to "prescribe the conditions of our political existence" by undermining or weakening our commerce and inducing our "passivity."[41] While commerce is not violent, it is competitive, and seeks supremacy and advantage, not merely opulence.

Nations use commerce to obstruct and retard their adversaries' growth and development, through which they can "influence the conduct" of their competitors, preventing their rise to preeminence. This may mean, for instance, that nations must choose, based on political criteria, who should have favored access to their markets. To evaluate such goals, statesmen must look to the non-obvious secondary or tertiary effects of a policy to comprehend its advantages. Commenting on his times, Publius argues that by banning British ships from American ports, America can inflate the costs of British goods by forcing Britain to pay the Dutch to transport their goods. America can thus make the Dutch the master of British commerce in America. Publius would consider the key calculation here as not the increased costs of consumer goods, the only criterion used today, but diminishing a competitor's influence and obstructing its long-term designs.

Trump and Publius agree on this understanding of trade: Consideration for long-term competition, and the national power and respect that come with it—rather than cheap goods for American consumers—constitutes the central goal of commercial policy. Trump has shown his understanding of this lesson on several occasions by observing the foolhardiness of America's many trade agreements with China:

> America became the world's dominant economy by becoming the world's dominant producer...The wealth this created was shared broadly, creating the biggest middle-class the world has ever known. But then, America changed its policy from promoting development in America...to promoting development in other nations...We allowed foreign countries to subsidize their goods, devalue their currencies, violate their agreements and cheat in every way imaginable, and our politicians did nothing about it. Trillions of our dollars and millions of our jobs flowed overseas as a result...This is a direct affront to our founding fathers...They wanted this country to be strong. They wanted to be independent and they wanted it to be free.[42]

For Publius, it would be preposterous for America to actively allow the enrichment of nations which, on account of this enrichment, will become viable competitors, as we have done in the recent past with China. Exploiting our errors, China's "1.3 billion customers have given it the leverage other countries don't have to demand technological transfers."[43] Dogmatic political commentators today have misidentified the naturalness of foreign desires to intervene in our affairs. In dreaming that competitors do not understand themselves as consciously competing with us through trade, these commentators have often countenanced exchanging America's long-term competitive advantages for market access.

Competitors will aim to slowly choke America's influence by suffocating our enterprising spirit and as such diminishing our self-confidence. Our enterprising spirit may flounder and can be "stifled and lost."[44] Today, it can be lost through the slow forfeit of America's commercial independence, which occurs through the loss—induced by competitors—of our advantages in intellectual property, communications technologies, financial systems, and medical innovations. The future of the nation, Publius thinks, largely rests upon our enterprising spirit: its loss will likely culminate in "poverty and disgrace," while its successful maintenance and projection will maintain our being the "admiration and envy of the world."[45]

Though odd-sounding to modern sensibilities, rather than seeking the approval of world opinion, a powerful America will become both envied and admired by other nations. Admiration seems to originate in sufficient fear which can restrain foreign ambitions and desires. Without this restraint, foreigners will have no "scruple and remorse" in directly or indirectly undermining our interests and self-confidence. Our power will be an important source of our respectability, without which competitors have "nothing to fear from us."[46] Admiration, moreover, would seem additionally to imply possessing something honorable and worthy of imitation, like our republican principles. Nevertheless, foreign fears, which only a great nation can inspire, will set the limits on their ambitions, and thereby limit, though perhaps never stop, the natural desire they possess to intervene in our affairs. Maintaining this psychological state, a combination of envy and admiration in our adversaries, Publius suggests, characterizes a good outcome.

CONCLUSION

Enlightened commerce generates national wealth, whose purpose, ultimately, is to establish and preserve national independence or sovereignty. Modern republicanism, for Publius, requires this form of national greatness. Yet this so far is an incomplete picture of greatness, for it characterizes only the means of obtaining it. Greatness must be choice-worthy for its own sake—it must either be the best thing in itself, or the best thing available. Publius, observes Thomas Pangle, "demands that republican self-government be treated as an end, not merely as a means toward prosperity." Indeed, Publius "associates liberty not only with 'happiness' but also with 'dignity.'"[47] Republican liberty is the choice-worthy and legitimate end of national greatness. Although Publius and Trump largely agree on the means of achieving national greatness, and while Trump does at times seem to emphasize the importance of self-rule, his references to national greatness overemphasize the means of becoming great at the cost of the proper end.

Finally, *The Federalist* opens by contrasting reflection and choice with accident and force. *The Federalist's* political experiment is staked on establishing the rationality of human beings over the power or need for prophets, accident, or history. In this regard, America will be the first non-theocratic country, an example of *human* dignity, and the reason for which *The Federalist's* political experiment is an example for all mankind.[48] The Constitution, explained and defended by *The Federalist*, is the product of human reason. Reason lives in the work of its writers or the "system" they erect, rather than in the people themselves. This is perhaps the highest meaning of the nation, and the Constitution which orders it, which entails the greatness of man himself.

NOTES

1. While most of my citations of Publius refer to essays written by Hamilton, this chapter does not contain an exhaustive review of Hamilton's work on the subject of national greatness. Rather, my focus deals with *The Federalist* alone. Accordingly, I refer to "Publius" instead of to "Hamilton."

2. Without reviewing the entire 40-year history of such assertions in the public square, consider the recent and prominent examples of Joe Biden, "Remarks by the Vice President to the Irish People" (speech, Dublin Castle, Dublin, June 24, 2016), https://ie.usembassy.gov/vice-president-biden-speech-dublin-castle/. Additionally, consider Hillary Clinton's now famous comment on the campaign trail that half of the Americans supporting Donald Trump are a "basket of deplorables" defined specifically as being "racist, sexist, homophobic, xenophobic, Islamophobic" people.

3. Many examples may substantiate this. Consider, for instance, the attempt to impose the disparate-impact standard on public schools' disciplinary policies, the usage of which presumed that institutionalized racism accounts for disparities of outcomes.

4. To list just one academic in the expansive and ever-growing chorus supporting such views, see Charles Wright Mills, *The Racial Contract* (Ithaca: Cornell University Press, 1997), pp. 9–19; 41–81; 91–109.

5. For remarks on the need for fundamental transformation of the nation, see Barack Obama's "Campaign Rallies Columbia, Missouri" (speech, Columbia, Missouri, October 30, 2008), https://www.realclearpolitics.com/articles/2008/10/obama_rallies_columbia_missour.html. See also, Barack Obama, "Barack Obama's Inaugural Address" (speech, District of Columbia, January 20, 2009), http://content.time.com/time/politics/article/0,8599,1872715,00.html.

6. Donald Trump, "An America First Economic Plan: Winning The Global Competition" (speech, campaign event, Detroit, Michigan, August 8, 2016), http://thehill.com/blogs/pundits-blog/campaign/290777-transcript-of-donald-trumps-economic-policy-speech-to-detroit.

7. Donald Trump, "Republican Nomination Acceptance Speech" (speech, Republican National Convention, Cleveland, Ohio, July 21, 2016), http://www.politico.com/story/2016/07/full-transcript-donald-trump-nomination-acceptance-speech-at-rnc-225974.

8. On the numerous voices during the founding opposed to national greatness, see Karl-Friedrich Walling, *Republican Empire: Alexander Hamilton on War and Free Government* (Lawrence: University Press of Kansas, 1999), pp. 101–103.

9. All references to *The Federalist* in this essay are to: *The Federalist*, eds. George W. Carey and James McClellan, (Indianapolis: Liberty Fund,

2001). I will provide essay number and page number. Citation in text refers to *Federalist* 1, p. 1, where Publius suggests that we will be an example to the world.

10. *Federalist* 11, p. 54.
11. For a clear articulation of the logic of China's imperial and mercantilist policies, see Peter Navarro and Greg Autry, *Death by China, Confronting the Dragon—A Global Call to Action* (New Jersey: Prentice Hall, 2011).
12. *Federalist* 9, p. 38.
13. See Thomas Pangle's succinct and pointed analysis of Publius' assessment of the problems of classical republics. Thomas L. Pangle, *The Spirit of Modern Republicanism: the Moral Vision of the American Founders and the Philosophy of Locke* (Chicago: University of Chicago Press, 1990), pp. 46–47.
14. *Federalist* 34, p. 163 (my emphasis).
15. *Federalist* 9, pp. 37 and 39.
16. Consider also *Federalist* 6, where Hamilton discusses the motives of Pericles and the effects of relying too much on great individuals. *Federalist* 6, p. 22.
17. *Federalist* 11, p. 55.
18. While the "noblest minds" may be attracted to the presidency, the president's powers are circumscribed and divided among other branches of government. The president's interests must be made to coincide with his duties (*Federalist* 72), although some measure of "independence [is] intended for him by the constitution" (*Federalist* 73, p. 381). Virtue is not entrusted with free reign; presidents will not rule like Homeric kings.
19. *Federalist* 12, p. 55 (my emphasis).
20. Trump campaign speech, Bismarck, North Dakota, May 26, 2016.
21. *Federalist* 11, p. 52.
22. Publius mentions that national poverty, on account of an underdeveloped commerce, is "an extremity to which no government will of choice accede." *Federalist* 12, p. 59.
23. "The industrious habits of the people of the present day, absorbed in the pursuits of gain, and devoted to the improvements of agriculture and commerce, are incompatible with the condition of a nation of soldiers." *Federalist* 8, p. 34.
24. *Federalist* 11, p. 52.
25. *Federalist* 12, p. 55 (quotation). In addition, see *Federalist* 10's statement on the purpose of protecting unequal acquisitive faculties. One may additionally consider the patent clause in the U.S. Constitution as seeking to encourage, among other things, the blossoming of the unequal faculties of the mind.

26. Niccolo Machiavelli, *The Prince*, trans. Harvey Mansfield, 2nd ed. (University of Chicago Press, 1998), p. 67.

27. *Federalist* 12, p. 55. Cf. John Locke, *Two Treatises of Government*, ed. Peter Laslett (Cambridge: Cambridge University Press, 1993), 5.50.

28. *Federalist* 11, p. 53.

29. *Federalist* 12, p. 57.

30. *Federalist* 12, p. 56.

31. Germany has insufficient paper money in circulation, the proximate cause of its dependence and weakness. Paper money, however, as Publius states in the previous essay, is connected to the liberation of avarice and the national spirit that it can generate.

32. Donald Trump, "Declaring America's Economic Independence" (speech, campaign event, Pittsburgh, Pennsylvania June 28, 2016), http://www.politico.com/story/2016/06/full-transcript-trump-job-plan-speech-224891.

33. *Federalist* 11, p. 49.

34. *Federalist* 11, p. 55.

35. David Epstein, *The Political Theory of* The Federalist (University of Chicago Press, 1984), p. 27.

36. *Federalist* 11, p. 51.

37. *Federalist* 11, p. 52.

38. For the best historical and theoretical analysis on the "scientific" theories based on natural history, then current in Europe, which claim to prove the natural weakness of all things American (the "degeneracy thesis") see James Ceaser, *Reconstructing America* (Yale University Press, 1997), pp. 19–42. For *The Federalist*'s understanding of political science as opposed to natural history see pp. 53–65.

39. *Federalist* 11, p. 54.

40. *Federalist* 11, p. 54.

41. *Federalist* 11, p. 52.

42. Trump campaign speech, Monneson, Pennsylvania, Time, June, 6, 2016, http://time.com/4386335/donald-trump-trade-speech-transcript/.

43. Christopher Caldwell, "The Globalization Swindle," *Claremont Review of Books* XVII, no. 2 (2017), pp. 20–23.

44. *Federalist* 11, p. 52.

45. *Federalist* 11, p. 52.

46. *Federalist* 11, p. 51.

47. Pangle, *The Spirit of Modern Republicanism*, p. 45.

48. See *Federalist* 1, p. 1, and *Federalist* 14, p. 67.

REFERENCES

Caldwell, Christopher. "The Globalization Swindel." *Claremont Review of Books* XVII, no. 2 (2017).

Ceaser, James. *Reconstructing America*. New Haven: Yale University Press, 1997.

Epstein, David F. *The Political Theory of the Federalist*. Chicago: University of Chicago Press, 1984.

Locke, John. *Two Treatises of Government*. Edited by Peter Laslett. Cambridge: Cambridge University Press, 1993.

Machiavelli, Niccolo. *The Prince*. Translated by Harvey Mansfield, 2nd ed. Chicago: University of Chicago Press, 1998.

Mills, Charles Wright. *The Racial Contract*. Ithaca: Cornell University Press, 1997.

Navarro, Peter, and Greg Autry. *Death by China, Confronting the Dragon—A Global Call to Action*. New Jersey: Prentice Hall, 2011.

Pangle, Thomas L. *The Spirit of Modern Republicanism: The Moral Vision of the American Founders and the Philosophy of Locke*. Chicago: University of Chicago Press, 1990.

Publius. *The Federalist*. Edited by George W. Carey and James McClellan. Indianapolis: Liberty Fund, 2001.

Walling, Karl Friedrich. *Republican Empire: Alexander Hamilton on War and Free Government*. Lawrence: University Press of Kansas, 1999.

CHAPTER 12

American Constitutionalism from Hamilton to Lincoln to Trump

Murray Dry

Introduction

Alexander Hamilton and Abraham Lincoln are among the most important figures in American political history. To my mind, Lincoln is the most important. Their writings and the actions they took merit study. Their allegiance was to the American Constitution and its modern republican form of government. Each understood the strengths and weaknesses of government that relies on popular consent. In what follows I hope to draw lessons from their thought and their actions for a consideration of Donald Trump's presidency, one which has caused consternation for many.

The Age of Trump is characterized by a populism on the Left and the Right and by a polarization between the two major political parties which appears greater in Congress than in the population at large. This divisiveness in our political life prompts questions like the following. First, how did Hamilton and Lincoln, respectively, understand the relationship between the government and the people, and what did they do to define and/or enhance or maintain that government? Second, how can what we learn from them inform our understanding of our current condition? In the first part of this essay, I'll show how Hamilton, who thought a

M. Dry (✉)
Middlebury College, Middlebury, VT, USA

© The Author(s) 2018
A. Jaramillo Torres, M. B. Sable (eds.), *Trump and Political Philosophy*,
https://doi.org/10.1007/978-3-319-74445-2_12

constitutional monarchy the best form of government, supported the
Constitution during the ratification debate and then implemented the
energetic executive government he thought essential to good government, as President George Washington's Secretary of the Treasury. As
important as Hamilton was to Washington, Washington's moderating
influence and his stature with the people was essential for Hamilton's successes. Lincoln, however, as I will show in part two, combined the excellences of Hamilton and Washington. With the coming of political parties
and the democratization of American government, Lincoln was the perfect populist president; he was an effective leader as he marshaled the elements of the presidency to preserve the Union and put slavery "in course
of ultimate extinction."[1] The recent election of Donald J. Trump as president confronts our government with a distinctive challenge. We have a
charismatic and impulsive individual holding this powerful office in the
age of nuclear weapons, and there is no easy or safe way to dislodge him
until the next election; our presidential system, unlike a parliamentary system, does not provide for a vote of no confidence. I turn to this in the last
part of this essay.

ALEXANDER HAMILTON, PRESIDENT WASHINGTON'S ESSENTIAL PARTNER

In Federalist 68, writing as Publius, Hamilton asserted that the proposed
Constitution's mode of appointing the chief magistrate "affords a moral
certainty, that the office of president will seldom fall to the lot of any man
who is not in an eminent degree endowed with the requisite qualifica-
tions." Hamilton was writing about the "electoral college" mode of election before the development of organized political parties, when the
presidential electors, chosen by the people but not bound by law or custom to vote for any specific candidate, would exercise their discretion. He
was advocating for the ratification of the newly proposed Constitution. As
he explained in Federalist 1, his support for the Constitution reflected his
preference for an energetic government over a weak one like the Articles
of Confederation. Moreover, he argued that the energetic government
would be less likely to degenerate into tyranny than a weak government.

[A] dangerous ambition more often lurks behind the specious mask of zeal
for the rights of the people than under the forbidding appearance of zeal for
the firmness and efficiency of government. History will teach us that the

former has been found a much more certain road to the introduction of despotism than the latter, and that of those men who have overturned the liberties of republics, the greatest number have begun their career by paying an obsequious court to the people, commencing demagogues and ending tyrants.[2]

This position accounts for Hamilton's own proposed plan for a constitution, which he presented in the Federal Convention. After criticizing both the Virginia and the New Jersey plans in his long speech on June 18, Hamilton proposed a plan of government that included a single executive and a senate, both elected for life. In James Madison's *Notes*, Hamilton expressed a concern whether republican government "could be established over so great an extent" of territory and population as the United States and praised the British government as "the best in the world." After defending a senate for life because "in every community where industry is encouraged there will be a division ... into the few and the many," Hamilton considered the Executive. In words anticipating Federalist 70, he suggested that people had better not assume that a good executive cannot be reconciled with republican government since good government requires a good executive. In proposing an executive for life, Hamilton stretched the understanding of republican government to its limit, and perhaps beyond, by asserting that "if all the Magistrates are appointed and vacancies are filled, by the people, or a process of election originating with the people," the government would be republican.[3] He went on to argue that "monarch" was an indefinite term, so that a unitary executive elected for a limited term was not qualitatively different from one elected for good behavior.

The Federal Convention chose an indirectly popular mode of election of the president, which allowed for reeligibilty. In Federalist 72, Hamilton argued in support of reeligibility, which was controversial, by suggesting that holding up reelection as a reward for good service would constructively direct ambition toward the public good. Hamilton has in mind both avarice and ambition. While each is actively or potentially a vice, offering up the reward of reelection could channel either desire to public benefits. Ambition, for example, could direct the avaricious man toward the higher goal of ambition for fame.[4]

Notwithstanding Hamilton's advocacy of a government that relies on interest, or perhaps because of it, he was aware of the problem posed by a demagogic appeal from a "man of the people." In addition to his statement about popular leaders challenging the need for strong government in Federalist 1, he expressed his private reservations about Madison's reliance on the extended sphere as a means of taming majority faction. In Hamilton's Notes on Madison's June 6 speech in the Federal Convention, which was a precursor of Madison famous Tenth Federalist, Hamilton paraphrased part of Madison's argument ("large districts less liable to be influenced by factious demagogues than small") and then noted:

> "This is in some degree true but not so generally as may be supposed. Frequently small portions of [mutilated] large districts carry elections—An influential demagogue will give an impulse to the whole—Demagogues are not always inconsiderable persons—Patricians were frequently demagogues—Characters are less known and less active interest taken in them."[5]

Hamilton made his most significant contributions to American government when he served as Secretary of the Treasury under President George Washington. He oversaw the funding of the national debt, the assumption of the state debts, and the establishment of the first national bank. Because Hamilton thought America would eventually rival Great Britain as a commercial republic, this pointed in the direction of manufacture, which, in turn, required a system of public credit with a program for managing public debt. To that end, Hamilton proposed paying off the federal debt from the Revolution at par, notwithstanding the fact that speculators had bought up many of the bonds for pennies on the dollar. He also proposed assuming all the state debts, though some states, such as Virginia, had paid off a greater share of their debt than others. These proposals, along with his proposal for a national bank, divided Madison and Hamilton. Eventually Madison joined Thomas Jefferson in opposing almost everything Hamilton proposed. Their opposition led to a deep division within Washington's Administration and finally to the factional conflict between the Federalist party and the newly emerging Republican Party. The Federalist Party division resulted in Jefferson's defeat of President John Adams in the election of 1800.

After Congress passed the bill establishing the Bank, over Madison's strong objections in the House, President Washington sought the views of Jefferson, his Secretary of State, as well as Hamilton. These "opinions," as they are called, represent the classic "strict" and "loose" constructions of the Constitution's "necessary and proper" clause, which comes at the end of the enumeration, of the legislative powers vested in Congress (I, 8, 18).

Hamilton argued that coming after an enumeration of powers in a constitution, the term "necessary" in "necessary and proper" can extend to
what is convenient or useful. When the bank issue came before the
Supreme Court, after Maryland taxed the Second National Bank, Chief
Justice John Marshall, writing for a unanimous Court, followed Hamilton's
argument and upheld the bank's constitutionality in McCulloch v
Maryland[6] (1819).

When the French Revolution, which broke out in 1789, developed into
a bloody civil war within France and a war with England and the rest of
Europe, the divisions within the Washington Administration became
intense. This was illustrated by the opposition that Jefferson and Madison
mounted to President Washington's decision, on the recommendation of
Hamilton, to declare America's neutrality in the war between France and
Europe.

The three paragraph Neutrality Proclamation, dated April 22, 1793,
acknowledged "that a state of war exists between Austria, Prussia, Sardinia,
Great Britain, and the United Netherlands, of the one part, and France on
the other," and then declared "the duty and interest of the United States
require that they should with sincerity and good faith adopt and pursue a
conduct friendly and impartial towards the belligerent Powers."[7]

The Administration faced a legal difficulty because the U.S. had a treaty
with France, its erstwhile ally in the American Revolution and War of
Independence. To fully live up to the obligations of the pre-(French)
Revolutionary treaty would most likely embroil the U.S. in war, a war
which would have been devastating for the new country. Both Jefferson
and Madison agreed that the best American policy was to avoid the
European War, but they also wanted to sidestep an overt break with France
and they viewed a formal neutrality declaration as supporting monarchical
England.

The constitutional question was whether the executive power, which
was lodged in the president, included the power to declare the condition
of the country with respect to war and peace. Under the pseudonym,
Pacificus, Hamilton wrote a series of essays advocating that the president's
executive power, along with his power to executive the laws, including
treaties and the law of nations, and his right to receive ambassadors and
other public ministers permitted him to declare the condition of the country and the requirements of the treaty. He allowed as how Congress could
reverse that decision by exercising its power to declare war, which would,
however, have to be presented to the president for his signature, and

hence would be subject to his veto.[8] James Madison, at the behest of Jefferson, reluctantly argued the latter position, in essays under the pseudonym Helvidius.

Hamilton argued that a change in the character of the French government allowed the United States to reconsider its treaty obligations. He also argued that France was the aggressor in the war and the treaty only provided for assistance in connection with a defensive war.

Today, constitutional scholars and the public generally accept the Neutrality Proclamation as prudent policy and constitutionally sound. The constitutional soundness derives from Hamilton's arguments described above, as well as his contention that the president's power to receive foreign ambassadors made the executive "the organ of intercourse between the nation and foreign nations...."[9]

HAMILTON AND WASHINGTON: THE JAY TREATY AND THE FAREWELL ADDRESS

Hamilton resigned from his post as Secretary of Treasury in January 1795, but he remained the intellectual force behind Washington's decision to sign and the Senate's decision to ratify the Jay Treaty, which also needed, and received, approval from the House for funding. He also influenced the president's Farewell Address in 1796. Hamilton's analysis of the Jay Treaty prompted Washington to write "I am really ashamed when I behold the trouble it has given you to explore and to explain so fully as you have done." After providing that quotation, Chernow writes "...Washington never shied away from differing with the redoubtable Hamilton but agreed with him on the majority of issues."[10] Chernow also reports that Washington chose Hamilton's draft of his Farewell Address, reducing and revising it with this result:

> If Hamilton was the major wordsmith, Washington was the tutelary spirit and final arbiter of what went in. The poignant opening section in which Washington thanked the American people could never have been written by Hamilton alone, conversely, the soaring central section, with its sophisticated perspective on policy matters, showed Hamilton's unmistakable stamp.[11]

Chernow's comment about the Washington-Hamilton relationship suggests that Hamilton's brilliance and industry needed the moderating influence of Washington to guarantee politically constructive results.

ABRAHAM LINCOLN: THE POPULIST PRESIDENT

If Hamilton was, like Tocqueville, a friend of American democracy without being an unqualified democrat, Abraham Lincoln was the perfect president for American democracy; he combined the best qualities of Washington and Hamilton and he was of and for the people.

Historians have noted how Lincoln, who grew up among the common people, kept in touch with them even while president. He did it by reading many newspapers, reading his mail, and replying to some letters himself, and to devoting some time to meet with people who came to the White House. His encounter with the people, "renew[ed] in me a clearer and more vivid image of that great popular assemblage out of which I spring ... I call these receptions my '*public-opinion baths*'; for I have but little time to read the papers and father public opinion that way."[12]

In addition to ambition, which Lincoln, like Hamilton, surely had, and his affinity with the common people, Lincoln was also comfortable working with the organizational framework of the political party. As the historian Richard Carwardine put it, as a peacetime politician Lincoln's "great achievement was to set ambitious but realizable political goals; to fathom the thinking of ordinary citizens and to reach out to them with common assurance; and to hone his impressive skills as a manager of the often unstable and fractious elements that made up the political parties to which he belonged."[13]

THE POLITICAL PHILOSOPHY OF A YOUNG WHIG: LINCOLN'S PERPETUATION SPEECH

Lincoln's 1838 speech to the Young Men's Lyceum on The Perpetuation of Our Political Institutions reveals a careful and engaging writer and a thinker with an appreciation of the challenge individual ambition puts to republican government.

The most arresting part of Lincoln's Address concerned his presentation of the problem of ambition. After a country has experienced a successful founding, especially one that involved a war for independence as well as the establishment of a new constitution, what chores remain for the talented and ambitious men, such as those, including Hamilton, of the founding generation? Hamilton himself made the case for reeligibility of the executive partly in terms of the inducement to great fame and perhaps other rewards that could be won by having more time to complete important projects for the country. But Lincoln, who read and studied Shakespeare and whose favorite play was *Macbeth*, said that will not suffice for "the family of the lion or the tribe of the eagle. What? Think you these places would satisfy an Alexander, a Caesar, or a Napoleon? Never! Towering genius disdains a beaten path."[14] As if that were not enough, Lincoln shows how this might play out in America: "It [the towering genius] thirsts and burns for distinction; and, if possible, it will have it, whether at the expense of emancipating slaves, or enslaving freemen."

While Stephen Douglas was hardly a towering genius bent on achieving personal fame at any price, his Nebraska Bill, later Kansas-Nebraska Act, repealed the 1820 Missouri Compromise, which forbade slavery in the federal territory north of 36:30 degrees latitude and replaced it with "popular sovereignty," or the settlers decide.

Lincoln reentered national politics in 1854, opposed to this Act because of the effect it was likely to have on public sentiment toward slavery. In his Peoria Speech (October 16, 1854), Lincoln said: "I particularly object to the NEW position which the avowed principle of this Nebraska law gives to slavery in the body politic. I object to it because it assumes that there can be MORAL RIGHT in the enslaving of one man by another."[15]

From that date on, Lincoln took a consistently firm position against the extension of slavery into the territories because of his abhorrence of the institution as well as from the conviction that "a house divided against itself cannot stand":

> Either the opponents of slavery, will arrest the further spread of it, and place it where the public mind shall rest in the belief that it is in course of ultimate extinction; or its advocates will push it forward, till it shall become alike lawful in all the States, old as well as new—North as well as South.[16]

Lincoln also prudently resisted the calls from abolitionists and radical Republicans for a complete attack on slavery. Lincoln's prudence reflected his awareness of the range of opinion among potential or actual Republican Party voters and his judgment that the necessity the framers were under to accept the existence of slavery as the price of union meant that slavery's existence within the states was left to state governments and slave owners had a constitutional right to the return of fugitive slaves.

In the Lincoln-Douglas Debates in 1858, Stephen Douglas tried to force Lincoln to identify himself with all propositions in the Republican Party platform of 1854. That platform included opposition to a fugitive slave law and to the admission of any more states allowing slavery, as well as the advocacy of the elimination of slavery in the District of Columbia and the abolition of slave trade between different states. In his reply to Douglas, Lincoln asserted that the 1856 Republican platform reflected the party's commonly agreed upon focus on opposing slave extension into the territories.[17]

Lincoln's position on slavery included an acknowledgement of the legal claim that slave owners had on that insidious form of property in human beings; it also comprehended Lincoln's awareness of the widespread aversion among white people to social commingling of the races. Lincoln confronted this fact directly in his Peoria Speech, and he returned to it in his Ottawa Debate with Douglas. Lincoln's plan to put slavery in course of ultimate extinction would seem to suggest the need to support integration, or a biracial or multiracial political community. We take this for granted today, notwithstanding continuing racial tensions and conflicts. It took some time before Lincoln came to support such a solution. It's hard to imagine his being nominated for president by the Republican party in 1860 had he advocated freedom and assimilation, and even more difficult to imagine his winning the election. In 1854, in 1858, and even after his election, Lincoln favored compensated emancipation and colonization. In 1854, he presented his position:

> What then? Free them and make them politically and socially our equals? My own feelings will not admit of this; and if mine would, we well know that those of the great mass of white people will not. Whether this feeling accords with justice and sound judgment, is not the sole question, if indeed it is any part of it. A universal feeling, whether well or ill-founded, cannot be safely disregarded. We cannot then, make them equals. It does seem to me that systems of gradual emancipation might be adopted; but for their tardiness in this, I will not undertake to judge our brethren of the south.[18]

Lincoln says something similar in his Ottawa Debate with Stephen Douglas, who aims to align Lincoln with the radical Republicans, whom Douglas constantly called Black Republicans. Lincoln continues to think the physical difference between the two races precludes "their living together upon the footing of perfect equality." But he also criticizes the Dred Scott decision and Douglas's "popular sovereignty" approach to slavery in the territories for preparing the people to regard slavery as an acceptable outcome of majority rule.

[L]et us see what influence he [Douglas] is exerting on public sentiment. With public sentiment, nothing can fail; without it nothing can succeed. Consequently, he who molds public sentiment goes deeper than he who enacts statutes or pronounces decisions. He makes statutes or decisions possible or impossible to be executed.[19]

Lincoln's forceful opposition to the extension of slavery during the debates of 1858 made possible his presidential victory in 1860. And while as president-elect Lincoln remained "inflexible" on the "territorial question,"[20] he was not prepared to attempt to change public sentiment on racial commingling until December, 1862, months after announcing what he would declare on January 1, 1863, the Emancipation Proclamation. While that Proclamation only affected the states in rebellion, it was clear that if Lincoln and the Union prevailed slavery would be abolished. That left the choice between colonization or a Reconstruction that would deal with granting the rights of citizenship to the newly freed race.

In his First Inaugural, Lincoln argued that the Constitution left the matter of slavery in the territories to the political branches of government to decide, not the courts, and he interpreted his election as a vote to restore the Missouri Compromise. At the same time, he opposed secession, which he called "sugar coated rebellion," by asserting that no organic law contains provision for its own termination and, besides, the union was older than the Constitution.

Lincoln also asserted a robust form of executive power while reporting his actions to Congress, allowing the legislative branch either to confirm or rescind his actions. After Fort Sumter fell, Lincoln "call[ed] out the war power of the government." This included calling for volunteers, raising money from the Treasury to pay for them, and suspending the privilege of the writ of habeas corpus. Acknowledging these extraordinary actions by the man charged with faithfully executing the laws, Lincoln put the question directly: "are all the laws but one [the writ of habeas corpus] to go unexecuted, and the government itself go to pieces, lest that one be violated?"[21] While Lincoln goes on to say that the Constitution "is silent" regarding who is authorized to suspend the writ, his statement justifying his actions immediately acknowledged that the placement of the power to suspend the writ in cases of rebellion, in Article One, implied that such authority was vested in Congress. Unlike more recent presidents, however,

Lincoln presented his case for his actions to Congress, leaving it to them to approve or disapprove, and Congress authorized what he had done.

Finally, Lincoln's decision to emancipate the slaves on January 1, 1863, but only in those parts of the country that were in rebellion, reflected a prudential judgment composed of expediency and morality. Lincoln knew that he had to wait on Emancipation until the common war effort would make the military necessity rationale acceptable to his diverse coalition, which included Abolitionists, Republicans and slave owners in the "border states." With the Emancipation Proclamation, there was no going back. If the Union forces prevailed under Lincoln, and his reelection in 1864 was not always certain, slavery was going to be permanently eliminated, as it was with the Thirteenth Amendment. Reconstruction would be a more difficult challenge, for which Lincoln attempted to prepare the country as early as his Annual Message to Congress in December 1862.[22]

In sum, I believe that Lincoln combined the excellences of Washington and Hamilton. Putting it another way, he was the perfect democratic, or populist president. His uncommon prudence included both the knowledge of what was right and the skill to attain his objectives by working with the people and directing, ever so patiently, their sentiments.

American Government Under President Donald J. Trump

Turning to American government today, the Trump presidency was preceded by a wave of hostility to established politicians, especially in the national government, and to political parties. What first arose in the Republican party, with the development of the anti-government "tea party" in 2009, and is described as "libertarian, populist, and conservative," also produced a similar split in the Democratic party, as Senator Bernie Sanders, an Independent and former Socialist, contested the Democratic party's nomination for the presidency with the party's established candidate, Hilary Clinton.

Donald Trump won the Republican party nomination and then the general election on the strength of his brashness, his reality TV celebrity and his ability to command the spotlight, and the electorate's dissatisfaction with establishment candidates. His impulsive behavior, including vulgar speech and action, seems to satisfy and even delight his supporters.

President Trump's behavior, so far, ranks as the opposite of what Hamilton said the indirectly popular mode of election would produce and he surely is the anti-Lincoln in terms of his inability to articulate a coherent position on any important topic of government. As for public opinion, he appears to have no interest in reaching out to those who did not support his candidacy. His loyal core supporters, while less than 40% of the electorate, are politically powerful enough to keep the support of most Republican members of Congress who intend to run for reelection in 2018.

Ironically, both Hamilton, in his comments on the limits of Madison's extended sphere argument, and Lincoln, in his youthful reflections on the "towering genius," were aware of what Plato wrote about: the danger of a man of the people arising to become a dangerous demagogue, if not a tyrant. The additional irony is that Hamilton expounded on the importance of an energetic executive and Lincoln took advantage of the office to mobilize its potential to lead the country against a powerful attack on its very existence. And now we have a person in the White House who has alienated our country's allies while befriending authoritarian rulers, and whose impulsive tweets and other off the cuff remarks are uncontrollable by his aides. We are confronted with the limits of a presidential, as opposed to a parliamentary, system, as neither the provisions for impeachment nor the disability provisions of the twenty-fifth amendment were designed to reach such a case. And this occurs at a time when an exchange of intemperate speech between the president and the North Korean leader could lead to a devastating war.

For many Republican party supporters of President Trump, however, the election simply threw out the big government party and replaced it with someone who will return the government to the people. For others, including some prominent Republicans, the presidential election of 2016 represented populism in decline. I think the latter interpretation is more accurate, and the source of the problem is popular distrust in government and political party organizations that have become too weak to restrain and direct excessive populist impulses. If we do not need an enlightened statesman like Lincoln, we do need someone, somewhat like Lincoln, who is able to work within political party organizations to strengthen the bonds between the people and their government. When popular government works, it is because, among other things, the two major political parties are able to present people with a choice of candidates in which either candidate would be well qualified to govern.

To illustrate this point, consider three recent critiques of the Trump presidency. In the October 2017 issue of the *Atlantic*, two former members of Republican Administrations, Jack Goldsmith and Eliot A. Cohen, and Atlantic Correspondent Ta-Nehisi Coates, critically assessed the Trump presidency. I think the first two criticisms reflect positions consistent with those of Hamilton and Lincoln, while the third resembles an abolitionist's criticism of Lincoln. Goldsmith a law professor who rescinded the Bush Administration's "torture memo" when he led the Office of Legal Counsel, argues that while the Constitution's checks and balances have so far prevented President Trump from violating the law, he has trashed numerous norms, such as respecting the independence of the courts and the Justice Department's administration of justice, and more generally the maintenance of civil and honest discourse.[23] Cohen, a professor at John's Hopkins School of Advanced International Studies who also served as Counselor of the State Department under Secretary Condoleezza Rice, expresses alarm over this president's brazen treatment of America's allies, his cozying up to Russian President Vladimir Putin, and his leaving unfilled hundreds of key positions in the State Department. Agreeing with Goldsmith concerning Trump's "disregard for constitutional norms and decent behavior," he fears something worse "on the treacherous stage of international politics": "Hearing him bully and brag, boast and bluster, threaten and lie, one feels a kind of dizziness, a sensation ... that accompanies dangerously high blood pressure, just before a sudden, excruciating pain"[24] (p. 73). The heart attack is a metaphor for a deadly war with North Korea or China.

Writing as an African-American and an advocate of "identity politics," Coates calls Trump "America's first white president" because he is "the first president whose entire political existence hinges on the fact of a black president."[25] This contribution reminds us that over fifty years after the Civil Rights Act of 1964 and the Voting Rights Act of 1965, the race question remains on the front burner of American politics. We must acknowledge that while Lincoln did extinguish slavery, and while Frederick Douglass paid him a worthy appreciation in 1876, violent incidents on our country's streets, often involving police, mainly white, and young men, mainly black, account for much of the turbulence of American politics today.

The civil disagreements and coalition building that we need today require a public that is wise enough to realize that race and class conflicts both need to be resolved. That might require the kind of enlightened statesmen that Publius warned us would not always be at the helm. It may also require America's voters to assume more responsibility when exercising their right to vote. The presidency is too important an office for a protest vote.

NOTES

1. This phrase comes from his "House Divided" Speech, delivered June 16, 1858, at Springfield, Illinois. *Abraham Lincoln: Selected Speeches and Writings*, selected by Don Fehrenbacher, introduction by Gore Vidal, (Library of America paperback classic, 2009), p. 131.
2. *The Federalist*, edited by Robert Scigliano (Modern Library 2001), Federalist 1, pp. 5–6.
3. Max Farrand, ed. *Records of the Federal Convention of 1787*, 1937 revised edition in four volumes, (Yale 1966), volume 1, pp. 288, 290.
4. *Federalist* 72, in Scigliano, pp. 464–5
5. Ibid., volume 1, p. 147.
6. 4 Wheaton 116 (1819).
7. Morton J. Frisch, ed. *The Pacificus-Helvidius Debates*, p. 1, from Papers of Alexander Hamilton, 27 volumes, edited by Harold C. Syrett et. al. (Columbia UP, 1961–1987) vol. 14, 308–309.
8. Pacificus #1 in Frisch, pp. 12–15.
9. Pacificus #1, in Frisch, p. 11.
10. Ron Chernow, *Alexander Hamilton*, (Penguin Books, 2004) p. 488.
11. Ibid., p. 506.
12. Richard Carwardine, *Lincoln: A Life of Purpose and Power*, (Vintage Books, 2007) p. 197; Carwardine's source is F.B. Carpenter, *The Inner Life of Abraham Lincoln: Six Months at the White House*, pp. 281–2.
13. Carwardine, Preface, p. X.
14. *Abraham Lincoln: Selected Speeches and Writings*, selected by Don Fehrenbacher, introduction by Gore Vidal, (Library of America paperback classic, 2009), p. 19.
15. Ibid., p. 96.
16. Ibid., p. 131, (June 16, 1858).
17. Paul M. Angle, ed. *The Complete Lincoln-Douglas Debates of 1858* (University of Chicago press, 1958) pp. 171–172.
18. *Abraham Lincoln: Selected Speeches and Writings*, p. 95.
19. Ibid., p. 170.
20. See his letter to John A. Gilmer, December 15, 1860, in ibid., p. 274.
21. Ibid., pp. 304, 307.

22. While he still favors colonization, Lincoln points out that "equally distributed among the whites of the whole country ... there would be but one colored to seven whites. Could the one, in any way, greatly disturb the seven?" see Special Message to Congress, December 1, 1862, in ibid., p. 362.

23. The Atlantic's cover features the three articles under the heading "The Trump Presidency: A Damage Report." Goldsmith's essay is entitled "Will Donald Trump Destroy the Presidency?" It appears on pages 58–66.

24. Cohen's essay is entitled "Is Trump Ending the American Era?" It appears on pp. 68–73. The quoted passages are on p. 73.

25. Coates' presentation, "The First White President," is part of his new book, *We Were Eight Years in Power*. It appears on pages 74–87. The quoted passage is from p. 76.

References

Angle, Paul A. ed. *The Complete Lincoln-Douglas Debates of 1858*. Chicago: University of Chicago Press, 1958.

Carwardine, Richard. *Lincoln: A Life of Purpose and Power*. Reprint ed. New York: Vintage, 2007.

Chernow, Ron. *Alexander Hamilton*. New York: Penguin Books, 2004.

Coates, Ta-Nehisi. "The Whitest White House." *Atlantic*, October 2017, 74–84.

Cohen, Eliot A. "Sudden Decline of a Superpower." *Atlantic*, October 2017, 68–73.

Farrand, Max, ed. *The Records of the Federal Convention of 1787*. Revised ed. in 4 Volumes. New Haven: Yale University Press, 1966.

Frisch, Morton J., ed. *The Pacificus-Helvidius Debates of 1793–1794*, from *Papers of Alexander Hamilton*, 27 Volumes. Edited by Harold C. Syrett, et al. New York: Columbia University Press, 1961–1987.

Goldsmith, Jack. "Will American Democracy Recover?" *Atlantic*, October 2017, 58–66.

Hamilton, Alexander, James Madison, and John Jay. *The Federalist: A Commentary on the Constitution of the United States*. Modern ed. Edited by Robert Scigliano. New York: Modern Library, 2001.

Lincoln, Abraham. *Selected Speeches and Writings*. Paperback Classics. Edited and Selected by Don Fehrenbacher, with and Introduction by Gore Vidal. New York: Library of America, 2009.

CHAPTER 13

The Lesson of Lincoln in the Age of Trump

John Burt

LINCOLN AND THE ETHICAL FOUNDATIONS OF DEMOCRACY

Lincoln teaches two lessons for the age of Trump, first, a morally responsible but unself-righteous strategy for occasions when one discovers the American people engaging in behavior that undermines the mores upon which democratic political culture depends, and second, a realistic and moderate method of approaching opponents who seem to have closed themselves off from persuasion.

Lincoln came out of political retirement in 1854 because he realized that he had mistakenly idealized the American people. He had assumed that most white Americans, slaveholding or non-slaveholding, outside of a few South Carolina eccentrics, looked forward to a time when slavery might end. He took for granted that most white Americans believed that although slavery was so deeply entangled in both the economy and the political culture of the United States that it would be difficult to eradicate without creating a host of intractable problems, nevertheless it was bound,

---

The Almighty has His own purposes. 'Woe unto the world because of offenses; for it must needs be that offenses come, but woe to that man by whom the offense cometh.'

J. Burt (✉)
Brandeis University, Waltham, MA, USA

© The Author(s) 2018
A. Jaramillo Torres, M. B. Sable (eds.), *Trump and Political Philosophy*,
https://doi.org/10.1007/978-3-319-74445-2_13

some day, either through continuous cultural erosion, through private manumission, perhaps even through colonization, ultimately to vanish.

It was the removal of the prohibition against slavery in Kansas and Nebraska territories with the passage of the Kansas-Nebraska Act in 1854 that shocked Lincoln out of these illusions. Lincoln discovered that he could no longer assume that the opinion leaders among slaveholders shared his wish that slavery should somehow pass away. And he could no longer assume that opinion leaders in the free states were willing to limit the growth of slavery if doing so risked straining the cross-sectional partisan alliances with slave state politicians upon which both parties depended. If, indeed, the prohibitions were off about where slavery could go, there was no particular reason it could not re-enter areas where it had earlier been forbidden, not merely the free territories, but the free states as well.

What most shocked Lincoln about the Kansas-Nebraska act was not what it portended about the future of slavery, which was shocking enough in itself, but what it meant about what he took to be foundational American values. Lincoln took the act as an attack upon the promise of equality articulated by Jefferson in the opening sentences of the Declaration of Independence.

Lincoln knew he lived in a slaveholding society, and that his society's behavior contradicted the idea that all men are created equal, as our society in different ways does even now, and as perhaps every society does. But there is a difference between recognizing a rule but not following it, on one hand, and on the other, treating what Jefferson had called a self-evident truth as "a self-evident lie," as Calhoun's disciples did, or interpreting away its sting, as Stephen Douglas did, by arguing that it was only meant to apply to white people. Lincoln understood the promises of the Declaration to be something that would make America unhappy until it fulfilled them. He had in mind what Robert Penn Warren did when he called the Declaration a "burr under the saddle of the Republic." A norm you recognize even if you betray it every single day is still something different from a norm you think of as an illusion or a norm you have qualified away into thin air.[1]

Equality has, Lincoln argued, a special, foundational role in democratic political culture. Republics are spaces of self-rule, and self-rule only happens in publics, in rule-bound associations of people who recognize each other's moral equality and agree to respect and conserve each other's agency. You and I inhabit a space of freedom only if we acknowledge each other as equals, only if we see each other as agents whose agency we cannot allow ourselves or anyone else to trample. If I violate (or allow others to violate) the agency of other citizens, I undermine my own.

Now all republics, not just liberal democratic ones, depend upon a culture of equality shared by their stakeholders. But what is unique to a liberal democratic republic, and what, Lincoln felt, American history existed to test the possibility of, was whether the ground of equality was not merely something shared by an in-group of social masters but was something that all people as people might have a claim upon. In the classical world, the clique of insiders, the members of the *polis*, enjoyed freedom in their relations with each other, but their freedom was made possible by the oppression of the members of the *oikos*, whose uncompensated labor freed the *polis* from some of the coercion of biological or economic necessity. The freedom of the Athenian democracy, like the freedom of the slaveholders in the South, was the freedom of a master class, a freedom made possible by the subjection of others. Southerners were very aware of the connection between their own freedom and slavery, a connection developed in persuasive detail by Senator James Henry Hammond in his "Mud-Sill" speech in 1858.[2] But in Lincoln's view the American republic had promised that freedom was not merely the privilege of an in-group who could keep others under their heels. The United States was "dedicated to the proposition that all men are created equal," a dedication that required the United States to erase the classical distinction between *polis* and *oikos* and to offer political self-rule to everyone.[3]

Equality is foundational to liberal democracy because the ethos of mutual recognition is its essential moral prerequisite. To attack the Declaration is to deny that respect for persons *qua* persons is a primary value and to argue that persons may be excluded from the *polis* because they are the wrong color or worship the wrong God or speak the wrong language. Rule by law, as opposed to rule by decree or by force, is conditioned upon reasonable consent, which is itself conditioned upon political equality; what is at stake in the promises of the Declaration is not merely democracy, but the idea that any social order might foundationally be the product of reflection and choice rather than of force and accident. The upshot of Lincoln's allegiance to the Declaration is a vision of politics as a rule-bound order founded on mutual recognition of agency and commitment to persuasion by reason, the world articulated in Kant's 1795 essay "Perpetual Peace." The problem of mutual respect concerning agency is central to the ethics of the *Critique of Practical Reason*, and to the politics of Kant's political essays. It is this fundamental concern with equality and agency that connects Lincoln's thinking with Kant's.[4]

What is at stake in Lincoln's view of the Declaration is not merely the place of racial equality in a democratic ethos (a place which Lincoln himself was not yet ready to proclaim) but the question of whether the essence of politics is the search for fair and general terms of cooperation among people with different interests and different ideas of the good who nevertheless seek to share a common public world, or whether the essence of politics is the power to draw the distinction between those who are friends, to whom one concedes equality, and those whom, answerable to no rationality other than one's own sovereign decision, one declares to be outside the circle of friendship, and whom one approaches in a spirit of contestation to determine who will be subjected and who will be master; in other words, what is at stake in this distinction is the distinction between a vision of politics that is fundamentally Kantian in character and a vision of politics which, whether in acknowledged or unacknowledged ways, is characterized in the writings of Carl Schmitt.

What Lincoln saw in the Declaration of Independence, and in the ethos of equality and freedom it proclaimed, was a new model of nationhood, founded not in ethnic accidents but in democratic principles, principles that stood in the place blood and culture had always stood before. This model, then and now, is America's great gift to the world, and one the world stands in need of urgently at this present moment, in this era of vicious conflicts along ethnic and religious lines. It is the idea that gives power to the poetry of Whitman and the fiction of Melville. And it is also the idea that the election of Donald Trump has called into question. Anyone who cares for equality has reason to fear the current administration. And anyone who fears what the American people have become or will become under this administration should look to Lincoln for guidance about what to do when the American people reject the values that made them a people.

CONSENSUS AMERICAN VALUES REJECTED BY TRUMP'S SUPPORTERS

Here are two things that after the election of 2016 you can no longer say about the United States, two things that I had thought were bedrock convictions, some going back to the Civil War, some going back to the Second World War, that turn out to be rejected by Trump and his ruling coalition:

1. That America sees itself as destined to be an equal multicultural society that will root its sense of being a nation in a common political culture rather than in common blood; that in attempting to become a multicultural democracy America will blaze a path for democracy worldwide.
2. That America is committed to a world order founded upon multilateral agreements (as opposed to two-sided bargains of a temporary and transactional kind), to international institutions of collective security ruled by open covenants openly arrived at, in short to an order which extends to the world the political culture of liberal democracy.

Both of these themes are consequences of the idea that legitimacy is the product of consent among equals whose agency all have an interest in respecting and conserving. The first theme is the vision of the meaning of America articulated by Lincoln in the Gettysburg Address. The second theme is the application of the principles of the first to the international sphere, developed in the long foreign policy tradition that was first set forth in the Fourteen Points and elaborated by presidents of both parties from Roosevelt to Obama. Neither of these themes has the slightest value to Trump and his supporters, and in rejecting them they are rejecting the key lessons the world has looked to the United States to teach. From Lincoln we should learn what to do when America seems ready to betray its foundational values, and what the limits are of the means he sought to use. But to learn that lesson we need to see clearly what that betrayal is; we must face what the American people have chosen to become.

Trump's election depended explicitly upon the widely held assumption that only some Americans are real Americans. Americans of Muslim descent are presumed to be in sympathy with foreign terrorists, and immigration from Muslim countries must be subject to "a complete and total shutdown," since even infant refugees might be the next generation's suicide bombers, and can be counted upon to cheer the next terrorist attack as their co-religionists in Jersey City, New Jersey (as Trump claimed and his supporters continue to believe) had earlier cheered the fall of the twin Towers.

Americans of Mexican descent, Trumpists say, are at the very least coming to America to freeload on the bounty of its welfare system, and include disproportionate numbers of rapists, drug dealers, and gang members, although "some, I assume, are good people." Undocumented persons who risked their lives for America in the armed services are also criminals worthy of rapid deportation, since their presence in the United States is itself a crime. And the American citizen children of undocumented persons deserve deportation too, since they are "anchor babies," unworthy of the protection of the Fourteenth Amendment, which was designed only for real Americans in just the way that the equality promised in the Declaration of Independence was really only equality for white people. That is why the crowd at Trump's July 26, 2017 speech at Youngstown cheered his railing against Mexican gang members who "slice and dice" innocent captive white women (as if the gang members were somehow representative of all undocumented people), rhetoric taken from the lynch mob rantings of the late nineteenth century.

Trump's attacks on the citizenship rights of African-Americans have been less frontal, although it should not be forgotten that Trump first came to political fame taking out a full page advertisement in the *New York Times* on May 1, 1989, demanding, in racially charged ways, the death penalty for the "Central Park Five," who turned out to be innocent of the crimes they were charged with (although Trump still does not concede this), and by promoting in numerous venues from March to May 2011 the false claim that President Obama was born in Kenya, not in Hawaii, a claim that can only arise out of racial animus. Resentment against civil rights legislation, usually expressed in the form of hostility to "political correctness" and to "reverse discrimination," and hostility to voting rights legislation, expressed in the form of bogus claims about impersonation fraud at the ballot box, have energized Trump's coalition by expressing racial animus in coded form.

If Muslims, Mexican Americans, and African Americans are not real Americans for Trumpists any more than the enslaved were for Calhoun or Taney, Trump's liberal opponents are to them the most un-American at all, because such people are, in the phrase of Trump's early adviser Sam Clovis, "race traitors," which is to say, people who sneer at ordinary Americans and advance outsiders at their expense. Such people are what Trump's advisor Stephen Miller calls "cosmopolitans," people who are more deeply enemies of American greatness than the intelligence services of a hostile foreign power. They are, as Michael Anton, Trump's new Deputy Assistant to the President for Strategic Communications on the United States National Security Council, called them, the "Davoisie," internationally oriented parasites who seek "the ceaseless importation of Third World foreigners with no tradition of, taste for, or experience in liberty," in order to provide for themselves a docile electoral majority and to humble an America they hate. (This same cast of traitors sometimes also includes the business-oriented conservatives who used to dominate the Republican party as well.)[5]

In the current political world, exemplified by Trump but preceding his rise, politics is not about persuasion in the hope of reasonable consensus or of fairly mediating ongoing conflicts but about the expression of identity-making resentments in symbolic forms. Symbolic issues are rallied for expressive purposes to secure tribal solidarity. Politics is not a debating society, not a scheme for dividing resources fairly, but only, in Carl Schmitt's famous phrase, an arena in which friends confront enemies, and in which besting the enemy is the only consideration.[6] This is why Trump's children and campaign chiefs, contacted by what were clearly operatives connected to a hostile foreign intelligence service, did not blink at treating that intelligence service as a friend, and the loyal opposition party as the enemy. And this is why Trump himself, confronted with evidence about that contact, argued that he could not imagine that anyone to whom a hostile intelligence service offers dirt about a political opponent would not accept the offer.

In America now there are two ruling passions in the governing party, *herrenvolk democracy* and *anti-elite resentment*. Historically these are two separate things, but political currents since the civil rights era have aligned them to the point of making them hard to distinguish. What George Fredrickson (1987) called herrenvolk democracy is the oldest political strain in American culture, going back to Bacon's Rebellion in Virginia in 1676. It was a powerful formation in all of the regions whose economy depended upon slave agriculture up to and beyond the Civil War, but it has shaped politics far beyond the confines of the poor whites of the former slave states, and the thinking of middle-class whites throughout the Union even now reflects themes whose origins are in the herrenvolk democracy of the slavery era.

Herrenvolk democracy underlies American political institutions in deep ways, for it reflects the original bargain that introduced slavery into Virginia.[7] Nobody can share rule with people they must exploit. The system of exploiting white indentured labor upon which Virginia depended proved politically unstable, because the indentured servant would eventually become free and would inevitably make demands for a say in the political order. Therefore coerced labor had to be supplied from another source, the African-American slave, who could be forever denied a place in the *polis*. Releasing the white laborer from subjection made it possible to give him the measure of self-rule which social stability required. The price of allowing the poor white a modicum of self-rule was providing that the enslaved black man be exploited in the poor white's place. The poor white knew from the beginning that the oppression of the black man was the condition of his own political freedom.

The classic herrenvolk democracy of the slavery era combined racial hatred and class resentment in a powerful way. For the poor white, it provided a way of claiming that shared whiteness trumps class inequality. It also provided a way for the poor white to extort recognition from the rich white: you must respect our shared whiteness or I will be a threat to you. But because the poor white knew that the recognition herrenvolk democracy won for him was extorted, he knew that it was inauthentic, and he was constantly surveying his imaginary ally in the race war for signs of defection.[8] He knew that that ally ultimately had contempt for him no matter how fervid his professions to the contrary.

For the rich white, herrenvolk democracy was a way to keep the poor white in line, and to prevent him from making class alliances across racial lines, something which even later populist figures who have gone down in history as angry race-baiters, such as Georgia's Tom Watson, were occasionally tempted by. But the rich white too knew that his alliance with the poor white was unstable, and needed continuous shoring up through inflammatory appeals to race loyalty. One might say that the rich white's strategy of enlarging racial hatred was so obviously manipulative that one wonders how it could possibly have been effective, except that herrenvolk democracy gave both the rich white and the poor white reasons to magnify racial hatred, reasons that have to do with their suspicions of each other.

The end of slavery, and even the end of formal legal segregation, left intact the grievances and fears which drove herrenvolk democracy and gave the current politics of white resentment its shape. The politics of white grievance is a familiar theme in conservative (and even moderate) politics of the last fifty years, and it has played out as strongly in the northern suburb as in the Southern town. It is also nowadays a politics embraced by middle class white people at least as strongly as by poor white people.

No politician recently has used the theme of white resentment as effectively as Trump has, because no politician has more successfully tied white resentment to hostility to the administrative class and to hostility to what he portrays as a self-proclaimed (and mostly white) moral elite of progressive bureaucrats, experts, activists, and do-gooders. When George Wallace in 1968 denounced the "pointy-headed bureaucrats" to whom he wished to "send a message," he struck a political nerve, but he remained a fringe figure. But now Wallace's ideas have completely captured one of the two major parties. The effect has been to make an upsurge in public racism seem to be an egalitarian groundswell. Anti-elite resentment makes embracing white supremacy seem to be the (white) people's rejection of their would-be moral superiors' attempts to dictate their lives to them and to police their morals and their language. If you care about racial equality, you obviously lack the common touch; you are a world citizen, but not an American.

There is a symmetry between Trumpist domestic policy and Trumpist foreign policy. In both cases the aim is to narrow the duty of care and to repudiate an ethos of responsibility for a common national public life and for a common world order. In his May 25, 2017 speech dedicating the September 11 memorial at the NATO headquarters in Brussels, Trump scolded the gathered heads of government about shortcomings in their defense spending, implying that they require the United States to bear too many of the costs of their collective defense.[9] Trump's remarks then are consonant with the foreign policy remarks in his inaugural address complaining that prior administrations had "subsidized the armies of other countries while allowing for the very sad depletion of our military," and had "defended other nation's [sic] borders while refusing to defend our own."[10] The foreign policy burden of Trump's inaugural address was chiefly directed at American allies, and it concerned not only whether they had shouldered a fair share of the expenses of the common defense but also their economic competition with the United States: "We must protect our borders from the ravages of other countries making our products, stealing our companies, and destroying our jobs."

These pugnacious lines, particularly startling because they were aimed at states that think of themselves as friends, came wrapped in what at first glance looks like a truism: "We will seek friendship and goodwill with the nations of the world—but we do so with the understanding that it is the right of all nations to put their own interests first." The practical meaning of that truism was not explicated until Trump's advisors, General H. R. McMaster, Trump's head of the National Security Council, and Gary D. Cohn, the Director of the National Economic Council, articulated them in an op-ed published in the *Wall Street Journal* just after Trump's return from his rebuke of the NATO leaders:

> The president embarked on his first foreign trip with a clear-eyed outlook that the world is not a "global community" but an arena where nations, nongovernmental actors and businesses engage and compete for advantage. We bring to this forum unmatched military, political, economic, cultural and moral strength. Rather than deny this elemental nature of international affairs, we embrace it.[11]

The reader should note the jeering tone embodied in the scare quotes around the phrase "global community." Only soft-headed people and believers in unicorns like Franklin Roosevelt and Dwight Eisenhower apparently believe in such a thing as global community, even as an ideal. One should also note the self-congratulatory tone McMaster and Cohn use to describe their own toughness of mind: they, like Trump, have a "clear-eyed outlook" that suffers no illusions and grasps substantial realities.

McMaster and Cohn postured as hard-minded realists. But what they articulated is not consonant with the half-century of realist policy applied in different ways beginning with Marshall, Kennan, and Acheson. During the Cold War it could not have been lost on the people of the allies of the Soviet Union that the United States was a far better ally to its own allies than the Soviet Union was. The Soviet Union made the economies of its allies serve its own; that any Soviet satellite might compete with it was unimaginable. By contrast, the United States encouraged the economic development of Germany and Japan, and not only tolerated but promoted them to become its own formidable economic competitors.[12]

That the US did not seek to suppress the economies of Japan and Germany is for Trump and his followers a sign of weakness, and something to be ashamed of. It's one aspect of what Trump referred to as "American carnage" in his inaugural address. But it was the consequence of the wartime generation's conviction that trade is the enemy of war, and part of the same thinking that produced other treaty-shaped, rule-bound international institutions, beginning with the Atlantic Charter, such as the western allies crafted in the years after the Second World War. Trump's resentment against the US allies is resentment against the institutions that have kept the western powers at peace with each other for seventy years.

It was a commonplace during the prelude to the Iraq War that Democrats saw the world in Kantian terms and Republicans saw the world in Hobbesian terms. Trump's "economic nationalism," with its rhetoric of muscular *realpolitik*, suggests that Trumpists have an attraction to a

Hobbesian, perhaps a Darwinian point of view. But the undercurrent of resentment, particularly resentment against democratic allies (authoritarian allies like Saudi Arabia, Poland, Hungary, the Philippines, and Turkey seem to get a pass), suggests that what is in play in Trump's foreign policy is not just clear eyed *realpolitik* but a burning desire to settle scores with those who have used professions of friendship to take advantage of us.

The politics of this angry, identity-shaping hostility to others arises not from Hobbes but from Schmitt. The assumption that there is no international order worth thinking about, that there is no persuasion or consensus, only friend or enemy, suggests a Schmittian rage behind the Darwinian hardness; Trumpist realism does not issue from the coolness of the detached intellect, but from the grim satisfaction one takes when one is about to let something rip, and damn the consequences.

In both the domestic and international arenas the chief theme of Trumpist policy is resentment and grievance, and the great philosopher of resentment and grievance, the great self-proclaimed unmasker of visions of world order and disinterested justice, is Schmitt, whom Trump has probably not read but who is his intellectual godfather. Furthermore, anyone who has followed the politics of the United States over the last few years must be forced to the conclusion that a large portion of the American electorate is animated by Schmittian political values. No democratic society can expect to survive a situation where Schmittian political values prevail in its people.

LINCOLN'S KANTIAN STRATEGIES AGAINST SCHMITTIAN POLITICS

The question with which this essay began was the question Lincoln faced in the wake of the Kansas-Nebraska Act: what is the proper response when the American people undermine the habits and mores upon which liberal democracy depends but which it cannot legislate?

The Schmittian world view underlying Trump's victory is unattractive relative to the Kantian views one might see as underlying both Lincoln's politics and the mainstream politics of the post-1945 era. But that world view does pose a challenge to Kantian politics which is hard to surmount: if the nature of politics is always a conflict between enemies, then it is easy to maintain that the attempt to resolve the conflict through appeal to a transcending common value must always be a bad faith attempt to subdue an opponent by blinding him in a golden fog of idealizations. The charge may be false, but it is rhetorical dynamite, and hard to defuse. As the edge of Schmitt's convictions was its argument that the vision of a peaceful world order elaborated in Wilson's Fourteen Points masked the Allies' ambition for conquest, so the edge of Trump's conviction is that the ideals of civil toleration and equality embraced (however imperfectly and grudgingly) by his opponents mask, for Trump's white middle-class and working-class supporters, their real aim of enriching the underclass, and particularly the black underclass, at their expense.

Trump's victory raises the question of whether Kantian ideals really are something human nature can sustain, since they are so vulnerable to attacks that arise from loyalty politics and resentment politics. In particular, I wonder whether Kantian politics is capable of holding its own against herrenvolk democracy, a central theme of the politics of Lincoln's own day and ours. After all, herrenvolk democracy did bring down Reconstruction, and perhaps it did so not just because the white supremacists of the Reconstruction era were more ruthless and single-minded than their opponents were, but because Lincoln's values depended upon an unrealistic idealization of human nature, since human nature is fallen in such a way as to make the liberal dream of fair dealing and the democratic dream of popular rule not only values in tension with each other but stark opposites.[13]

Lincoln argued in his 1838 Lyceum Address that liberal democracy was vulnerable because its stability depended upon a cultural structure of commonly held but only partly conscious assumptions and norms that law could not establish by itself.[14] In the 1854 Peoria speech he argued that Stephen Douglas, by treating the choice of whether to have slavery or not as a purely economic choice subject to majority will, was corrupting those cultural preconditions for freedom.[15] It is only mores and customs, Lincoln argued, not laws and constitutional arrangements, that keep the liberal ideal of fair toleration and the democratic ideal of popular rule from destroying each other. Those cultural preconditions seem on very thin ice now.

Lincoln was not the only person to see that the American democracy was under existential threat during the political crisis of the 1850s, but his response to the threat was more thoughtful than most. He did not, like Thoreau in "Resistance to Civil Government," conclude that the public order was so irremediably corrupt that the only alternative was withdrawal from the public arena, except for engaging in what at this distance seem to be mostly symbolic acts of resistance. Nor did he, despairing of worldly justice, come to see himself as an instrument of divine justice, as John Brown did, since Lincoln understood that that position could lead one to do and become almost anything. Nor did he, as in different ways Stephen Douglas and William Seward did, simply try to make the best concrete bargain he could persuade the other side to agree too, since he was aware that if your side believes it has to bargain and the other side does not then the other side will invariably drive your side to the wall. Nor did he, like Salmon Chase or Charles Sumner, simply accept the fact that the descent of the republic to war had opened ways to settle by force the moral question that the impasses of politics had previously closed.

Lincoln strove to keep alive the possibilities of persuasive engagement with his political opponents that his friends and enemies alike had striven to kill off. In the 1854 Peoria Speech, for instance, Lincoln imagined a version of the slaveholder with whom it was possible that he could come to political terms. He began by disclaiming that he had any prejudice against the people of the south. Southerners of the current day, he argued, had inherited slavery, and would not have invented it had they not inherited it, being neither better nor worse than other people. Further, he conceded that they acted under practical constraints that made emancipation, although not impossible, difficult enough that he did not believe that he had the right to denounce them for their lack of courage in not attempting it immediately. He was skeptical that merely freeing the slaves and keeping them as underlings would improve their condition, and he believed that the burden of ugly racial feeling, even if unjust, would complicate making freed slaves the equals of white citizens, since even an unjust universal feeling cannot be safely disregarded. Similar practical difficulties—not to mention moral ones—ruled out colonization as well. Although it did seem to him that systems of gradual emancipation might be adopted, he conceded that "If all earthly power were given me, I should not know what to do" about slavery, and because of that concession he understood that he could not blame Southerners for not doing what he should not know how to do himself (I: 316).

To modern readers, Lincoln's position here seems pretty weak. But its weakness served a strategic purpose, that of persuading Southerners to agree that slavery should not go into the western territories, something that his taking a hard moral line might well rhetorically have put out of reach by getting his opponents' backs up. Lincoln's eye was on the immediate purpose, talking the South off a high horse about the Kansas-

Nebraska Act. Those purposes were modest, and involved what seem to be deep moral concessions on his part. But Lincoln's purposes were also merely a first step, and they made possible second steps, equally modest, which make possible further steps. Also, Lincoln's concessions were temporary, made in order to evade resistance but not to surrender to it. Lincoln didn't ask to end slavery, but he did ask the South to take measures that would weaken it and make its end more imaginable. He didn't ask for social or political equality for black people, because he knew that doing so would foreclose the possibility of any concession by slaveholders, and that many white non-slaveholders would defect to supporting the slaveholders if equality were made an issue of right then. But he also did not concede that racism accords with "justice and sound judgment," conceding only that it is a very powerful bad habit, a bad habit he admitted (with some shamefacedness) that he himself shared, and one that could not be broken in an afternoon. The concessions he asked of his opponents were small, but each one elevated the possibility of a further concession, and each one brought the political culture one step further toward the horizon of political and social transformation.

In making this argument, Lincoln imagined his opponents in an idealized way. He saw the typical slaveholder as someone like Thomas Jefferson, or like his friend Joshua Speed, slaveholders who hated slavery and longed for a way to end it, but perhaps lacked the courage, or were too far in debt, to do so. For all his faults, this kind of slaveholder offered the possibility of persuasive engagement. With such an opponent one does not have to see one's self as engaged in a conflict over principle but instead in a conflict over means. At worst, with such an opponent, one shares the underlying value, what H.L.A. Hart would call a legal "concept," and differs with the opponent about how to realize that value under concrete conditions of time and space and history and institutions, what Hart would call a legal "conception."[16] To see a political conflict as turning on alternative conceptions that derive from a shared concept is to keep alive the possibility of a shared political life even in the face of a deep conflict; to see the conflict instead as a conflict between law and higher law, or between man's law and God's law, by contrast, is to raise the stakes of the conflict and to increase the chances that only violence can solve it. Those who share a concept recognize that that concept has what in *Lincoln's Tragic Pragmatism* I called "implicitness." They recognize that the concept is saturated with implications and entailments, many of which are not obvious to one at any particular moment, and many of which one would deny the presence of at the moment, even if later one would concede that those entailments were so inevitable that it is a matter of wonder that they were ever doubted.

In his speech on the Dred Scott decision of June 26, 1857, Lincoln conceived of the promise of equality, made by Jefferson in the Declaration of Independence, as having the kind of implicitness I have in mind. The promise of equality was made knowing that under present circumstances it would not be fulfilled, but would raise the pressure to create the conditions which would make its fulfillment possible. Furthermore, the boundaries of the promise of equality are unknown, and each development of the meaning of the promise opens the door to further developments, impossible to imagine before the door opens, and inevitable once it does. The "new birth of freedom" Lincoln speaks of in the Gettysburg Address is not just Emancipation, the consequence of the promise of the Declaration that the republic was in the bloody process of securing, but political equality across racial lines, which it had mostly not yet begun seriously to imagine.

The way Lincoln sought to deal with the actual slaveholder by constructing an idealized model with which he encouraged the actual slaveholder to identify might seem to suggest a good way for decent people to deal with the politics of Trumpism. The difficulty is that the kind of slaveholder Lincoln imagined had in fact been becoming extinct, suspected of disloyalty to the South and crushed by the increasingly brutal loyalty politics of the slavery era. That slaveholder had been replaced by disciples of Calhoun who believed that slavery was not a regrettable legacy but a positive good and that slaves were property in exactly the way mules were property.

Lincoln was well aware that if the slaveholders really believed this, they were beyond persuasion, and sooner or later violent confrontation with them would become inevitable. But Lincoln also wondered how far slaveholders really believed professions like this (after all, Lincoln remarked at Peoria, they allow their children to play with their slaves' children, but not with the slave-dealer's children). People often do take hard-minded positions because they are forced into them by the loyalty politics of their own side. And people often throw hard-minded arguments into the faces of their opponents because they seem to be trumping and unanswerable, even if those arguments don't do justice to the nuances of their actual convictions. In *Lincoln's Tragic Pragmatism* I called such arguments "suicidally apodictic," and suggested that much political argument one hears even now is suicidally apodictic, designed to shut the other guy up rather than to advance one's own beliefs honestly. Suicidally apodictic arguments are thrilling, not only because they brace up one's own side, but also because they give those who make them the ability to claim that they are more loyal to their side than those who avoid them are. Suicidally apodictic arguments tempt politicians to compete for leadership of their faction by leading a race to the bottom. Lincoln sought to woo southerners away from suicidally apodictic arguments by attempting to appreciate the arguments that actually moved them. If such a strategy could work, it would be a valuable strategy at the present moment.

Promising as the strategy of the Peoria speech sounds, it was a failed one. Lincoln was very slow to recognize that the politicians of the slave states had closed their minds to persuasion, because he recognized that where persuasive engagement is impossible violence is sure to follow, and violence is never a test of who is right, only a test of who is stronger, and transforms even the victor is ways one might be reluctant to contemplate. But Lincoln's reluctance to despair of persuasion and deal-making was not soft-headed.

After his famous demonstration in the 1860 Cooper Institute speech that the thirty-nine men who wrote the Constitution favored federal control over the future of slavery in the territories, Lincoln sought to address a few words directly to his slaveholding opponents. He was aware, however, that they had turned away from persuasive engagement, and behaved in ways rather similar to what one sees in the comment threads on news sites today.

Lincoln's strategy was to address the fears which he believed had closed southern minds. He proceeded to work through the particular arguments he understood that his opponents might lodge: that his party was sectional; that it proposed a revolutionary reinterpretation of the Constitution; that it encouraged slave insurrections, such as the still-recent John Brown raid on Harper's Ferry; that it would seek to deny to the slave states rights granted in the Constitution; even that the election of a Republican president would itself be sufficient grounds to break up the United States. Lincoln's point was that none of these arguments were plausible; Lincoln's Republicans may have sought to prevent slavery from moving into the western territories, and they may have had in mind setting slavery in the course of ultimate extinction, but they did not represent an immediate existential threat to the south.

Having disposed of all these fears, Lincoln admitted that even for his side to give in on the immediate demands for the protection of slavery in the western territories that the slave states were pressing was unlikely to resolve the sectional conflict, because what the slaveholders wanted was not actually to have their way about the concrete issues in dispute but that the people of the free states stop criticizing slavery and recognize it as a positive good.

Lincoln had begun by conceding that the southern people were unlikely to listen to his argument, and he concluded by showing why whatever he said was unlikely to change their minds. Lincoln describes a south in an argumentative death-spiral, in which, ratcheted into issuing ever-escalating ultimata by its underlying insistence that the free states come to see slavery as a positive good, the south finally demands what the north cannot concede without a fatal sacrifice of interest or principle. The escalation of demands is enforced by loyalty politics—only the most extreme fire-eater is really loyal to the south—and also by wounded moral narcissism, since southerners could not help but feel that even the most craven surrender by the free states to their demand that slavery be embraced as a good thing was, because it was coerced, an inauthentic surrender, motivating a further demand.

Why would one bother to make arguments to those who have closed their ears to persuasion? The traditional interpretation of Lincoln's move in the Cooper Institute speech is that he was seeking to reassure fellow northerners that he was, unlike Seward perhaps, no radical, and that he wasn't actually addressing southerners at all. But Lincoln may well have sought to provoke in his southern interlocutors a kind of self-recognition. Actual people often entertain their convictions with more ambivalence than they let on, and usually entertain those convictions together with many other convictions, some of which pull in a morally different, and perhaps more morally wholesome direction. Lincoln asks, in effect, are your convictions on this issue suicidally apodictic ones? Are they convictions you embrace out of fear that your neighbor may stigmatize you as disloyal if you said what you really believe? Are the convictions that divide us really deeper, more close to your moral center, than the convictions that join us?

As it turned out, this strategy too was a failed one. And even the very broad concessions and the last-ditch, poetical appeal to the memory of the Revolution and to the "better angels of our nature," in Lincoln's First Inaugural Address was received in the South not as a peace offering but as a declaration of war, although some contemporary observers wondered whether the editors of those Southern newspapers who denounced what the *Richmond Enquirer* called the "cool, unimpassioned, deliberate language of the fanatic" of the address had even read it before writing their responses.

And the war came. But Lincoln's strategy of attempting to keep open the possibility of persuasive engagement remained a useful one, not because that engagement ever happened but because seeking it kept Lincoln, even as he prosecuted the most violent war in the West between Waterloo and the Somme, from a fatal and self-destructive illusion, the illusion that he himself had divine sanction in his back pocket, and wielded the terrible swift sword of God. And Lincoln's strategy, and his caution, provides some insights into how to proceed today.

A good immediate strategy to meet the threat of Trumpism might indeed be the one that Lincoln laid out in the closing lines of the Cooper Institute address. That strategy was two-fold. First, it involved avoiding a stance of pure confrontation, in which whatever the other side proposes is to be opposed because it is proposed by the other side. If the other side has a point, it should be recognized. Where the concession they ask is reasonable and can be given without a fatal sacrifice, the concession should be made. Second, we must also affirm that there are lines we won't cross, concessions we won't make no matter how high the price of firmness is; we must "dare to do our duty as we understand it."

A more important strategy is taught by the Lincoln Second Inaugural Address. The speech is famous for its forbearing and unself-righteous last paragraph. But it is still a very angry speech, willing even to hold that if God should will that the Civil War should continue "until all the wealth piled by the bondsman's two hundred and fifty years of unrequited toil shall be sunk, and until every drop of blood drawn with the lash shall be paid by another drawn with the sword," that "the judgments of the Lord are true and righteous altogether." The speech did not propose moral surrender, or splitting of the moral difference. It did not even quite propose that the two sides were morally equivalent. But it did propose that all parts of the United States shared responsibility for slavery, and that whatever policy follows the war it must not be one that turns on rewarding the pure and punishing the impure but upon atoning for the shared crime which led to the war. It proposes reconciliation on the basis of a recognition of shared complicity.

The lesson is that people on my side of the fence too share the burden of a history of herrenvolk democracy; it has opened possibilities for us, and it has shaped our political identities in ways we might find hard to acknowledge. Even our own anger with the Trumpists shows us how easy it would be to settle into a politics of resentment and score-settling. They too are our countrymen. We can disavow them no more than we can disavow the crimes of our own ancestors. And we have to take responsibility for them the way we take responsibility for the crimes of our ancestors, by recognizing a human fallenness we share with them.

PROSPECTS

So where do we stand now? Our country has betrayed the most important contribution it has made to the moral evolution of world politics. And unlike other periods in recent history, in which the United States has made moral compromises in order to defeat real world threats, this time the United States has itself decided to lead the way down to darkness, to a world driven by ethnic nationalism and authoritarianism. At other times in our history the United States has stood for things progressives in the world have admired, while using means they criticized. This time those who have most admired the United States have most reason to fear it.

What will the coming years be like? Will the Trump era be merely a wobble, like the Watergate era, or a passing episode that leaves behind a lasting bad taste and sense of shame, like the McCarthy era? Or will it be the beginning of several decades of determined reaction, in the way the Compromise of 1877 began seven decades of Jim Crow?

It was always wrong to believe that American history is characterized by innocence, success, and prosperity, as C. Vann Woodward pointed out more than fifty years ago.[17] But despite everything America has stood for something, has had a lesson to teach the world. That lesson began with a concept of nationhood that did not depend upon blood, religion, or culture, but on allegiance to key political ideals. America also offered the promise of moral equality: embracing the claim that "all men are created equal" means that recognizing the freedom and moral dignity of other people as people is a foundational political value, and that that recognition is the condition of one's own freedom and moral dignity. It is from that vision of the meaning of equality that other things Americans have cherished, such as the consent of the governed and the rule of law, descend.

America had already betrayed that value as deeply as it was possible to do at the very moment it articulated it, since many of the founders who proclaimed that all men were created equal also owned other men and women as slaves. But the idea of freedom has the strength of implicitness. Even as Americans betrayed that ideal, it worked on them. And we have seen it unfold in new ways over the years, haltingly advancing first religious toleration, then gender equality, more recently equality for people with different sexual orientations, and always the unfinished but continuing advance of racial equality. All these things were fermenting under the surface even as the levers of power were controlled by forces of reaction. This was as true in the Gilded Age, the apogee of Jim Crow and lynch law, as it was in the era of the overseer and the slave patroller.

I have some faith that the era of reaction we are now entering will pass. But I don't think it will pass in two or four years. Ultimately, though, I do think that this era will pass, because Trumpism promises impossible things and is riven with internal contradictions, as George F. Kennan once said of Communism. The era that began in 1877 passed, but not for eighty years. I have to hope that somehow America will regain its moral balance. Even in the Gilded Age, the values America betrayed kept moving it.

NOTES

1. The "self-evident lie" phrase struck in Lincoln's craw, and he cites it repeatedly, famously during the Galesburg debate with Douglas. See Abraham Lincoln, *Speeches and Writings 1832–1858*, ed. Don E. Fehrenbacher (New York: The Library of America, 1989) I: 794–795.
2. For the text of the "Mud-Sill" speech, sometimes called the "Cotton is King" speech, see James Henry Hammond, "Speech of Hon. J.H. Hammond, of South Carolina, in the Senate, March 4, 1858", *Congressional Globe 35th Cong., 1st sess. app.*, 35th Cong., 1st sess. app. 71, 1858, 68–71.
3. For how the distinction between *polis* and *oikos* applies to the slavery question, see John Burt, *Lincoln's Tragic Pragmatism: Lincoln, Douglas, and Moral Conflict* (Cambridge, MA: Belknap Press of Harvard University Press, 2013) 309. See also Hannah Arendt, *The Human Condition* (Chicago: University of Chicago Press, 1958).
4. See Steven B. Smith, "Abraham Lincoln's Kantian Republic", in *Abraham Lincoln and Liberal Democracy*, ed. Nicholas Buccola (University Press of Kansas, 2016), 216–238. See also Hannah Arendt, *Lectures on Kant's*

Political Philosophy, ed. Ronald Beiner (Chicago: University of Chicago Press, 1982).

5. For Clovis, see http://www.cnn.com/2017/08/02/politics/kfile-sam-clovis-blog-posts/index.html. For Miller, see http://www.politico.com/magazine/story/2017/08/03/the-ugly-history-of-stephen-millers-cosmopolitan-epithet-215454. For Anton, see Michael Anton, "The Flight 93 Election", Author given as "Publius Decius Mus", *The Claremont Review of Books*, September 5, 2016, visited on August 2, 2017, http://www.claremont.org/crb/basicpage/the-flight-93-election/. See also https://theintercept.com/2017/02/12/dark-essays-by-white-house-staffer-are-the-intellectual-source-code-of-trumpism/

6. On Schmitt, see Carl Schmitt, *The Concept of the Political*, Expanded edition, tr. George Schwab, Orig. 1932 (University of Chicago Press, 2007).

7. The argument in this and the next few paragraphs derives from Edmund S. Morgan, *American Slavery, American Freedom: The Ordeal of Colonial Virginia* (New York: W. W. Norton, 1975).

8. For more on how class conflict and racial conflict entangle each other see C. Vann Woodward, *Origins of the New South* (Baton Rouge: Louisiana State University Press, 1951).

9. For the text of the speech, see https://www.whitehouse.gov/the-press-office/2017/05/25/remarks-president-trump-nato-unveiling-article-5-and-berlin-wall.

10. For the text of the speech, see https://www.theguardian.com/world/2017/jan/20/donald-trump-inauguration-speech-full-text.

11. The op-ed can be found at https://www.wsj.com/articles/america-first-doesnt-mean-america-alone-1496187426.

12. See John Lewis Gaddis, *We Now Know: Rethinking Cold War History* (Oxford: Clarendon Press of Oxford University Press, 1997).

13. For a meditation on the idea that liberal fair dealing and tolerance and democratic popular rule may oppose each other see Chantal Mouffe, *The Democratic Paradox* (New York: Verso Books, 2005). As will be seen, I accept Mouffe's diagnosis, although I propose a different solution to the problem she describes.

14. About this structure of mores and assumptions in the Lyceum Speech, see John Burt, "Prosperity and Tyranny in Lincoln's Lyceum Address", in Buccola, *Abraham Lincoln and Liberal Democracy*, 13–43.

15. For a telling analysis of the consequences of Douglas's position, see Harry V. Jaffa, *Crisis of the House Divided: An Interpretation of the Issues in the Lincoln-Douglas Debates* (Garden City, NY: Doubleday and Company, 1959). See also Lewis E. Lehrman, *Lincoln at Peoria* (Mechanicsburg, PA: Stackpole Books, 2008).

16. For the distinction between concept and conception see H. L. A. Hart, *The Concept of Law* (Oxford: Oxford University Press, 1961). See also Ronald Dworkin, *Law's Empire* (Cambridge, MA: Harvard University Press, 1986).

17. See C. Vann Woodward, *The Burden of Southern History* (Baton Rouge: Louisiana State University Press, 1960).

REFERENCES

Anton, Michael. "The Flight 93 Election". Author Given as "Publius Decius Mus". *The Claremont Review of Books*, September 5, 2016. Visited on August 2, 2017. http://www.claremont.org/crb/basicpage/the-flight-93-election/.

Arendt, Hannah. *The Human Condition*. Chicago: University of Chicago Press, 1958.

———. *Lectures on Kant's Political Philosophy*. Ed. Ronald Beiner. Chicago: University of Chicago Press, 1982.

Buccola, Nicholas, ed. *Abraham Lincoln and Liberal Democracy*. Lawrence: University Press of Kansas, 2016.

Burt, John. *Lincoln's Tragic Pragmatism: Lincoln, Douglas, and Moral Conflict*. Cambridge, MA: Belknap Press of Harvard University Press, 2013.

———. "Prosperity and Tyranny in Lincoln's Lyceum Address". In Nicholas Buccola, *Abraham Lincoln and Liberal Democracy*. Lawrence: University Press of Kansas, 2014, 13–43.

Dworkin, Ronald. *Law's Empire*. Cambridge, MA: Harvard University Press, 1986.

Fredrickson, George M. *The Black Image in the White Mind: The Debate on Afro-American Character and Destiny, 1817–1914*. Orig. 1971. Middletown, CT: Wesleyan University Press, 1987.

Gaddis, John Lewis. *We Now Know: Rethinking Cold War History*. Oxford: Clarendon Press of Oxford University Press, 1997.

Hammond, James Henry. "Speech of Hon. J. H. Hammond, of South Carolina, in the Senate, March 4, 1858". *Congressional Globe 35th Cong., 1st sess. app.*, 35th Cong., 1st sess. app. 71, 1858, 68–71.

Hart, H.L.A. *The Concept of Law*. Oxford: Oxford University Press, 1961.

Jaffa, Harry V. *Crisis of the House Divided: An Interpretation of the Issues in the Lincoln-Douglas Debates*. Garden City, NY: Doubleday and Company, 1959.

Lehrman, Lewis E. *Lincoln at Peoria*. Mechanicsburg, PA: Stackpole Books, 2008.

Lincoln, Abraham. *Speeches and Writings 1832–1858*. Ed. Don E. Fehrenbacher. New York: The Library of America, 1989.

Morgan, Edmund S. *American Slavery, American Freedom: The Ordeal of Colonial Virginia*. New York: W. W. Norton, 1975.

Mouffe, Chantal. *The Democratic Paradox*. New York: Verso Books, 2005.

Schmitt, Carl. *The Concept of the Political.* Expanded edition, tr. George Schwab, Orig. 1932. Chicago: University of Chicago Press, 2007.

Smith, Steven B. "Abraham Lincoln's Kantian Republic". In Buccola, *Abraham Lincoln and Liberal Democracy*, 2016, 216–238.

Woodward, C. Vann. *Origins of the New South.* Baton Rouge: Louisiana State University Press, 1951.

———. *The Burden of Southern History.* Baton Rouge: Louisiana State University Press, 1960.

CHAPTER 14

The Great Emancipators Oppose the "Slave Power": The Lincolnian—and Aristotelian—Dimensions of Trump's Rhetoric

Kenneth Masugi

One should be struck by similar themes and strategies in the surprising campaigns of Donald Trump and Abraham Lincoln. To be sure, Lincoln and Trump have in common superficialities such as a crude sense of humor, a reliance on conspiracy theories, and a reputation for being unqualified for office. And they certainly both harbored enormous ambitions. Though candidate Trump made casual references to Abraham Lincoln, as any Republican would, he did not wrap himself in Lincoln's cloak and rhetoric the way some recent presidents have.

While Trump's Lincolnian tropes include his frequent reference to "government of the people" and giving a major policy speech on limited government at Gettysburg, his key theme of "Making America Great Again" was Lincolnian: American nationalism was the central theme of his campaign. His campaign rhetoric echoed that of the Whig Party and Lincoln's own political career, including policies on tariffs, internal improvements, immigration, conspiracies against the liberties of the people, and war. Above all, Trump champions the Whig regard for striving Americans.[1]

K. Masugi (✉)
Claremont Institute, Upland, CA, USA

© The Author(s) 2018
A. Jaramillo Torres, M. B. Sable (eds.), *Trump and Political Philosophy*,
https://doi.org/10.1007/978-3-319-74445-2_14

235

Aristotle illuminates these disparate presidents in distilling the significance of political rhetoric. "Rhetoric is a counterpart of dialectic," his treatise on rhetoric begins (*Rhetoric*, I.1). He thereby compares and contrasts the words of politicians and the arguments of philosophers. He suggests that knowing one requires knowing the other. Thus, political philosophy seeks to understand that relationship between political and philosophic *logoi*. Aristotle's two definitions of human being in the *Politics* connect these human activities: "Man is by nature the political animal" and "Man is the animal having *logos*" (reason or speech). Rhetoric exists in the space between these two descriptions of human being. Politics and *logos* are intimately related but not identical. Without rational speech we are barbarians, able to govern only through brute force. Speech saves us for higher purposes. But speech full of lies and threats corrupts us and becomes another form of our degradation; far from protecting us from tyrants, speech becomes their tool. And nothing could be sillier in politics than to think that speech alone is sufficient to govern and to protect nations. Speech is successful when it convinces the audience to have trust in the speaker's character (*ethos*), to agree with the speaker's arguments (*logos*), and to give their hearts to the speaker (*pathos*), which means the listeners act the way he wills. Both Lincoln and Trump, as do all successful democratic politicians, appeal to voters following Aristotle's ancient principles.

Trump's emphasis on patriotism and duty of Americans toward each other reflects Lincoln's strategy. Both Lincoln and Trump insist that common citizenship counts for more than one's region, ethnicity, race, or sex. The patriotism of his campaign speeches is further refined in Trump's most important presidential speeches—the Inaugural Address, the Address to Congress, the Warsaw admonition, and the United Nations address. Though their circumstances and crises differ, the 16th and 45th presidents advanced similar arguments on the nature of American patriotism. Both presidents confronted the challenge to patriotism in a nation fractured over sectional injustice and over race. Though neither president was a scholar of the ancients, classical political philosophy, especially its teaching on the best regime and friendship of virtue, illuminates their intentions and provides the standards of success and failure. Viewed from that perspective both presidents are great emancipators and facilitators of new births (or re-births) of American identity.

On closer examination several other comparisons come to mind. These come to light in Lincoln's rhetoric and strategy, which saved the Union and have taught future Americans the meaning of their country.

LINCOLN'S RHETORIC AND THE "SLAVE POWER"

The leading Lincolnian theme is his peculiarly principled opposition to the "slave power." Lincoln saw an America whose political institutions were dominated by pro-slavery forces—the Congress, the judiciary, most presidents from Jefferson on, and the dominant Democratic Party. In other words, Lincoln saw what James Madison had earlier labeled a "majority faction," an injustice against the people, perpetrated under the guise of democracy. Trump decried "a rigged system," with no relief in the establishments of either party. (His condemnation found bipartisan support in the leftist populism of Senator Bernie Sanders.) The prospect of an appalling choice between yet another Clinton and yet another Bush forced discontented citizens toward other possibilities, an outsider who did not hesitate to assail his opponents in dramatic ways and assert his independence.[2]

Lincoln made no less unexpected a conquest of the new-born Republican Party of the 1850s than Trump did of the geriatric Republicans of 2016. Thus the Compromise of 1850, crafted by giants of Senate, including Douglas and his hero Henry Clay, bought peace at a fearful price. Even more telling was the Kansas-Nebraska Act, which scrapped the Missouri Compromise and invited slavery into the entire country ... and triggered his re-entry into politics from his flourishing legal career. His October 16, 1854 Peoria Address outlined his principles and strategy of the 1850s. Rejecting the extreme of abolitionism, Lincoln denounced the recent "declared indifference" to the evil of slavery and accordingly its spread. Practically, this meant toppling Senator Stephen Douglas, the leader of the national Democracy (or Democratic Party) and replacing him as the nation's leading politician, heaving a new political party.[3]

As Don Fehrenbacher, among other historians, has noted, the pro-slavery faction dominated American national institutions since the Revolution of 1800. The 3/5 clause, the Louisiana Purchase, the Mexican War, and the formation of slaveholding states produced national majorities that protected slavery. Amid one-party Democratic rule, even three of the four Whig presidents owned slaves. While Democrats Franklin Pierce and James Buchanan did not own slaves, the prevalence of slaveholding presidents illustrated how both parties collaborated in deepening the "slave power."[4]

Lincoln denounced political deal-making that would "blow out the moral lights around us, and extinguish that greatest torch of all which America presents to a benighted world—pointing the way to their rights, their liberties, and their happiness." America's greatness lies in its founding mission, which elevates its citizens beyond the constraints of mere self-interest. Lincoln refers to the Declaration of Independence, which calls for elevating and revolutionary but ultimately also sobering conduct. Thus, the expansion of slavery must not be taken as another instance of the "sacred right of self-government" (Eulogy of Henry Clay, July 6, 1852).

Until recently, Lincoln lamented, Americans accepted a moral consensus on the wrong of slavery—after all, who embraces the slave-dealer? It follows that there must not be moral preening on the side of the North against the South: "They are just what we would be in their situation." The South does not have a monopoly on "natural tyrants." Finally, most sobering of all, "A universal feeling, whether well or ill-founded, can not be safely disregarded." But at the heart of that recognition of the limits of laws is the belief that one might leave a black person alone rather than enslaving them, thus honoring the "sacred right of self-government." That recognition points to the importance of moral consensus for self-government to work (All quotations from the Peoria Address, October 16, 1854).

But even that bare minimum is no longer assumed: now politicians and academics speak of the Declaration as "a self-evident lie." The Declaration did not necessitate "political and moral equality" between black and white. No such rashness there. A kind of political fanaticism had taken over politics, manifested in pro-slavery manifestoes and in abolitionism (and its frequent companions of communism, sexual equality, and temperance). Lincoln's Temperance Address was intended to address all these power-drunk excesses.

Thus Lincoln referred to the Declaration as "the white man's charter of freedom" (see also his eulogy of Henry Clay, July 6, 1852). Not for white men only, the Declaration rather gives freedom to white men *provided* they extend it to *all* men. What keeps white men (including immigrants) free will also have to free, eventually, black slaves as well. Thus, Lincoln in his speech on Dred Scott observed about a black woman that she need be neither his slave nor his wife. "In some respects she certainly is not my equal, but in her natural right to eat the bread she earns with her own hands without asking leave of any one else, she is my equal, and the equal of all others" (Dred Scott speech, June 26, 1857). (The Lockean capacity for work makes the black woman the equal of other humans. Lincoln chose the least threatening comparison to make.) In a celebration of the Fourth of July he observed, "this argument of the Judge [Stephen Douglas] is the same old serpent that says you work and I eat, you toil and I will enjoy the

THE GREAT EMANCIPATORS OPPOSE THE "SLAVE POWER"... 239

fruits of it ... whether it come from the mouth of a King, an excuse for enslaving the people of his country, or from the mouth of men of one race as a reason for enslaving the men of another race, it is all the same old serpent..." (Chicago Independence Day Celebration, July 10, 1858).

Lincoln would further intrigue his audiences by proclaiming an amazing conspiracy theory: "we find it impossible not to believe that Stephen and Franklin and Roger and James all understood one another from the beginning, and all worked upon a common plan or draft drawn up before the first blow [for spreading slavery nation-wide] was struck" ("House Divided" speech, June 16, 1858). Lincoln's uncompromising position led to the rupture of the Democratic Party and his eventual national political triumph.

To succeed politically, Lincoln's argument for equality had to transcend mere charitable appeal. In this he is far from contemporary liberalism and multiculturalism. His understanding of the human soul explains his political rhetoric. Toward the end of his Dred Scott speech, Lincoln, arguing for a policy of colonization of free blacks to be paired with his emancipation goal, noted the need for a "hearty will" toward that uncertain (and implausible) end. "Will springs from the two elements of moral sense and self-interest." People need to believe in the rightness and goodness of a policy and also believe it is in their self-interest (or "at least, not against our interest"). Politics fails when it becomes all about duty or all about self-interest. The task of politics is to combine the two human passions, with the motive of duty having become ever more powerful in a nation of Christians. Lincoln would practice this basic prudence throughout the Civil War, combining "moral sense and self-interest" toward the cause of preserving the Union. He then further refined the Union by restoring its principles in a "new birth of freedom."

The high expression of this unity of duty and interest is found in the Gettysburg Address, the psalm of American political religion. Only Lincoln's Second Inaugural transcends it, with biblical religion dominating political life. The first poem glorifies civil religion, the second the political consequences of divine revelation. Explicating the Gettysburg Address's powerful themes will aid in understanding Trump's appeal to American traditions. That poem became America's way to summarize its principles and express how Americans feel about them.

The psalm depicts an "organic and sacramental" union, one both natural and divinely rooted. "[T]he central metaphor of the Gettysburg Address is that of birth and rebirth ... This new birth [of freedom] is not ... mere renewal of life but the origin of a higher life."[5] Americans are united with each other more closely than could previously be imagined by either nature or God. The founders described Americans as uniting for the sake of self-interest in a world where the clash of factions induces moderation and "ambition must be made to counteract ambition," to cite *The Federalist*, #51. Washington elevates this constitutional achievement into a glorious consummation. Lincoln takes this unity of space, over an empire of liberty, and extends it over time, spanning generations. His psalm takes Americans from a continent to a graveyard and then back out to the whole earth, from founding fathers to a new birth, from people of "a proposition" to people who have been chosen and tested, from the word to the deed and then always back to the word that renews them for the sake of more deeds.

For a country that was split by civil war then and by general discontent and partisan ill-feeling today, it may seem implausible that Lincoln (and Trump) were inspired by a notion of the best political way of life, or the best regime. But in fact such inspirations are a cause as well as an effect of division. Far from utopianism, this focus on friendship is the ultimate "realism" of ancient political philosophy, which takes its bearings by what it sees and experiences directly. The best regime or political order's leading traits of common good and self-sacrifice guide the wise statesman in arranging institutions and recommending policies. A nation needs a political passion greater than either the Hobbesian fear for one's own life or desires for the lives and possessions of others. A nation must unite its citizens in a familial way yet not turn them into a family of perpetual children—George Washington was well aware of this danger. How can a nation be both united (a condition of its existence) and free (a condition of its purpose or happiness)? That was Aristotle's question, Lincoln's question, Trump's question, and the question of the entire history of statesmanship. It is a first question that precedes contemporary ideological debates.

TRUMP'S RHETORIC AND POLITICAL PRACTICE: DEFENDING THE NATION

As we see in George Washington's Farewell Address, national unity requires a combination of what is necessary, such as property rights and national defense, and what is noble or splendid, including religion, benevolence, and national pride. While some candidates pursue policies of redistribution (e.g., Bernie Sanders), others emphasize opportunity and growth. Trump challenged the bipartisan agreement on the benefits of global trade agreements and immigration (e.g., Bush). Again Aristotle helps us understand that "Oligarchies change most often in two most obvious ways. One occurs when they treat the multitude unjustly, for then any champion is sufficient, especially when it turns out that the leader comes from the oligarchy itself..." (*Politics* V.6). Class resentment can be mollified if the candidate is a traitor to his class. While moral and religious beliefs can unify, they can also foster division (e.g., Ted Cruz). Trump proclaimed his support on key moral/religious issues such as abortion and won over evangelical and Catholic voters in the general election, despite vehement denunciations of his character. He got the political benefit of "values voters" without bearing the stigma of being a moralistic prig. Chortling at saying "merry Christmas" again did not sound threatening.

On foreign policy, Trump appealed to frustrations with the Obama and Bush foreign policies and in particular the Middle East wars. Not isolationist, his slogan was an unapologetic "Make America Great Again." In the primaries Trump campaigned and held rallies in states throughout the country where he had no chance of winning electoral votes but showed him proclaiming a consistent message. A national celebrity long before he became a candidate, he presented himself as a national candidate, above all speaking for those whom both parties had ignored. Rather than raise funds from interest groups, he accepted invitations from national media and held enormous rallies, relying on social media from attendees to spread enthusiasm about his candidacy. Constantly on the attack, rarely specifying reforms, Trump always stood for radical change in a direction that cut him off from major policies that found agreement between both parties. In these ways, Trump argued that he (and only he) could unite the country in a combination of self-interest and higher duty.[6]

A comparison of Trump and Lincoln is not justified by his conscious imitation of Lincoln but rather through the similarity of the challenges each president faced and their politically ingenious responses. To restate Trump's challenges: the new "slave power;" the economic, strategic, and political policies that draw upon and revive a deep, abiding American patriotism; opposing the establishments of both parties and creating a new one. Underlying these ambitions is an unremitting assault on "political correctness" and identity politics, which often took on unsettling language, such as rebuke of a "Mexican judge." All this would promote a new birth of freedom, preceding the semiquincentennial (250th) anniversary of the United States in 2026. Neither Lincoln nor Trump can be understood apart from knowing national or human ultimate goals and knowing the partisan and short-term goals as well as the long-term ones. Just as for Lincoln, it would be folly to reduce Trump to short-term ambitions or political necessities.

Trump seeks to establish what Aristotle described as political friendship (*politike philia*). Friendship is the topic discussed most in length in the *Nicomachean Ethics* (with two whole books of ten devoted to it). In fact, Aristotle thought of the best regime in terms of friendship among its citizens. Opening his discussion of friendship, he describes *philia* as a "certain kind of virtue or accompanies virtue and is most necessary for life." More than mere affection, such a serious friendship

> seems to hold cities together, and lawgivers seem to take it more seriously than justice, for concord (like-mindedness, *homonoia*) seems to be something similar to friendship, and they aim at this most of all and banish faction most of all for being hostile to it. And when people are being friends, they have no need for justice, but when they are just, they still need friendship, and among just things, the most just of all seems to be what inclines toward friendship.

> And friendship is not only necessary but also splendid... (*Nicomachean Ethics*, VIII.1; 1155a23–30)

How such a friendship-driven political community is possible is the task of Aristotle in the *Ethics* and in parts of the *Politics* and *Rhetoric* as well.

What Rousseau proposed in the general will and Marx in social man, Aristotle saw in political friendship. He posits three types of friendship: with utility, pleasure, and virtue or excellence (*arête*) being their origin and purpose. Most commentary on Aristotle on friendship tends to dismiss the friendship of utility (co-workers or teammates) as even craven and the friendship of pleasure (sorority sisters or lovers) as fleeting. The friendship of virtue (fellow philosophy students) abides and is for the sake of a higher purpose. But this artificial approach ignores the obvious overlap in friendships we know from everyday life.[7] The three types of friendship are working materials for the statesman, who blends them in various combinations to produce political friendship, with all its benefits. Political friendship brings together citizens for all the practical purposes of politics, identifies common enemies, enables citizens to cheer and laugh together and enjoy each other's company, and affirms patriotism, courage, pride, solidarity, and other virtues that each esteems. Is this not what a Trump political rally did? His rallies were microcosms of political friendship.

We may feel such longing more powerfully today, when the individualism of contemporary life, driven by the internet, seems to dissolve the bonds of neighborhood and nation. But we are also aware of the threat of romanticism's *"Alle Menschen werden Brüdern,"* culminating in Communism or fascism, international or national socialism. The failure to distinguish between the bonds of private life and the bonds of political life can destroy liberal democracy. Lincoln had warned of such extremism in his Temperance Address (February 22, 1842), a political satire whose real subject was not alcohol abuse but rather those who are drunk on power. This tension between the rights of the individual and what we call community is at the heart of the Gettysburg Address. Trump sees two things: that justice in different forms of false friendship has taken over both parties, and neither party can unify the country. The collusion between these parties produced the crisis of American politics today, which allowed an unlikely candidate such as Trump to win: America has lost its ability to have a politics both unifying and liberal, that is, freedom-loving principles. In place of such a best regime, Trump sees an America where patriotism has been replaced by political correctness, a foreign policy of national greatness by the United Nations, a political community united by liberty and justice for all by identity politics fueled by open borders. In looking at the ills of his own country, Trump has struck the vein of not only the great theme of American political history but also that of Western civilization.

It is neither utopianism nor intellectual striving that leads citizens to think of their nation in terms of the best regime. While Trump disdains the term "American exceptionalism," it is clear that he regards America as the best regime; this is the natural way for a thoughtful person to think of one's own political community, whether a Spartan, Athenian, Roman, or American. One could say that for Trump it was natural for him to think in terms of America as the best regime brought to earth, just as for Lincoln it was natural (as well as divinely urged) to think of America as having a universal mission.

Making America great again means recovering the America of Lincoln and the founders. Trump's first three major speeches as president articulate how his presidency intends to restore American greatness. This means rescuing American politics from the constraints of identity politics and replacing it with commonalties: land, blood, faith, and ideals. Each speech emphasizes a different dimension of greatness as political friendship in the classic sense. The Gettysburg Address, as we have seen before, distills all these themes of political friendship. Trump's inaugural exalts America as a common country, one for strivers; his speech to Congress portrays an America whose citizens sacrifice for each other and accordingly is to be honored; his Warsaw speech describes America, together with Poland and other nations who have experienced suffering, as the leader in the crisis of the West. "Our freedom, our civilization, and our survival depend on these bonds of history, culture, and memory," he reminded the Poles. It is both noble and necessary that nations think of themselves in terms of their heritage. And for an American it requires both moral and intellectual virtue to do so, this nation founded on self-evident truths.

The Enlightenment of the "Dark" Inaugural

The heights of the Warsaw speech required grounding in Trump's initial defense of politics in his inaugural address. Often misleadingly decried as a "dark" speech, Trump defied the pretensions of many recent inaugural speech conventions—e.g., George H.W. Bush's decrying partisanship and George W. Bush's calling for an end to tyranny. Trump denounced previous administrations, both Republican and Democrat, for promoting a faction, "a small group in our nation's Capital [which] has reaped the rewards of government while the people have borne the cost." This faction's triumphs were not "your triumphs." "The establishment protected itself, but not the citizens of our country."[8] By contrast, Trump affirmed the result of democratic politics in his victory, one that promised an end to bipartisan collusion against the rights of the people. In response, "we are transferring power from Washington, D.C. and giving it back to you, the American People."

At the heart of the Inaugural Address is a defense of self-interest—not crass self-interest merely for oneself but as a necessary part of the common good that recent administrations had misperceived and ill-defined. The failure to defend one's rights robustly has been disastrous trade deals, wars, and domestic policies. The new president reminds the American people—and even more those sitting on the dais—of some simple truths that immediate past presidents had ignored: "What truly matters is not which party controls our government, but whether our government is controlled by the people."

Trump reaffirmed President Reagan's warning in his first inaugural that "From time to time we've been tempted to believe that society has become too complex to be managed by self-rule, that government by an elite group is superior to government for, by, and of the people. Well, if no one among us is capable of governing himself, then who among us has the capacity to govern someone else?" For Trump, such a "righteous public" demands justice and an end to the "carnage" that characterizes life in American inner cities, suburbs, and rural areas alike. This waste of American lives is an American failing, not one of a class or race. In this, "We share one heart, one home, and one glorious destiny." This unity means that "From this moment on, it's going to be America First."

In this civic partnership, we rise from self-interest and a commercial partnership to a higher political friendship:

> We will follow two simple rules: Buy American and Hire American...

> At the bedrock of our politics will be a total allegiance to the United States of America, and through our loyalty to our country, we will rediscover our loyalty to each other.

> When you open your heart to patriotism, there is no room for prejudice.

Self-interest becomes refined into the greatest generosity of all: committing one's life to others. An America pursuing "solidarity" is "totally unstoppable." If it has such civic friendship, it deserves to be regarded as the preeminent nation. But then there is a qualification: "In America, we understand that a nation is only living as long as it is striving." This is not Wilsonian or any other Darwinism, but old Lincolnian Whiggism, the praise of the striving, rising American. Do Americans still have the energy to succeed? "Your voice, your hopes, and your dreams, will define our American destiny." This is not mere populism but republicanism; the massive rallies are a republican substitute for the securities of the administrative state. The Inaugural Address makes clear the need to restore republican government from bureaucratic tyranny.

A CALL TO DUTY: THE PRESIDENT'S MOMENT IN THE DECLARATION'S TIME

By contrast, the president's speech before Congress brought out the nobility and splendor of American political life. Republican government, as President Reagan noted, requires heroes for its survival, not just the founders and Lincoln, but ordinary citizens who behave heroically. Even Trump critics had to acknowledge the effectiveness of his address to

Congress. "Tonight Donald Trump became President of the United States," conceded CNN commentator Van Jones.[9]

As Abraham Lincoln at Gettysburg did in four score and seven years from its birth, President Trump envisioned an America 12 score and 10 from its birth, its 250th birthday or sestercentennial. (That would be in 2026, a year and a half following an eight-year Trump presidency.) Within this framework of time, the president initially placed his audience in biblical and political time, reminding them that Black History Month ended that day and declaring that all were united in condemning desecrations and violence directed against Jews. Slaves in Egypt, slaves in America. We are now free, but our liberty remains threatened. What protects our liberty is the Constitution.

President Trump emphasized the executive's duty under the Constitution to enforce the laws, not only the Constitution and the laws of the land but the natural law America is based on. In that spirit, Trump posed Congress an unanswerable question that reflected these principles: "To any in Congress who do not believe we should enforce our laws, I would ask you this question: what would you say to the American family that loses their jobs, their income, or a loved one, because America refused to uphold its laws and defend its borders?" In unity with the Declaration of Independence, Trump maintains that "safety and happiness" are the great purposes of legitimate government; rights exist for ultimate ends, not just for their own sake. "My job is not to represent the world. My job is to represent the United States of America." (Earlier, he had even quoted Congressman Abraham Lincoln's thoughts on the benefits of tariffs from December 1, 1847).[10]

The ultimate meaning of constitutional duty became vivid in the president's recognition of the widow of Navy Special Operator Ryan Owens, killed in action in Yemen. "Ryan's legacy is etched into eternity. For as the Bible teaches us, there is no greater act of love than to lay down one's life for one's friends. Ryan laid down his life for his friends, for his country, and for our freedom—we will never forget him."

Our relationships as citizens are largely those of commerce and utility, but they can flourish into something higher, such as the friendship of virtue that the president and Congress celebrated with Ryan's widow. The higher friendship and its patriotism are dependent on the success of the lower, the prosperity of the country. America cannot project power around the world unless we have a robust economy. Our higher purposes can flourish only when necessary goods exist.

When we have all of this, we will have made America greater than ever before—for all Americans. This is our vision. This is our mission. But we can only get there together. We are one people, with one destiny. We all bleed the same blood. We all salute the same great American flag. And we all are made by the same God.

When we fulfill this vision, when we celebrate our 250 years of glorious freedom, we will look back on tonight as when this new chapter of American Greatness began...

LINCOLN IN POLAND

The fundamental question of our time is whether the West has the will to survive. Warsaw, July 6, 2017

And above all, we value the dignity of every human life, protect the rights of every person, and share the hope of every soul to live in freedom. That is who we are. Those are the priceless ties that bind us together as nations, as allies, and as a civilization. Warsaw, July 6, 2017

Trump's most profound speech of his presidency took place in Warsaw, Poland, the "land of great heroes." It has great practical implications for his foreign policy (and not only his view of Russia) and reflected domestic concerns as well (the meaning of nationalism). He raised the question of how we survive as free human beings, not slaves, not masters, but free and equal citizens.[11]

What defines the West? Are we free men to be ruled by reason or by the force of others? In a dialectical ascent, he reached the highest plain of American political rhetoric: its nexus with the divine and transcendent, a height achieved in, to give the greatest example, Lincoln's Second Inaugural. To ask these questions is to raise the themes of Plato's *Republic*: what is the best way of life and how do we discover it?[12]

Plato's (and Lincoln's) comparison of the human soul and the body politic becomes vivid in Trump's description of the valiant Polish sacrifices at Jerusalem Avenue during the uprising. The key to understanding the West is its heart: "Poland is the geographic heart of Europe, but more importantly, in the Polish people, we see the soul of Europe. Your nation is great because your spirit is great and your spirit is strong." When Pope John Paul II visited Soviet-dominated Poland for the first time as Pope, the people sang, "We want God."

Knowing the soul of one's own nation does not require scholarship; knowledge of one's own comes from being aware of one's biography, and history and culture. But how can we maintain strong spirits?

> Our own fight for the West does not begin on the battlefield—it begins with our minds, our wills, and our souls. Today, the ties that unite our civilization are no less vital, and demand no less defense, than that bare shred of land on which the hope of Poland once totally rested. Our freedom, our civilization, and our survival depend on these bonds of history, culture, and memory.

"The fundamental question of our time is whether the West has the will to survive." We recall Lincoln's words in concluding his *Dred Scott* speech: "Will springs from the two elements of moral sense and self-interest." The elites may have lost both elements, in Lincoln's time and ours, hence his appeal to the Declaration and Trump's appeal to "the people."

For Trump the West is embodied in the people of each nation:

> [I]t is the people, not the powerful, who have always formed the foundation of freedom and the cornerstone of our defense. The people have been that foundation here in Poland—as they were right here in Warsaw—and they were the foundation from the very, very beginning in America.

The political and intellectual elites, as Trump has often stated, lack the spirit of freedom, in Poland, in America, and throughout the West. It is the people who will decide this struggle. The people in Poland who sang "We want God," and the people in America who attended the Trump rallies—descendants of those who heard the Lincoln-Douglas debates. They saw the heights of Western civilization in their embrace of revelation and reason for the sake of freedom.

CONCLUSION: IN THEIR BEGINNINGS WERE THEIR WORDS

How far can one sustain the Trump-Lincoln comparison as viewed through the lens of political friendship, the great theme that informs their campaigns and Lincoln's presidency? Trump's speeches, while abrasive on many counts, also drew him closer to those who saw him as the one finally defending their interests.

Perhaps the most revealing comparison between Trump and Lincoln occurs on the subject of race. In the workers' party that Trump is seeking to replace the Republicans would contain a large portion of black voters.

This is not fantasy but a part of his political friendship or patriotism project. Only Trump can unify a country hopelessly divided by identity politics, left and alt-right, and its violence. Lincoln had once declared that, "The strongest bond of human sympathy, outside of the family relation, should be one uniting all working people, of all nations, and tongues, and kindreds." (Reply to New York Workingmen's Democratic Republican Association, March 21, 1864.) Thus, Trump has courted union leaders, supported policies that would increase manufacturing jobs, and hailed "uneducated" voters as part of his coalition. Moreover, beyond economic issues, he has protected morally conservative policies without appearing moralistic.[13] Unlike any Republican candidate in generations Trump has the close support of a decades-long hero of black Americans and now Secretary of Housing and Urban Development, Dr. Ben Carson. His campaign stop at Carson's childhood Detroit home and an inner city church may have swung Michigan into his victory column. Exit polls estimate that 13% of black men voted for Trump (http://www.cnn.com/election/results/exit-polls). By appealing to both morally conservative and blue collar black Americans Trump might effect a political revolution—one that addresses the demands of Lincoln's Second Inaugural. This in turn is all part of a broader political strategy of opposing the degeneration of politics into that of a royal court and returning politics to the citizens, thus reviving American republicanism.

Notes

1. As a "methodological" issue: Why even bother to look at speeches? Isn't the real Trump the tweeter? Aren't his books ghost-written? But this overlooks the purpose of the tweets and the message in the books. We need not inquire into the extent of Trump's Jesuit education in logic and rhetoric at Fordham University.

   In the 1980s columnist George Will offered an insight into Trump's national outlook and ambitions.

   > Donald Trump is not being reasonable ... But, then, man does not live by reason alone, fortunately. Trump, who believes that excess can be a virtue, is as American as Manhattan's skyline, which expresses the Republic's erupting energies. He says the skyscraper is necessary because it is unnecessary. He believes architectural exuberance is good for us [and] he may have a point. Brashness, zest and elan are part of this country's character.

George Will, as quoted in Donald Trump, *The Art of the Deal*, (New York: Ballantine Books, 2015, originally published 1987), p. 341.
The March 1990 *Playboy* interview reveals something of Trump's self-understanding and his long-standing political ambition: http://www.playboy.com/articles/playboy-interview-donald-trump-1990.

Playboy: How large a role does pure ego play in your deal making and enjoyment of publicity?
Trump: Every successful person has a very large ego.
Playboy: *Every* successful person? Mother Teresa? Jesus Christ?
Trump: Far greater egos than you will ever understand.

2. The "slave power" label originated from the fleeting flash of the now defunct, iconoclastic pro-Trumpism website *The Journal of American Greatness*, succeeded by *American Greatness*, https://amgreatness.com/.
3. The study of Lincoln here relies on Harry V. Jaffa, *Crisis of the House Divided* (Chicago: University of Chicago Press, 1982, originally published 1959).
4. Don E. Fehrenbacher, *The Slaveholding Republic*, compiled and edited by Ward M. McAfee (New York: Oxford University Press, 2001).
5. Jaffa, *Crisis*, 228.
6. "[James] Ceaser's characterization of Trump as "post-ideological" misses that Trump is in fact *pre*-ideological—he thinks in terms of the whole American nation, not in terms of the groups that comprise it. Trump is more like Lincoln at Gettysburg than Madison in *Federalist* 10." See my reflections on Trump's campaign in this book review of James Ceaser, et al., *Defying the Odds: The 2016 Elections and American Politics*, https://amgreatness.com/2017/06/30/coarse-correction-real-significance-2016-election/.
7. See Marc Sable, "Learning and Humor, Friendship and Democratic Politics," in "Lincoln's Virtues and Aristotle's Ethics," unpublished manuscript, 2016. On the compromise of friendship, see Eva Brann, "On Compromise," a lecture delivered at the John M. Ashbrook Center, Ashland University, October 27, 2017. http://ashbrook.org/event/eva-t-brann/.
8. Inaugural Address, January 20, 2017. https://www.whitehouse.gov/inaugural-address. Key Lincoln speeches on similar themes include his First Inaugural, March 4, 1861; Speech to Wisconsin State Agricultural Society, September 30, 1859; and his speech to the 166th Ohio Regiment, August 22, 1864.
9. "Remarks to Congress," February 28, 2017. https://www.whitehouse.gov/the-press-office/2017/02/28/remarks-president-trump-joint-address-congress. Key Lincoln speeches on similar themes include his July 4, 1861 Message to Congress; his Cooper Institute speech, February 27, 1860; speech at Independence Hall, February 22, 1861; and Sanitary Fair speech, April 18, 1864.

10. http://quod.lib.umich.edu/l/lincoln/lincoln1/1:423.1?rgn=div2;view=fulltext.
11. The Warsaw speech is here: https://www.whitehouse.gov/the-press-office/2017/07/06/remarks-president-trump-people-poland-july-6-2017. For foreign policy purposes, this speech should be compared and contrasted with his Saudi Arabia Summit remarks. May 21, 2017. https://www.whitehouse.gov/the-press-office/2017/05/21/president-trumps-speech-arab-islamic-american-summit.
12. Indeed, Trump sees the West as founded on Socratic inquiry: "And we debate everything. We challenge everything. We seek to know everything so that we can better know ourselves." Lincoln speeches on similar themes include his Second Inaugural, March 4, 1865; Chicago, July 10, 1858; and his early Perpetuation, January 27, 1838, and Temperance Addresses, February 22, 1842.
13. See the op-ed by F.H. Buckley, "How Trump Won: In Two Dimensions," *Wall Street Journal*, August 10, 2017. https://www.wsj.com/articles/how-trump-won-in-two-dimensions-1502320256.

References

Brann, Eva. "On Compromise," a Lecture Delivered at the John M. Ashbrook Center, Ashland University, October 27, 2017. http://ashbrook.org/event/eva-t-brann/.

Buckley, F.H. "How Trump Won: In Two Dimensions," *Wall Street Journal*, August 10, 2017. https://www.wsj.com/articles/how-trump-won-in-two-dimensions-1502320256.

Fehrenbacher, Don E. *The Slaveholding Republic*. Compiled and Edited by Ward M. McAfee. New York: Oxford University Press, 2001.

Jaffa, Harry V. *Crisis of the House Divided*. Chicago: University of Chicago Press, 1982. Originally Published 1959.

Journal of American Greatness. On-line Journal. Succeeded by American Greatness. https://amgreatness.com/.

Lincoln, Abraham. Available Online. https://quod.lib.umich.edu/l/lincoln/. His major writings may be found in Lincoln, Abraham. *Writings of Abraham Lincoln*. Edited and with an Introduction by Steven Smith, New Haven: Yale University Press, 2012.

Masugi, Ken. "Coarse Correction." Review of James Ceaser, et al., *Defying the Odds: The 2016 Elections and American Politics*. https://amgreatness.com/2017/06/30/coarse-correction-real-significance-2016-election/. *American Greatness* Online Journal, June 30, 2017.

———. Bimonthly Postings. *American Greatness*. Online Journal. https://amgreatness.com/author/ken-masugi/.

Trump, Donald. Donald Trump Interview. *Playboy*, March 1990. http://www.playboy.com/articles/playboy-interview-donald-trump-1990.

———. *The Art of the Deal*. New York: Ballantine Books, 2015. Originally Published 1987.

———. Presidential Speeches. Inaugural Address, January 20, 2017; "Remarks to Congress," February 28, 2017; Warsaw Speech, July 6, 2017; Saudi Arabia Summit Remarks. May 21, 2017; United Nations remarks, September 19, 2017. https://www.whitehouse.gov/briefing-room/speeches-and-remarks.

———. Trump Campaign Speeches and Remarks Are Collected at Various Websites, Including C-SPAN. https://www.c-span.org/person/?donaldtrump, and the American Presidency Project, Hosted by the University of California, Santa Barbara Site. http://www.presidency.ucsb.edu/2016_election_speeches.php?candidate=45&campaign=2016TRUMP&doctype=5000.

PART III

Continental Perspectives

CHAPTER 15

Charisma, Value and Political Vocation: Max Weber on the 2016 US Election

Marc Benjamin Sable

Max Weber's sociology provides a powerful framework for interpreting the defeat of Hillary Clinton as a crisis of legitimacy and the election of Donald Trump as an example of charismatic leadership. Even so, the effectiveness of Trump's demagogy places in grave doubt Weber's normative analysis of political leadership, which implicitly depends on his understanding of charisma.

My analysis will proceed in five parts. First, I explain Weber's notion of legitimacy and show that it ultimately depends on the charismatic postulation of absolute values; charismatic legitimacy in this sense is personal. In the second section, I show how charisma is embodied in institutions and status groups. This routinized or institutionalized charisma is essential to

A highly similar version of this argument was previously published as "Charisma, Value and Political Vocation: Max Weber on the 2016 US Election." *Study of Comparative Cultures* (Morioka University, Japan) 27 (2017): 5–19.

M. B. Sable (✉)
Universidad Iberoamericana, Mexico City, Mexico

Universidad de las Américas, Mexico City, Mexico

A. Jaramillo Torres, M. B. Sable (eds.), *Trump and Political Philosophy*,
https://doi.org/10.1007/978-3-319-74445-2_15

255

all social meaning. Next I explain how charisma is intimately related to his concept of statesmanship, both in terms of specifically political values and in the way politics governs all values. Fourth, I apply the concepts of institutional and personal charisma to Clinton and Trump, highlighting how Clinton's failure to rebut Trump's personalist appeal reflected an overconfidence in American institutions and an obliviousness to a deep crisis of legitimacy in the United States.

Finally, I argue that although Weber's sociology of charisma provides an effective analysis of recent American politics, he misunderstands the relationship between personal charisma and statesmanship by idealizing the former; In fact, personal charismatic leadership may be neither creative nor principled. Trump, despite exhibiting charisma, would certainly fail to meet Weber's standards for political vocation, thus revealing how that concept of statesmanship is itself flawed.

CHARISMA AND LEGITIMACY

Weber understands legitimacy as the acceptance by members of a community that its authorities have the right to enforce their decisions by physical force. Modern political legitimacy, which principally concerns the nation-state, can have three forms of inner justification. These "basic legitimations of domination" are tradition, charisma and legalism.[1] Although Weber lists them (in multiple contexts) in this order, I will take up traditional and rational-legal legitimacy together, because conceptually they have only an indirect relationship to ultimate values.

By traditional legitimacy, he means that people obey—or rather, that they feel a duty to obey—because a form of authority has been sanctioned by long usage. We obey because this is the way we've always identified leaders to whom obedience is due. This is authority justified by "the 'eternal past,' i.e. of custom sanctified by a validity that extends back into the mists of time and is perpetuated by habit."[2] At its outer limit, traditional legitimacy becomes blind habit. By legalistic legitimacy, he means that community members obey due to their belief that authorities have been selected according to formally rational rules. The notion of a purely formal legality as the grounds for legitimacy strikes me as untenable, since it seems that if I accept a decision because the authority is duly constituted, I implicitly believe it sanctioned by some other normative belief.[3] In practice when one cannot give an account of why one thinks an authority rightly-constituted, this implies that acceptance of its legitimacy has become blind habit. For this reason, I would argue that rational-legal legitimacy is really a species of traditional legitimacy, albeit one which derives from faith in reason as a value.[4] While traditionally and legalistically legitimated authorities differ in their organizational efficiency, in both cases the value or normative meaning of obedience must derive from a source outside it.

That source can only be, by inductive reasoning, the third and final inner motivation of legitimacy: charisma. Weber describes this as "the wholly personal devotion to, and a personal trust, in the revelations, heroism, or other leadership qualities of an individual."[5] It is exercised by prophets, and in politics, "by the elected war lord or the ruler chosen by popular vote, the great demagogue, or the leaders of political parties."[6] We obey charismatic leaders because we trust them: Something about their character creates an inner acceptance of their decisions as binding.

The current United States presidential transition illustrates all three types of legitimacy. Hillary Clinton, Barack Obama and tens of millions of Americans who rejected Donald Trump personally in the most vehement terms accepted his legitimate right to assume the presidency. This is Weberian rational-legal legitimacy par excellence: Trump was indeed elected according to the legally recognized procedures. On another level, these procedures are accepted as binding because we consider them as tradition: Accepting election results is the American way. As Clinton said in her November 9 concession speech, "Our constitutional democracy enshrines the peaceful transfer of power and we don't just respect that, we cherish it." As Obama noted a day later, "The peaceful transition of power is one of the hallmarks of our democracy." The rules are sanctioned by the belief that they are *our* rules.

But given the clear contempt and mistrust that both Obama and Clinton had for Trump, one has to ask: Why did they still consider this rule inviolable? In Weberian terms, this occurred because, at the deepest level, constitutional democracy in the United States is posited as value: As an end which is good in its own terms.

Weber distinguishes between instrumental and substantive rationality. Instrumental rationality defines the most effective means to an end, but cannot determine the validity of ends. Following Nietzsche, he holds that the correct determination of ends is not a matter that can be rationally determined. The substantive rationality of ends consequently is an existential choice (and so not rational in any obvious meaning of the term). Deciding that a particular goal is good simply—a value—is thus neither calculated nor reasoned to: It is merely posited as a value. Accordingly, the positing of values is sacred—it is both mysterious and un-caused. Since the meaning of human action can only come from ultimate values, and yet there is no way to determine them rationally, values are in fact the "gift of grace"—precisely how he defines charisma in "Politics as a Vocation."[7] For Weber, adherence to the ultimate values of any regime stems from a *faith* in those values which cannot be rationally defended, and which implicitly comes from charismatic founders.

Communities and Impersonal Charisma

The above provides a hint that charisma is much more than just an inner attitude toward authority: Charisma is the very substance of community. For Weber, Community is individuals identifying with one other, rather than struggling against one another.[8] "The *communalization* of social relationships occurs if and insofar as the orientation of social behavior—whether in the individual case, or on the average or in the ideal type—is based on a sense of solidarity: the result of emotional or traditional attachments of the participants."[9] Here Weber only speaks of emotional and traditional attachments, but these are precisely those elements which transcend self-interested calculation. A sense of solidarity means that individuals in community believe they share a common good, rather than merely shared interests. While shared interests can produce coordination to achieve a given end—e.g., a business enterprise or an alliance—this sort of reasoning, being essentially instrumental, necessitates that the relationship will end when the interests cease to be shared. Alliances end when one party or both ceases to feel threatened; business partnerships end when one partner can make more money elsewhere. Communities only end when the "sense of solidarity" ends, i.e., when their emotional or traditional attachments attenuate and ultimately break completely.[10]

Although Weber's sociology always pays close attention to self-interest and conflict, he also believes that social relations are permeated by communalization: To some extent, almost all social relationships are communities. "Every social relationship which goes beyond the pursuit of immediately obtainable common ends involves a relative degree of permanency between the same persons and such relationship cannot be limited to activities of a purely technical nature."[11] While some organizations are predominantly defined by shared interests and technical rationality, social life can rarely be defined entirely by interest and calculation. Any on-going relationship implies a deeper connection, one which recognizes some non-technical goal, i.e., is the domain of either affect or an ultimate value. *"Communalization* may be based on any kind of emotional, affectual or traditional link: e.g., a spiritual brotherhood, an erotic relationship, a relationship of personal loyalty, a national heritage, or the comradeship of a military unit."[12]

From whence does a sense of solidarity come? How do group members come to have emotional or traditional attachments to each other? While Weber does not provide a general answer, the structure of his thought does. Implicit in his analysis of status groups is the notion that communities are made by charisma.

The typical group which is defined by common qualities, situation and mode of behavior is a social class. Famously, a class can be in itself without being for itself. In other words, unless the proletariat, for example, sees itself as a community, it cannot act: Workers will see themselves as individuals who are exploited without identifying with other workers as a community, as a whole.[13] "In contrast to classes, *status groups* are normally communities ... we wish to designate as 'status situation' every typical component of the life fate of men that is determined by a specific, positive or negative, social estimation of *honor*."[14]

Because status groups "are normally communities," it stands to reason that their essential characteristics are characteristics of communities.[15] Now, since status groups are defined by social estimation of honor, it seems that solidarity due to either emotional or traditional attachment is tied to honor. And honor is more than just valuing something or someone, because goods may be merely instrumental. Honor implies valuation of something as good in itself, not merely as a means. This is the difference between honorable and useful. Indeed, under extreme situations, the honorable act may be extremely inconvenient—as prominent #NeverTrump Republicans can now attest. As noted earlier, legality depends, logically on some rational justification external to itself (principally tradition), while tradition itself ultimately reflects a prior belief about shared values, a commonly-held belief that has been handed down. This social origin of all value—all ultimate ends—is in fact charisma. Since belief in the greater or lesser status of a group is based in its greater or lesser proximity to honored activities, status derives primarily from charisma. Communalization is principally the result of charisma.

Charisma is thus not just a form of allegiance, but rather the social dimension of the positing of ends, of substantive rationality, i.e., of ultimate value. It is important to realize that for Weber this is not just a question of politics. Naturally, because it arbitrates conflicts between and within communities, politics more than any other activity necessarily postulates value. But charisma is present in any activity that its participants consider a value rather than simply a tool. For example, Weber's analysis of the Protestant ethic and the rise of capitalism shows how religious ideas translate into specific forms of charismatically-charged economic activity. Charisma may also be present in normal economic activities,[16] e.g., Apple under Steve Jobs. Likewise, when art is seen as a life's ultimate purpose, then art partakes of charisma.[17] For Weber, all activity is ultimately validated by choosing to posit its intrinsic value, even the activity of evaluating choices (or rather, the consequences of choices), as in the rigor of social scientific thought. Thus all activity must be justified existentially, and that justification *is* charisma. Not just the devout or the militant, but artists and even entrepreneurs can be seen as members of communities based on the charismatic positing of value. To rigorously live according to a value—whatever that value may be—is what Weber calls "vocation."

Indeed Weber believes that science, as much as art, religion or politics, cannot substantiate its activity rationally: "Natural science gives us an answer to the question of what we must do if we wish to master life technically. It leaves quite aside, or assumes for its purposes, whether we should and do wish to master life technically and whether it ultimately makes sense to do so."[18] For Weber, modern science has disenchanted the world: it has exposed the hard truth that values are in conflict and nature does not rank order them. Those who think the growth of knowledge necessarily makes human life better are "overgrown children in their professorial chairs or editorial offices"; No one else "imagines nowadays that a knowledge of astronomy or biology or physics or chemistry could teach us anything about the *meaning* of the world."[19] Indeed Weber also argues that natural law legitimacy had charismatic roots. The Enlightenment project was itself an enchantment—a product of charisma. In explaining the French Revolution, he states explicitly that, the "charismatic glorification of Reason ... is the last form charisma has adopted in its fateful historical course."[20] Because ultimate meaning can only be posited as value, charisma is present wherever ultimate ends are posited.

Thus, more important than personal charisma is the *institutionalization* of charisma, which is exemplified in virtuosi committed to ultimate ends. Institutionalized charisma not only privileges certain groups, rendering them higher status that others—it privileges certain ideas. The identity of the United States as a constitutional democracy thus represents, in Weberian terms, the institutionalized charisma which holds that civil liberties are sacrosanct, that elections should be free and fair, that power should be divided vertically and horizontally. In short, institutionalized charisma is culture.

This may sound strange, but Max Weber is a methodological individualist. At the end of his life, in *The Basic Concepts of Sociology*, he very carefully defined authority, legitimacy, and other key concepts, as the *probability* of that individuals will act in certain ways.[21] Cultural systems are the accumulation of probabilities that people in specific contexts will hold certain ideas. Charismatic breakthroughs occur when cultural certainties—conventions that have been more or less uniformly acceded to—are suspended. A traditional king is legitimate as long as it is accepted that he is right to demand obedience. Disobeying the king openly and without shame implies a rejection of traditional deference. In describing the "charisma of Reason" as the cause of the French Revolution, he shows that charisma is less a question of personalities than of ultimate values. And revolution—the quintessential charismatic breakthrough—can only occur when faith in the ancien regime has become purely traditional, i.e., largely a matter of blind habit. In such cases, charismatic leaders gain power in the personal sense because existing institutions have lost their charismatic hold on key social groups.

We are left now to wonder about the relationship between charismatic legitimacy in the personal sense and charisma as the social and institutional positing of ultimate ends. To address this question, we must examine politics as a vocation.

STATESMANSHIP, OR POLITICS AS A VOCATION

Weber argues that to have a true political vocation, "three qualities, above all, are of decisive importance: passion, a sense of responsibility, and a sense of proportion."[22] The statesman balances a passionate commitment to an ideal with a deep sense of responsibility for the consequences of his actions.

To analyze this vocation, Weber's creates two ideal types of political action. First, political leaders can be guided by an "ethic of responsibility", the principle that effective action is the measure of the political good. They hold themselves responsible for the consequences of their actions. Under the ethics of responsibility "you must answer for the (foreseeable) consequences of your actions."[23] The paradigm here is something like

262 M. B. SABLE

Machiavelli's teaching that to be a good prince one must sometimes do evil. The ethic of responsibility agrees with his observation in *The Discourses* that, "When the deed accuses him, the effect excuses him."[24]

Secondly, Weber describes an "ethic of absolute ends." In its purest form, this ethic holds that actions must be done for their own sake, without regard to consequences. The paradigm he mentions is the "Sermon on the Mount." The ethic here is Kantian: Good action is good in itself and done for its own sake. Since meaningful action requires a purpose, something not done for something else must be posited. However, since values are inherently incommensurable, a true leader simply commits to a value as his lodestar. "The *nature* of the cause in whose service the politician strives for power and makes use of is a matter of belief ... He may be motivated by a powerful faith in 'progress' (however this is defined), or he may coolly reject faith of this kind."[25]

A true political vocation requires both instrumentally rational action and action for its own sake. On the one hand, politics is about states and states have historically pursued all manner of ends. Moreover, the defining characteristic of the state is the use of violence.[26] Thus, political leadership is essentially about taking responsibility for achieving goals at the price of real bads, particularly those involving violence. Likewise, since the accrual of power is a means to achieve greater goods, the (partial or temporary) sacrifice of one's ultimate ends is also justifiable under the ethic of responsibility. On the other hand, since states have no given ends, they lack intrinsic goals, and political activity will devolve into pointlessness unless ends are posited from outside it. Thus meaning must come from an extrapolitical ethic of absolute ends. The two ethics exist in permanent tension: "The genius, or the demon, of politics lives in an inner tension with the God of love as well as with the Christian God as institutionalized in the Christian churches, and it is a tension that can erupt at any time into an insoluble conflict."[27] For Weber, a political vocation is an agonistic balance between absolute ends (values) and politically instrumental thinking.

The 2016 Democratic primary campaign provides fair examples of these two political ideal types. On the one hand, Bernie Sanders exemplified a political vocation that veered sharply toward an ethic of absolute ends. Sanders posited as ultimate ends social rights such as universal healthcare, college and higher wages. As we have seen, belief in natural law is an example of a value—something posited as good in itself.[28] As the spokesman for his values, Sanders embodied a kind of charisma to his followers. His politically inconvenient self-identification as a socialist in the United States and his rejection of corporate campaign contributions also illustrate his belief that doing the right thing is more important than obvious or immediate political efficacy. On the other hand, advocates of responsible liberal politics criticized Sanders' vagueness about *how* he would achieve those goals: He was vague about how his nomination would achieve a "political revolution," and why the likely consequence would be to sweep Democrats into power, rather than merely repeating McGovern's 1972 landslide loss.

Such criticisms came naturally to Hillary Clinton, because she adhered closely to an ethic of responsibility.[29] Meeting with activists from Black Lives Matter early in the campaign, she said, "I don't believe you change hearts. I believe you change laws, you change allocation of resources, you change the way systems operate."[30] For Clinton, politics was the art of the possible. For example, both her 1994 and 2008 healthcare proposals were designed with major concessions to reduce opposition by powerful insurance companies. Her career as a senator likewise reflects this desire to maximize political effectiveness by compromising in the face of hostile public opinion (supporting the Iraq War) or powerful interests (Wall Street). This mentality also included making compromises at times for the immediate objective of advancing personal political power, under the assumption that it would later be put to good use. This was documented in the WikiLeaks emails which showed how the Clinton campaign defined her policy positions: While they often discussed public policy on the merits, there was also much discussion of the impacts of policy stances on voting groups and special interests.[31] Given how biased human beings are with respect to their own motives and self-interest, it is no wonder that many perceived Hillary Clinton not as exemplifying an ethic of responsibility, but rather its decay into what Weber labels "unprincipled opportunism."

HILLARY CLINTON: INCARNATION OF ATTENUATED INSTITUTIONAL CHARISMA

We are now in position to apply Weberian concepts of legitimacy to the 2016 presidential election. It seems obvious that Trump had charisma and Clinton did not. Why did she lack charisma?

As we just saw, Clinton focused on calculating the consequences of political action, identifying the means necessary to achieve ends and accepting the trade-offs between ends. Still, she did hold some ultimate values: not everything was up for negotiation.[32] For example, conceding defeat to Trump, despite a popular vote majority, demonstrated a principled commitment to the American constitutional system. Likewise, consider her characterization of half of Trump supporters as a "basket of deplorables" who are "racist, sexist, homophobic, xenophobic, Islamophobic—you name it. ...Now some of those folks—they are irredeemable, but thankfully they are not America."[33] This too implies a substantive idea of America, although to appreciate it, one must read into the labels an implicit argument for civic nationalism.[34] Unfortunately, reducing the argument to labels assumes so much that links to foundational values are inarticulate.

Looking back on the general election campaign, it seems painfully obvious that Clinton was incapable of adequately articulating the ultimate ends of the policies she advocated. Consider her Acceptance Speech at the Democratic National Convention: Explicit references to the central values of the republic—freedom, equality and justice—were few and vague. She referred to equality exactly three times: once to assert simply, "There's too much inequality," once to call for equal pay between men and women, and once to assert that America was great, because it has the "most enduring values. Freedom and equality, justice and opportunity." Likewise freedom was mentioned twice, once in that list of enduring values, and once to assert that in every generation, Americans "come together to make our country freer, fairer, and stronger." Her lone reference to democracy asserted opaquely that "our economy isn't working the way it should because our democracy isn't working the way it should." Finally, she referred to justice only three times: once when referring to the killing of Osama Bin Laden, once when thanking Sanders for putting social and economic justice "front and center," and finally, again in that list of "enduring values."

Consider how she "articulated" the meaning of the American regime: We have the "most enduring values. Freedom and equality, justice and opportunity. We should be so proud that these words are associated with us. That when people hear them—they hear … America." This is a platitude and not in any sense an interpretation. In Weberian terms, a true political leader inspires the people, motivates them to allegiance to his or her vision of the ends of the polity. Whether or not you agreed with

Obama's vision of America, one cannot deny that he *interpreted* key American values, tying them to the public policies advocated by liberals.

During her debates with Trump, she likewise failed to articulate general principles with which to reject Trump's policies or his notion of American "greatness." For example, Trump asserted that immigrants were a threat to American jobs, security and identity. Rather than defend America as a nation of immigrants, as a refuge for those seeking political freedom and economic opportunity, Clinton merely used the issue to accuse Trump of hypocrisy for being the son and grandson of immigrants. The only reference she made to the Statue of Liberty, that grand symbol of immigration to the United States, was as a device to mock his sexism at the Al Smith Memorial Dinner.

At a rally in September, Clinton asked, "Why am not 50 points ahead?"[35] She never managed a referendum on American values, and so depended on institutional charisma, rather than feeding it. Her slogan, "Stronger Together," itself constructed through a group process, was a claim to institutional charisma. She characterized the possible election of Trump as the "apocalypse"[36]—yet ran as if she were facing a normal political opponent. There was no sustained, coherent defense of fundamental principle. She assumed that racism and sexism were disqualifying, and while she made the case against Trump as fomenting racism in her August speech in Reno, she never followed up. Fully 76 percent of her television ads were attacks on Trump's personal character.[37] There was no sustained argument about the core values of the republic.

Clinton lacked charisma because she assumed that Americans agreed about what American values were: But for a political vocation to augment rather than diminish the charismatic power of communal institutions, a leader must articulate the values of those institutions. Instead she merely reflected them: she never nourished them. As someone working within the system who could implement (her interpretation of) core values, but not articulate them, she was the embodiment of an overly routinized charisma. In her, the liberal interpretation of those core values was presented as blind tradition.

TRUMP'S VICTORY: A WEBERIAN LEGITIMACY CRISIS

Trump likewise did not appeal to the ultimate values of the American regime, appealing instead to "American greatness." His Acceptance Speech at the Republican convention illustrates clearly how far he deviates from traditional understandings of American values of freedom, equality, justice and democracy.

His single reference to equality is early in the speech, when he promises, without any elaboration, to "treat all our kids equally." His only references to justice are two: (a) to assert that he has no patience for injustice, and (b) to note scathingly that his opponent received a rebuke from the FBI Director instead of punishment. And, while it is true that he claims to speak for his supporters who have been cheated by a "rigged system", in the Acceptance speech he never explicitly referred to democracy as an ideal, while in other contexts he praised a dictator, Vladimir Putin as a better leader than Barack Obama and said he would accept the election results "if I win."[38]

Trump's unwillingness to mobilize traditional American values was most glaring in his rare references to the central political value of American conservatism: freedom. In his Acceptance Speech, he referred to freedom precisely five times. Three times he referred to the freedom in the sense of national sovereignty—the freedom of the United States from constraints by trade agreements, vowing to make America "free and independent and strong," and to free it from "the petty politics of the past." Once he mentioned freedom in the sense of license—speaking of illegal immigrant criminals "roaming free to threaten peaceful citizens." And finally, he vowed to repeal the Johnson rule which denies tax-free status to churches which directly support political candidates. Thus, for Trump, freedom is almost entirely a question of collective power.

But while Trump does not posit traditional conservative American values as ultimate ends, he possesses personal charisma, and he posits another value: a nation restored to power, wealth, and prestige. His appeal is a nakedly personal form of charisma, based exclusively on his personal qualities. He says often, "Trust me" and "believe me." His supporters typically praise him because, "He tells it like it is," "He's not politically correct," and "He speaks his mind." When confronted about some obvious untruth, they employ technicalities to say he didn't mean it. If faced with an argument about the dangerous consequences of one policy suggestion or another, they suggest that it's all posturing, or they rationalize it. This is faith in a person more than anything else. In January he claimed, in what is now barely a hyberbole, "I could stand in the middle of 5th Avenue and shoot somebody and I wouldn't lose voters."[39] His supporters *want* to believe he will "make America great again." And they project onto him whatever it is they imagine American greatness to be. A telling example is the assertion by Michael Anton, writing as "Decius", that Trump will help dismantle the modern administrative state.[40]

Trump ran explicitly as strongman, which directly contradicts traditional American values of the separation of powers, checks and balances and the rule of law. He said the American political system was broken and, "I alone can fix it."

Indeed, his supporter, Governor Paul LePage of Maine, said explicitly, "Sometimes I wonder that our Constitution is not only broken, but we need a Donald Trump to show some authoritarian power in our country and bring back the rule of law."[41] Quite clearly, for some on the right, American institutions have become so illegitimate that democracy itself has been called into question.

No moment in the 2016 campaign better illustrates the legitimacy crisis than a brief exchange between Clinton and Trump over the carry-over interest deduction exchange during the second debate on 9 October:

CLINTON: Well, here we go again. I've been in favor of getting rid of carried interest for years, starting when I was a senator from New York. But that's not the point here.[42]

TRUMP: Why didn't you do it? Why didn't you do it?

COOPER: Allow her to respond.

CLINTON: Because I was a senator with a Republican president.

TRUMP: Oh, really?

CLINTON: I will be the president and we will get it done. That's exactly right.

TRUMP: You could have done it, if you were an effective—if you were an effective senator, you could have done it. If you were an effective senator, you could have done it. But you were not an effective senator.

COOPER: Please allow her to respond. She didn't interrupt you.

CLINTON: You know, under our Constitution, presidents have something called veto power. Look, he has now said repeatedly, "30 years this and 30 years that." So let me talk about my 30 years in public service. I'm very glad to do so.[43]

This exchange neatly encapsulates the dynamic between Trump and Clinton. First, Trump displays a total disregard or ignorance of the system of checks and balances that defines American constitutional democracy. Underlying his ignorance (or disdain) for the give and take of political decision making is the implicit claim that a strong man can solve American's problems by force of will. Second, this faith in willfulness is reflected in Trump's disregard for simple courtesy, his interruptions and not accepting her right to completely present her views: Civility is an implicit norm necessary for democratic debate. Finally, we see Clinton's blithe arrogance that she will win.

In Weberian terms, American constitutional principles and the core values of freedom, equality and democracy are the institutionalized charisma which have defined the ultimate ends of the United States since its founding. Trump's popularity—and his electoral victory—thus constitutes a legitimacy crisis. It signifies that for his core supporters the original ends of the American polity became mere traditional, indeed blind, habit.[44]

WEBERIAN POLITICAL ETHICS
AND THE PROBLEM OF CHARISMA

Weber would be personally appalled by Trump: He would certainly deny that he had a true vocation for politics, despite his surprising success. Viewing statesmanship as the proper combination of a sense of responsibility and commitment to ultimate ends, he would deem Donald Trump lacking on both counts: as without seriousness of political purpose and as failing to take responsibility for the consequences of his actions.

Weber's notion of political responsibility includes the scientist's commitment to inconvenient facts. Those interested "only in the practical point of view" should still find science useful, because it forces them to "acknowledge *inconvenient facts*," i.e., "facts that are *inconvenient* for their own personal political views."[45] Acceptance of inconvenient facts is necessary for a true political vocation because serious responsibility for the consequences of political choice requires knowing objectively what those consequences are.

Yet Trump is famous for launching a post-factual politics, asserting without evidence, for example, that Obama was not born in the United States and then claiming the allegation began with Hillary Clinton's 2008 campaign. He further claimed that Obama "founded ISIS," that Ted Cruz's father was involved in the assassination of John Kennedy, that the election system was rigged to elect Hillary Clinton and that Russia did not interfere in the election in his favor. Trump's complete disregard for truth—going as far to repeat outrageous assertions even after being refuted—means that he can literally promise anything or stoke any fear he feels will advance his immediate purpose. His promises to bring back heavy industry and coal are good examples. Being indifferent to facts makes his demagogy truly without constraint.

Still, Weber distinguishes politics from science, going so far as to say that in politics, "If you speak about democracy at a public meeting ... The words you use are not tools of academic analysis, but ... swords to be used against your opponents: weapons, in short."[46] From this perspective, Trump's demagogy could in the abstract be justifiable, provided it was in the service of serious political purpose.

What *are* Trump's purposes? We can read his campaign in two distinct ways: Either (1) he has craftily packaged ethnic nationalism in a crowd-pleasing, attention-grabbing form, perfectly suited to the times—or (2) he simply sought the Presidency for fame and wealth, as the ultimate branding opportunity. In the first case, interpreting Trump's charisma as aimed at the ethno-nationalist reconstruction of the American regime, those of us committed to a civic nationalist vision will be forced to conclude that charismatic leadership can generate political nightmares as easily as cultural renaissance. In the second case, if we see Trump's political ambitions as simply a spectacular example of "living off politics," then he lacks a true political calling in the Weberian sense, while still displaying charisma.[47] The former case reveals that Weber's political ethics provides us with no means for distinguishing good from bad charismatic leadership, nor good from bad political vocations. In the second case, charismatic leadership as an empirical phenomenon is shown to have no necessary connection with value creation at all. One could respond that only charismatic leaders with a sense of responsibility and seriousness of purpose are capable, in the long run, of institutionalizing their charisma and installing stable socio-political orders—but that would sound pollyannish to Weber himself.

Clearly, empirical charisma and political vocation are not necessarily in accord. The example of Trump reveals clearly the flaws in Weber's normative assessment of charismatic leadership and political vocation: We neither know how to identify a positive from a negative charismatic reordering of values nor how to distinguish a constructive from a merely destructive charisma. Yet Weber is a better sociologist than political theorist. As we have seen, Weber's notion of charisma is much more than just a form of legitimacy: social value depends on it. While he incorrectly expected true political vocation and charismatic leadership to coincide, his analysis of the social necessity for charisma to legitimate political order appears validated by Trump's rise.

When political values atrophy, when they become mere platitudes sanctioned only by habit and interest, legitimacy will pass to charismatic figures with whom the masses can identify. Whether that personal charisma will be transformed into enduring legitimacy is an open question, depending precisely on the degree to which the charismatic leader actually has a true vocation for politics.

NOTES

1. Max Weber, "Politics as a Vocation," in *The Vocation Lectures*, ed. David Owen and Tracy B. Strong (Indianapolis: Hackett Publishing Company, Inc., 2004), 32. See also Max Weber, *Basic Concepts in Sociology*, Reissue ed. (New York, NY: Citadel, 1976), 120.
2. Weber, "Politics as a Vocation," 34.
3. David Beetham makes the same point, although in much greater detail, "Max Weber and the Legitimacy of the Modern State," *Analyse & Kritik*, 13 (1991): 39–40.
4. See below, Sect. 2.
5. Weber, "Politics as a Vocation," 33.
6. Weber, "Politics as a Vocation," 33.
7. "Second, there is the authority of the extraordinary, personal *gift of grace*, or charisma." Weber, "Politics as a Vocation," 33. Emphasis original.
8. "Communalization is, in the sense used here, normally the opposite of 'struggle.'" Weber, *Basic Concepts*, 93.
9. Weber, *Basic Concepts*, 91. Emphasis original.
10. See Aristotle's discussion of use-friendships in the Nicomachean Ethics, book VIII.
11. Weber, *Basic Concepts*, 92.
12. Weber, *Basic Concepts*, 92. Emphasis original. Moreover, this implies that even sustained relationships whose end is economic acquisition are to some extent communities. Anyone who has enjoyed having dinner with a colleague or client knows this.
13. This is most obviously the case in situations of "cross-cutting cleavages", as described in such pluralist theorists as Seymour Martin Lipset, Stein Rokkan, Robert Dahl, and in earlier writers like David Truman, and ultimately in the theory of the extended republic articulated in Federalist Paper No. 10 by James Madison.
14. Max Weber, *On Charisma and Institution Building (Heritage of Sociology Series)*, ed. S. N. Eisenstadt (Chicago: University of Chicago Press, 1968), 177. Emphasis original.

15. The typical example of a communalized relationship which is not a status group would be lovers, whose shared sense of solidarity stems from their emotional attachment. Friendships, too, would fall under the heading of communal but not status groups.

16. Eisenstadt, "Introduction," in Weber, *On Charisma and Institution Building*, xxxii. I am indebted to Eisenstadt for showing the crucial linkage between social order and institutionalized charisma.

17. Weber, *On Charisma and Institution Building*, 22.

18. Weber, "Science as a Vocation," 18. He rejects immanentist solutions to this problem, whether by Aristotle or Hegel.

19. Weber, "Science as a Vocation," 17, 16.

20. Max Weber, *Economy and Society*, 1209. Quoted in Guenther Roth and Wolfgang Schluchter, *Max Weber's Vision of History: Ethics and Methods*. (Berkeley: University of California Press, 1979), 134. See also Weber, *Basic Concepts*, 82.

21. For example, "A system of authority will appear to be (a) *conventional*, where its validity is externally guaranteed by the probability that deviation from it within a definable social group will be met with relatively general and significantly perceptible disapproval. (b) Such a system of authority will be considered as *law* if it is externally guaranteed by the probability that unusual behavior will be met by physical or psychic sanctions aimed at compelling conformity or at punishing disobedience..." Weber, *Basic Concepts*, 75. Emphasis original.

22. Weber, "Politics as a Vocation," 76.

23. Weber, "Politics as a Vocation," 83.

24. I: 9. Niccolo Machiavelli, *Discourses on Livy*. (Chicago: University of Chicago Press, 1996), 29.

25. Weber, "Politics as a Vocation," 78.

26. This is built into his definition of politics as "only the leadership, or the exercise of influence on the leadership, of a *political* organization, in other words, a *state*," and the state as defined "only sociologically by the specific *means* that are peculiar to it, as to every political association, namely, the use of physical violence." Weber, "Politics as a Vocation," 32–33. Emphasis original.

27. Weber, "Politics as a Vocation," 90.

28. "'Nature' and 'Reason' are the substantive criteria of what is legitimate from the standpoint of natural law." Weber, *On Charisma and Institution Building*, 100.

29. For a defense of this mindset, see Ezra Klein, "Hillary Clinton and the audacity of political realism," *Vox.com*, January 28, 2016. Accessed December 12, 2016. http://www.vox.com/2016/1/28/10858464/hillary-clinton-bernie-sanders-political-realism.

30. Russell Berman, "Hillary Clinton's Blunt View of Social Progress," *Atlantic.com*, August 22, 2015. Accessed December 12, 2016. http://www.theatlantic.com/politics/archive/2015/08/hillary-clintons-blunt-view-of-social-progress/402020/.

31. Jeff Stein, "What 20,000 pages of hacked WikiLeaks emails teach us about Hillary Clinton," *Vox.com*, October 20, 2016. Accessed March 15, 2017.

32. A fascinating example of this is her response to the question, "Have you always told the truth?" She replied, "I've always tried to. Always, always." While lying is negotiable, *she would not lie about lying*. Liz Kreutz, "Hillary Clinton Says She's 'Always Tried' to Tell the Truth to Americans," *abc-news.com*, February 18, 2016. Accessed December 13, 2016. http://abc-news.go.com/Politics/hillary-clinton-shes-truth-americans/story?id=37043658.

33. Reuters, "Clinton: Half of Trump Supporters Belong in 'Basket of Deplorables,'" September 10, 2016. Accessed December 13, 2016. http://www.reuters.com/article/usa-election-clinton-idUSL1N1BM05L.

34. For this distinction, see for example, Tom Nairn, *The Modern Janus: Nationalism in the Modern World* (London: Hutchinson Radius, 1990).

35. John Wagner, "Clinton asks why she isn't beating Trump by 50 points," *Washington Post*, September 21, 2016. Accessed December 12, 2016. https://www.washingtonpost.com/news/post-politics/wp/2016/09/21/clinton-asks-why-she-isnt-beating-trump-by-50-points/?utm_term=09c3b49ca1d2.

36. Mark Leibovich, "'I'm the Last Thing Standing Between You and the Apocalypse'," *New York Times Magazine*, October 11, 2016. Accessed December 12, 2016. http://www.nytimes.com/2016/10/16/magazine/hillary-clinton-campaign-final-weeks.html?_r=0.

37. Associated Press, "2016 presidential advertising focused on character attacks," Accessed December 13, 2016, http://bigstory.ap.org/article/6be6a1391cfe48598c5f65b0bc607426/2016-presidential-advertising-focused-character-attacks. The AP adds, "Between 1952 and 2008, 31 percent of the general election ads were character-based."

38. BBC.com, "Trump says Putin's a leader far more than our president"", September 8, 2016. http://www.bbc.com/news/election-us-2016-37303057. CNN.com, "Donald Trump: 'I will totally accept' election results 'if I win'", October 20, 2016. http://edition.cnn.com/2016/10/20/politics/donald-trump-i-will-totally-accept-election-results-if-i-win/. Trump also praised the dictator of North Korean, Kim Jong Un, saying, "You gotta give him credit … he was like 26 or 25 when his father died … he goes in, he takes over, and he's the boss … It's incredible. He wiped out the uncle, he wiped out this one, that one. I mean this guy doesn't play games." *abcnews.com*, January 10, 2016. Accessed December 12, 2016,

http://abcnews.go.com/Politics/trump-north-korean-leader-kim-jong-gotta-give/story?id=36198345.

39. Trump at rally in Sioux Center, Iowa, January 23, 2016.

40. "Publius Decius Mus," "The Flight 93 Election," *Claremont Review of Books*, September 5, 2016. Accessed December 13, 2016. http://www.claremont.org/crb/basicpage/the-flight-93-election/.

41. Andrew Prokop, "Governor of Maine: maybe we need a Donald Trump to show some authoritarian power," *Vox.com*, October 11, 2016. Accessed December 13, 2016. http://www.vox.com/policy-and-politics/2016/10/11/13243344/trump-authoritarian-paul-lepage.

42. The carry-over interest deduction allows general partners in certain businesses to pay taxes on income made for profits as capital gains rather than as individual income, typically at 20% instead of the top individual rate of 39.6%. For hedge fund managers on Wall Street—the quintessential one-percenters—this tax differential can be worth tens of millions of dollars. Both Clinton and Trump agreed the deduction should be eliminated.

43. "Second U.S. Presidential Debate," October 10, 2016. Accessed October 16, 2016. http://www.nytimes.com/2016/10/10/us/politics/transcript-second-debate.html?_r=0.

44. Foa and Mounk have documented a dramatic decline in support for democracy in the West generally and in the United States in particular. Roberto Stefan Foa and Yascha Mounk, "The Democratic Disconnect," *Journal of Democracy* 27, no. 3 (July 2016): 5–17.

45. Weber, "Science as a Vocation," in *The Vocation Lectures*, 22. Emphasis original.

46. Weber, "Science as a Vocation," in *The Vocation Lectures*, 20.

47. "There are two ways of engaging in politics as a vocation. You can either live 'for' politics or 'from' politics ... Whoever lives 'for' politics makes 'this his life' in an *inward* sense. Either he enjoys the naked exercise of power he possesses or he feeds his inner equilibrium and his self-esteem with the consciousness that by serving a 'cause' he gives his life a *meaning*. In this inner sense, probably every serious person who lives for a cause also lives from it. The distinction, then, refers to a far weightier aspect of the matter: its economic dimension." Weber, "Politics as a Vocation," in *The Vocation Lectures*, 40. Emphasis original.

References

Anton, Michael [Publius Decius Mus]. "The Flight 93 Election." *Claremont Review of Books*, September 5, 2016. http://www.claremont.org/crb/basicpage/the-flight-93-election/.

Aristotle. *Nicomachean Ethics*. 2nd ed. Indianapolis: Hackett Publishing Company Inc., 1999.

Beetham, David. "Max Weber and the Legitimacy of the Modern State." *Analyse and Kritik* 13 (1991): 34–45.

Berman, Russell. "Hillary Clinton's Blunt View of Social Progress." *Atlantic.com*, August 22, 2015. http://www.theatlantic.com/politics/archive/2015/08/hillary-clintons-blunt-view-of-social-progress/402020/.

Coates, Te-Nahesi. "The First White President: The Foundation of Donald Trump's Presidency Is the Negation of Barack Obama's Legacy." *The Atlantic Monthly*, October 2017. https://www.theatlantic.com/magazine/archive/2017/10/the-first-white-president-ta-nehisi-coates/537909/.

Foa, Roberto Stefan, and Yascha Mounk. "The Democratic Disconnect." *Journal of Democracy* 27, 3 (2016): 5–17.

Klein, Ezra. "Hillary Clinton and the Audacity of Political Realism." *Vox.com*, January 28, 2016. http://www.vox.com/2016/1/28/10858464/hillary-clinton-bernie-sanders-political-realism.

Machiavelli, Niccolo. *Discourses on Livy*. Translated by Harvey C. Mansfield and Nathan Tarcov. Chicago: University of Chicago Press, 1996.

Nairn, Tom. *The Modern Janus: Nationalism in the Modern World*. London: Hutchinson Radius, 1990.

Roth, Guenther, and Wolfgang Schluchter. *Max Weber's Vision of History: Ethics and Methods*. Berkeley: University of California Press, 1979.

Sable, Marc. "Charisma, Value and Political Vocation: Max Weber on the 2016 US Election." *Study of Comparative Cultures* (Morioka University, Japan) 27 (2017): 5–19.

Weber, Max. *On Charisma and Institution Building (Heritage of Sociology Series)*. Edited by S. N. Eisenstadt. Chicago: University of Chicago Press, 1968.

———. *Basic Concepts in Sociology*. Translated by H. P. Secher. Reissue ed. New York: Citadel, 1976.

———. *The Vocation Lectures*. Edited by David Owen and Tracy B. Strong. Indianapolis: Hackett Publishing Company, Inc., 2004.

CHAPTER 16

The Common Sense of Donald J. Trump: A Gramscian Reading of Twenty-First Century Populist Rhetoric

Kate Crehan

> But nobody's ever had crowds like we're having. It's a movement. It's a movement for common sense. (Donald Trump on the Rush Limbaugh Show, October 25, 2016)

> Common sense is not a single unique conception, identical in time and space. ...it takes countless different forms. Its most fundamental characteristic is that it is a conception which, even in the brain of one individual, is fragmentary, incoherent and [inconsistent[1]].... (Gramsci 1971: 419)

A photograph taken at a Trump rally in Alabama captures the almost messianic fervor Donald Trump aroused in his core supporters in the course of his presidential campaign—a fervor that seems remarkably unaffected by his performance as president. Amidst a throng of devotees, one woman holds aloft a sign that reads 'Thank You, Lord Jesus, for President Trump'.[2] Throughout his campaign his supporters' unshakeable belief in their savior baffled liberal commentators. Pointing out the errors and outright lies in his speeches and tweets, their internal contradictions, the lack of

K. Crehan (✉)
CUNY, New York, NY, USA

© The Author(s) 2018
A. Jaramillo Torres, M. B. Sable (eds.), *Trump and Political Philosophy*,
https://doi.org/10.1007/978-3-319-74445-2_16

information on how all the promises might actually be fulfilled, seemed to have little effect. The Trump faithful just *knew* he was right and that he could, and would, carry them back to a lost golden world when "America was great". An interchange between Matt Mayberry, New Hampshire's Republican Vice Chairman and a male Republican voter shortly before that state's primary is a good example this blind faith:

Mayberry: Who you gonna vote for?
Voter: Trump. He's gonna make America great again.
Mayberry: How's he gonna make American great again?
Voter: I don't know. He just is. (Quoted in Lake and Enda 2016: 45)

To begin to explain Trump's extraordinary power to inspire his faithful, it is instructive to go back to the prison notebooks of Antonio Gramsci.[3]

Mussolini's Prisoner

Antonio Gramsci, born in 1891, was one of the founders of the Italian Communist Party in 1919. Politically active from an early age, he was elected to the Italian Parliament in 1924, two years after the fascists came to power, and their leader Benito Mussolini was named Prime Minister. As a parliamentary deputy, Gramsci should have had legal immunity from arrest, but the fascists had little concern for such legal niceties and in 1926 he was arrested. He and twenty-one other leading communists were then subjected to a show trial. Gramsci received one of the longest sentences, 20 years, 4 months and 5 days, the prosecutor famously declaring: "we must prevent this brain from functioning for twenty years". The Communist deputy and his brain would remain in prison until a few days before his death in 1937. The now celebrated prison notebooks he wrote during his years of incarceration are proof that while the fascists might have locked up his body, they spectacularly failed to prevent his brain from functioning.

The notebooks cover a vast range of topics related to questions of power. Writing in his prison cell at a moment when the Italian left seemed to have been defeated, its leaders incarcerated, dead, or in exile, Gramsci seeks to understand the structural reasons for the left's failure and the rise of Mussolini. Twenty-first century America is not twentieth-century Italy, and Trump is not Mussolini, nonetheless the notebooks' reflections on the appeal of right-wing populism, and what is necessary to defeat it, seems particularly resonant in our historical moment. In this essay I focus on Gramsci's concept of *senso comune*, which can help us understand, it seems to me, both Trump's appeal, and how his narrative of 'making America great again' can be effectively challenged.

One problem faced by Gramsci's Anglophone readers is that *senso comune* has no simple English equivalent. The standard translation, common sense, is a mistranslation. For English-speakers, common sense has come to denote, in the words of the Oxford English Dictionary, "good sound practical sense; combined tact and readiness in dealing with the every-day affairs of life; general sagacity." *Senso comune*, by contrast, is a more neutral term that lacks these strong positive connotations. In the notebooks it refers to that accumulation of taken-for-granted "knowledge" to be found in every human community. In any given time and place, this accumulation provides a heterogeneous bundle of assumed certainties that structure the basic landscapes within which individuals are socialized and chart their individual life courses. Despite it being a mistranslation, I have nevertheless chosen to use the English term. Coupling "common sense" and Gramsci's radically different understanding of the taken-for-granted in everyday life will, I hope, help draw attention to some of the hidden baggage that comes with the English term, and in addition provide Anglophones with an alternative way of thinking about this apparently "self-evident" word, and what it names.[4] The reader needs, however, to bear in mind that the notebooks' common sense is not the same sturdy touchstone of "practical sense" that it is in English.

Common sense for Gramsci is inherently heterogeneous and contradictory. It is "a chaotic aggregate of disparate conceptions, and one can find there anything that one likes" (Gramsci 1971: 422). And it is an aggregate that is continually shifting: "Common sense is not something rigid and immobile, but is continually transforming itself" (Gramsci 1971: 326). Confronted with the confusion of common sense, it is the analyst's task to sort through the mass of beliefs and opinions, identifying its different components, tracing out the links between particular "truths" and social realities. How are the different elements disseminated? What is it that makes them appear self-evident, and self-evident to whom? Whose common sense are they—men's, women's, poor people's, the better off, the more educated, the less educated, the old, the young, particular religious groups? What are the mechanisms through which they are, or are not, internalized by individuals—what indeed does it mean to internalize them? To what extent do different elements hang together? Do individuals pick and choose between them? How do they choose between them? And on and on.

Gramsci is scornful of intellectuals who celebrate common sense. He quotes the assertion of the philosopher and fascist politician, Giovanni Gentile, that "Philosophy could be defined as a great effort accomplished by reflective thought to gain critical certainty of the truths of common sense", ridiculing it as "yet another example of the disordered crudity of Gentile's thought" (Gramsci 1971: 422). Common sense is rather "an ambiguous, contradictory and multiform concept, … to refer to common sense as a confirmation of truth is a nonsense" (Gramsci 1971: 423). Gramsci's attitude to common sense is not wholly negative however. Embedded within the chaotic confusion of common sense he identifies what he terms "good sense" (*buon senso*). For instance, taking the common expression, "being philosophical about it", he notes that while this expression may contain "an implicit invitation to resignation and patience", it can also be seen as an "invitation to people to reflect and to realise fully that whatever happens is basically rational and must be confronted as such." This appeal to use reason rather than blind emotion constitutes "the healthy nucleus that exists in 'common sense', the part of it which can be called 'good sense' and which deserves to be made more unitary and coherent" (Gramsci 1971: 328). Note that this "good sense" still needs to be made "more unitary and coherent"; work that Gramsci sees as the task of intellectuals.

All the different manifestations of common sense, including good sense, do share one characteristic: they do not need to be proved or supported by evidence. A common sense "truth" merely needs to be stated; a "truth" that is not immediately obvious to any "reasonable" person, is not common sense. Common sense, we might say, is the polar opposite of critical thinking, which demands that we accept no "truth" unquestioningly, but always carefully scrutinize the evidence on which it is based.

In modern democracies the realm of "common sense" is a crucial domain. Politicians of all stripes, especially, but not only those of a populist bent, like to present their particular "truths" as common sense, and as such beyond debate. And this has certainly been Trump's strategy. The very vagueness of Gramsci's concept of common sense, its broad, inclusive quality that can encompass contradiction and facts that shift over time, coupled with its recognition of the importance of emotional persuasion, make it an illuminating way of approaching the peculiar power of Trump's narrative.

Trump Voters

Six months into Trump's presidency, Emily Ekins (research fellow and director of polling at the Cato Institute) published a paper challenging the idea that Trump voters constitute "a homogeneous bloc with similar tastes and motivations" (Ekins 2017). Using data from a survey of 8000 voters, Ekins identifies five distinct types of Trump voter.

Staunch Conservatives—(31 percent), fiscally conservative with traditional values, who worry about legal and illegal immigration.

Free Marketeers—(25 percent), in favor of free trade and smaller government, with moderate-to-liberal views on immigration and race, whose vote was a vote against Clinton.

American Preservationists—(20 percent), who favor higher taxes on the rich, back the social safety net, believe the economic and political systems are rigged, and are skeptical of both free trade and immigration.

Anti-Elites—(19 percent), who believe the economic and political systems are rigged.

Disengaged—(5 percent), who don't follow politics, are skeptical of immigration, and support a temporary Muslim travel ban.

Despite the heterogeneity, the five types of Trump voter share certain attitudes: a hatred of Hillary Clinton, strong support for a temporary ban on Muslim immigration, and pessimism about their personal financial situation. In addition, with the exception of the Anti-Elites, they are all hostile to a path to citizenship for unauthorized immigrants.

Trump's political message is that America has taken a wrong turn and only he can get it back on track. Under Obama, he warned, the country has become ever more vulnerable to its enemies: Mexicans, Muslims and all those "others" defined in opposition to "real" Americans, who are becoming ever worse off. Only when its enemies are excluded or defeated will America be made "great again". And the former star of reality TV has proved to be remarkably adept at whipping up hostility. During the long months of his campaign he managed to turn his Democratic opponent, Hillary Clinton, into a one-woman embodiment of the out-of-touch elite who have nothing but contempt for those living in rural America and the flyover states. Her unfortunate reference to certain Trump supporters as "deplorables" only reinforced this perception. More significantly, "crooked Hillary", as Trump referred to her, was transformed into a living symbol of corruption and government malfeasance. According to Jared Sexton, two of the most popular chants at his rallies were "Lock her Up" and "Trump that Bitch". When the then FBI Director James Comey announced in July 2016 that he would not seek charges against Clinton over her use of a private email server, the vitriol intensified. Now there was a new chant: "Hang that Bitch" (Sexton 2016). And the hate intensified. On July 15 one Michael Folk, a West Virginian lawmaker tweeted: "Hillary Clinton You should be tried for treason, murder, and crimes against the US Constitution … then hung on the Mall in Washington" (Quoted in Lake and Enda 2016: 161). This demonization of Hillary, it should be noted, was achieved over the course of Trump's campaign. In 2016 all of Ekins' five types of Trump votes expressed an intense dislike of her, even though four years earlier nearly half of the American Preservationists and Anti-Elites had positive views of Clinton (Ekins 2017).

Once Clinton had lost the election, President Trump needed to find a new hate figure around which to focus his supporters' resentment. CNN, the *New York Times*, and other media that have not displayed unquestioning support have now been demonized as "fake news" and enemies of the American people, as in his tweet (Trump's favorite form of communication) from February 2017: "The FAKE NEWS media (failing @nytimes, @NBCNews, @ABC, @CBS, @CNN) is not my enemy, it is the enemy of the American People!"[5] "The FAKE NEWS media" may not be his enemy but they are, he insists, engaged in a "witch hunt" against him. Commenting on a Fox reporter's claim that the Russians spread negative information about Trump when he was a candidate, in July 2017 Trump tweeted: "So why doesn't Fake News report this? Witch Hunt! Purposely phony reporting."[6]

Trump's rhetoric of hate reinforces the idea that the defeat of evil requires violence. He has repeatedly called for the killing of terrorists. At the same rally where Sexton heard the "Hang the Bitch" chant, Trump had some words of praise for Saddam Hussein: he was "a bad guy, a really bad guy. But you know what he did well? He killed terrorists". The blood-lust of the rally reminded Sexton of a 2010 Tea Party informational meeting he attended in Indiana:

> Speakers equated President Barack Obama with Mao Zedong and Joseph Stalin. They alluded to the Great Famine and the Great Purge. If Obama had his way, they argued, we should all be ready to report to work camps. After the presentation, I listened to farmers and factory workers alike wonder whether to take up arms and march on Washington. If the time had come, as one speaker put it, to 'refresh the tree of liberty with the blood of tyrants.' (Sexton 2016)

It is not only its undercurrent of violence that links Trump's rhetoric with that of the Tea Party. His diagnosis of the ills afflicting America runs along grooves carved out by Tea Partiers.

Channeling the Tea Party

In his history of the Tea Party Ronald Formisano summarizes the Tea Partiers' demands as "limited government, debt reduction, no higher taxes, and no new spending" (Formisano 2012: 1). The narrative of an overreaching government that spends irresponsibly, lavishing benefits on immigrants and other unfairly privileged minorities, while overtaxing the corporations that create jobs, thus encouraging those corporations move jobs overseas, is one to which Trump has repeatedly returned. He promised his supporters that he would be their savior. As Lake notes, he

> never pretended to be Joe Six-Pack. That would have been implausible, and a little too ordinary. Instead he won over working-class Republicans by playing ... a golden colossus who would gladly strike down all that displeased "real" Americans. *Let the market govern big corporations?* No. The golden colossus would bend corporations to the people's will. Punish Ford and Carrier for outsourcing American jobs. Punch China in the *face*. (Lake and Enda 2016: 92)

At the same time a Trump administration, he promised, would roll back all the burdensome regulations that prevent American businesses from creating jobs. The contradiction here was lost in the sweep of an intoxicating narrative that held out a vision of a return to a lost golden world. As a candidate, the all-powerful, former boss of *The Apprentice* spoke to the same cry of pain that Skocpol and Williamson heard from a male Tea Party supporter in 2010: "I want my country back!" (Skocpol and Williamson 2012: 7) His supporters (such as the New Hampshire man quoted at the beginning of this essay) were convinced that once the great dealmaker was president, they *would* get their country back.

In essence, Trump succeeded in weaving together a series of assertions about the threats facing native-born Americans into a narrative that to his supporters seemed no more than common sense, even if the mainstream media, dominated by out-of-touch elites, fail to recognize it. This narrative is rooted in racism; it is no accident that when Trump first began flirting with the idea of running for president, he continually questioned whether President Obama was really born in the U.S. I would argue that the plausibility of Trump's birther lie, which was easily and repeatedly disproved, depended on a gut sense that no one who looked like the president and had the name Barack Hussein Obama had a right to be president. As Bernie Sanders put it to Chris Matthews on MSNBC:

> what the birther movement was about, Chris, was not being critical of Obama. This is a democracy. We can criticize Obama. It was delegitimizing the first African American president in the history of our country. And the reason for that was clear. There are racists in this country who could never accept the fact that we had a black president. And that's what Trump was trying to do, delegitimize the president, not disagree with him.[7]

A bumper sticker I saw in Maine the summer before the 2016 elections, reflects the deep resentment of those perceived as not being genuinely American: "To Hell with Diversity: Keep America American." Trump's narrative is one of us and them, where the menacing "them" includes Mexicans who control the drug trade and take jobs away from native-born Americans, Muslims (all potential terrorists), and an out-of-touch elite who despise "ordinary" Americans, and are bent on repealing the Second Amendment.

This angry common sense underlies the rallying cry of Trump's campaign "Make America Great Again." Despite Trump's claim to have coined this slogan (which he trade-marked), it was first used by Ronald Reagan in his 1980 presidential campaign, although on Reagan's campaign merchandise it appeared as the softer, more inclusive "Let's Make America Great Again". In both its Reaganite and Trumpian incarnations, "Make America Great Again" promises a return to post-war American prosperity, conjuring up a lost and sunnier world, one in which "ordinary" Americans, implicitly assumed to be white, had good-paying jobs. Trump's version is undoubtedly angrier, and places the blame for the loss of American greatness on immigrants, and underserving non-white Americans, more explicitly. Both narratives, however, lay the blame for the loss of greatness on external or internal enemy 'others' rather than the inherent dynamics of a globalized capitalism.

Trump's success in connecting with such a broad swathe of angry Americans is in large part based on endlessly repeated sound bites. As Gramsci noted, "repetition is the best didactic means for working on the popular mentality" (Gramsci 1971: 340). Trump's rhetorical style makes this repetition especially effective. His simplified language—he speaks at just below 6th grade level (Spice 2016)—and his flouting of the norms of educated, "politically correct" speech seems to his supporters a welcome return to a time when they could speak their minds and tell jokes without fear of the political-correctness police. Demonstrating Trump's factual inaccuracies, providing evidence of his lies, has no hope of dislodging his supporters' profound sense that he, unlike the beltway elites, grasps the reality that ordinary white Americans, are living. In Trump's words they hear articulated all their own frustrations and anger at the metropolitan elites' perceived disdain for them, their way of life, their worldview. That this was coming from a New York real estate mogul, born into wealth was not important. It is true that the great dealmaker's own life hardly reflects the values championed by conservative Republicans, but "sometimes", as Jeff Sessions, Trump's pick for Attorney General, and a devout Methodist, is reported to have said: "God uses ungodly people to do his will" (Lake and Enda 2016: 103). What mattered was that Trump, honed by his years as a reality TV celebrity, was giving voice to his supporters' anger in a language they recognized: a language rough and unpolished but seemingly "authentic," which gave all those elites the middle finger. Those who believed in him heard him expound a vision of turning back the clock expressed not in the slick language of experts and spin doctors, but in the form of an inarticulacy that rang true to those who feel excluded and belittled by Washington's power elite. The message that came through loud and clear was that what had once been, could and should come again. The faithful did not need to hear detailed plans of how this might be achieved; its simple commonsense rightness was proof enough.

As Katy Waldman has noted, there is a certain brilliance in Trump's speaking style. For instance, he

> tends to place the most viscerally resonant words at the end of his statements, allowing them to vibrate in our ears. ...Ironically, because Trump relies so heavily on footnotes, false starts, and flights of association, and because his digressions rarely hook back up with the main thought, the emotional terms take on added power. They become rays of clarity in an incoherent verbal miasma. ...If Trump were a more traditionally talented orator, if he just made more sense, the surface meaning of his phrases would likely overshadow the buried connotations of each individual word. As is, to listen to Trump fit language together is to swim in an eddy of confusion punctuated by sharp stabs of dread. (Waldman 2016)

Hillary Clinton's campaign speeches with their dogged laying out of specific policies designed to tackle specific problems may have been fact-based and practical, but they lacked her opponent's rhetorical power. In mass democratic systems all politicians, wherever they stand on the political spectrum, need *emotionally* powerful narratives, narratives that reflect back to their supporters compelling, and seemingly obvious, common sense truths. Clinton's rival in the democratic primaries, Bernie Sanders, demonstrated his understanding of this with his continual reiteration of the same simple message of America's palpable and increasing economic inequality. This was a message that spoke directly to the lived experience of so many, especially perhaps that of millennials who reached adulthood during the Great Recession and the subsequent anemic recovery that seemed to have exacerbated inequality. Effective challenges to Trump would seem to demand such compelling and easily graspable narratives. Gramsci's reflections on the need for these kinds of progressive narratives, and on where and how they emerge, although written in a fascist jail cell more than seventy years ago, remain relevant.

TOWARD A NEW COMMON SENSE

Gramsci was very much a Marxist. He believed that the material circumstances of people's lives shape their worldview, but he never saw those material circumstances as determining those worldviews. Running through the notebooks is a concern with the ways in which people's understanding of the world are fashioned from the narratives they have available to them. All of us, even the most sophisticated theorists, are molded by the ideas and beliefs of the world, or worlds we inhabit. For Gramsci, human beings are profoundly cultural beings. Culture is a crucial dimension of any state's power, and those who would bring about social transformation need to exercise cultural leadership. Progressives must, he writes, attach "'full weight' to the cultural factor, to cultural activity, to the necessity for a cultural front alongside the merely economic and merely political ones" (Gramsci 1995: 345).

Central to Gramsci's insistence on the importance of cultural struggle is his concept of hegemony, one of his most influential concepts. Part of what hegemony names is the ability of those in power to make the way the world appears to them (as they view it from their vantage point) the authoritative viewpoint. Alternative narratives that challenge the hegemonic status quo seem unrealistic, or no more than the pleadings of special interests, or simply wrong. A Trump, whose basic message never challenges traditional capitalist pieties, has a far easier task than those who go against the hegemonic narrative. Any serious challenge to existing power relations demands carefully thought-out, intellectually coherent accounts of the world as it is, but it also requires: "new popular beliefs, that is to say a new common sense and with it a new culture and a new philosophy which will be rooted in the popular consciousness with the same solidity and imperative quality as traditional beliefs" (Gramsci 1971: 424).

Coming up with easily graspable narratives that people recognize as true to their experience, and that call into question the hegemonic accounts, is hard. From where might such "new popular beliefs" come? Unlike some Marxists, Gramsci never believed that intellectuals on their own could come up with radically new understandings that reflect the world as seen from the vantage point of the subordinated and oppressed. For him, while intellectuals play a crucial role in the generation and dissemination of new ways of understanding the world, effective oppositional narratives are ultimately the fruit of dialog between intellectuals and the collective experience of those who are subordinated, those the notebooks term "subalterns."[8] Intellectuals are necessary because while the subordinated and oppressed certainly generate their own explanations of their oppression, these remain incoherent and fragmentary; their "good sense" scattered among the general confusion of common sense. It is intellectuals who bring these fragments together into a coherent whole.

It is important to note here that Gramsci's definition of intellectuals rejects the standard understanding of what defines the intellectual[9]: "[t]he most widespread error of method", he writes, is the notion that intellectuals are defined by "the intrinsic nature of intellectual activities". What defines intellectuals is rather "the ensemble of the system of relations in which these activities (and therefore the intellectual groups who personify them) have their place within the general complex of social relations" (Gramsci 1971: 8). In other words, it is not a specific expertise or set of skills that defines the intellectual but the social context in which they exercise their expertise. As he observes in a clarifying footnote, "because it can happen that everyone at some time fries a couple of eggs or sews up a tear in a jacket, we do not necessarily say that everyone is a cook or a tailor" (Gramsci 1971: 9). The category "intellectual" in the notebooks is also a broad one: "at the highest level would be the creators of the various sciences, philosophy, art, etc., at the lowest the most humble 'administrators' and divulgators of pre-existing, traditional, accumulated intellectual wealth" (Gramsci 1971: 13). The following passage from the notebooks indicates the breadth of this former Communist Party activist's definition, and what he takes to be the essence of the intellectual function.

> That all members of a political party should be regarded as intellectuals is an affirmation that can easily lend itself to mockery and caricature. But if one thinks about it nothing could be more exact. There are of course distinctions of level to be made. A party might have a greater or lesser proportion of members in the higher grades or in the lower, but this is not the point. What matters is the function, which is directive and organisational, i.e., educative, i.e., intellectual. (Gramsci 1971: 16)

The intellectuals who craft effective, oppositional narratives remain, however, dependent on the raw, fragmentary beginnings generated by subaltern experience itself: "Is it possible that a 'formally' new conception can present itself in a guise other than the crude, unsophisticated version of the populace?" (Gramsci 1971: 342). It is imperative that progressive intellectuals listen carefully to these embryonic stirrings, developing them into coherent and sophisticated political narratives. It is equally necessary, however, that those more sophisticated narratives are also translated into a new, easily graspable common sense.

One consequence of the decline of the left in the U.S., and the ever-smaller role of labor unions, has been a dramatic shrinking of the spaces in which accounts of the world that challenge the triumphant capitalist narrative have room to emerge, develop, become common sense, and spread. As the popular media has shifted to the right over recent decades, the dominant popular narratives are those broadcast on Fox News, and other right-wing TV stations, talk radio shows, and an increasingly segmented social media. All of these tend to echo and amplify a view of the world that is deeply suspicious of government, and is convinced that things would be better run if business executives, not politicians, were in charge. Given this, from where might oppositional common sense narratives emerge— narratives with the power to become "rooted in the popular consciousness with the same solidity and imperative quality as traditional beliefs"? The Occupy Wall Street (OWS) movement that erupted in 2011 perhaps provides an example.

OWS has been dismissed by many as having achieved nothing lasting. It did succeed, however, in making economic inequality something that politicians of all stripes found themselves having to address. And crucial here was the slogan "We are the 99 percent!" As Todd Gitlin has written, OWS created "a new center of gravity in what we are pleased to call 'the national debate.' Inequality of wealth was now widely recognized—and seen as a problem, not a natural condition. 'The 1 percent' and 'the 99 percent' were commonplaces" (2012: 232). Using Gramscian language we could say that OWS with its occupation of Zuccotti Park—a site associated with big capital—created a space that allowed a new common sense to emerge, namely that the contemporary US is a country of savage inequality in which a tiny minority benefits at the expense of everyone else. Intellectuals were certainly important. The OWS dialog was framed by arguments made by progressive thinkers such as the economists Joseph Stiglitz and Paul Krugman, but it was the army of occupiers who articulated their experience through a forest of handcrafted signs, which seemed not the slick products of media professionals but authentic, heartfelt cries of distress, welling up from the day-to-day experience of inequality. "We are the 99 percent!", the slogan that emerged out of this dialog, did not require explanation; it simply captured the lived experience of inequality.

Prior to OWS, politicians who talked about inequality were regularly accused of advocating class warfare. On September 18, 2011, for example, just a month before the occupation of Zuccotti Park, Fox News had a story on its website quoting Paul Ryan, then chairman of the House Budget Committee, who "accused President Obama of appealing to Americans' 'fear, envy and anxiety' by pushing a new tax rate on people making more than $1 million annually: 'Class warfare ... may make for really good politics, but it makes for rotten economics'. The 'class warfare path' will only hurt the economy."[10] Obama's own skittishness around this issue is suggested by an incident recorded in David Remnick's (2014) New Yorker profile of the president. At the 2011 annual White House dinner for American historians, held the summer before the occupation of Zuccotti Park, the president "asked the group to help him find a language in which he could address the problem of growing inequality without being accused of class warfare" (Remnick 2014: 44–45). The "We are the 99 percent!" slogan, which emerged from OWS, did precisely that. This powerful, albeit vague, cry of outrage was effective because it seemed to many to do no more than state an obvious truth. Anyone who felt that the decent life the American system was supposed to provide was slipping beyond their grasp could feel themselves included within the embrace of the 99 percent: those with degrees who had been left with a mountain of debt but no job; those whose homes had been foreclosed, not because they had borrowed recklessly but because the recession had cost them their jobs; workers whose hard-won benefits and pensions were being slashed as "unfeasible"; and jobless veterans. "We are the 99 percent!" provided a name for lived experience that demanded articulation. And whereas Trump's "Make America Great Again!" slogan is so easily heard as a racist explanation of America's decline, "We are the 99 percent!" explains the sense of a broken America in terms of a narrative of class. And it explains it the form of a commonsense truth—a truth that seems undeniable to so many who see the ladder of prosperity receding ever farther beyond their reach.

Conclusion

As I am writing this essay in July 2017, Trump has a national approval rating of around 36 percent, the lowest six-month approval rating of any president in the last 70 years of polling (Langer 2017). His support among the Trump faithful, however, remains remarkably strong even if there are some signs it may be beginning to erode (Silver 2017). Many in the Democratic Party and on the left seem to share the optimism recently expressed by Al Gore that even his supporters will come to recognize the disconnect between his message and the reality of what his Administration is doing: "I think it is only a matter of time before a great many of those who supported President Trump realise that what he is doing in office is directly contrary in so many ways to what he promised ... I just have enough faith in the American people to believe that it's only a matter of time before people realise what he's doing" (Gore 2017). The problem with this optimism is that people rarely become aware of even the most apparently objective realities in any simple, direct way. All of us, whether we are intellectuals or those Gramsci termed the popular element, make sense of the world we inhabit using narratives we have available to us. Whether we have unconsciously absorbed these through osmosis from our environment, or arrived at them through critical reflection, the world we perceive is rendered intelligible by the assumptions we bring to it— assumptions that have become such a familiar part of our mental furniture we are scarcely aware of them.

Effective politicians, of both left and right, draw on pre-existing elements within the heterogeneous confusion that is common sense to create narratives that are emotionally powerful while reflecting 'realities' their supporters recognize. Before hearing what seems such common sense truth, they would have been hard put to articulate it, but now it seems no more than what they already knew. Trump's rhetoric with its transformation of immigrants, Muslims, the media, and above all Hillary Clinton, into figures of hate, explains to his supporters in an emotionally convincing way, why they feel they are losing their country, while holding out the promise that he, Trump, will take it back for them. And if his Administration is unable to fulfill his campaign promises, the story continues, it is the fault of a biased, elite media bent on destroying him. This kind of political narrative is relatively impervious to demonstrations of its factual inaccuracy. Those, like Al Gore, waiting for his supporters to realize "that what [Trump] is doing in office is directly contrary in so many ways to what he promised", are likely in for a long wait. Progressives who would counter Trump need a narrative with the same *emotional* power. Even if it soon flamed out, the collective energy and enthusiasm of the Occupy Movement can be seen as creating collective spaces that generated the beginnings of just such an emotionally resonant common sense.

It should be stressed that neither Trump's nor OWS's common sense diagnosis of the ills of contemporary America represent pre-existing narratives. It was over the course of his campaign that Trump wove together a general feeling of disempowerment, distrust of Clinton, suspicion of immigrants, Muslims and the media, into a fever pitch of visceral hatred. In contrast to this top-down creation of common sense, the physical occupation of a site signifying Wall Street and big capital, Zuccotti Park, by a mass of "ordinary people" created a space in which the simple but effective slogan, "We are the 99 percent!", could well up from collective experience of the inequalities of twenty-first century capitalism.

These very different struggles over political narratives take us back to Gramsci's insistence on the importance of attaching full weight "to the cultural factor, to cultural activity, to the necessity for a cultural front alongside the merely economic and merely political ones" (Gramsci 1995: 345). Whoever we are, and wherever we are, we make sense of the world we inhabit through stories that tie together the fragments of our day-to-day lives into some kind of meaningful coherence. Cultures consist in part of those stories. As our worlds move through history, continually shifting, so, too, do the cultures through which we perceive and experience that history, albeit in complex and sometimes very indirect ways.

If we want to map the continually shifting accumulations of certainty that tie cultures together, Gramsci's inclusive and flexible concept of common sense provides a powerful tool that directs us to look for shared beliefs and taken-for-granted assumptions while making no assumptions as to their character or contents. It recognizes the importance of emotional persuasion, but also that common sense is ultimately grounded in lived experience. Trump, the self –proclaimed leader of a movement for common sense, has proved himself a master at fashioning an emotionally resonant account of twenty-first century America that speaks to his supporters' sense that the country's leaders have abandoned them. Gramsci's notion of common sense can help us see past the smoke and mirrors to discover how the trick was done.

Notes

1. Gramsci writes *inconsequente*, translated in Gramsci (1971) as *inconsequential*. In this context inconsistent is a more accurate translation. I am grateful to Frank Rosengarten for pointing out this mistranslation.
2. https://www.cbsnews.com/pictures/extreme-donald-trump-fans/7/, accessed 16 November 2017.
3. See Crehan (2016) for an extended discussion of Gramsci's theorisation of power, and its relevance for our twenty-first century world.
4. For an argument for staying with the Italian term, see Thomas (2010: 16).
5. https://twitter.com/natemezmer/status/832818957702672384, accessed 16 November 2017.
6. https://twitter.com/realdonaldtrump/status/890568797941362690, accessed 17 November, 2017.
7. http://www.msnbc.com/hardball/watch/donald-trump-and-the-birther-movement-767215171717, accessed 17 November 2017.
8. Gramsci's use of the term subaltern in the notebooks is explored in Crehan (2016).
9. See Crehan (2016) for an extended discussion of Gramsci's definition of the category intellectual.
10. "Republicans Accuse Obama of Waging 'Class Warfare' with Millionaire Tax Plan". FoxNews.com, September 18, 2011, http://www.foxnews.com/politics/2011/09/18/rep-ryan-accuses-obama-waging-class-warfare-with-millionaire-tax-plan/. Accessed 23 January 2014.

References

Crehan, Kate. 2016. *Gramsci's Common Sense: Inequality and Its Narratives.* Durham, NC: Duke University Press.

Ekins, Emily. "The Five Types of Trump Voters: Who They Are and What They Believe." *Voter Study Group.* June, 2017. https://www.voterstudygroup.org/reports/2016-elections/the-five-types-trump-voters. Accessed 20 July 2017.

Formisano, Ronald P. 2012. *The Tea Party: A Brief History.* Baltimore: Johns Hopkins Press.

Gitlin, Todd. 2012. *Occupy Nation: The Roots, the Spirit, and the Promise of Occupy Wall Street.* New York: itbooks.

Gore, Al. Interview on National Public Radio's *All Things Considered*, July 21, 2017. http://www.npr.org/2017/07/21/538067710/al-gore-climate-change-issue-will-be-a-much-bigger-political-plus-for-democrats. Accessed 21 July 2017.

Gramsci, Antonio. 1971. *Selections from the Prison Notebooks of Antonio Gramsci.* Edited and Translated by Quintin Hoare and Geoffrey Nowell Smith. London: Lawrence and Wishart.

———. *Further Selections from the Prison Notebooks/Antonio Gramsci.* Translated and Edited by Derek Boothman. Minneapolis: University of Minnesota Press, 1995.

Lake, Thomas, and Jodi Enda. 2016. *Unprecedented: The Election that Changed Everything.* New York: Melcher Media Inc.

Langer, Gary. "6 Months in, a Record Low for Trump, with Troubles from Russia to Health Care (POLL)," July 16, 2017. http://abcnews.go.com/Politics/months-record-low-trump-troubles-russia-health-care/story?id=48639490. Accessed 17 July 2017.

Remnick, David. "Going the Distance: On and Off the Road with Barack Obama." *New Yorker*, January 27, 2014.

Sexton, Jared Yates. "There Will Be Blood." *New Republic*, July 6, 2016. https://newrepublic.com/article/134892/will-blood. Accessed 7 July 2017.

Silver, Nate. "Donald Trump's Base Is Shrinking." *FiveThirtyEight*, May 24, 2017. https://fivethirtyeight.com/features/donald-trumps-base-is-shrinking/. Accessed 17 July 2017.

Skocpol, Theda, and Vanessa Williamson. 2012. *The Tea Party and the Remaking of Republican Conservatism.* Oxford: Oxford University Press.

Spice, Byron. "Most Presidential Candidates Speak at Grade 6–8 Level." Carnegie Mellon University. *News*, March 16, 2016. https://www.cmu.edu/news/stories/archives/2016/march/speechifying.html. Accessed 25 June 2017.

Thomas, Peter D. 2010. *The Gramscian Moment: Philosophy, Hegemony and Marxism.* Chicago, IL: Haymarket Books.

Waldman, Katy. "Trump's Tower of Babble." *Slate*, November 2, 2016. http://www.slate.com/articles/news_and_politics/politics/2016/11/how_donald_trump_uses_language_and_why_we_can_t_stop_listening.html. Accessed 25 June 2017.

CHAPTER 17

"I Alone Can Solve": Carl Schmitt on Sovereignty and Nationhood Under Trump

Feisal G. Mohamed

The title of this paper arises from—what else?—one of Donald Trump's tweets. As a candidate responding to a March 2016 terror attack in Pakistan, Trump emphasized that this "radical Islamic attack" targeted "Christian women and children," before adding "I alone can solve."[1] This final statement had no period, as if beckoning us to a future of glorious possibility ready to unfurl itself with his sanctifying touch. As a whole the post expressed core national security ideas of the campaign, making clear that terrorism has been insufficiently associated with radical Islam and that Trump would be uniquely vigorous in combatting it. (That he can express the full range of his thought on any given subject in 140 characters or less is, of course, Trump's great strength and his great weakness.)

Christian innocents are identified in this tweet as especial targets of radical Islam. That most victims of Islamic terrorism are in fact Muslim never enters Trump's worldview. Though he had, and continues to have, a more complicated relationship with the Christian right than most leaders within his party, he does use with remarkable ease the apocalyptic language that is their stock in trade. The world has reached a moment of crisis. The elect

F. G. Mohamed (✉)
CUNY Graduate Center, New York, NY, USA

© The Author(s) 2018
A. Jaramillo Torres, M. B. Sable (eds.), *Trump and Political Philosophy*,
https://doi.org/10.1007/978-3-319-74445-2_17

must cast out the damned. Emphasizing the martyrdom of Christian women and children is more than a simple ploy by a Republican candidate to tickle the sensibilities of the party base. It also contributes to a larger narrative of evil running amok, victimizing the righteous in a way that now demands the balm of unfettered state violence. Trump offered a fully secular millenarianism, casting himself in the role of Christ returned.

These messages of the campaign were crystallized in Trump's speech at the Republican National Convention, which centered on two key themes: the threat of violence by terrorists and undocumented immigrants, and cultivation of a republic bound by strong ethno-nationalist sentiment.[2] In this view, the very presence of Muslims and Mexicans in America is a wrench in right order preventing true political community from emerging. By heightening hatred of elements defined as irredeemably foreign, Trump sought to thicken the meaning of the nation as a category. Put differently, he aimed to restore the racial and familial implications always at play in its Latin root, *natio/-onis*. Tacitus plays on such associations in the *Annals*, when Gaius Cassius declares that the only way to maintain unity in a nation where family and nation have been severed is through terror: "Now our households [*familiis*] comprise nations [*nationes*]— with customs the reverse of our own, with foreign cults or with none, you will never coerce such a medley of humanity except by terror."[3] Trump focused his terrorizing aspect on the foreign while conjuring an American nativism united by blood. In this respect it was fitting that he was introduced at the Convention by his daughter Ivanka, and that the week featured his children much more prominently than it did the usual party functionaries. We were being invited to join them under the beneficent wing of his paternal care, and with such familial bonds to reconstitute a nation atomized by the financialization and globalization to which the liberal state, and liberal politics, had become beholden.

It will not be a surprise that one of the most infamous alt-right gadflies drawn to the Trump campaign, Richard Spencer, counts Carl Schmitt among his intellectual heroes—in an image of his office bookshelf appearing in *The Atlantic*, Spencer's copy of *Legality and Legitimacy* tops an unabashedly sparse pile, which also includes Alain de Benoist's *Carl Schmitt Today*.[4] Many aspects of Trump's campaign performances are reminiscent of Schmitt's thought. "The specific political distinction to which political actions and motives can be reduced," Schmitt famously intoned, "is that between friend and enemy."[5] It is a statement meant to be descriptive, rather than prescriptive: the friend-enemy distinction is central to politics in the same way that a good-evil distinction is central to ethics and a beautiful-ugly distinction is central to esthetics. All other considerations are peripheral to this core concern. And the considerations that Schmitt especially wishes to strip away are the legal and procedural ones central to defenses of the liberal state. Such defenses ignore the question of the political at their own peril, by reducing public life to a constant competition among interest groups and political factions with no overarching sense of purpose. "Liberalism is the enemy of enemies," as David Dyzenhaus describes it in his clear-sighted exegesis of Schmitt, because "it seeks to win the political battle by establishing a pluralist state built on an avoidance or eternal postponing of decision, and the fiction of the end of politics....Vitality can be restored only by a decision to establish a state properly based in the life of an utterly homogeneous people."[6] In Schmitt's view, liberal thought distracts subjects with abstract threats to be endlessly managed and regulated, whereas a true politics identifies actual enemies disturbing the concrete situation of a people attached to a homeland. Such are the enemies of a people that has exercised its *pouvoir constituant*, the power to form a constitution, and thereby become an organic unity. In the modern state, not given to recognizing the authority of monarchs as legitimate, this "democratic notion of legitimacy" is the norm.[7] As a candidate, Trump sought time and again to speak on behalf of true Americans attached to the land: the constituted *Volk* directly threatened by actual groups of brown bodies in their midst, be they Muslim or Mexican. That "Build the Wall" became the most common rallying cry of Trump's supporters gives outward expression to this central aspiration: it is an affirmation of the land-folk nexus. As in Schmitt's thought on the nature of the political, the distinction between friend and enemy was everywhere raised "to the utmost degree of intensity."[8]

So much for the campaign. Now that the world is living with the consequences of Trump's unthinkable victory, the more interesting and important question is whether he is governing in a style also in stride with Schmitt's thought, and especially his emphasis on sovereign decisionism. If we were to focus only on Trump's campaign rhetoric, then we would be using an association with Schmitt for primarily polemical ends: this would be a liberal appropriation of his work that forecloses the hard questions Schmitt puts to the liberal tradition, one of the chief values of his work. Eschewing such an approach, we will examine some of the most controversial measures of the Trump presidency: the so-called "Muslim ban" and his pardon of Sheriff Joe Arpaio. Throughout we will see him operating within his constitutional powers, though also seeking to stretch recent practice in ways consistent with the sense of national emergency that he seeks to cultivate. Or, in more explicitly Schmittian terms, he governs in a way making visible the state power that exists over and above the law within the terms of the U.S. Constitution. To truly read this in light of Schmitt's thought is to ask whether that sense of emergency reflects the nature of the political situation in which we find ourselves. In closing, we explore the ways in which Trump reflects, rather than invents, aspects of the American political imaginary that have been especially pronounced during the war on terror.

TRUMP AS COMMISSARIAL DICTATOR

At this writing Trump has been president for ten eternal months. It is within the realm of possibility that at some point in his term of office he will shift course or choose, spurred by boredom or sloth, to delegate responsibility to competent hands. Even at this early stage, we can discern actions in office illumined significantly by Schmitt's work. Trump's dictatorial style has become a leitmotif of casual political discourse. Parsing the actual workings of that tendency may be guided by the distinction central to *Dictatorship* between "commissary and sovereign dictatorship."[9] During the campaign, Trump certainly spoke as though he was poised to become a sovereign dictator, an avatar of "true" Americans reclaiming their *pouvoir constituant*. Of course it is not possible for an elected president to wield such power without dissolving the other branches of government. As Schmitt rightly observes, sovereign dictatorship arises in a climate of revolution, where sovereign power must be reconstituted.

That is not to say, however, that Trump is not dictatorial at all. Schmitt's commissarial dictator works within legally defined limits to preserve an existing constitutional order. Here the dictator does not acquire the status of an omnipotent lawgiver, but can deploy extralegal authority to resolve a situation of crisis. As an example, Schmitt points to Machiavelli's reading of the Venetian republic: "The dictator cannot change the laws; neither can he suspend the constitution or the organization of office; and he cannot 'make new laws' (*'fare nuove leggi'*). In a dictatorship, according to Machiavelli, the official administration subsists as a kind of control (*guardia*). Therefore dictatorship was a constitutional instrument for the Republic."[10] This definition of dictatorship guides Schmitt's reading of the presidential powers delineated in the Weimar constitution, and especially those of Article 48, which authorizes the president of the Reich to "take all the measures he deems necessary for the restoration of public security and order when these are seriously threatened."[11] Though this means that during the emergency the president is not constrained by limits on his power found elsewhere in the constitution—such as the prohibition against setting up extraordinary courts—and though it entails a fundamental reorganization of constitutional powers, it is not equivalent to sovereign dictatorship because the exercise of these powers depends on resolving an existing state of emergency. As Schmitt has it, the power exercised is defined by the nature of the lawless action threatening a given constitutional settlement. The specific form of such action cannot be perfectly anticipated by statutes and court decisions, so that the executive's emergency powers resemble an individual's right of self-defense, which is legally guaranteed without being attached to a definition of the specific acts comprising legitimate self-defense:

> For analogy, in self-defense, when the conditions are met—that is, an illegal attack, in the now—it is permitted to do anything it takes to counter the attack, and there is no specification, in the legal statutes, about the content of what is allowed to happen, because the law does not name the actual measures; it only advises what is *necessary* for defense. In the same way, once the conditions setting up the state of emergency have occurred, the action made *necessary* by the concrete circumstances occurs too. The analogy goes further. It is the essence of the right to self-defence that its conditions will be determined through the deed itself; hence it is not possible to create an institution that could prove legally [*justizförmig*] whether the conditions for self-defense obtain or not. In the same way, in a real case of emergency, the one who acts in self-defence cannot be differentiated from the one who decides whether there is a case of self-defence to answer.[12]

This explicates the dictum with which Schmitt opens *Political Theology*: "Sovereign is he who decides on the state of exception."[13] An emergency necessarily occurs in the aporiae of the law: it is a situation to which regular legislative and judicial bodies cannot adequately respond. And this is why the framers of constitutions leave a reserve of power in the executive not only to respond to emergency, but to determine the existence of a state of emergency. In Schmitt's mind these two things cannot be separated: to deprive a sovereign of the latter power is to neutralize the former power; it is equivalent to saying that an individual has a right to self-defense against a life-threatening physical attack, but no right to determine when such an attack is taking place.

Even at this early point in his presidency, we can see that this is the constitutional zone in which Trump has sought to wield power: he has exploited aspects of his office allowing him to take insuperable unilateral action, reflecting his various statements on the existence of a state of emergency. This was clear from his very first days in office, with his January 27 attempt to bar entry into the United States from seven Muslim-majority countries, Iraq, Iran, Libya, Somalia, Sudan, Syria, and Yemen. Clearly a case of executive overreach, this first attempt was quickly corrected by the courts: within seventy-two hours, it had been blocked by the Eastern District of New York, the Eastern District of Virginia, the Western District of Washington, and the District of Massachusetts.[14] In an appeal before a three-judge panel of the Ninth Circuit, the government's lawyers argued that the executive must be given a wide berth by the courts on matters of national security. When pressed by the judges to provide a factual analysis leading the president to conclude that measures already taken by Congress were insufficient, the response was refusal.[15] To present such analysis would be to suggest that the decision is subject to judicial review. The government simply declined to offer evidence supporting the decision to undertake emergency immigration measures, seeking instead to preserve a space of executive decisionism that the law cannot touch. This is precisely the space that Schmitt seeks to defend throughout his thought, in which the president decides on the existence of an emergency and the measures that it demands.

The Ninth Circuit responded as many of Schmitt's liberal interlocutors did during the Weimar era: by declaring that the space in question is in fact covered by law, and especially that the executive's emergency powers cannot impinge upon constitutionally guaranteed rights. Here they cited *Holder v. Humanitarian Law Project* (2010), in which the Supreme Court declares that its "precedents, old and new, make clear that concerns of national security and foreign relations do not warrant abdication of the judicial role," though that decision concedes that the courts have limited ability to collect evidence and draw factual inferences in these areas.[16] Despite this precedent, it is entirely likely that the Supreme Court may not see things exactly as the Ninth Circuit has done—term after term, it is the circuit that the court most often reverses.[17] While it is difficult to read the Court's inclinations at this time, or to predict how Trump's own appointee, Neil Gorsuch, will affect the outcome of this matter, it does seem likely that the Court will leave in place portions of the executive order pertaining to classes of individuals, such as refugees, whose due process rights are most tenuous and least likely to be construed as including access to federal courts. Trump does have behind him a sweeping statute by which Congress has given the executive a great deal of discretion: "Whenever the President finds that the entry of any aliens or of any class of aliens into the United States would be detrimental to the interests of the United States, he may by proclamation, and for such period as he shall deem necessary, suspend the entry of all aliens or any class of aliens as immigrants or nonimmigrants, or impose on the entry of aliens any restrictions he may deem to be appropriate."[18] Not only is the finding left to the president, but the standard implied in triggering action in the executive, "detrimental to the interests of the United States," is endlessly malleable. The Supreme Court is not likely to impose strong limits on the executive branch when Congress has so clearly resigned oversight. Judicial review of the entry ban has been complicated by the issuance of a third version adding North Korea, Venezuela, and Chad to the list of nations whose citizens are barred entry to the United States.[19] Understandably, the Court has asked for clarification on this rewriting of an order already rewritten.

This is the most infamous of Trump's attempts to deploy executive authority, and to be seen as deploying executive authority, but there are others. The Tomahawk strike against an airfield held by Bashar al-Assad's forces also comes to mind. The launching of these missiles prompted Fareed Zakaria infamously to declare on CNN that "Donald Trump became President of the United States last night," as though this single action had whisked away the sense of illegitimacy that is a persistent feature of his term, whether voiced by protesters shouting "Not My President" or by mounting revelations of his entanglements with Russia.[20] Legal objections to these airstrikes were fairly muted, as domestic law clearly and intentionally extends to the president the authority to engage in military strikes without the approval of Congress: the War Powers Resolution (1973) allows a president to initiate military action so long as he reports to Congress within forty-eight hours and so long as the action is terminated within sixty days.

Both the entry ban and the Syria airstrikes pertain to matters of security and foreign policy, where presidential powers are at their fullest. More unusual in terms of the recent history of the presidency has been Trump's inclination to decide the exception in the sphere of domestic law. Several examples might suggest themselves here, such as his general posture of aggression toward the courts, or his dismissal of an FBI director who declined to express enthusiastic loyalty, or his haranguing of his own Attorney General. All of these show impulses directly at odds with rule of law. But most pertinent to this discussion is the pardon of Joe Arpaio. Reading the significance of that pardon narrowly might lead us to see it as a simple favor to a sheriff who was a friend to the Trump campaign—as the corrupt Canadian Prime Minister Brian Mulroney was wont to say, in politics "you dance with the one that brung ya," a kernel of insight explaining both the Arpaio pardon and the president's tender handling of neo-Nazis and other white supremacists after the Charlottesville protests. But the pardon's broad implications make this narrow reading insufficient. Arpaio was a sheriff notorious for violating the due process and habeas corpus rights of Latinos, who on his watch were routinely subjected to racial profiling, arbitrary arrest, cruel and unusual jailing practices, and extended detention without trial.[21] The specific offense of which he was convicted, however, was criminal contempt for disregarding a court order to stop detaining suspected undocumented immigrants. Presidential pardons are not generally praised, especially when granted to one's political connections. But Trump's use of the pardon power seems especially unsettling in its direct assault on due process, by exonerating a public official who prided himself in overseeing systematic due process violations, and by vacating a contempt charge and thus disrupting the courts' ability to conduct a criminal trial. Trump declared that Arpaio was guilty only of "doing his job"—one is inclined to note that if his job was to uphold the law, he was in fact doing the exact opposite of his job. That this pardon comes very early in a presidential term suggests that Trump is signaling his intention to protect other police and public officials pursuing vigilantism against potential violations of immigration law; if that is his intention, then this could augur a very far-reaching assault on due process. As with our discussion of the entry ban, however, we must note that he is exploiting existing presidential powers, rather than inventing new ones. Every president since Reagan has used 8 USC 1182 (f) to limit the entry of one class of individuals or another.[22] Every president since Washington has granted pardons, the only exceptions being William Henry Harrison and James Garfield, both of whom died shortly after taking office. Thus far Trump has not done anything that could be described as a major innovation in his constitutional authority. Put differently, the executive powers outlined in the U.S. Constitution and the American legal tradition rhyme well with the commissarial dictatorship that Schmitt finds in the republican tradition, a point to which we shall return.

We must also emphasize, however, that considering the Trump presidency exposes a flaw in Schmitt's work—in fact it exposes the same flaw as does the rise of the Nazis. In his writings of the Weimar era, Schmitt has many things to say about the necessity of flexing presidential power in a time of emergency. He has a great deal less to say about presidents who manufacture a state of emergency for the sole purpose of expanding their power. Setting for himself the task of defending executive decisionism, even if it includes dissolution of the legislature, Schmitt rarely considers the legal means by which a baseless declaration of emergency ought to be confronted. The passage from *Dictatorship* quoted above stipulates that a "*real* case of emergency" triggers commissary dictatorship, but Schmitt offers few theoretical tools by which rule of law might counter false emergencies promulgated by mere presidential ambition.

Though the parlor game of comparing Trump's rise to that of the Nazis is generally uninstructive, I will tentatively draw a narrowly circumscribed parallel to the Reichstag fire of February 1933, an assault on the seat of German democracy then used to justify a sweeping abrogation of constitutional rights in the Enabling Act passed the following month. Whether the Nazis were responsible for the fire remains contested.[23] But it can be hardly disputed that they exploited the event to advance their own power by crushing their enemies. And these were not political enemies in Schmitt's sense of the term, but quite the opposite: not enemies of the German people but opponents of a particular political faction who were styled enemies of the German people. Schmitt's response to this curtailment of constitutional rights was to join the National Socialists on May 1, standing in line to add his name to party rolls with his friend Martin Heidegger.[24] From then until the attacks in the SS newspaper *Das Schwarze Korps* that caused him to resign his party offices in 1936, he enters the darkest phase of his career, one where he is willing and eager to argue for the legitimacy of the Nazi regime, most visible in his organization in 1936 of a conference on eliminating the Jewish influence from German law, in which he urges in a closing keynote that books by Jewish authors be confined to shelves labeled "Judaica" and that the state should keep a complete register of Jewish intellectuals.[25]

Both as a person and a theorist, Schmitt seems largely unable to respond to opportunism masquerading as the sovereign's legitimate expression of the will of the people. It has been Trump's position throughout his campaign and presidency that the nation is a house on fire, teetering on the brink of collapse, subject to marauding Muslims and Mexicans, resting on a false foundation of Chinese steel. And yet the country's core institutions are perfectly intact, facing no existential threat from foreign or domestic enemies. The aura of emergency that Trump uses to justify his flexion of executive power is a fabrication, a theater of distraction orchestrated by this devoted student of cable news and reality television.

AMERICAN EXCEPTION

I say that Schmitt is "largely unable" to theorize a counterbalance to such opportunism because he does recognize in *Dictatorship* that commissarial dictatorship is often limited in duration by a legislative body, so that its powers expire once a specific situation of emergency is resolved. The dictator is a "direct commissar of the people" empowered to bring about a specific result: "the content of the measures deemed necessary in a dictatorship is unconditionally and exclusively determined by the actual situation. In consequence, there is an absolute balance between the task and the authorisation, discretion and empowerment, commission and authority."[26] That he does not emphasize this "balance" is largely due to the specific situation from which many of his writings emerge: that of a conservative legal theorist seeking to defend the Weimar Constitution in a moment of real political turmoil.[27] In this context, he saw rigid liberal adherence to legislative procedure as insufficient and cynical, the program of bourgeois parties seeking to advance their own interests rather than attempting to serve the nation's needs. His emphasis on exercising the presidential powers described in Article 48 of the Weimar Constitution must be read in this light.

Seeing Schmitt's arguments in this way impresses upon us one of the dangers of modern constitutionalism: once a founding document, supported by a powerful modern state, grants emergency powers to the executive, the executive will devote every ounce of its ingenuity to finding emergencies. The framers were fully aware that they had granted the president enormous war powers, which Hamilton described in *Federalist* 70 as necessary to the "energy" of the office. Such energy depends upon its "unity," defined as the "decision, activity, secrecy, and dispatch" much more typical of the "proceedings of one man" than "of any greater number."[28] The long-standing solution to containing the destructive potential of these powers is thoroughly Schmittean: allowing the president unilaterally to exercise force against external enemies, while expecting rule of law to be observed in handling internal friends. This is the constitutional bargain spelled out by the Supreme Court in *United States v. Curtiss-Wright* (1936): the limited and enumerated powers of the Constitution apply only to domestic matters; in "the field of international relations" the president is the "sole organ of the federal government" and exercises a "delicate, plenary, and exclusive power."[29] In *Harrisiades v. Shaughnessy* (1952), the Court applied this broad deference on matters of foreign affairs to immigration: "any policy toward aliens is vitally and intricately interwoven with contemporaneous policies in regard to the conduct of foreign relations, the war power, and the maintenance of a republican form of government. Such matters are so exclusively entrusted to the political branches of government as to be largely immune from judicial inquiry or interference."[30] That lack of interference is narrower still, given, as we have seen, that Congress in 8 USC 1182 (f) has deposited in the Executive sweeping power to deny entrance to foreigners. We can readily imagine Schmitt assenting to the equation in *Shaughnessy* of war powers, the handling of strangers, preservation of the republic, and the political.

The nature of American sovereignty long tended to be overlooked by liberal political theorists, who present the nation's militarism as an aberration to its core commitments rather than as expression of its core political qualities. This is one of the central insights of Paul W. Kahn's recent application of Schmitt's thought to the American case: "Rawls and his followers never took seriously the violence of the state....It is as if the violence of the United States is simply an accidental characteristic of an essentially liberal political order."[31] Despite the rhetoric of *Marbury v. Madison*, in which the Court styles itself the voice of the People, Kahn finds that sovereignty manifests its presence through the executive in the American constitutional tradition:

> with respect to foreign policy and national security, the Court has traditionally been at its weakest point in asserting an identity with We the People, while the president has been at his strongest. The issue is not one of better "representing" the national interest. Rather we have seen the nation through the president in moments of national crisis: his rhetorical role is to present the nation to itself, configuring himself as the universal, sacrificial citizen.... Fully to understand this, we must turn from the theology of creation to that of Christology as the frame of the imagination, for the question is no longer one of miraculous creation but of who embodies the whole.[32]

It is significant, and apt, that Kahn uses the term "Christology," rather than messianism, in this passage: this is not a Messiah whose arrival is perpetually deferred, which might place us in the philosophy of Lévinas or Derrida, but an actual god-man walking among us whose life is taken as synecdoche of the community as a whole. "I am the way, the truth, and the life"; "I alone can solve." The latter is unintelligible to a citizen whose political imaginary does not include the former. Kahn here importantly directs our attention away from veneration of the Constitution and its interpretation by the Supreme Court, a legalist political theology that liberal theorists might view as relatively benign—the kind of political experience explored by Sanford Levinson in *Constitutional Faith*.[33]

Setting himself against a legal positivism and political liberalism that ignored what he saw as the true nature of the political, Schmitt favored what he described in *Political Theology* as a "sociology of a concept" that takes an accurate reckoning of the state of political ideas in a given situation: "this sociology of concepts transcends juridical conceptualization oriented to immediate practical interest. It aims to discover the basic, radically systematic structure and to compare this conceptual structure with the conceptually represented structure of a certain epoch."[34] The rise of Trump has certainly made clear the affinity in broad segments of the American population for sovereign action against enemies, including the deployment of lethal extralegal state violence. Liberal theory cannot account for the ways in which this expresses long-standing values in the American imaginary, and also reflects the growing affinity for authoritarianism of a neoliberal epoch rapidly eroding liberal institutions. A "sociology of the concept" of American sovereignty would reckon the conflicting demands of faith and reason in its political consciousness. It is an Enlightenment republic that attempts to institutionalize a civic culture of rational debate and consensus, but nonetheless demands love and sacrifice, as well as obliging hatred of enemies posing an obstacle to its out-sized aspirations. And the war on terror has created a doctrine of perennial threat mobilizing a largely unquestioned militarization of American society, and with it a mobilization of a politics of tribal hatred. The key Supreme Court decision noted above, *Holder v. Humanitarian Law Project*, came during the administration of Barack Obama, which was deemed to have exceeded just bounds in prosecuting the war on terror. It seems obvious in this light that Trump's rise is a mere symptom of a perennial American mentality on sovereignty especially pronounced over the past fifteen years.

While I have emphasized here that the state of emergency Trump has sought to exploit is a manufactured one, that may not always be the case. If, as has been persuasively argued, it is the effect of neoliberalism to erode the public institutions central to liberal democracy, then the age of Trump might be a grim prelude to more robust expressions of sovereign decisionism underwritten by populist nativism. Democratic society certainly is not characterized by the defunding of public education at all levels, the corruption of the electoral process, the steepening of economic inequality and racial segregation, the highjacking of public discourse with misinformation, and the transformation of local police and immigration officers into paramilitary groups residing above the law. In the years to come, conditions on the ground may lend more substance to anti-democratic declarations of emergency from reactionary forces. And those who have always favored preserving the constituted *Volk* via sovereign decisionism and extralegal violence will accept such declarations all too eagerly.

Notes

1. Donald J. Trump, Twitter post @realDonadTrump, 27 March 2016, available at http://mobile.twitter.com/realDonaldTrump/status/714189569793646597. For their comments on earlier drafts of this essay, I am grateful to Peter Catapano and the editors of this volume.
2. This paragraph and the next adapt material from my "Arendt, Schmitt, and Trump's Politics of 'Nation,'" which appeared in the series "The Stone," edited by Simon Critchley and Peter Catapano, *NYTimes.com*, 22 July 2016.
3. Tacitus, *The Annals*, trans. John Jackson, Loeb Classical Library (1937; Cambridge, MA: Harvard University Press, 2006), 14.44 ("Postquam vero nationes in familiis habemus, quibus diversi ritus, externa sacra aut nulla sunt, conluviem istam non nisi metu coercueris").
4. Graeme Wood, "His Kampf," *The Atlantic*, June 2017; available at theatlantic.com. Admiration of Schmitt certainly informs Spencer's core political yearning for "something as robust and binding as Christianity had once been in the West."
5. Carl Schmitt, *The Concept of the Political*, Expanded ed., trans. George Schwab (1996; Chicago: University of Chicago Press, 2007), 26.
6. David Dyzenhaus, *Legality and Legitimacy: Carl Schmitt, Hans Kelsen and Hermann Heller in Weimar* (Oxford: Oxford University Press, 1997), 41.
7. Schmitt, *Political Theology*, trans. George Schwab (Chicago: University of Chicago Press, 2005), 51. See also 49 on the "organic unity" of a people.

8. Schmitt, *Concept of the Political*, 26.
9. Schmitt, *Dictatorship: From the Origin of the Modern Concept of Sovereignty to Proletarian Class Struggle*, trans. Michael Hoelzl and Graham Ward (Cambridge: Polity, 2014), 2. For brief but detailed background on Schmitt's views of dictatorship, see Duncan Kelly, "Carl Schmitt's Political Theory of Dictatorship," in *The Oxford Handbook of Carl Schmitt*, ed. Jens Meierhenrich and Oliver Simons (Oxford: Oxford University Press, 2016), 217–244.
10. Ibid., 4.
11. Ibid., 180. Schmitt includes an extended commentary on Article 48 as an appendix to *Dictatorship*.
12. Ibid., 154.
13. Schmitt, *Political* Theology, 5. The Schwab translation has "Sovereign is he decides on the exception," though commentators on Schmitt tend to prefer "Sovereign is he decides on the *state of* exception." See, for example, Giorgio Agamben, *The State of Exception*, trans. Kevin Attell (Chicago: University of Chicago Press, 2005), 1.
14. See Orin Kerr, "Four Federal Judges Issue Orders Blocking Parts of Trump's Executive Order on Immigration," *WashingtonPost.com*, 29 Jan 2017; Benjamin Wittes, "Malevolence Tempered by Incompetence: Trump's Horrifying Executive Order on Refugees and Visas," *Lawfare*, 18 Jan 2017, available at lawfareblog.com. See also my "The Trump Entry Ban: Is it Legal? (Or, the Toddler-in-Chief Beats the Drum of War)," *HuffingtonPost.com*, 30 Jan 2017. Full text of Protecting the Nation from Foreign Terrorist Entry into the United States, Exec. Order No. 13769 (27 Jan 2017), is available at whitehouse.gov. This order was later superseded by Exec. Order 13780 (6 Mar 2017); text also available at whitehouse.gov.
15. For video of the oral arguments before the Ninth Circuit, see Tim Harris, "Full Replay: Oral Arguments for Trump Immigration Ban Hearing, Ninth Circuit Court of Appeals," *RealClearPolitics.com*, 7 Feb 2017. See also my "Trump Entry Ban: The Ninth Circuit Lands a Stiff Jab, but the Fight is in the Early Rounds," *HuffingtonPost.com*, 10 Feb 2017.
16. *Holder v. Humanitarian Law Project,* 561 U.S. 1, 34 (2010); cited in *State of Hawaii v. Donald J. Trump*, 859 F.3d 741, 769 (2017).
17. For statistics on the Supreme Court's decisions, see the "Stat Pack Archive" at SCOTUSblog, available at scotusblog.com/reference/stat-pack/.
18. Inadmissible Aliens, 8 USC 1182 (f).
19. Presidential Proclamation Enhancing Vetting Capabilities and Processing for Detecting Attempted Entry Into the United States by Terrorists or Other Public-Safety Threats, 24 Sep 2017, available at whitehouse.gov.

20. See Mark Hensch, "CNN Host: 'Donald Trump Became President' Last Night," *TheHill.com*, 7 Apr 2017. On these airstrikes, see my "Trump's Syria Air Strikes: A Perverse Advance in International Law?," *DissentMagazine.org*, 14 Apr 2017.

21. See Julie Hirschfield Davis and Maggie Haberman, "Trump Pardons Joe Arpaio, Who Became Face of Crackdown on Illegal Immigration," *NYTimes.com*, 25 Aug 2017. For an argument that the pardon is unconstitutional, see Laurence H. Tribe and Ron Fein, "Trump's Pardon of Arpaio Can—and Should—Be Overturned," *WashingtonPost.com*, 18 Sep 2017.

22. See the annotated code on Inadmissible Aliens, 8 USC 1182, available at http://uscode.house.gov.

23. For a recent, full-length study of this event, surveying evidence of Nazi responsibility, see Benjamin Carter Hett, *Burning the Reichstag: An Investigation into the Third Reich's Enduring Mystery* (Oxford: Oxford University Press, 2014).

24. See Gopal Balakrishnan, *The Enemy: An Intellectual Portrait of Carl Schmitt* (London: Verso, 2000), 181.

25. Schmitt's association with the National Socialists from 1933–1936 is oft-discussed. See Balakrishnan, 176–208; Stephen Holmes, *The Anatomy of Antiliberalism* (Cambridge, MA: Harvard University Press, 1993), 37–39; Ellen Kennedy, *Constitutional Failure: Carl Schmitt in Weimar* (Durham: Duke University Press, 2004), 11–37. Joseph W. Bendersky, "Carl Schmitt at Nuremberg" and translations of Schmitt's Nuremberg testimony, special issue "Carl Schmitt: Enemy or Foe?," ed. Paul Piccone and G.L. Ullmen, *Telos* 72 (Summer 1987): 91–129, as well as Bendersky's generally sympathetic biography of Schmitt, *Carl Schmitt: Theorist for the Reich* (Princeton: Princeton University Press, 1983), 195–218.

26. Schmitt, *Dictatorship*, xliii.

27. On Schmitt in the context of constitutional failure, see Kennedy, 154–183.

28. Alexander Hamilton, "The Federalist No. 70," in *The Federalist*, intr. Edward Mead Earle (New York: Modern Library, n.d.), 455.

29. *United States v. Curtiss-Wright*, 299 U.S. 304, 320 (1936).

30. *Harisiades v. Shaughnessy*, 342 U.S. 580, 588–589 (1952); see Louis Henkin, "Is There a 'Political Question' Doctrine?," *The Yale Law Journal* 85 (1976): 597–625.

31. See Paul W. Kahn, *Political Theology: Four New Chapters on the Concept of Sovereignty* (New York: Columbia University Press, 2011), 7.

32. Ibid., 86. Kahn's *Political Theology* is the culmination of his applications of Schmitt's thought to an American context, and especially the politics of the war on terror. See also his *Putting Liberalism in its Place* (Princeton:

Princeton University Press, 2005) and *Sacred Violence: Torture, Terror, and Sovereignty* (Ann Arbor: University of Michigan Press, 2008). Also relevant is Ashraf H.A. Rushdy's work on lynching, which argues that throughout American history extralegal collective violence has often been deemed a legitimate expression of popular sovereignty; see his *American Lynching* (New Haven: Yale University Press, 2012a) and *The End of American Lynching* (New Brunswick: Rutgers University Press, 2012b).

33. Sanford Levinson, *Constitutional Faith* (1988; Princeton: Princeton University Press, 2011). The 2011 Afterword takes into account the "constitutional fundamentalism" of such movements as the Tea Party.

34. Schmitt, *Political Theology*, 45.

REFERENCES

Agamben, Giorgio. *The State of Exception*. Trans. Kevin Attell. Chicago: University of Chicago Press, 2005.

Balakrishnan, Gopal. *The Enemy: An Intellectual Portrait of Carl Schmitt*. London: Verso, 2000.

Bendersky, Joseph W. *Carl Schmitt: Theorist for the Reich*. Princeton: Princeton University Press, 1983.

———. "Carl Schmitt at Nuremberg." Special Issue, "Carl Schmitt: Enemy or Foe?" Ed. Paul Piccone and G.L. Ullmen. *Telos* 72 (Summer 1987): 91–129.

Dyzenhaus, David. *Legality and Legitimacy: Carl Schmitt, Hans Kelsen and Hermann Heller in Weimar*. Oxford: Oxford University Press, 1997.

Hamilton, Alexander. "The Federalist No. 70." *The Federalist*. Intr. Edward Mead Earle. New York: Modern Library, n.d.

Henkin, Louis. "Is There a 'Political Question' Doctrine?" *The Yale Law Journal* 85 (1976): 597–625.

Hett, Benjamin Carter. *Burning the Reichstag: An Investigation into the Third Reich's Enduring Mystery*. Oxford: Oxford University Press, 2014.

Holmes, Stephen. *The Anatomy of Antiliberalism*. Cambridge, MA: Harvard University Press, 1993.

Kahn, Paul W. *Putting Liberalism in Its Place*. Princeton: Princeton University Press, 2005.

———. *Sacred Violence: Torture, Terror, and Sovereignty*. Ann Arbor: University of Michigan Press, 2008.

———. *Political Theology: Four New Chapters on the Concept of Sovereignty*. New York: Columbia University Press, 2011.

Kelly, Duncan. "Carl Schmitt's Political Theory of Dictatorship." In *The Oxford Handbook of Carl Schmitt*. Ed. Jens Meierhenrich and Oliver Simons. Oxford: Oxford University Press, 2016, 217–244.

Kennedy, Ellen. *Constitutional Failure: Carl Schmitt in Weimar*. Durham: Duke University Press, 2004.

Levinson, Sanford. *Constitutional Faith*. 1988. Princeton: Princeton University Press, 2011.

Rushdy, Ashraf H.A. *American Lynching*. New Haven: Yale University Press, 2012a.

———. *The End of American Lynching*. New Brunswick: Rutgers University Press, 2012b.

Schmitt, Carl. *Political Theology*. Trans. George Schwab. Chicago: University of Chicago Press, 2005.

———. *The Concept of the Political*. Expanded ed. Trans. George Schwab. 1996. Chicago: University of Chicago Press, 2007.

———. *Dictatorship: From the Origin of the Modern Concept of Sovereignty to Proletarian Class Struggle*. Trans. Michael Hoelzl and Graham Ward. Cambridge: Polity, 2014.

Tacitus (Cornelius). *The Annals*. Trans. John Jackson. Loeb Classical Library. 1937. Cambridge, MA: Harvard University Press, 2006.

INDEX[1]

[1]Note: Page numbers followed by 'n' refer to notes.

© The Author(s) 2018
A. Jaramillo Torres, M. B. Sable (eds.), *Trump and Political Philosophy*,
https://doi.org/10.1007/978-3-319-74445-2

G

Gaddis, John Lewis, 231n12
GDP, 63, 66
General will, 9, 166–169, 174, 176, 242
Geneva, 9, 166, 170, 171
Genius, 71n22, 86, 202, 206, 262
Gentile, Giovanni, 278
Gentleman, 4, 47n3, 61, 93–112
  compare *jūnzi*, 君子, 95, 97, 98, 111
Germany, 108, 138, 186,
  193n31, 220
Gessen, Masha, 25, 31n11,
  31n12, 31n13
Gettysburg Address (Lincoln),
  11, 215, 239, 243
Gilded Age, 230
Girard, René, 110
Gitlin, Todd, 287
Glaucon, 4, 33–40, 46, 47n3
Globalism, 6, 294
Globalization, *see* Globalism
Glory, 76, 88–90, 150, 152, 183
God, 21, 79, 80, 96, 98, 106, 152,
  154, 173, 213, 224, 228, 240,
  247, 262
The Godfather, 158
Goldsmith, Jack, 207
Good sense, *see* Common sense
Good, the, 1, 2, 7, 20, 22, 23, 30,
  31n9, 35, 37–40, 47n3, 55, 56,
  60, 61, 66, 71n22, 76, 77,
  83–90, 90n2, 95, 97, 98,
  100–102, 105, 108–111, 118,
  120–123, 125, 135, 139, 141,
  143, 145, 163, 165, 166,
  169–171, 173, 176, 188–190,
  196, 197, 199, 214, 225, 227,
  228, 240, 244, 246, 249n1,
  257–259, 261–263, 269, 276,
  278, 282, 287, 295
  compare common good, 13, 77,
    141, 170, 240, 244, 258

Gore, Al, 288, 289
Gorgias, 21, 22, 39, 40, 85
Gorka, Sebastian, 108
Government, 1, 55, 97, 137, 167,
  168, 192n18, 195, 196, 205,
  219, 246, 298, 303
Gracchus, Gaius, 294
Gracchus, Tiberius, 166
Grace, 99
Gramsci, Antonio, 12, 275–278, 282,
  284–286, 288–290, 290n1,
  290n8, 290n9
Great Recession, 284
Greatness, 7, 25, 65, 76, 80, 81, 107,
  164, 172, 175, 179, 191n1, 191n8,
  216, 237, 243, 247, 266, 282
Green Party, 62
Greenblatt, Stephen, 4, 150–153
Grifter, *see* Con artist

H

Habits, 192n23
  See also Mores (mouers)
Hal, 4, 5, 150, 152–155, 157–159
Hamilton, Alexander, 3, 5, 8, 68n10,
  70n16, 191n1, 192n16,
  195–208, 208n7, 302
Hammond, James Henry, 213, 230n2
Happiness, 36, 61, 88, 123, 124, 142,
  183, 184, 237, 240, 246
Harmony, 99, 102, 105, 111, 135, 182
Harrington, James, 138
Harrisiades v. Shaughnessy (1952), 303
Hart, H.L.A., 224, 232n16
Hate, 75, 109, 217, 280, 289
Healthcare, 62, 262, 263
Heaven
  compare to natural law, 98
  compare to natural right, 98
  compare to religion, 98
Hegemony, 9, 93, 284

Sumner, Charles, 223
Supreme Court, 23, 26, 199, 298, 299, 303, 304
System, 145

T
Tacitus, Cornelius, 294
Taney, Roger B., 216
Taylor, Frederick Winslow, 6, 132, 142, 145, 147n38
Tea Party, 12, 205, 280–284
Territories, 165, 197, 202–204, 212, 223, 226, 227
Terrorism, 67n7, 69n15, 215, 280, 282, 293, 294
Theologico-Political Treatise (Spinoza), 120
Thoreau, Henry David, 222
Thucydides, 8, 9, 75–90
Tiān, 天 (heaven), 96, 98, 113n9
Tillerson, Rex, 30
Tocqueville, Alexis de, 177n3, 201
Toleration, religious, 230
Trade, 52, 71n21, 109, 122, 172, 175, 185, 187, 203, 220, 241, 244, 266, 279, 282, 293
Tradition, 1, 2, 4, 7, 8, 12, 42, 45, 94–99, 109, 215, 216, 239, 256, 257, 259, 265, 295, 300–301
Transgender people, 29
Trans-Pacific Partnership, 23
Tribune, 182
Trogneux, Brigitte, 103
Trump University, 55, 156
Trump Voters, 157, 164, 171, 241, 248, 249, 279
Trump, Donald J.
  and pardon of Joe Arpaio, 300
  and white supremacists, 222
  as dictator, 8, 266, 296
  handshake, 100, 102

rhetoric, 1, 220, 235–249, 275, 295
Syria airstrikes, 299
See also Acceptance Speech (Trump); Demagogy; Inaugural Address (Trump); Speech at the United Nations (Trump); State of the Union Address (Trump); Trump, tweets; Warsaw Speech (Trump)
Trump, Donald J. Jr., 28
Trump, Melania, 103
Trump, tweets, 90n1, 108, 160, 280, 293
Trumpism, 3, 13, 225, 228, 230
Truth, 2, 6, 8, 13, 14, 17–30, 38, 42, 43, 45, 46, 48n37, 61, 69n14, 79, 80, 84, 86, 87, 114n19, 117, 121, 123, 139, 153–155, 173, 177, 187, 198, 212, 230, 244, 260–262, 264, 266, 268–270, 277, 278, 283–285, 287, 288, 294–296, 304
Two Treatises on Government: Locke, 193n27
Tyranny, 1–14, 17–31, 33, 40, 44, 45, 53, 89, 196

U
Undocumented immigrants, *see* Illegal immigrants
Union, 105, 151, 183, 185, 186, 196, 202, 204, 205, 217, 220, 236, 239, 249, 286
United States Constitution, 110
  See also Founding
United States v. Curtiss-Wright (1936), 303
Unity, 294, 295, 302
Universal, 6, 18, 21, 76, 84, 85, 88, 121–123, 132, 138, 166–168, 203, 223, 238, 243, 262, 303

Made in the USA
San Bernardino, CA
24 August 2019